key passages - 6, 55/35, 64, 76, 87ff, 144, 191, 210, 235, 268

38 - silliness of separating out a religious economy;
144   religion competes in broader cultural economy

45 - impossibility of separating "religious motives", or interest
in salvation, from other motives for buying rel. products of various
sorts -- shows silliness of (R.Z) tradeoff (56)

64 - key idea that rel.'s attempt to influence cultural
144   market involves it in the market - attempt to
147   use religion to influence market results in commodification of religion; underlying point that commodification
of religion is a cultural achievement; not a
universal feature of the phenomenon. (also 91)

69 - rel. on every side of every issue in 19th cent.
81 - emergence of political competition at same time also
speaks to this - 85 - , both driven by expansion
of "market-based liberalism" (89)

- [theme of how to study culture] ⊛ 45 - rel. influences how culture
   marketed, to whom, in what
   formats, etc. - 275
- also, theme of extradenominational face of religious culture.
   - lots of action outside denoms (92); raises question of
   appropriate unit of analysis for study

99 - eg of "thin" claim for cultural influence of rel. over market

108 - recurring theme of rel. tendency to influence what
113   it cannot ban or control. - 119

115 clear case of rel. influence - invention of b-ball & v-ball as
   result of evangelizing through gyms

- me: Answer why is religion as commodity apparently so popular now
   item: this book seems independent of resources of religion in
                                                                      soc.
   - not influence of rel. economies
   - not that "reality" has changed to make
      religion more of a commodity
   - for same reason, it seems more
      important to us at this particular
                           moment to call

attention to the ways in which religion works like a
commodity - why is that?

137 - early Adventist a buddy of a Garrisonian
abolitionist in 1830s

— cultural products we owe to rel. influences in
market: basketball, volleyball, graham crackers,
chiropractics, osteopathy, Xmas, movie ratings

142 - ties presence ♂ ♀ in certain 19th cent. movements
to fact that there were health movements

145 - to say religion is commodity isn't to say it is
peanut butter —

196 - another theme: businesses + religion cooperate
to promote moral regulation

me: the claims about how rel. influences
pop. culture need comparative data -- is
US pop culture so much more moral than
pop culture in Eng. or France or Ger? Maybe it is

209 - on financing churches

256 - cheese analogy -

255b - what changes when rel. auth. narrows
its scope —

273 - on "nonprofit" activities of rel. orgs

SELLING GOD

SELLING
GOD

American Religion
in the Marketplace
of Culture

R. LAURENCE MOORE

New York   Oxford

OXFORD UNIVERSITY PRESS

1994

Oxford University Press

Oxford   New York   Toronto
Delhi   Bombay   Calcutta   Madras   Karachi
Kuala Lumpur   Singapore   Hong Kong   Tokyo
Nairobi   Dar es Salaam   Cape Town
Melbourne   Auckland   Madrid

and associated companies in
Berlin   Ibadan

Copyright © 1994 by Oxford University Press, Inc.

Published by Oxford University Press, Inc.
200 Madison Avenue, New York, New York 10016

Oxford is a registered trademark of Oxford University Press

Library of Congress Cataloging-in-Publication Data
Moore, R. Laurence (Robert Laurence), 1940–
Selling God : American religion in the marketplace
of culture / R. Laurence Moore.
p. cm.   Includes bibliographical references and index.
ISBN 0-19-508228-1
1. United States—Religion—Economic aspects.
2. Religion and culture—United States.
I. Title.
BL2525.M67   1994   200'.973—dc20
93-19624

9 8 7 6 5 4 3 2 1

Printed in the United States of America
on acid-free paper

For Lauris

Acknowledgments

Not everyone who has provided inspiration for this book would wish to be thanked. I think especially of a businessman friend of my father who declared to the author, then an impressionable adolescent, that preachers could say anything, so long as they promoted capitalism. From what I saw of Houston, Texas, in the 1950s, he did not have much to worry about. But my perspective then was narrow. Time, I hope, has made it broader.

I started writing this book while I was a fellow at the Woodrow Wilson International Center for Scholars. I want to thank Michael Lacey, who runs the American program at the center; my fellow scholars in residence, especially James Gilbert and Elliot Brownlee; and William R. Taylor, who participated in a public discussion of my work-in-progress. During my residence at the Smithsonian, Brian Kassof acted as an unfailingly helpful research assistant. Gary Kulik, who was across the way at the Museum of American History, invited me to submit an early version of my thoughts to the *American Quarterly*.

In the same year, an invitation from the University of Notre Dame allowed me to begin thinking about the material that is now Chapter 3 of this book. Thomas Kselman is a good questioner and generous host, who published the lecture in his edited volume *Belief in History. Innovative Approaches to European and American Religion*. Another opportunity, this time to deliver the Tanner Lecture at the annual meeting of the Mormon Historical Society, started me thinking about the problems now contained in Chapter 4.

Viola Sachs, who directs the Laboratoire de Recherche sur l'Imaginaire Américain at the Université de Paris VIII, has for a number of years been inviting me to conferences in Paris. I am especially grateful to her and her colleagues for an opportunity to present a portion of my book at a 1993 colloquium held at the Maison des Sciences de l'Homme.

I could implicate many other individuals in this enterprise, individuals whose brains I have picked at meetings over the years. Since many of them will be called upon to review this work, I will not try to compromise their judgment by special citations. Their names are all in the notes. To my colleagues at Cornell, however, I need to issue a collective thanks for twenty years of intellectual stimulation. It is hard for me to write without imagining them reading over my shoulder. In this project, Isabelle Lehuu, one of my former graduate students, has been especially important. I must also acknowledge a special debt to the late William McLoughlin. For what he taught me through his writings and for other kindnesses to a person he never met, I am very grateful.

I wrote the last half of this book at Franklin and Marshall College, where my wife teaches anthropology. To Kathleen Spencer and her staff at the Franklin and Marshall Library, I am grateful for permission to spend quiet hours, virtually alone, scribbling away in The Academy Room.

This is my fourth book with Sheldon Meyer at Oxford. As always it has been a pleasure to work with him. Scott Lenz, my copy editor at Oxford, learned what a careless speller I am but was supportive and helpful all the same. My children, Alissa, Patrick, and Greta, could not read when I published my first book and remained indifferent toward the others. I am thrilled that they now each have coffee tables for this one.

As for Lauris McKee, the dedication is small thanks indeed. She has made the days of writing this book joyous and serene. She is my smartest critic and my best friend.

Lancaster, Pa.   R. L. M.
June 1993

Contents

SELLING GOD

Introduction

As I purposed to make a considerable stay
here, it gratified me to learn that there is
no longer the want of harmony between
the townspeople and pilgrims. . . . Many
passengers stop to take their pleasure or
make their profit in the Fair, instead of
going onward to the Celestial City. Indeed,
such are the charms of the place, that
people often affirm it to be the true and
only heaven; stoutly contending that there
is no other, that those who seek further are
mere dreamers, and that, if the fabled
brightness of the Celestial City lay but a
bare mile beyond the gates of Vanity, they
would not be fools enough to go thither.

> Nathaniel Hawthorne, "The Celestial Railroad"
> (on entering Vanity Fair)

I follow religion with much the same exuberant spirit that many of my friends follow baseball. Readers offended by the suggestion that religion exerts an appeal analogous to that of a form of commercial entertainment might as well stop here. Much more of the same will follow. However, my intention in making the suggestion is not in the least flippant. Religion is a curious and somewhat unique national passion (in that way, quite like baseball) that demands an explanation beyond the observation that Americans are especially pious. The assertion of piety explains nothing. Moreover, it often emanates from sources that render it suspect; for example, from Madison Avenue ads invented to elect politicians who find a divine national mission easier to invoke than a set of cogent policy proposals. A lot in this book suggests that there are significant ruptures between religion and piety. That is not my primary point in drawing a connection between religion and various forms of commercial entertainment. I am trying to explain how Americans managed a formal separation of church and state while leaving religion a central component of their traditions of laicity. Besides, the connection is not my own invention.

For example, a media analysis in the *New York Times*, dated April 2, 1987, directed some rare appreciative comments at the PTL (Praise The Lord) television ministry of Jim and Tammy Bakker.[1] This was shortly after the couple had been exposed for the sexual and tax scandals that would wipe out their audience of an estimated fifteen million viewers and result in a jail term for Jim Bakker. In reflecting on their past success, the analyst John Corry gave Jim and Tammy high marks for their good-humored, relaxed programs. It was effective and sincere presentation, not fraud, that accounted for the willingness of viewers to send them money. "The evangelists will continue," Corry concluded, "because they're good at what they do." The sophistication, the slickness of "wonderful packaging," and the suspected play-acting all might constitute a degradation of religion. But the Bakkers and the other TV evangelists had moved with the times. According to the analyst, "we are a long way here from a revivalist tent show."

Are we indeed? Lying behind the analysis of the Bakkers in the *New York Times*, as well as the more usual hostile reaction to their work, is a notion about the growing worldliness of religion. For Corry the TV evangelists had simply learned rules about how to appeal to a television audience from successful talk-show hosts, especially Johnny Carson. Carson had demonstrated just how far "sheer amiability" could go in producing income both for himself and for his sponsors. Folding up their revival tents forever, the Bakkers, Jimmy Swaggart, Robert Schuller, Rex Humbard, Jerry Falwell, and Pat Robertson revamped their format in careful imitation of the entertainment media. With evidence of this sort

3

of shameless clerical capitulation to worldly fame and fortune, never mind the sexual misbehavior and high living, who could doubt that we live in a secular age?

Yet leaving aside the Bakkers and their former associates, some of whom fell by the wayside, we need to think carefully about what we mean when we use the word "secular" to differentiate contemporary religious life in the United States from what preceded it. Was religious life in the United States ever demonstrably less "worldly" than what one now finds on TV? Maybe, depending on what you mean by the terms. But equivalents to televangelism are easy to find and were always widespread and popular. The road to the PTL cable network was a long time in the making. Anyone wishing to affirm the reality of a present-day secular world has more to do than point to the gulf separating Jonathan Edwards from Oral Roberts.

In 1991, 90 percent of all Americans identified themselves as religious.[2] Most Americans go to church—in percentage terms as many as a hundred years ago and vastly more than most contemporary Europeans. National leaders lace their public statements with religious sentiments with a frequency surpassed perhaps only in Middle Eastern countries. Religious symbols and references crowd into our marketplaces, our commercial media, our sporting arenas, and our places of entertainment. Even our public schools, now supposedly denuded of every trace of formal religion, remain embroiled in religious controversy.

However, if secularization inadequately describes contemporary culture and society in the United States, the mere statistical counter-assertion that organized religion remains important obscures much that has happened over time. Most students of the American past, trained to spot what has changed, view claims about the lessening importance of religion as generally valid. Some important things are not the same as they once were. For example, there is measurable truth to the proposition that organized churches lost much of their power to enforce moral sanctions during the course of the nineteenth century, even against their own members. Many Americans, especially well-educated Americans, do not go to church these days and suffer no social stigma as a result. For a long time the most privileged part of being Protestant in the United States was the freedom to walk away from that identification without becoming socially lost. Now many American Catholics and Jews are equally privileged. Religious controversy, something that once provided young children with their first taste of intellectual argument and debate and furnished the chief rationale for "higher" education, no longer plays a necessary part in stimulating academic curiosity and growth. The history of the changing curriculum offered by American universities since the middle of the nineteenth century tells this tale sufficiently. As an influence over what is deemed "acceptable" in the public life of the nation, individual religious denominations exercise clout in ways that are not very different from the ways of local PTAs, Rotary clubs, or the Modern Language Association.

Yet, I insist, religion is pervasive, even if it is also compartmentalized and in some contexts marginalized. A major thesis of this book is that much of what we usually mean by speaking of secularization has to do not with the disappearance of religion but its commodification, the ways in which churches have grown by participation in the market, or more specifically how religious influences established themselves in the forms of commercial culture that emerged in the nineteenth century, turning the United States into a flowering Eden of leisure industries by the middle of the twentieth. This is not a history of the fortunes of individual denominations. It is a study of religious influence in determining the taste of people who were learning to purchase "culture" as a means of self-improvement and relaxation.

"Commercial culture" (or comparable terms such as "marketplace of culture" and "culture industry") is a problematic concept, but it has, I think, a reasonably clear meaning in this book. One way to define it is by setting it against other uses of the word "culture." To Matthew Arnold and to many other aesthetically minded people in the nineteenth century, culture was a quality of being, the attainment of elevated taste and refinement that came with proper breeding and education. It was most certainly not something that one purchased. The idea of commercial or marketed culture also differs from the meaning that anthropologists assign to culture. Their view of culture as the sum total of humanly created symbol systems, artifacts, ideologies, and behavior codes through which people order and understand their world is a relevant concept herein. I often use the word culture in the anthropological sense. But the particular term "commercial culture" denotes something narrower, a more restricted arena.

"Commercial culture" sits awkwardly between the meanings of culture used by Arnold and by anthropologists. On the side nearest to Arnold, it designates a number of commodities that are marketed with the promise of their being helpful, indeed essential, to any person wishing to attain "culture." To consume them in large quantities is a way to indicate that one is "cultured." Such commodities include art, opera, ballet, legitimate theater, and the "Five-Foot Shelf of Harvard Classics." "Aids" to culture were sold before the nineteenth century, but for various reasons industrialization vastly expanded the market for them. More important, in the United States the expansion of the marketplace of culture in the nineteenth century entailed a significant democratization that brought commercial culture and popular culture into close proximity. The cultural

5

commodities just mentioned were directed mainly at people of wealth and education. A larger market for culture (the vast majority of it related to what we now call the entertainment and leisure industry) grew up to meet the consuming tastes of ordinary folk. In pre-industrial societies, popular culture rested on traditional folkways that were only marginally related to buying and selling. That was no longer the case after large industries grew up to sell cheap fiction, newspapers, melodrama, minstrel shows, baseball, and movies to the democratic masses. In this sense mass culture is commercial culture carried to the largest possible number of consumers.

Religion's role "in the marketplace of culture" began in the nineteenth century as an effort to influence and in some cases to ban altogether the commodities being offered for sale. Protestants had special problems with markets that existed to make various forms of leisure and entertainment attractive. Religious leaders were not themselves selling anything. Their censorship efforts and prescriptive commentary were intended to exert an independent control over what sorts of items and activities became available for consumption. In these endeavors they extended the hand of cooperation to all laypeople who shared their values and their view that just because people might be willing to pay to do something did not mean that they ought to be able to.

However, the work of religious leaders and moralists in the marketplace of culture was immediately entangled in a related but distinguishable enterprise. Rather than remaining aloof, they entered their own inventive contributions into the market. Initially these were restricted to the market for reading material, but their cultural production diversified. Religious leaders even sponsored "non-profit" organizations with moral and reform goals that competed with the appeal of popular entertainments. By degrees, religion itself took on the shape of a commodity. Supposedly an item that promoted culture in Arnold's sense, religion looked for ways to appeal to all consumers, using the techniques of advertising and publicity employed by other merchants. Many religious leaders tried to stay on the high road of elevated taste. However, America's boom market in religion operated most effectively at the popular end of the market in cultural commodities.

Since I have mentioned Jim Bakker, it may seem disingenuous to say that I am not writing a tale of declension. The narrative does suggest a trend in which religion's initial role "in the marketplace," its acting as an independent influence, gives way to its second role, its cooperation in making itself a competitive item for sale. However, both roles are relevant at the beginning and at the end of the story. Most often they complement each other. Readers who are interested in my judgmental voice will have to wait until the epilogue. At this point, I will offer only a few more observations and disclaimers.

The argument is not that religion has only recently found it necessary to embrace techniques of commercial expansion to get ahead. Commercial aspects of religion are traceable in any century. Markets once flourished in cathedral towns, and the Church shared the profits. Martin Luther complained about the sale of indulgences. Protestants made their crucial conquests in Europe among urban merchants. To say that religion is involved in market trade is not to pose a unique problem of modernity. In fact, the years I intend to cover, a relatively brief and parochial moment in the long course of developing religious traditions in the West, only about two centuries of America's past, is misleading like all chronological frames. The general historical problem about the worldly and commodity aspects of religion would take us back to the origins of Christendom and the organization of religion in Europe.

I will not go back so far, because I am persuaded that transformations of market societies in the nineteenth century as they affected the United States did transform the issues, changing the whole texture and meaning of activities labeled "spiritual." Clearly the First Amendment was a major factor in accelerating the process of religious commodification. Even before it was enacted, as Harry Stout has demonstrated in his work on the eighteenth century, religious leaders, in order to "make religion popular," understood that they had "to compete in a morally neutral and voluntaristic marketplace environment alongside all the goods and services of this world."[3] The environment of competition among denominations created by the First Amendment's ban on religious establishment simply accelerated the market rationale. The logic carried a long way. Peter Berger has observed: "The pluralistic situation is above all a market situation. In it religious institutions become consumer commodities. And . . . a good deal of religious activity comes to be dominated by the logic of market economies."[4] I do not think it perverse to suggest that contemporary religion operates in the marketplace of culture under the purest rules of *laissez-faire* left extant in our "modern" state. Government regulators and tax people put it in a separate category and try to ignore it. No one dares suggest that neon signs blinking the message that "Jesus Saves" may be false advertising.

A great part of our analytical problem lies in the slipperiness of the meanings we attach to terms. A short historical perspective tempts us to imagine that the word "spiritual" only became problematic when Thoreau heard the railroad whistle echo through the woods around Walden Pond. In fact, the categories "religious" and "secular" are social constructions that do not have steady historical meanings. Neither do their binary equivalents like "worldly" and "otherworldly," or "mundane" and "spiritual." "Secular" as a category for understanding historical experience depends for its meaning on the existence of something called "religion," and vice versa. At a formal level we are stuck with a dialectic that can produce any number of historically different syntheses.

It is even more complicated because for most people in the past the distinctions that elites found useful to settle jurisdictional disputes between church and state were meaningless. In Protestant lands and Catholic lands ordinary people went about their lives, working and worshiping and playing, without drawing impermeable boundaries between the spirit and the flesh. The habit has not vanished. Contemporary American Protestants may take offense when they see, as they certainly do in southern Europe and in Latin America, images of the crucified Christ and the grieving Virgin hanging between political posters and cheesecake calendars. But they have their own special ways to blur boundaries. They are the ones who gave sacred significance to the counting house. Protestants have zealously pledged themselves to God's business. However much we conceptualize with binary minds, however much bureaucratization encourages us to differentiate functions, reality remains hybrid.

My own historical perspective is, for all that, a secular one. It seems axiomatic to me that religion as a system of belief is not inherently different from any other system of belief. It is a construction of human invention and assumes social forms that are both reflective and productive of class, gender, and politics in various historical contexts. The fact that religion is usually bound up with claims about extra-worldly and non-material realities provides it with special content, but not content distinct in its social and cultural production from other ideologies that give direction and meaning to human lives. It does not take much cleverness to see that in all past epochs, despite the distinguishing postures assumed by the church and by the state, each regarding the other as a potential enemy or usurper, the religious and the secular, understood in the least problematic ways, freely intermingled and confronted each other on the same very earthly soil.

I am aware that my analysis does not pay much attention to the intricate appeal and complexity of religious ideas. In privileging a secular understanding of spiritual claims, it opens itself to the charge of functionalism or, worse, reductionism. That possibility worries me only a little bit since one of the most egregious forms of reductionism is to place special boundaries around the concept of religion. The history of religion in the United States has suffered from being placed in a category separate from the general issue of understanding culture. On the other hand, I do not want to seem insensitive to the autonomous power of ideas, a power that can never be fully explained by stretching ideas over a grid of socio-economic factors. The human mind is not open-endedly inventive, and what it can know and believe is always conditioned by specifiable historical circumstances. However, I am a soft, not a hard, determinist. What makes history fascinating is not our undoubted ability to entrap human behavior in circumstances but our surprise in seeing humans outwit circumstances. Every now and again they accomplish something that takes our breath away by its sheer nobility. The people in my narrative do not do that, but they are not pawns.

I do not deny that when people call something "religion," it makes a difference in how they respond. Religion, even conceived as a very earthbound cultural construction, yields a different sort of allegiance than most other things, whatever the close analogues. Yet one benefit of treating religion in most ways like other ideologies is that you equalize blame. Religion is not, as some would have it, uniquely responsible for all the crimes of a divided humanity or for the problems of American capitalism. I may even be arguing something comforting to religious people—to wit, that religion is not clearly worse off or less "spiritual" than it once was. After all, if religion is to be culturally central, it must learn to work with other things that are also central. Previously that might have been feudalism, kings, or Platonic philosophy. More recently it has been market capitalism responsive to consumers with spare time and a bit of money to spend. If contemporary religion in America seems to lack anything suggesting transcendence, it may be because it has not had much to work with. Religion by itself never made any age great.

In fact, I discount "golden ages" of any kind, and perhaps especially a religious "golden age" of New England Puritanism when everyone went to church, feared God and ministers, trembled before a still mystified universe, and tested notions about God with an intellectual rigor that reduced all other interests to insignificance. By anybody's reckoning, the account that follows is not a Whiggish one. But it is an effort to redress a balance. American history was once cheerfully written with the assumption that Americans were a religious people. They were because God wanted them to be. Even Perry Miller, an atheist impressed not with God but with the ideas of godly men, managed to leave that impression. As a breed, political historians have been more nervous than intellectual historians in assigning a positive role to religion. Religion either leads people to overmoralize issues that demand rational analysis and compromise or prompts them to vote blindly in affirmation of group identity rather than in accord with economic self-interest. Many narratives of American history firmly consign religion to the private sphere, something occasionally interesting when supportive of a progressive social philosophy but otherwise best left out of the account. In my opinion no centrally important cultural component of American life is more regularly neglected in synthetic accounts of American history than religion.

That is because most American historians since World War II have not only become secularists, as I classify myself, but have accepted Weberian assumptions that a secularization finally destructive of religion is an inevitable tendency of modernization. In the long run, the final-solution secularists may be right. But at the moment the intriguing question is why they have proved to be so dead wrong. The answer that I spin out in this book is that religion, with the various ways it has entered the cultural marketplace, has been more inventive than its detractors imagined. As an independent influence, it won some important victories. And as a commodity, it satisfied many buyers.

In the most objectively measurable terms, the great age of religion in the United States was not the seventeenth century, however remarkable the theological inventiveness of the Puritans, but the nineteenth century. Christianity was carried in all of its forms, including some newly invented ones, across an expanding nation. The people in the South, both black and white, went from being the least religious folk in the nation, to arguably the most religious. Everywhere, church membership rose from a small plurality of people to a majority. Non-Christian religious traditions, especially Judaism but also Buddhism, Hinduism, and Islam, began building institutional structures in the United States. Elaborate church architecture was a visible sign of "worldly success."

The quotation marks are meant to remind us that we are always talking about significant fictions. Commercial culture in America developed new forms of "worldliness." At the same time, it developed new ways to be "religious." As usual, what was worldly and what was religious did several things at once, engaging in angry confrontation, somehow coexisting, commonly intermingling. The sheer diversity of ethnic cultures in the United States made the patterns intricate and unpredictable. Almost any generalization can be contradicted. However, it is always the pattern of the religious and secular, not the assumed eclipse of one by the other, that is interesting.

In one respect I will concede declension because I can think of no neutral way to talk about it. Religious ideas are not as philosophically powerful as they once were. Although I cannot prove that average religious Americans are less theologically sophisticated than their forebears, I can nonetheless assert without any hesitation that they are no more so. They can buy and read vast numbers of religious books, yet survey after survey suggests that they are stupefyingly dumb about what they are supposed to believe. When religion began to sell itself in earnest, it contributed to a process of democratization that did not yield impressive enlightenment. Maybe that is the point. American religious leaders cannot expect everything. If they had clung to their best religious ideas and compromised nothing, their churches would be as empty as they are in many European countries, and lay people would expect them to keep their mouths shut in public places outside of ecclesiastical boundaries.

For that very reason we need to be careful about what we dismiss as unworthy of serious attention. We may sneer at TV evangelism. But religion has always been most popular in its intellectually debased forms, even in eras when cardinals worked for kings and theologians were better philosophers than now. Again, the interesting historical story is about the changed ways in which religion learned to exert its influence in the United States. In telling this story, I have tried to rein in my urges to "deconstruct" claims about what was or was not religion, and what was or was not secular. I do not enter the debate about whether a church-sponsored raffle empties a church of religion; nor does my argument proceed by trying to demonstrate that everything suggestive of what psychologists call "peak experiences" can be called religion, however blatantly secular its purport. This is not to say that there will not be confusions. Wait until we get to the New Age.

Let us begin, keeping always in mind that something important happened in the United States when religion could no longer be defined by legal privilege. It had to sell itself not only in the competitive church market but also in a general market of other cultural commodities that were trying in many cases to break free of religious disapproval rooted mainly in Protestant animosities. Culture became an industry, related both to Arnold's high-minded aspirations and to less high-minded leisure activities that soon defined popular culture. Technology, industrialization, class and gender formation, urbanization, immigration—all these things created bewildering complexities that demanded adjustments. The wonder is not that under the circumstances religion sometimes pandered to mass audiences, that one group of people used it to exert social control over another group of people, that the prophetic voice of religion was a minor key, or that churches in a broad sense became profit conscious. The wonder is the skill with which religious leaders negotiated the new circumstances, indeed the aggressively leading role that religion played in shaping society and culture.

We will eventually get back to Jim Bakker and his set. There is a long story to unfold first, one in which leaders of all shades of religious opinion played a role. I completed the final chapter and revisions of this book in Lancaster, Pennsylvania, where the Amish have struggled to show what religion might look like if left untouched by the processes of commodification. Yet anyone who has traveled east from Lancaster on Route 30 and viewed the manufactured Amish attractions that draw tourists by the thousands to the area will recognize the futility of attempted isolation. If you do not commodify your religion yourself, someone will do it for you. That fact also plays a significant part in my analysis.

CHAPTER ONE

Moral Sensationalism
and Voracious Readers:

Religious Strategies in
the Antebellum Book Market

I thank God there are no free schools nor
printing, and I hope we shall not have
[either] these hundred years, for learning
has brought disobedience, and heresy, and
sects into the world; and printing has
divulged them, and libels against the best
government.

Governor William Berkeley of Virginia

According to a celebrated notion deeply rooted in the Western tradition, reading is a subversive practice. The matter is debatable. Until recently the general view among partisans of democracy has been that the ability to read is an equalizer; it empowers the weak at the expense of the privileged. Skeptics now argue, however, that the practice of reading only occasionally threatens settled ways of thinking; more commonly the aid it provides to collective memory promotes centralized authority and works to the advantage of entrenched interests. This soured view reflects disenchantment with power manipulations attendant to our age of mass culture. According to the argument, the potential intellectual liberation promised by the diversity of print material works within exceedingly narrow boundaries set by men and women who lay claim to the privileges of professional standing. For most people, reading is no more than a ticket to enter a market stocked with printed ideas that have been shorn of any threat to the status quo. They wander tamely through it observing carefully controlled rules of conduct and purchase.

A jaundiced assessment about how print promotes the hegemony of elite groups has considerable appeal in our era when even reading enthusiasts suppose a connection between the staggering amount of print material available in any supermarket and the banal, repetitive, committee-constructed sound bytes that television news programs broadcast as substantive public debate. Nonetheless, it took time, a long time, before elites regarded the habit of reading as a reasonably safe practice to encourage in large numbers of people.[1]

For perhaps obvious reasons the history of reading has been bound closely to the history of religion. Clerics took the lead in saying what was good and bad about exposure to the printed word.[2] They wrote the books that prescribed reading practices. Before the Reformation, reading was a restricted privilege. There were practical reasons for this. Despite the famous innovations of Johann Gutenberg (circa 1440), a book printed from movable type remained for a long time an expensive commodity unknown in most households. Class and education also circumscribed boundaries for a society of readers. What was printed was in Latin, and the vast majority of Europeans could not make out the written signs of that language or of any other language.

Religious leaders deliberately kept other barriers in place that retarded the passage to literacy. Long before literary critics (our contemporary clerics) discovered that reading is not a passive exercise and that readers reshape texts to their own fancies, those charged with maintaining religious orthodoxy worried about how the dissemination of print material might contaminate the "truth." From the time that we can speak of a commercial circulation of texts, heretics have wanted to get published. It was not merely, or even primarily, the possibly unorthodox content of printed material that was worrisome. More threatening was the likelihood that printed orthodoxy (and what could be more orthodox than the Bible?) would be misconstrued by people who were functionally literate but who were not trained to see meaning on the page that matched what religious councils had struggled mightily to construct.[3] The practice of reading, then, was deliberately discouraged in Christian Europe, and the truth that was preserved in print was conveyed to the people through oral instruction. Reading without oral commentary was unthinkable. The first communities of readers beyond the monasteries did not learn to read silently. Reading, where it was possible, was more a public than a private practice.[4]

With the Reformation, Protestants changed many of the assumptions that governed reading. That, in any case, is how Protestants like to remember their liberating influence. The Bible printed in the vernacular became a book for the people. Priests no longer had the authority to command the meanings that were read into it. What God had chosen to communicate was available to ordinary human beings. To place themselves in the most favorable circumstance to receive his instructions, they had a positive duty to master reading and to study incessantly his revealed words. In market terms this meant a stimulus to demand. Printers and booksellers began to make money on the rising tide of literacy. Clerics quickly detected a downside to a situation in which popular taste rather than authoritative pronouncement determined what was printed. Broadsides, chapbooks, and almanacs appealed to an insatiable consumer appetite for gossip, heroics, and violence. Nonetheless, in Protestant lands the most typical commodity that the print market offered for sale was some form of devotional material.

Despite gibes at Catholics for looking suspiciously at efforts to promote universal literacy, the encouragement that Protestants gave to reading and the private study of religious material was cautious and bounded by all sorts of restrictions. Pushed to an extreme, the Protestant ideal of *sola fide* made churches and ministers unnecessary to an individual's intellectual and spiritual grasp of God's word. To guard against the rampant spread of this invitation to anarchy, Protestant countries required church attendance, with severe penalties for non-attendance. Although ministers had no power to impart God's grace through the sacraments and no authority to forgive in his name, they were, through their training and in their office, assigned a role as primary interpreters of God's word. Telling people what the Bible meant was the function of sermons, often very long sermons, that came to prominence in Protestant worship. The Bible was available to everyone, but within a system that taught people not to challenge men who held offices that God had instituted. Wherever the Reformation was able to control what it had unleashed, its leaders regarded the printing press as an ally in the cause of building godly communities. They also believed that unless they controlled what was printed, they could find themselves in deep trouble.

In the seventeenth century in some parts of colonial America, Protestantism's encouragement of literacy seemed to be working in exactly the right way. Many people could read; but their reading habits reinforced orthodoxy rather than encouraged questioning.[5] People read to sustain their faith. To be sure, the widespread ability to read also spread news of religious dissent that stirred all the American colonies both in the seventeenth and the eighteenth centuries. Yet interestingly, the dissenters who caused the most trouble, antinomians of one sort or another and emotional revivalists, were often the ones who placed the least emphasis on reading and intellectual discourses shaped by reading. If anything can be judged by quantifying the various categories of colonial print material, we may cautiously conclude that Protestant religion was the great beneficiary of the colonial press. Reading did not undercut the large amount of deference accorded to appointed and elected leaders.

We know most about New England, admittedly a misleading example.[6] There we would expect a predominance of godly books, written in the main by ministers who had ample occasion to interpret them to captive audiences. By the end of the seventeenth century, more "corrupting" written material—jestbooks, chivalric tales, romances, ballads, plays, poetry, and especially almanacs—was a source of profit for printers and booksellers. These often sensational tales competed with the steady sellers of piety, and though not as closely read and reread as the Bible, they were avidly consumed.[7] Their circulation bothered ministers. In retrospect, it is easy to say that all reading material, including the Bible, was in the process of being commodified; that is, assigned value based on its sales potential. Even so, the balance had not tipped. The books that ordinary people preserved and willed to their heirs were godly books whose use value transcended cash transactions. Piety remained the chief justification for the extraordinary New England venture of trying in systematic ways to teach people to read.

In other parts of the American colonies, although literacy and reading habits were less pronounced and less dependent on church encouragement, theology remained a central component of reading practice. This was true even in areas where religious control was notoriously lax.[8] Evidence drawn from southern library collections suggests that the southern planters of the eighteenth century gave pride of place to books about history, politics, and law. However, according to one careful estimate, religious works were in the eighteenth century, as in the seventeenth, the most widely read books in library collections.[9] In any case, colonials did not set theological and devotional books in opposition to works dealing with history, politics, and law. In the South, as in New England, clerics believed that much of the reading material that we routinely classify as "secular" directly supported religious instruction. This was certainly true of the many kinds of school books that appear in inventories of colonial libraries—geographies, histories, and spellers that were more often than not written by ministers. In effect, Protestant ministers welcomed virtually all learned tracts except those of Papists or freethinkers. Thus, the Anglican Society for the Propagation of the Gospel stocked its libraries with works by classical authors who predated the Christian era.

To be sure, reading in the late eighteenth century could veer in directions that challenged, if not God's architecture of the world, then many of the irrational decrees that ministers attributed to divinity. By the end of the century, the number of non-devotional books offered for sale easily exceeded specifically religious titles. We may still say that the difference in numbers is misleading because religious leaders regarded many of the "secular" books as "serious" reading that complemented the Protestant temperament.[10] On the other hand, something in the balance signaled a significant change not only in readers' taste but also in the ways that the merchants of books responded to taste. With the beginning of the nineteenth century, a strong market demand for non-prescribed types of reading—novels and certain newspapers, for example—posed a severe test to the encouragement that Protestants had given to universal literacy. The problem of wayward reading was not exactly new, but it grew in import for Protestant leaders who believed that America's venture into republican politics depended for its survival upon strong religious faith and the moral order it was presumed to sustain.

The circumstances that turned reading into everyday practice and at the same time into a problem that demanded innovative responses from people who feared that Satan had seized control of the book trade were in part the results of technology. In the early nineteenth century the introduction of stereotype printing and steam-power presses made possible the production of print material on a scale that was revolutionary in its proportions. These innovations at the same time represented significant capital investments and required publishers to find ways to expand their market by advertising, better distribution, and providing a product with mass appeal. A book market had existed in colonial America, but it relied primarily on a local clientele and was not highly differentiated. In the first half of the nineteenth century, print material became a leading industry that by degrees shifted profits to the entrepreneurs with the heaviest capital investments and the ability to distribute a relatively cheap product to a vast number of potential buyers.

The question that ministers faced was whether they could exercise more than a marginal influence upon the directions taken by commercial publishing houses in the United States. Their social and political position had altered. In 1740 clergymen had constituted 70 percent of all learned professionals in Massachusetts. In 1800 the figure had been cut down to 45 percent.[11] Lacking the apparatus of an established church, they carried no weight in the realm of public opinion unless they could find ways to make people want to listen to them. Small wonder that many of them spoke of a crisis. If Protestant ministers could not control people's reading habits and turn them toward spiritually rewarding material, then what hope was there for a virtuous republic.

What happened was rather remarkable. Once they understood the challenge, many religious leaders decided to fight fire with fire. They entered the marketplace of reading culture with circumspection but with an eye toward opportunity. Religious societies founded specifically to spread the message of Christianity first demonstrated the possibilities of the new print technology, showing the way for profit-making applications. Ministers became authors, not only of devotional material with greater popular appeal but of books that competed directly with despised forms of fiction. In time they even wrote fiction. The sorts of experiments that ministers and their close allies launched varied by denomination. Unitarians and Methodists did different things. In sum, however, we may credit them with an influence upon popular taste that gave a religious and moral tone to many kinds of print material that did not emanate from the clerical camp or have its approval. In the first part of the nineteenth century, this was largely a Protestant achievement. Protestants solidified a new base for religious authority in the United State that depended heavily on market strategies. In so doing, they crucially affected the nature of commercial culture that came into being in the course of the nineteenth century.[12]

Bibles, Tracts, and the Printing Revolution

The Protestant faith in the benevolent power of the printed text was at no time more fervently expressed than through missionary organizations formed in England late in the eighteenth century and in the United States a decade or so later. On this side of the Atlantic, the most famous of these was the American Tract Society, which resulted from a merger in 1825 of some forty smaller societies. One of the merged entities, the Massachusetts Society for the Promoting of Christian Knowledge, had been in operation for over twenty years. Of roughly equal importance to the American Tract Society was the American Bible Society (founded in 1816) whose evangelical aims are perpetuated in our own time by the quite separate The Gideons International. Modern American business travelers, utterly reliant on the tools of instant commercial transactions, find it easier in their hotel rooms to put their hands on a Bible than on a telephone directory.

In commercial terms the importance of the nineteenth-century societies, funded primarily by Presbyterian and Congregational laymen, was in demonstrating the economic feasibility of vastly increasing the scale of production. By 1827 the Tract Society printed over three million items for distribution. That number went to over five million in 1828 and to over six million in 1929. The Bible Society by the end of the 1820s was producing three hundred thousand editions annually, not enough to put the New Testament into the hands of every man, woman, and child in the United States but an ambitious step in that direction. Probably no other publisher at the time printed as many volumes annually, and only one or two others took in more cash receipts.[13] The missionary and tract societies were, to use the language of modern tax codes, non-profit organizations. That label, however, should not obscure the implications of their activities for developing a market logic. Books (a cultural product) and reading (a cultural practice) were being drawn into a system that measured utility by profit, hence the term "commercial culture." Ministers were important figures in a network of critics who tried to separate good books (morally uplifting ones) from bad books. But they had to think in creative ways. If readers did not choose good books, publishers would not print them.

The mass production of relatively cheap material held out great promise for turning daily newspapers, magazines, and serial fiction into major growth industries. The first publishers of the penny press, Benjamin H. Day and James Gordon Bennett, seized their chance for enrichment in the middle of the 1830s; within a few years many others did as well, including Sarah Hale, the editor of Godey's Lady's Book; George Wilkes, the editor of the National Police Gazette; and Irwin and Erastus Beadle, the famous promoters of the dime novel. However, religious leaders had a jump on the competition. Religious publishers had first demonstrated the possibilities of scale. They pioneered in innovative ways to sell a message to consumers.

Their inventions made the line between business and non-business, profit and non-profit, almost irrelevant. Methodists turned their chaplains into colporteurs who aggressively sold tracts. By 1830, several years before any of the undertakings named above were launched, the Methodist weekly *Christian Advocate and Journal* claimed a circulation of twenty-five thousand, a figure much larger than that of any other American serial. The *Christian Advocate* aimed to be "a good, virtuous well-conducted newspaper," and it succeeded because it was livelier than most of the competition.[14] It eschewed dogma for genial aphorisms and general advice. "Parents," "youth," and "children" had different departments to read; and the paper did not neglect "Domestic Economy," "Medical Intelligence," and "Foreign Intelligence." It finally carried a variety of information useful to consumers including bank-note tables, New York prices, and advertising. The appeal of the *Christian Advocate* caught the attention of both religious and secular publishers. Gaylord P. Albaugh estimated that in the years between 1800 and 1830 the number of subscribers to religious journals climbed from five thousand to around four hundred thousand.[15]

Something besides cheapness determined the success of publishing ventures. Formats and content had to be adjusted to appeal to large numbers of Americans who had the time and money to read but who also had diverse reading interests and varying attention spans. Religious authors who understood that the nation's tolerance for religious instruction depended on innovations in the use of the printed word became cultural entrepreneurs of the first rank. These religious leaders recognized that they faced serious competition in trying to attract audiences of nineteenth-century readers, and they urged Protestants to broaden their definition of what constituted acceptable reading material. In 1834 the American Tract Society, in heralding a list of "steady sellers" for children, phrased the problem as it was widely perceived: "While, on the one hand, the Committee wish to issue publications rich in the glorious truths of salvation, and to do what they can to *counteract* the prevailing thirst in the rising generation for the mere entertainment of high wrought fiction—a thirst which, it is feared, some writers, professedly religious, are injuriously cherishing—they are aware, on the other hand, that the young demand something more entertaining than mere didactic discussion."[16]

For a religious publisher to talk about the need for entertainment was an enormous concession to the changing times. Almost any statement about the use of non-work time could set a fierce quarrel going in the first half of the nineteenth century. Many Protestant ministers never uttered the word "entertainment" with an approving tone without placing it next to the words "useful" and "instructive." Therefore it was a big step for the mainly Presbyterian and Congregational sponsors of the

Tract Society to portray their material as enjoyable reading. They wrote pleasure into their advertising. Tracts were "short," "interesting," "striking," "clear," "plain," "pungent," and "entertaining," the same adjectives picked up by copywriters to sell popular serials and fiction.[17] By 1850 the American Tract Society had published some sixty-nine volumes intended to attract young people, titles divided between a "Youth's Biographical Series" and a "Youth's Narrative Series." To heighten the appeal, directors of the society hired some of America's best artists and engravers to add illustrations.

In one important respect the Tract Society made no concession to popular taste. It refused to print fiction, frequently repeating the well-established Protestant view that fiction degraded morals. The reasons for this bias went beyond the common association of novels with sexually bawdy themes. What bothered religious writers more was the novel's frank departure from "truth," and the pleasure it gave to readers by appealing to the free play of their imagination. A fear of the imagination affected Protestant attitudes toward all forms of "art" well into the nineteenth century. Although most religious objections to "virtuous fiction" disappeared in the latter half of the nineteenth century, clerical opinion in the first half adjusted by stages. In the first stage it endorsed "true narratives" or "truthful tales." The instructive narratives and stories printed by the Tract Society were "authentic."

It is no small point to note that a "true tale" published as a moral warning to the young might include racy material that made many novels written at the same time seem tame by comparison. They were every bit as made-up, just more report-like in style. However, genuflecting to "truth" was essential, and the formula, if transparent, served a purpose. Religious moralists satisfied popular taste with stories that denounced fiction-reading, gave inexpert readers something almost as entertaining, and taught conventional moral messages. "True narratives" replaced dogmatic treatises and devotional books as the most popular form of religious publishing and one of the most popular forms of any sort of publishing in the first half of the nineteenth century.

For that result, a lot is owed to Mason Locke Weems. He was an innovator of considerable importance. William Gilmore Simms, in summing up his achievement, wrote: "He had no fear of the vulgar." To critics of this ordained minister of the Protestant Episcopal Church, Simms was understating the case. In their opinion, Weems loved what was vulgar and was determined to drag American culture down to the lowest level of democratic taste. Simms added about Weems that "the social aspects of a tavern . . . found favour in his sight."[18] It was an accurate statement. Weems's partisanship to "motley folk" raised a big-

ger controversy in some minds than the one about how far he had stretched the truth in his famous biography of George Washington. Weems was an itinerant bookseller who never tired of instructing Mathew Carey, the Pennsylvania publisher for whom he worked, about the necessity of giving ordinary people what they were supposed to read in formats they would buy. Typically he wrote back to Philadelphia pleading for Carey, who was Roman Catholic, to stop "oppressing and crushing me to the earth by ten thousand puritannical books."[19] Rather than gloomy tomes that threatened both him and local book merchants with insolvency, he asked for books "of the gay and sprightly kind, novels, decent plays, elegant histories. Let the moral and religious be as dulcified as possible. Divinity for this climate should be natural and liberal, adorned with the graces of style, and clothed in splendid binding."[20] Weems viewed religion as a commodity, and he made a close study of attractive packaging.

Weems had learned something about the book trade before he had gone to work for Carey in 1794. Traveling the countryside in 1791, he had found success with an "edifying" book entitled *Onania*, a treatise warning of the "heinous sin of self-pollution and all its frightful consequences." The "edifying" label was important to Weems. He was, after all, a Protestant. To sell a book was a commercial transaction, but it was also a missionary enterprise whose social goal was to promote virtue. A graphic and frank description of the wages of sin, according to Weems, invited authors to explore new ways to capture and sustain reader interest. The benefits for moral instruction and profit were already apparent in the most famous didactic tracts that had flowed from Weems's own pen. These included *Hymen's Recruiting Sergeant, The Drunkard's Looking Glass, God's Revenge Against Adultery, God's Revenge Against Murder, The Bad Wife's Looking Glass*, and *God's Revenge Against Gambling*. These volumes, and others like them, constituted a genre that might aptly be labeled "moral sensationalism."

A few examples convey the flavor. Weems began *The Drunkard's Looking Glass* with the tale of a man, who, after falling before Satan's temptation to get drunk, violates his sister, kills his father, and hangs himself. Calamity follows upon calamity, all bloody, all violent. Drunkards die in their vomit. One inebriated young man falls from his horse, and the brutal impact leaves "no sign of a nose remaining on his face . . . completely scalping the right side of his face and head. . . . One of his eyes . . . was cleanly knocked out of its socket; and, held only by a string of skin, there it lay naked on his bloody cheek."[21] In his other small volumes, women are "defiled," parents die of grief, and annoyed lovers ready to move on to new conquests murder those they have ru ined. In one case an unfortunate girl is pushed from a canoe by her betrayer. He drowns her by striking her with an oar, beating her hands away from the sides of the craft, and "barbarously" pushing her backwards, "as she cried for mercy, unto the bubbling, blood-stained wave."[22] Theodore Dreiser was considered daring over a century later for fictionalizing this sort of incident in *An American Tragedy*.

To make his words more graphic, Weems searched for engravings to accompany them. His tracts usually boasted a frontispiece as a clear "come-on" for readers. The illustrations were, without exception, violent. In one, a man shoots another in the head, saying "There! G—d D—n you. Take that."[23] To illustrate another, he wrote to Carey asking that he put it "instantly into the hands of some artist good at design who would give us at once the likeness of a very beautiful woman distorted or convulsed with Diabolical passion, in the act of murdering, with up-lifted axe, her husband in sleep."[24] This from a man who also begged Carey to send him no books of "bad morals."[25]

Weems's marriage of aggressive marketing with a moral mission was one important starting point of America's nineteenth-century culture industry. Weems intended a didactic point in depicting the murders, the broken skulls oozing with blood, the twisted faces with strangled purple tongues, and the suicides of violated women. The gory passages were always tagged with a direct moral message to readers. No sooner does a drowned young woman sink under the waves than Weems writes words as if from her mouth: "O' hear my counsel. Shun, as you would a demon, the man who scorns religion: our helpless sex's only guardian, whose divine power alone exalts a husband's soul. . . ."[26] To readers reeling from the image of a wife who has sunk an axe deep into her husband's brain, Weems says: "Oh young men! young women draw nigh—and from this bloody bed come learn that lesson which pulpits so often have preached in vain. Learn at this scene of death the *worth* of religion."[27] We may imagine readers of this material who easily separated the sensationalism from the morals and were interested only in the former. However, although Weems was an author determined to make money (his letters to Carey make that abundantly clear), his intentions were to find literary formulas that blended "amusement" with "instruction" in religion and virtue. What he perfected proved to be popular, and the basic formula was recycled endlessly through the course of the nineteenth century. Moral sensationalism remained a staple of commercial publishing. It convinced many American religious leaders to pay attention to popular taste as reflected in consumer choices. It was one of the factors that turned the public influence of religion away from dogma toward moral issues. It is a subject of endless fascination.

Secular Appropriations of Moral Sensationalism

The key to appreciating Weems's success lies in his off-handed juxtaposition of daily banalities, commercial shrewdness, humor, horror, and piety. This mixture resulted from Weems's calculation of the popular pulse. Weems moved daily among a variety of people and grew sensitive to the opportunities created for him by their desires. As one sort of archetypal white American male, his career provides us with a number of different historical images. On the negative side, he might handily be used to illustrate the intellectual decline of the Protestant cleric, the pettiness of the small-time American businessman, or the crafty exploitative drives of the pornographic writer. More positively, he might stand for the practical inventiveness exemplified just prior to his era by Benjamin Franklin and a pattern of autodidactic learning that clever youths followed to make their fortunes for the rest of the nineteenth century.

What is so intriguing about Weems is something else. His career reflected changes in the ways that American print material was published and distributed during the first five decades of the nineteenth century. Although he did not start the process, what he wrote and sold speeded up transformations in reader taste. Colonial readers had proved themselves to be avid consumers of sensational tales comparable to what Weems provided. Perhaps somewhat fewer broadsides and chapbooks had circulated in colonial America than in Europe at the same time.[28] But printed accounts of executions, Indian captivity tales, and novel-like stories of sexual passion had exposed American colonials to prurience and violence. For that matter, even a book that had passed the strictest standards of piety, Foxe's *Book of Martyrs*, pandered to what must be a natural human curiosity about bodily dismemberment. Widely circulated "penny godlies" supplied Weems with plenty of evidence that terror sold.[29]

Weems also had before him the example of the novel, a genre associated in the late eighteenth century with the names of Daniel Defoe, Samuel Richardson, and Henry Fielding. The controversy over the moral and religious suitability of what those men had written was of long standing. Whether Defoe's Puritan upbringing influenced the themes in *Moll Flanders* (1722) was not a question resolved to everyone's satisfaction by the author's claim that "there is not a wicked action in any part of it, but is first and last rendered unhappy or unfortunate." Religious moralists who hoped that something good might come of the novel took encouragement from Samuel Richardson's *Pamela* (1740). Ian Watt, whose pioneering book on the rise of the novel merits special mention, suggested that part of *Pamela*'s popularity owed to the fact that it "enabled readers to enjoy the attractions both of fiction and of devotional literature at the same time and in the same work."[30] It was a notion that had early champions. However, the work of Henry Fielding (*Joseph Andrews* in 1742 and *Tom Jones* in 1749) ground the moral acceptance of the novel to a halt. The religious denunciation of Fielding was widespread and not limited to humorless Puritans.[31]

The problem with the novel went beyond the question of whether virtue and vice were rewarded and punished in appropriate ways. The novel's appeal to the imagination was dangerous in itself. The first English novelists, and Richardson was no exception, made the situation worse by writing plots in which female chastity hung in the balance. Pamela may have emerged intact from the snares that were placed in her path, but religious critics deemed it pornographic even to have raised another possibility. Richardson's story encouraged readers to imagine a ravished Pamela. With Clarissa he gave their imagination full satisfaction.

Explicit sexual content complicated the moral acceptance of fiction into the nineteenth century. A case illustrative of the American debate is Susanna Rowson's *Charlotte: A Tale of Truth* (1791). The novel was a resounding success, selling nearly forty thousand copies by 1800.[32] The plot was moral enough. Charlotte Temple, a young girl of immense virtue, is seduced and carried off by a thoroughly dissolute rake. Sexual passion had less to do with her fall than an almost saintly desire to sacrifice herself for a man who desperately needed the saving touch of someone absolutely pure. Abandoned with a bastard child, the unwed mother, although a paragon of pure feeling, dies finally for the sin that cannot be washed away. Meanwhile ruinous debts crash down upon her betrayer to ensure his punishment. Virtue and vice get their customary due, yet even the alleged "truth" of this morality tale did not save it from clerical scorn and condemnation.

A good deal of the problem that Charlotte Temple presented to religious moralists lay between the lines of the text in what readers might make of Charlotte's situation. The book's plot turned the sexual innocence of women into a complex problem. Charlotte Temple "fell" because she had no understanding of sexual passion and the dangers that attended the awakening of those passions. She was fucked before she knew what the word meant, leaving readers to infer that prior knowledge of the mechanics of sexual intercourse might have enabled her to avoid what happened. However, religious moralists were not prepared to see Charlotte and other women educated about sexual feelings. They preferred a discourse of silence or the less ambiguous warnings about female sexuality written into Weems's "truthful tales."

The novels that began to find an approved place in America's cultural hierarchy abandoned sex as a subject and gave no room to the purient imagination. They copied the narrative style of the truthful tale, leaving in some of the adventure but deleting the sensationalism. They were so moral that it is difficult to distinguish the appeal of novels written by antebellum American women and that of the "authentic" stories written about the lives of female missionaries.[33] Children's fiction produced in England and the United States for the Sunday school movement provided a model. The most important British author in this genre was without doubt Hannah More who led other religious writers to strive for moral tales "so plain" that they cannot "possibly be misunderstood."[34] Her success was repeated in America by Samuel G. Goodrich, the son of a Congregational minister. His Peter Parley tales sold some seven million volumes from the mid-1820s until the mid-1850s.[35] Goodrich's stories were acknowledged as fiction, but factual information stiffened them. The moral tone was serious and designed to dampen any laughter, any emotional response, any inclination to daydream.

Much of the English fiction that became enormously popular in the United States in the first half of the nineteenth century, beginning with the books of Walter Scott and extending through those of Edward Bulwer Lytton and Charles Dickens, enhanced moral claims for the novel simply by reducing the attention given to seduction. In a more emphatic way, that was true of the fiction written by the most popular American female authors of the antebellum period. The academic reputation of books by Catharine Sedgwick, E.D.E.N. Southworth, Caroline Lee Hentz, Susan Warner, and Harriet Beecher Stowe is on the upswing, though they have yet to re-kindle the reader enthusiasm they once stirred.[36] Unviolated and untempted chastity no longer provokes much interest.

Many novels in the second and third quarters of the nineteenth century are noteworthy because of the moral force they assign to women. "Bad" men, such as Aaron Burr in Stowe's *The Minister's Wooing*, either stand outside the story or "work their will" on peripheral, "foreign" characters. "Good" men are whisked into the plot to effect a marriage but are largely irrelevant to the moral development of the heroines. Ellen Montgomery, the young girl in Susan Warner's huge success, *The Wide, Wide World* (1850), finds temptation not in any sexual precociousness but in doubts about whether she can overcome pride and make herself the proper instrument of God's will. The wide world to which she is exposed turns out to be a good bit less interesting than the one Adam and Eve set out to discover at the end of Milton's *Paradise Lost*.

Clerics, at least the more liberal ones, seized upon this sort of fiction to inch their way toward reconciliation with the novel. Their endorsement of what people were choosing to buy anyway did several things. It helped to boost the market for "safe" fiction and to encourage publishers to provide a steady supply of it. It updated the guidelines for distinguishing good literature from bad literature. And, perhaps most important, it provided ministers with an activity whereby they might believably assert authority over the production of cultural commodities. The bonds that Unitarian, Universalist, and Episcopal ministers formed with women writers had important consequences for antebellum American culture.[37] Ministers from the fastest growing Protestant denominations—Methodist and Baptist—saw almost as quickly the need to rethink their resistance to popular reading practices. The battle for cultural correctness had to be carried beyond the churches, beyond the revivals, through benevolent societies, learned societies, belles lettres, and the press.

Purer in tone and content than some pamphlets turned out by the American Tract Society, women's novels even provided a justification for fiction that encouraged some Protestant ministers to try their hand at it. By far the most successful pioneer was Joseph Holt Ingraham who throughout the 1840s managed an annual production ranging between ten and twenty-five novels. By himself, he was responsible for 10 percent of the fiction titles published in the United States in that decade.[38] Ingraham was not ordained as an Episcopal minister until after he had completed most of his opus of hack fiction. Once he took up his pastoral role, he thought it best to change formulas in fulfilling his ongoing desire to write for the commercial market. His output in the 1850s turned toward historical fiction based on the Bible, a highly successful genre that was still going strong in post–World War II America. Predictably, once ordained, Ingraham no longer thought it prudent to call his work fiction. It was "commentary on the gospel of the life and acts and words of Jesus."

His caution was no longer absolutely necessary. When Henry Ward Beecher published *Norwood* in 1867, the appropriateness of the action still caused controversy. But the hard cultural work that allowed a famous minister to market an unabashed novel for purposes of personal gain and public instruction had already been done. We can read the signs of the times in the religious press. Almost all of it carried a cautious attitude toward fiction into the 1840s, even though *Graham's Magazine* and *Godey's Lady's Book* by that time ran stories that many ministers covertly approved. The Episcopal-managed *The Evergreen* warned against romance and pathos and "fictional embellishments." The Reverend D. W. Clark's *Ladies' Repository* opposed novel-reading as late as 1851 because it inspired the "love of excitement which will become habitual, like a drug, and unfit the mind for more healthy and useful exercises."[39] By the mid-1850s, a general retreat from an absolute ban on fiction was evident. Episcopal and Unitarian journals reviewed fiction in an effort to warn their readers of "trashy, infidel, licentious romances" and to provide them with titles of "religious fiction."[40] A Baptist review took a peek at the work of Washington Irving in 1850. The *Methodist Quarterly Review* did not review a novel until 1856 but was prepared soon thereafter, in 1860, to show how the "modern novel" was becoming morally acceptable.

From Moral Sensationalism to Moral Pornography

Religious moralists, even after they cautiously found ways to approve some best-selling novels, still had plenty to worry about. Women authors and their clerical allies represented only one part of the commercial expansion of the book trade in the first half of the nineteenth century. In fact the main path from the graphic moral sensationalism of Parson Weems led not to the domestic novels of Stowe and Warner but to George Lippard's American gothic serial *The Quaker City; or the Monks of Monk Hall* (1844). As a product of popular culture, Lippard's book poses interesting problems of interpretation. It was part of a growing body of antebellum popular fiction that did not follow the example of sentimental novels in abandoning erotic passages and themes. Since the long tale involved, among other things, seduction, rape, enforced prostitution, torture, and infanticide, critics understandably dismissed Lippard's training for the evangelical Methodist ministry as something that had shaped his motives as a writer.

We enter historical terrain where nothing can be proved with certainty. How can we ever know what people make of the books they read? As contemporary critics we are puzzled by nineteenth-century American novels that were laced with moral asides yet sneered sarcastically at society's moral and religious guardians. Their authors endorsed moral platitudes while filling their stories with episodes that we might ordinarily label pornographic. How did readers react to moral messages written into passages depicting torn nightgowns that reveal naked, heaving female breasts ("full globes in all their virgin beauty")? One plausible surmise is that the salacious episodes kept readers turning the pages so quickly that they did not notice the moral instruction. It was there only to infuriate the clergy. Thus, we may ignore Lippard when he tells us that the male sexual "pleasures" he depicted were "atrocities," when he insists that his purpose is not to satirize religion and encourage freethinking but to promote faith in the work of the "Savior Jesus." The trouble with this course of action is that we are left with the question of why Lippard and other writers took so much trouble to mark their moral intentions, of why line for line the moral messages outweighed all other passages of direct authorial address to readers.

If the seemingly obligatory moral inclusions had resulted from the pressures of censors, explanations would be simple. However, the many ministers who thought that Lippard pandered to vice had no power to halt or significantly discourage the strong sale of his work.[41] Lippard did not seek, nor did he need, their approval. As in our day, attacks by churchmen could boost reader interest. We have no evidence to sustain the suspicion that Lippard used devious and hypocritical strategies to get around the moral voices of his time and address the lust of his readers with the sole aim of making money. Lippard was not a libertine seeking to subvert morality. He was, if anything, a muckraking Puritan seeking to expose the evil in those who tried to use high social position as a sufficient proof of virtue.

What was subversive in Lippard's text was the strong anti-clerical tone, the explicitly underscored theme that ministers, not the honest people he addressed, were society's real hypocrites. His clearly delineated category of villains prominently included members of the clergy who mouthed the platitudes of righteousness but who either averted their eyes from the victims of urban vice or surrendered themselves to the pleasures of vice.[42] In Lippard's mind any moral improvement in the general population sufficient to impress a returning Christ needed stronger action than what organized churches in his day were providing. Ministers charged him with worldly corruption, but in his mind it was the other way round. Lippard's attitude was a product of the democratization of Christianity, not of a plot of free thinkers.[43] As had been true for Weems, he wished to sensationalize moral and religious instruction so that it sold a lot of books.[44]

The amount of violence and sex in Lippard's book was not especially greater than what good Christians encountered in their approved reading. Indian captivity stories, for example, remained popular market items and were recommended for children.[45] These contained ample descriptions of intestines ripped from "innocent" victims, of men stripped naked and burned alive, of Christians lying in their blood, throats cut, surrounded by a company of "roaring, singing, ranting hell-hounds." In the captivity narrative of Frederick Manheim, readers savored an image of "two sixteen year old girls, tied to saplings with their hands extended above their heads, flesh pierced from knees to shoulders with six hundred sharpened splinters, five inches in length and dipped in melted turpentine, these set afire on the bleeding victims." It took three hours for them to die.[46]

Temperance stories, another genre that generally won clerical endorsement, were equally graphic. Timothy Shay Arthur's runaway best-seller *Ten Nights in a Barroom*, first published in 1854, was one among many such tales of domestic violence. Husbands beat their wives and were then killed by sons. Daughters generally died of remorse. Drink did terrible things to people which could be described because they were true. Protestants had long been expected to have a strong stomach to learn their moral lessons. Thus, clerical suspicion of George Lippard did not convincingly take from him the claim to represent an honorable moral position. What his success, in fact, indicated was just how deeply moral and religious controversy affected the commercial book market.

Comparison with a work that was very different from Lippard's helps illustrate why many writers thought it necessary to bring boldness to moral instruction. The Reverend John Todd, a Yale-educated Congregationalist, kept a pastorate in Philadelphia for six years beginning in the late 1830s. Todd was a prolific author, and the didactic pieces that he wrote in the early 1830s, *Lectures to Children* and *The Student's Manual*, sold widely. Like Lippard, Todd decided to expose the moral corruption of Philadelphia. Unlike Lippard, he wrote a most unsensational religious treatise. *The Moral Influence, Dangers, and Duties Connected with Great Cities* (1841) proved to be short on specific information. Todd's listing of "temptations peculiar in great cities" included such pious abstractions as the temptation to overlook the guilt of sin, the temptation to neglect the religion of the heart, the temptation to be uncharitable to one another, and the temptation to be jealous. In one chapter on worldly amusements, Todd broached the dangers of cards, balls, and the theater only to retreat. He boasted that he had never been in a theater. Getting too near a detailed examination of what truly went on in urban pleasure palaces, he said: "I shall not degrade you so much as to begin to enumerate the abominations which are seen, and known, and heard in these places of amusement."[47] Todd was a grand master of let-down. Interestingly but perhaps not surprisingly, his book died after a single edition.

Although church publications in the United States by no means put aside this sort of pious social inquiry, many antebellum Protestants, without getting too close to Lippard, began to appreciate the need to sponsor books that people would not only buy but read. Church-sponsored missionaries who were setting up work stations among the urban poor in the 1840s learned to describe the horrors of urban vice in plainer terms than Todd used. As far as the commercial market for print was concerned, a market that result-oriented religious moralists were forced to notice, Todd's book was studied dullness. Common sense tells us that Lippard and other authors who were serving up the temptations of urban vice in more sensational form in the 1840s had a better chance of impressing readers with the damnable wages of sin. What remained uncertain was how clerics could learn from Lippard without renouncing their pretensions of exercising an independent moral influence in the marketplace of culture.

We know that moral sensationalism sold well and became a formula for many kinds of print material other than the novel, especially all forms of journalism. The *National Police Gazette* is a particularly interesting example. Begun in 1845, its mission, stated in each issue, was to protect its presumably male subscribers from vice and crime, not merely from criminal acts perpetrated by the already fallen but also from the potential corruption of their own selves ("the allurements of vice and the temptations that eventuate only in destruction"). Its regularly featured column "Lives of the Felons" consisted of serialized "truthful" tales of the horrific consequences of adultery, drinking, and gambling. The numerous and unfailingly violent illustrations ("Frank Florin Cutting His Wife to Pieces," "A Negro Ravisher Pulling the Tongue Out of His Victim") sought both to satisfy the curiosity of readers and to remind them that God punished wickedness.[48] Ministers were not impressed, especially since the "religious section" of the *Gazette* was devoted to exposing the sexual misbehavior of well-known clerics. Still, they knew that the *Police Gazette* reached at least some churchgoers.

Moral sensationalism had no more commercially successful nineteenth-century expression than in various books that purported to guide readers through the "mysteries and miseries" of great American cities and expose their dark and dangerous secrets. Their vogue began in the 1840s. Copied from European models, especially Eugène Sue's *Les Mystères de Paris* (1842–43) and G. W. M. Reynold's *The Mysteries of London* (1845–48) which sold well in the United States in pirated editions, this genre of exposé had both fictional and factual formats. Both used sexual titillation as a formula to sell books and, according to publishers' claims, as a strategy of moral instruction.[49] Sue's American publisher was the firm of Harper and Brothers, good Methodists who apparently believed that the scenes of low life that stimulated reader curiosity heightened the moral purity of the tale.[50]

Similar claims surfaced again and again. In the preface to *The Secrets of the Great City: A Work Descriptive of the Virtues and the Vices, the Mysteries, Miseries and Crimes of New York City*, James Dabney

McCabe stated that his book "is designed to warn the thousands who visit the city against the dangers and pitfalls into which their curiosity or vice might lead them, and it is hoped that those who read the book will heed its warnings. The city is full of danger. The path of safety which is pointed out in these pages is the only one—a total avoidance of the vicinity of sin. . . . His curiosity can be satisfied in these pages, and he can know the Great City from them, without incurring the danger attending an effort to see it."[51] This obviously is not the way that Puritan divines in the seventeenth and eighteenth centuries phrased a moral prohibition. McCabe acknowledges his reader's curiosity about vice as natural, perhaps even laudatory, and promises not to spare details in telling him (the audience addressed is the young male) all about it. The assumption is that reader lust can be stilled by graphic description coupled with stern warnings not to seek personal verification. The strategy may have backfired. Young men may have prepared for their first visit to a brothel by devouring McCabe's book, although on that level of detail the book does not deliver much. What is more interesting is the possibility that readers followed its words of warning.

The most severe testing of the parameters of book selling, moral instruction, and hypocrisy involves Ned Buntline (E. Z. C. Judson), a "great rascal" who became one of the most successful of the "dime novel" authors. He was a temperance lecturer and a drunk, a writer who condemned gambling and a man who built his life around risk, a crusader against male sexual conquests and an utterly irresponsible bigamist and womanizer.[52] This moral reprobate wrote the most widely sold book in the genre of urban exposé, *The Mysteries and Miseries of New York*, a book dedicated with an irony stronger than anything Lippard mustered to "the Reverend Clergy of New York . . . with a fervent hope that they may see and remedy the evils which it describes." Why the dedication at all and why the running commentary throughout the book that chastises men of the cloth for sending missionaries abroad while ignoring the problems of vice and poverty at home?

In view of the moral and religious failures of the author, hypocrisy may in this case seem a thoroughly sufficient explanation. Even so, what are the reasons for the hypocrisy? Judson had to satisfy his readers who expected books to contain moral messages. To sell books, Judson needed to claim respect for "the *true* minister of God" and to insist that the aim of his writing was "to do good." A popular writer, that is, had to assume the role of a morally serious man. Commercial culture constructed an anonymous relationship between authors and readers. The rules that governed the intimate relationship between a pastor and his parishioners did not apply. A minister's real character mattered; an author's real character had become irrelevant. Religious and moral messages commodified in the book trade existed apart from the person who sent them abroad. Markets make everything impersonal.

Judson's fiction followed the success of many examples of antebellum fiction by constructing a melodramatic wall between good and evil. The wall did not in this case protect the book's reputation from moral assault, but it allowed readers who relished the opportunity to challenge clerical opinion to do so without lowering their own estimate of their moral worth. They could establish a distance between themselves and the crimes that enlivened the plot. If we can be reasonably confident that middle-class churchgoers were not the chief purchasers of Judson's book, we can be as reasonably sure that its readers were not men who spent their idle hours drinking, gambling, and visiting brothels. For the tale to win popular favor, readers had to be shocked by the horrors of vice and made to feel sympathy for the victims. Judson's readers, whether they belonged to a church or not, were likely sympathetic to the religious chords that it struck. Insofar as the book made religious controversy appear to be a pressing public issue, it did an important service for clerics of all denominations. People who argued about reading material in antebellum America were not choosing between morality and immorality, between religion and atheism. Their arguments were about what sort of reading practice best promoted virtue and how best to establish the proper habits.

This is not the only way to look at the cultural issues. Possibly, as one critic has argued, authors committed to sensational fiction "were inventing moral disguises for notably immoral, sometimes even sacrilegious ponderings."[53] Yet even if the "occasional pious rhetoric and the overall righteous intent are obligatory obeisances to the powerful moral conscience bred by American Puritanism," the consequences may have been more supportive than subversive of religious and moral sensibilities. Obeisance is obeisance and signifies that someone or something has the power to force it. Granted, the bizarre and explicit sexual fantasies that we find in books by Weems, Lippard, and George Thompson, a writer who outdid everyone else, must have operated as powerful stimulants upon the minds of readers. The frontispiece of one of Thompson's books, *The Countess; Memoirs of Women of Leisure*, depicted naked women with exposed pubic hair, one sporting a moustache. These unsettling images had nothing to do with the plot, although the story line had plenty to interest the sexually inquiring mind: episodes of sadomasochism, necrophilia, incest, and sexual assault. A different author seems to have written the passages of moral discourse. And yet there they are. Thompson may be the example that shows where the formula failed. But whose failure was it? Thompson's, who had lost the skill and interest to make the formula work? Or the clerics, who had suddenly discovered that moral sensationalism never worked to their advantage?

There is another example of religious leaders clashing with an important innovator in commercial culture who insisted that his enterprises promoted the cause of true religion and morality. James Gordon Bennett founded in 1835 the *New York Herald*, not the first but the second successful penny newspaper in the United States. It was a controversial venture. A Scottish-born Catholic, Bennett locked horns in his adopted homeland with John Hughes, the powerful Catholic archbishop of New York City. Hughes called him "decidedly the most dangerous man, to the peace and safety of the community, that I have ever known." Bennett's fight with his own church put him in the unenviable position of being anathema to both Protestant and Catholic clergymen. In 1840 they joined together as "Holy Allies" to make him the target of a "Moral War," a battle to destroy his newspaper that, in their minds, made scandalous gossip and reports of criminal violence more interesting than the word of God to New Yorkers.[54]

Bennett, who would be buried in a Catholic church in Washington Heights that he had generously endowed, held a different view of his moral and religious influence. In a tribute to his mother, he wrote: "Moral and religious sentiment has been the cornerstone in the character of every great benefactor, every great genius, every great being, that the world ever saw." Bennett was not inclined to write himself out of that company, and he repeatedly affirmed what he viewed as his religious mission: "to show that religion stripped of cant hypocrisy, and sectarianism, is the only foundation on which the prosperity and happiness of nations or individuals can repose." He even attributed his career in journalism to the influence of the Scriptures. They were the first readings that he had done as a child. To the Bible, he wrote, "I am indebted for that force, brevity, spirit, and peculiarity which makes the style of the *Herald* as popular with the uncontaminated masses of a community who are yet imbued with the spirit and literature of the Bible."[55] Among the journalistic innovations that may be attributed to Bennett was his printing, in the Monday editions of his "secular" newspaper, reports of notable sermons delivered the day before. Religion was part of the news.[56]

What does the example of Bennett's protestations, along with those of other non-clerical print merchants who defended their religious intentions, prove? In the first place, their words show the constraint of a particular context. They were in response to a powerful claim, which echoed through all of America's cultural institutions, that the United States was a religious nation. What commerce did in culture's name had to follow this popular assumption, however amorphous and pliable its content. That the claim was powerful owed something to clerical activity. In the first fifty years of the nineteenth century, ministers and their close allies had been in the vanguard of innovators who revolutionized the habits of American readers. As cultural merchants, they commanded respect. They had demonstrated the commercial feasibility of new printing techniques. They had invented ways for writers to attract readers whose attention needed to be caught in a hurry. They had authored or published short, snappy stories that turned sensationalism to moral purposes.

Not all Protestant leaders interacted with the marketplace of culture with equal ease. Some warned about the dangers of commercialization and suggested that the only obligation of religious leaders toward the reading public was to ensure that those people who wanted devotional material got the real thing. Still, the temptation to work as tastemakers using whatever strategies found audiences was overwhelming. The opportunities seemed great and the dangers manageable. The four Harper brothers, by the end of the 1820s, ran the largest print establishment in the United States. Their staunch Methodism and their role in consolidating the publishing industry into large firms based in New York City and Boston suggested a natural alliance. The brothers lived frugally and honestly, believing that character rather than capital lay at the base of their business.[57] In 1830 they advertised that "no works will be published by J. & J. H. but such as are interesting, instructive, and moral." Among the authors deemed worthy of that claim were Washington Irving, Henry Longfellow, Richard Henry Dana, William Prescott, and, of course, Eugène Sue.

The perfect symbol of the way that the Harper brothers joined religion and commercial culture came with their publication in 1844 of *Harper's Illuminated and New Pictorial Bible*. Handsomely illustrated, beautifully bound, immensely profitable, the Harpers realized that in the new reading world of the early nineteenth century the Bible was no longer one book; it was many books, at different prices, in different sizes, in various bindings of many colors, with different illustrations. A well-known passage in Susan Warner's *Wide, Wide World* brilliantly captures the confusion of a young female consumer who had to decide which of the many Bibles for sale was the one for her. (Her mother had sold her ring to make the purchase possible.) The confusion is rapturous; "she pored in ecstasy over their varieties of type and binding." The passage in Warner carries not a hint of criticism about the commodification of Holy Writ into just another pretty material object on the shelf. It passed at the level of unconscious acceptance that religion and book merchants could be enriched in symbiotic association. With hindsight, we can manage a bit more shock. Once the Bible was offered as an item for display and sale, as a proof of the affluence of capitalism and its ability to invent endlessly in service to the pleasures of consumerism, what restraints remained on thinking about religion not merely as an influence on the taste of buyers but also as something that itself had to satisfy the reigning taste?

The Unresolved Problem of Popular Taste

Reading material was diverse, and so were readers. The uncertainties about how people responded to what they read grew. Who, then, can fail to understand why Protestant leaders, even as they urged people to read more and struggled to make more and more print material available to everyone, worried incessantly that reading was destroying the moral fiber of the country. Were the people who most needed moral guidance reading the right books and for the right reasons? Did they understand what they read? Although literacy was essential to proselytizing, was it possible that proselytizing worked with most effect on the reading taste of the already converted and left the rest of the population with a dangerous ability to read in the wrong directions? The young daughter of a prosperous merchant might devour a popular romance without serious danger and possibly with some positive moral effect. Her father could read the daily press and not threaten his immortal soul. A young male mechanic might even read the *Police Gazette* and stay mindful that what he read provided a catalogue of situations to avoid. However, put the same material into the hands of an Irish-born maid, a saloon owner, or a young unmarried working man who strolled along the Bowery in New York City and who could predict the result? Reading meant one thing to people who were learning to think of themselves as middle class or as aspirants to middle-class status. But suppose such people were not a majority and that their number was decreasing. What then?

One thing was clear. The effects of books, the safe ones and the questionable ones, were not uniform across class, racial, and ethnic lines.[58] Reading habits and reading skills most certainly varied with social position. Basic literacy is not the issue. Most people who lived in the United States in the nineteenth century could read some language. Young men and women of higher and lower social status, immigrant workers, and even African-American slaves have all left testimony, often poignant testimony, to the importance of reading in their lives. Academics like to collect this evidence because they are professionally committed to the proposition that reading is good for people.

However, to say that people could read reveals nothing about how often they read, in what circumstances they read, or why they read. People needed different information from reading. They had different tastes. Not all people had leisure time to devote to reading or strong motivations to improve their facility with difficult texts. Protestants still placed more emphasis upon reading skills than Catholics did, and that was an important differential among working-class people. So was money. Despite the trend toward cheapness, a novel or a magazine remained a relatively costly item. Only the penny-press magnates produced a product that almost anyone who earned an income could routinely afford. Aside from what the tract societies distributed, reading material that ministers agreed was morally rewarding had a restricted audience.

In the early nineteenth century, these considerations gave Protestant reading enthusiasts much to ponder. Might it be better that some people read nothing rather than some of the coarse material that the market was putting in their way? In the case of African-American slaves, the answer for a large and significant group of white Protestants was "yes," although it was difficult for them to explain what was "coarse" about the Declaration of Independence. Aside from the case of slaves, coercive restrictions did not help much to resolve the imagined problems about reading. In the North, questions about how strongly to encourage reading hovered over the issue of how to manage the behavior of working-class people, especially immigrants. Yet no one proposed discouraging the spread of literacy. It was already too strong an imperative. Thus, Protestant leaders had created a dilemma for themselves. They had laid the basis for the popularization of reading material. Their missionary efforts to invent and distribute "virtuous" books and tracts had provided crucial encouragement to the modern commercial forms of publishing. They now had to invent ways to control what they had helped start.

Many of their proposals were aimed at shaping the taste of readers in the process of teaching them to read. Atmosphere was all-important. Moralists applauded the formation of workingmen's improvement associations because they encouraged reading as a means of self-advancement. Generous lay donations built Sunday schools. The most dramatic American experiment was universal schooling for people of all social classes. Nineteenth-century school curriculums sought to lessen worries about reading by concerted endeavors to link literacy training to moral and religious training. Nothing, of course, guaranteed success, as was evident in many "disapproved" books that found readers. By 1850 the variety of the book and periodical market lay well beyond the firm control of those who sought ways to ensure their virtuous content. The cornucopia of printed delights had turned reading into a private practice in which moral authority and influence operated at a considerable distance from reader reception. Readers displaced authors, rewriting books in their own imaginations to find the messages they wanted.

Protestant responses to the problem varied, as did their definition of the problem. Some denominational leaders, especially Unitarians, Episcopalians, and Presbyterians, regarded a hierarchy of readers as inevitable. Books of a high quality were for people like themselves. When some of them ventured into the task of writing fiction, they did not expect their stories to have much influence beyond their own social class, although trickle-down culture, like trickle-down economics, was always a sort of middle-class faith. Mostly they left the moral work necessary for people of lesser social rank to the tract societies. When tracts seemed to encourage the popular market for sensationalism, most of them recoiled. Methodists and Baptists, although in some significant ways more comfortable with popular styles, tended to be no less suspicious of the misuses of reading.

Part of the religious work in the marketplace of culture was done by authors who were not approved by the religious leaders themselves. Ministers had shaped taste, but they did not always follow it. We stand in a better position to appreciate their accomplishments. A spiritual economy did guide many commercial publishing decisions. Almost everyone agreed that authors, publishers, and booksellers had moral responsibilities. The trick was to balance the decline in religious titles with books that had a comparable moral benefit. That was where consensus ended. A culture war raged around disagreements over what sorts of reading had a comparable benefit. What mattered in the long run was that "religion" remained the key term of reference for almost everyone who was party to the controversies.

Antebellum American readers, whatever the clergy said, in fact demanded a sufficient number of specifically religious titles to keep them securely a part of the popular book trade. That fact was evident in book advertising that listed religious books alongside novels, histories, and self-help manuals. Glance at the back of virtually any book published by a major publisher in the mid-nineteenth century. The back pages itemized other titles available from the publisher that might interest readers. Advertisements listed Dickens's *Life of Martin Chuzzlewit* next to Reverend Henry Anthon's *The True Churchman Warned Against the Errors of the Time*; *An Encyclopedia of Science* next to Dr. Pusey's *Sermons*; Kendell's *Life of Jackson* next to *Harper's Illuminated Bible*; Joe Cowell's

Thirty Years Among the Players in England and America next to Nathan Bang's *Life of Arminius*.[59]

Emerson, with his disdain for a foolish consistency, was born in the right place at the right time. Americans remained a religious people because religious leaders, and sometimes their opponents, found ways to make religion competitive with other cultural products. Although nineteenth-century Protestant ministers and many entrepreneurs of commercial culture on occasion furiously attacked each other, they had to learn to work the same audiences using a market model that compelled them to adopt techniques of persuasion rather than coercion. Neither could afford, quite literally, to ignore what the other was doing. Together they mixed the sacred and the profane in ways that made nineteenth-century America distinctive.

The revolution in reading that had a major impact on the development of consumer culture and the commodification of religion was not merely a phenomenon that put more books into the hands of more people. It involved a more basic shift in psychology, one that fed a habit of addictive buying. People learned to read through a book quickly, less to savor its story or to pore over its wisdom again and again than to get done with it and buy something else. Scholars call this a shift from intensive to extensive reading. Colin Campbell has noted that and something more. Oddly, compulsive, insatiable buying that distinguishes consumption in the industrial world became prominent first among Protestants rather than Catholics, the same Protestants who were supposed to be applying the habit of steady work and "frugal asceticism" to the cause of industrialization.[60] In Campbell's mind the imagination that was crucial to modern consumerism was nineteenth-century Romanticism. But Romanticism, he argues, depended in turn on the prior creation, by Protestantism, of an extreme subjectivism that turned inward to search for signs of personal salvation. Protestants thereby constructed elaborate mental images not in response to real events but from prior emotionally laden mental images. Protestants learned to store their images of guilt and redemption, to call upon them later at will, and to manipulate them for interior pleasurable consumption. This was fecund imagination indeed. Since the Protestant imagination was free to venture forth on its own without the intervention and control of priests, it luxuriated in novelty. Protestantism was excellent preparation for the pleasures of reading novels and more generally for modern consumer hedonism.

If Campbell is correct, the ferocity of nineteenth-century Protestant attacks on the imagination becomes more understandable. We are simply witnessing an effort, common in cases of unwelcome responsibility, to compensate for something that had gotten out of control. Rather than seeing their own invention in the impulse to daydream and to seek the stimulation of powerful emotions, Protestant moralists blamed Catholics; they blamed libertines; they blamed immoral publishers and authors. They also began to adjust. Ironically, their most innovative efforts to control imaginative desire usually legitimated an expansion of the cultural marketplace that fed on desire, including a desire for the comforts of religion. Just as production and consumption chased each other and became mutually dependent values in the Protestant world of antebellum America, so did public religion and public entertainment.

CHAPTER TWO

The Spoken Word, Stage Performance, and the Profits of Religious Spectacle

Indeed, what with their anxious seats, their
revivals, their music, and their singing,
every class and sect in the states have even
now so far fallen into Catholicism that
religion has become more of an appeal to
the senses than to the calm and sober
judgment.

Captain Frederick Marryat, *A Diary in America*
(1839)

In a diary recalling the early years of his life, George Whitefield records a moment when he first suspected that God was planning a special business for him. The adolescent Whitefield is reading a play to his sister and suddenly tells her: "Sister, God intends something for me which we know not of."[1] Whitefield's future readers, as the evangelist anticipated, already knew most of the rest of the story. Within a few years of that domestic scene, Whitefield entered Oxford and came under the aegis of a group of earnest young Christian men which included Charles and John Wesley. God imparted to the "re-born" Whitefield the gifts of a powerful preacher; and before his death in 1770, he had used his talents to convert tens of thousands of English-speaking sinners, both in the British Isles and in England's colonies. Of equal importance, Whitefield's style of preaching, which reportedly could hold as many as eighty thousand people spellbound in open fields, turned a portion of the Protestant Christian ministry away from intellectual preparation and instruction toward emotional exhorting. Following Whitefield's example, the evangelical preacher set the Christian faith ablaze and made revivalism essential to its future growth and prosperity.

Too much is claimed in the above summary, but the boastful Whitefield is a figure to be reckoned with. His career signals some significant alterations both in how many individual Christian ministers viewed the task of preaching and in how virtually all Protestant churches in the United States worked to influence the sinful world around them. To understand why that happened, we must not miss a significant detail in the diary entry just quoted. Whitefield was reading a play to his sister. All of his biographers have mentioned the great man's youthful interest in the theater, a fact he made no effort to conceal. His journal recorded that he "was very fond of reading plays and have kept from school for days together to prepare myself for acting them."[2]

To accentuate the miraculous transformation that God wrought in him at Oxford, Whitefield emphasized the sins of his youth. If his journals are honest, there were not a great many and none on a par with theft or "impure" sexual practices that were the stuff of many Christian confessions. But play-acting was a grave enough transgression. Whatever the primordial connections between drama and religious ritual, not to mention the importance of the medieval Christian church to the development of the theater, a censorious Puritanism rendered many English Protestants insensitive to what Elizabethan drama had achieved. They banned Thespis from Cromwell's island kingdom. His subsequent re-entry during the Restoration left English Christians with divided judgments. Those who were strictest about "worldly asceticism" grimly continued a moral war against the theater. Whitefield made certain that "my repentance as to seeing and acting plays," "my abhorrence of my former sin and folly," was declared publicly.[3]

Yet the revelatory association remains. Whitefield first spoke of his suspicions about a special divine mission for himself while reading a play aloud, doubtlessly with as much dramatic skill as he commanded. This early zeal for the theater had a great deal to do with what ensued. Whitefield rejected the stage only to re-invest his acting talents—good elocution, a trained memory, the ability to project intense emotion—into his career as a preacher. His critics quickly got the point and attacked him with the same arguments they used against actors. In fact they said most of the things that are now said about televangelists. Whitefield was turning preaching into a performance, a performance as carefully timed and calculated as one by his famous contemporary David Garrick of Drury Lane who liked to attend Whitefield's meetings. His religious presentations transformed church services into entertainment, and the money paid for the spectacle went to enrich Whitefield. Much later, in the 1830s, Walt Whitman summed up the most controversial consequence of Whitefield's life on Christian proselytizing when he wrote: "The most important of our amusements" are the churches, "especially the Methodist ones, with their frequent 'revivals.'"[4]

Whitefield never admitted that his holy mission had something to do with profit-oriented, pleasure-giving performance. The analogy between what he did and commercial culture took time to develop. Like any actor, Whitefield wanted all eyes riveted on him. According to his most recent biographer, the historian Harry Stout, he was a "self-promoter with sure business instincts" who "wanted to be a star." He carefully logged the signs of his popularity, the hosannas and tears of the multitudes, and the body count of the crowds he attracted and subdued. Always he gave God credit for his effect upon sinners, but those who detested his stage style saw only a sham humility. To them, Whitefield's infamous meetings in open fields, where he exposed religion "to the scorn of infidels and atheists," was bravura that had nothing to do with God. According to one critic, Whitefield "had sunk the house of God below a play-house, and turned religion into a farce."[5] Stout puts the matter more kindly. Whitefield presented religion as "a product that could be marketed," a force competing "for a market share according to new rules governed less by mercantile controls and elite institutions . . . than by market forces and the sheer power of public opinion."[6]

We may quarrel about every aspect of Whitefield's career except its success. About his power over crowds, he had no need to exaggerate. However we define what he did, however we explain it, however we judge it, Whitefield exhibited a rare skill. That skill, and the genuinely benevolent intentions behind it, made a strong and, to many, an unlikely impression upon Benjamin Franklin. The warm friendship between Franklin and the evangelist is puzzling since the emotional piety of the latter seemed poorly matched with the skeptical rationalism of the former. Yet both men sought to improve human behavior, and both men admired concrete results. Franklin was also a self-promoter who made a living as a communicator. He naturally was impressed that Whitefield attracted some thirty thousand people to a single meeting in Philadelphia and made his voice carry to the furthest reaches of the throng. Whitefield's theology was no improvement over what Franklin had long dismissed as drivel, but at least it stayed clear of the doctrinal controversies that kept too many churchmen uselessly closeted in lonely studies, far removed from the world's daily, urgent business. The stunning effect of Whitefield's oratory demonstrated that religion could yet be a powerful agent of moral order. Franklin was pleased and increased his income publishing the evangelist's words.

In the United States, Protestant revivalism became a major social force beginning with the famous Cane Ridge meeting at the outset of the nineteenth century. It was a defining feature of the early republic and a primary factor in churching the American people. The intention was to save souls, but in a brassy way that threw religion into a free-for-all competition for people's attention. Revival religion sought to influence American institutions. It did that, but not without being itself swept forward in unexpected ways by the tides of popular taste it had helped set in motion. Revivals quickly became entangled in controversies over commercial entertainments which they both imitated and influenced. Revivalism in fact, like the peddled books of Parson Weems, shoved American religion into the marketplace of culture. Very visible consequences have endured down to the present day.

The Nature of Oral Culture and the Antebellum Revivals

A curious twist developed in the phobic attacks made by revival preachers against the theater. In the early nineteenth century the American heirs of Whitefield, in the same breaths that they swore enmity against the stage, expressed envy at the talents and training of professional actors. An uneven rapprochement went forward, opening the possibility for people to re-define the theater in moral terms. In some avant-garde cases, ministers collapsed the gulf that formerly had yawned between the stage and the pulpit and argued that a good play, performed under proper con-

ditions, had the same spiritualizing effect upon spectators as a good sermon. Most Protestant religious moralists never went as far as that. Yet
American theater, in fancy if not in fact, was in 1850 a good bit less
wicked than it had seemed only a few decades before.

Both theater and revivalism depended upon being *heard* to achieve
their effects. During the early nineteenth century, plays and sermons
circulated in book and pamphlet form, but the printed versions did not
cause the ardent enthusiasm or the angry hostility that led to pitched
battles in the street over plays and actors. We need to recover in our
imaginations a period when Americans were still conditioned to listen to
oral performances that sometimes went on for hours.[7] In colonial New
England the average churchgoer of a ripe old age may have heard as
many as seven thousand sermons. That translates into about fifteen
thousand hours of listening time, 625 days stuck in a meetinghouse.[8] In
a busy week, ministers gathered an audience four or five times, not only
for the usual Sunday sermons but also for the special-occasion messages
prepared for fast days, elections, and executions.

That rather staggering pace of preaching fell off. By the early decades
of the nineteenth century, Americans, even in New England, depended
less upon the spoken word of ministers to pattern their world. Their
channels of information were more diverse, in large part because of the
explosion of published material. However, print culture did not replace
oral culture. In most societies, what is written and what is oral interact.[9]
Americans in the nineteenth century had abundant reading material and
a growing number of reasons to actually read it. This fact did not make
listening less popular. If anything, the printed versions of various forms
of speech—sermons, political addresses, lectures, and plays—increased
the demand for a diversity of oral performance. And even though preaching had been reduced to one form of speech among many, revivalism
kept it a very important form. With its populist accents, it was a major
source of novelty. The inventiveness of good revival preaching set standards for oral performance across a wide range of non-religious cultural
offerings.

It is probably true that orality, however serious or instructive the occasion for its use, is bound up with fun. Walter Ong, who along with
others has challenged us to think about the different effects of the written and the spoken word, has argued: "In an oral culture, verbalized
learning takes place quite normally in an atmosphere of celebration and
play. . . . Sound situates man in the middle of actuality and in simulta-
neity, whereas vision situates man in front of things and in sequen-
tiality."[10] The idea is certainly relevant to thinking about revivalism, for
antebellum revivals and revival camp meetings were arguably the first,

large-scale popular entertainments in the United States. The controversy that they caused was related to more general controversies about the moral uses of leisure time.

Saying that revivals and camp meetings made going to church fun and exciting does not mean that participants were not interested in salvation. It only points to the complexity of the phenomenon. Many motives drove people to travel sometimes long distances to attend camp meetings. Along with religion, they sought comraderie, diversion from routine, and relaxation from labor. The gratification and the pleasure were not even disguised. People looked forward to revivals in the same way they looked forward to a "mammoth picnic"; campsites came complete with concession stands selling gingerbread, lemonade, and, in the days before temperance took over, liquor.[11]

Significantly, memoirs of camp meetings stress noise, communal noise, rather than pious silence and private meditation.[12] The spoken and sometimes shouted word provided the drama and the evidence of God's presence. The words usually made sense, but that was not completely necessary, as in the groans, grunts, and barks that emerged in the early revival days from the mouths of new converts. The central attraction was the revival preacher. His were the words that riveted attention, that converted at the same time they entertained, that gave people the sense of being present at something "theatrical." Whitefield's shocked detractors would have felt themselves fully vindicated by what happened in the United States. Not all revival meetings were characterized by emotional outbursts, and not every revivalist preacher was a mesmerizing orator. A full understanding of the social meanings of revivals requires us to see them as part of a quest for order. Still, it is impossible to imagine their popularity without the drama and entertainment they provided. That was true even in revival meetings in which disruptive emotion was kept under a close check.

At the outset of the nineteenth century, the many references that connected revivals and stage plays were almost always hostile. But familiarity with both things softened the tone, and some early remarks were casual, unintentionally friendly. A preacher at one camp meeting remarked with no sense of inappropriateness: "It was like a theater. It was a theater in the open air, on the green sward, beneath the starry blue, incomparably more picturesque than any stage scenery."[13] Like the world of the theater, the revival meeting of whatever degree of emotional heat created a special sense of time during which the normal constraints upon sentiment and behavior were deliberately modified. It is tempting to say that a better analogy to "enthusiastic" camp meetings than the theater is carnival. Antebellum Protestant America was not known as a festive country. Charles Dickens and Frances Trollope were among the European visitors who commented on the disagreeable joylessness of life in the New World. They were not prepared to appreciate ways in which revivals might provide the same emotional outlets that street performances did in England. A Catholic visitor to the United States was in no better position to notice possible analogies between the clamorous rituals of Baptist and Methodist encampments and those of European Catholics in the days just before the Lenten season.

In 1854 the Methodist minister B. W. Gorham justified camp meetings in the following way: "All nations, ancient and modern, have held their great festivals, political and religious, a still further proof that there is an element in man which demands occasional excitement by such means."[14] This is a remarkable statement for a Protestant evangelical, especially a Methodist. Gorham candidly linked the religious revivals in the United States with a long tradition of festival that recognized "excitement" not as a special sign of conversions wrought by the Holy Spirit but as a psychological component of human nature that needed scheduled ventings. Carnival periods, stage performances, revivals—they all permitted role reversals and the relaxation of customary behavioral norms. Women frequently took on the role of preachers at revival meetings, thus usurping the place of the male speaker. Critics complained, but the setting of the revival, for the space of a few hours or days, often protected practices that were elsewhere forbidden.

Even African Americans and young children found themselves ministering to miserable sinners. A visitor to Cane Ridge reported that a seven-year-old girl was set upon a man's shoulders and spoke "until she appeared almost exhausted."[15] Others reported startled reactions to similar sights: "To see a bold and courageous Kentuckian (undaunted by the horror of war) turn pale and tremble at the reproof of a weak woman, a little boy, or a poor African; to see him sink down in deep remorse, roll and toss, and gnash his teeth, till black in the face, entreat the prayers of those he came to devour. . . . who can say the change was not supernatural?"[16] If not supernatural, then certainly unusual, for the behavior was not common outside the boundaries of camp meetings. The "unnatural" submission of "strong" white males to those they usually controlled was a ritual bit of "play-acting" that both subverted and reinforced social and cultural norms. The terms "holy fair" and "religious holiday" that were used to describe camp meetings suggest that revivalism was an American counterpart to European festivals.[17]

Yet carnival as a concept will not quite do. Dickens and Trollope had their point about American Protestant joylessness. As has been recently demonstrated, American revivalists were not the wildest of the breed.

Scottish Presbyterians (of all people!), whose eighteenth-century communion rites, in fact, prefigured much of what happened at Cane Ridge, easily surpassed Americans in their celebratory enthusiasm.[18] American revivals only started up after the elaborate and lengthy eucharist rituals in Scotland began to calm down and highland passions wax less ecstatically and spontaneously. True, the emotional heat of American Methodism in the early nineteenth century was great, greater than in England.[19] Still, the most uncontrolled features of American revivalism did not last long. The many critics of American revivals, who were loath to neglect a negative point, never thought to mention carnival. Carnival was pre-modern, pre-Protestant, pre-bourgeois market. By concentrating on the analogy to commercial theater, they had a better target.

It is significant that the improvement in the manners of theatrical patrons in antebellum America paralleled the trend of revival exhorters to calm down their meetings. Revivalists and theatrical managers were working on a shared problem of establishing respectability. For a time, antebellum theater mixed many different sorts of people together—the high-minded and the low-minded, married men (only sometimes with their wives) and young single men who sought the company of prostitutes in the infamous third tier, workers and their employers. Religious moralists deemed such audiences dangerous because the settings reduced everything to the lowest common moral denominator. The loudest objectors to Whitefield's practice of preaching in open fields had made a similar point: it brought the godly into contact with atheists and scoffers. Lyman Beecher feared the antebellum revivals because of their "promiscuous" mingling of "all the passions of all the classes of human society." They pressed "the mass of the community out of their place," and shook them together "in one cauldron of effervescence." The women who entered such a confusing atmosphere ran the risk, according to Beecher, of sinking to the level of actresses.[20]

Beecher's objections to revivals, which he partly overcame, reflected the tremendous problems that evangelical Christianity faced in adapting to the social circumstances of the young American republic. Beecher was accustomed to churches in which the congregation was made up of the church members (God's visible saints) and a sizable portion of the rest of the community. In such gatherings, social contamination posed no risk because all who attended church knew one another. They shared the same theological outlook and the same moral norms. Any stranger who came to scoff was quickly put out. The early revivals created a very different world of piety. Going to a camp meeting was to enter a crowd of strangers. No one screened the arrivals. A great deal of testimony, both from those who supported the revivals and from those who opposed them, suggests that unsympathetic interlopers were common, usually young men who came to make trouble and to have a good time at the expense of religion.[21] Revival meetings brought together as broad a cross section of antebellum Americans as any other sort of gathering until the formation of mass political parties late in the 1830s.

Precisely because revivals were a successful way to bring large numbers of people together, an opportunity to expand greatly the effect of evangelical preaching beyond the resources of organized churches, they were dangerous. At least that was how many people viewed the situation. What sure ways existed to control any sort of popular cultural activity? In "promiscuous" gatherings people, in effect, paid a price of admission and mixed with others whose reputations were unknown to them. What critics of the revivals worried about, and they worried about it for a long time after behavior at camp meetings had settled down, was a prolonged period of what social scientists call "liminality." People are placed in a setting where they lose the bearings of normal everyday life. People return from liminal situations somehow changed. That is the purpose.[22] From the standpoint of the opponents of revivalism, the changes were bad.

The list of "theatrical" horrors associated with revivals went on. Critics drew parallels between the "new methods" designed to convert "excited" revival participants and the techniques of clever staging used in the commercial theater. The "anxious bench," one of the most controversial innovations of nineteenth-century soul-saving, was a sort of "hot-seat" for people on the verge of accepting Christ. Their placement on the bench put them in full view of the congregation so that the prayerful emotion of the meeting could be focused on their anxious souls. According to one skeptic who doubted that conversion could be hurried along in this "dramatic" way, "the movement of coming to the Anxious Bench . . . is always more or less theatrical." Like the theater, it produced not permanent change but "transient excitement to be renewed from time to time by suitable stimulants presented to the imagination. . . . The pulpit is transformed, more or less, into a stage. Divine things are so popularized, as to be at last shorn of their dignity as well as their mystery."[23] Another critic mused: "And where is the mighty difference between the dissipation of the [revival] church . . . and the dissipation of the ballroom, the theatre, or the tea-table? . . . Many of those who now run after every preacher . . . are the very people, who, engaged by objects of another class, would be seen at every dance, raree show, and assembly, the foremost of the forward and the giddiest of the giddy."[24]

If the emotionalism generated by theatrical and revivalistic performance had been merely ephemeral, critics might have comforted themselves by saying that at least no permanent damage had been done. But they viewed the demand for spectacle as an addiction. Having tasted novelty, they wanted more of it. Revivals thus fed the psychology of consumption. The only cure was total avoidance. In some scandalous cases that critics never tired of citing, the damage from unlicensed emotionalism was permanent and devastating. They all involved sex. Zealous and lust-filled young preachers, who had no name for what drove them, put young girls under the spell of their words. They both lost control. One incident involved a female mill worker who was allegedly violated by a Methodist revival preacher and then murdered by him when she became pregnant. A jury found the minister not guilty. But Catharine Read Williams, who partially fictionalized the story in *Fall River, An Authentic Narrative*, clearly thought otherwise.

In an appendix to her book, she recounted her impressions of a camp meeting in Rhode Island. It was worse, she said, than attending the theater. At the theater the dangers were well known, and people could guard against them. At a revival, the drunks, gamblers, lechers, horse jockeys, and pickpockets came as a surprise. In the confusion, the deafening uproar, and the "unseemly riot," the defenses of otherwise careful people became impaired. Women who gave into the "strange expressions" and "violent gesticulations" of revival prayer, who were carried away by the groans, shouts, and shrieks of the crowd, were asking for trouble.[25] Emotionally aroused men were prepared to supply it. It is hard to read through these accounts without thinking of modern rock concerts. Music, joyous, rousing music, became extremely important to camp meetings.[26] The spoken word became the sung word, and the emotion they produced together crushed intellectual understanding and any resistance to sensuality. Is not that what critics of rock music maintain?

Are We Actors, and If So, Do We Compete With or Reform the Commercial Stage?

Supporters of the revivals, and the masterly actor/preachers who led them, were not sitting still through this criticism. Most Baptist and Methodist evangelicals associated with revivalism remained foes of the theater throughout the nineteenth century, more adamantly opposed, in fact, than Episcopal and Unitarian ministers who scolded them for being theatrical in their religious practice. Their opposition, however, was confused by their self-defense. Like Whitefield's opposition to the stage, it proved to be wonderfully equivocal, invariably working to neutralize their warnings about the moral menace of the stage. As soon as revivalists began to codify the rules of their craft, they found themselves admitting guilt to the charge that they emulated stage techniques. Religion had to be popular. And to be popular, it had to "adapt the style of her operations to the characteristics of the minds on which she see seeks to act."[27]

The earliest revivalist ministers liked to believe that they were doing what came naturally. Two of the most colorful early Methodist circuit riders, Lorenzo Dow and Peter Cartwright, said little in a systematic way about how they aroused crowds. But the hints were there to collect. They "directly" addressed individuals in a "warm fashion"; they used common speech; they told stories and sang songs; they prayed on their knees. By the time we get to Charles Grandison Finney, the most celebrated of the antebellum revivalists who started preaching in the 1820s, the calculation and codification of method-preaching were well along. "Practical" guides to revival preaching replaced guilelessness. Finney threw over his law practice but not the studied common touch that had made him successful in addressing juries. Ministers, he said, had to compete for people's attention if they would be a counter-force to "political and other worldly excitements." To do that, they did not need a Harvard or a Yale education. They needed a style with popular appeal. Reading a learned sermon was poor style. "In delivering a sermon in this essay style of writing, it is impossible that nearly all the fire of meaning and power of gesture, and looks, and attitude, and emphasis should not be lost."[28] Ministers should aim for excitement.

Finney counseled revivalists to adopt a style that we might call "practiced spontaneity." Stage-acting was the model. "Now what is the design of the actor in a theatrical representation?" Finney asked. The actor sought "to throw himself into the spirit and meaning of the writer, as to adopt his sentiments, make them his own, feel them, embody them, throw them out upon the audience as living reality." Should not preachers give their own words—or the Word of God [Finney's phrasing equivocates]—the same treatment? "And if ministers are too stiff . . . to learn even from an actor . . . the best method of . . . diffusing the warmth of burning thought over a congregation . . . let them remember, that while they are thus turning away and decrying the art of the actor, and attempting to support 'the dignity of the pulpit,' the theatres can be thronged every night."[29]

Finney never ceased to believe that the theater was off-limits for Christians. He agreed with critics of the stage that the moral nature of actors was perverted because of their necessarily close identification with an endless variety of characters.[30] One day they might "play" the incarnation of virtue, but the next evening they "became the metaphor" of evil. What saved the evangelistic preacher from a similar corruption, according to Finney, was the steadiness of his role. Many of the same talents and training made good actors and preachers alike, but the "pulpit is a fact," the stage, "an imagery."[31]

By the 1840s, manuals designed to improve the speaking effectiveness of ministers were a part of a growing body of self-help literature available to Americans. A printed manual setting down the rules of spontaneous speaking is arguably a gross conceptual oxymoron. But the mixture did not bother the authors. Even Henry Ware, the Unitarian professor of pulpit eloquence and pastoral care at Harvard, urged preachers "to find more warmth in the declamation, more earnestness in the address, greater animation in the manner, where the eyes and the fingers can speak." From printed texts, ministers learned that they should not be guided "by the dumb and lifeless pages of a book." Those who tried to win people to Christ had to recognize that "the mass of men . . . judge by the eye and ear, by the fancy and feelings, and know little of the rules of art or of an educated taste."[32] One manual quoted the actor David Garrick on the need for "earnestness and directness."[33]

Present-day college students who are assigned Finney's sermons to read are understandably bewildered when informed that his words once mesmerized audiences. Print can reveal stylistic elegance and closely reasoned theological points. That is not what revival preaching was about. Its greatness sprang from the lips of the minister. A sensibility "not formed from books" gave a sermon its force. Books, even those of Parson Weems and other writers who elaborated the style of moral sensationalism, were not up to the task of conversion that, in theory, motivated effective preaching.

It is useful, however, to think of Weems's little tracts and revival sermons as two aspects of religion's immersion into the landscape of commercial culture. Weems and Finney were both searching for ways to make religion popular in an era in which commercial-culture options were growing. That fact led Finney to adjustments that Weems would have endorsed as eminently sensible. The cry became general. Ministers needed to learn the techniques of self-promotion and rely, like other people who had causes or products to sell, upon handbills, newspapers, and the telegraph.[34] Advertising created expectations. How the preacher spoke, not what he said, became a marketable commodity. Audience enthusiasm did not happen by accident. It had to be created.

Finney's career ought to keep us mindful that revivalism was a sophisticated enterprise. In his case, preaching with a common touch had nothing to do with an unlearned ministry that his critics kept talking about.

He was, after all, a Presbyterian who started his career as a lawyer and ended it as a college president. Finney wanted ministers to think in innovative ways about the expertise that went into preaching. Finney's first counseling words about pulpit style stressed the importance of holding an audience. He grasped the connection between democratic culture and a competitive market better than most of his clerical contemporaries. Everything depended on learning how to make religion attractive to crowds of people who were free to develop their own consumer tastes for intellectual and cultural products. The successful revival preacher who followed Finney's prescriptions was no witless, untutored country bumpkin. According to Reverend Calvin Colton, he was someone who had carefully ascertained as far as possible "the character and temper" of the targeted community.[35]

The spontaneity appropriate to revival preaching required the minister to discard his notes before he mounted the pulpit. It did not preclude memorization and repetition of words that reliably aroused a crowd. Phrases and stories that proved effective with audiences were used over and over again. Itinerant preachers had an advantage. They could do the same thing in every town and still impress their audience as a bright, new presence. "Settled" preachers had to be inventive in a different way and enliven the content of sermons with fresh anecdotes culled from history, biography, and science as well as from current events. In all cases, the successful antebellum preacher had to become something of an actor.[36]

The Sermon on the Wicked Stage: Theater for the Family Audience

The clerics who objected to these huckster-like formulas for selling religion to Americans were not immune to the pressures that forced religion to make concessions to people's desire for novelty and entertainment. Trying to resist what they viewed as the cruder forms of concession was the whole point of their criticism. At the same time, they were aware that future success of religion in America required conscious competition with commercial entertainment. Almost everyone in the Protestant camp came to recognize the importance of emotion and feeling in religious life. What many non-revivalists sought to do was distinguish refined and uplifting religious emotions from the sort of hysteria they said was encouraged by untrained clerical upstarts. Theatricality had high and low forms. Evangelical-minded Baptists, Methodists, and some Presbyterians took what Episcopals and Unitarians regarded as the low road. The high road was aesthetic. The suspiciously Catholic Episcopals, who had never had much use for plain dress and plain settings, elaborated their costumed rituals to achieve theatrical effects. Well-born Protestants in the early nineteenth century increasingly serviced their emotional needs with superb organs, trained choirs, and stained glass. Many wealthy urban Protestant churches in antebellum America embraced the dramatic Gothic architectural forms of the medieval Roman church.[37]

Aestheticism, which carried with it an appreciation for some of the secular offerings in the cultural marketplace, led many liberal Protestant churchmen to seek a religious reconciliation with commercial theater. Naturally, in their minds reconciliation depended upon their being able to establish rules in the marketplace that respected their moral concerns. Even so, it represented an important shift in strategy. Protestant liberals were moving rapidly to the view that religion could countenance anything with a moral purpose. This logic suggested that religion's role in the world of commercial culture was not to forbid people in all cases the enjoyment it offered. There were ways to make churches more attractive environments, but men and women did have lives outside of church that were growing in complexity. Religious leaders therefore had to work with commercial agents to extend the sway of religious morality in places they had once regarded as strictly off-limits.

Henry Ward Beecher, the son of Lyman Beecher, became one of the most famous ministers of the nineteenth century. In many ways, his advice to clerics was the same as Finney's: "a minister without feeling is no better than a book." "Somewhere," Beecher said in recognition of the strong empathy that spoken words might create, "there must be that power by which the man speaking and the men hearing are unified; and that is the power of emotion." He drew comparisons between ministerial performance and stage performance, recommending to young ministers that they worry less about doctrine and more about their training in voice, posture, and gesture. According to his own account of his career, he had practiced public speaking from his sophomore year in college.[38]

Yet there were important differences as well. Although Beecher had once been a militant opponent of stage presentation, he later became a patron of "legitimate" theater. Ministers could copy the techniques of actors because the stage could be Christian. Finney never accepted that logic. Beecher took some of the lessons of revival preaching and gave them an up-scale mission. Unlike the early Methodist circuit riders and Baptist revival preachers, Beecher had proper social credentials. He was a man of taste, education, and established family. In addition to his success as a minister, he was an author and art collector.[39] As pastor of Brooklyn's Plymouth Church (the "playhouse church"), Beecher taught the middle class a popular style and urged them to join that style with a moral purpose to demand uplifting commercial entertainments.

Henry W. Bellows, a Unitarian minister, also endorsed the actor's skills along with the theater in an address to the Dramatic Fund Society of New York in 1857. He was prepared to privilege the performance of a play over its reading. The classic Protestant argument against the theater had stressed how performance overheated the imagination. Bellows argued instead that the private reading of a play in "parlours and bedrooms" was a more dangerous activity than attending the theater. An immoral play was exposed for what it was when performed before an audience of sensibility and taste.[40] Audience reactions provided instant reinforcement for virtuous sentiments and instant condemnation for evil ones. No one could miss the moral lessons of the drama. In this manner Bellows sought to demonstrate that theater, with the proper sponsorship, could actually serve religion. The differences between a good sermon delivered in church and a virtuous play performed in a "reformed" theater dwindled to the vanishing point.

Bellows and others who shared his views did not argue that all theater or even that most theater was virtuous. They argued only that efforts to reform the theater had produced positive results, that clerics should cooperate in consolidating the gains, and that as a reformed amusement the theater could be a powerful means to promote proper religious sentiments among Americans. Following his logic, good and caring Christians had a positive, compelling duty to patronize stage productions of the virtuous sort. If the commercial theater was immoral, it was because the church had abandoned it, unwisely trying to set a distance between itself and the world. The re-entry of virtuous people into the audience would change the atmosphere.[41] It was the only way for churches to influence "the customs, affections, and policies of the world at large."[42]

Bellows's irenic ploy very nearly collapsed the distinction between actors and ministers. Along with politicians, their oratorical skills gave them a special opportunity to advance public enlightenment. They also shared dangers common to "talking vocations." Their job required them to make themselves "an object of interest to masses—where strong temptations exist, to substitute immediate reputation for self-respect— and to make fine words and skillful manoeuvres do the work of sound principle and patient performance of duty." The temptations to cultivate outward show at the expense of character formation were constant.[43] Some actors and some ministers succumbed to them. They fell victim to the passion of adoring admirers who threw themselves at their feet.

Performance always carried risk. What Bellows wished to demonstrate was that no firm line separated the work of actors and ministers. Without a true regard for religion, their performances were empty. Ministers needed to acknowledge their kinship with other public figures. If they continued to think that the protection of religion was somehow their peculiar responsibility, they bore the blame for whatever decline they detected in commercial entertainments.

Beecher and Bellows were, of course, rationalizing. They could not halt the rising popularity of commercial theater. Besides, they liked stage performances. They had to come to terms with at least this much of secular commercial culture and to convince themselves that they did so in the service of religion and morality. Many ministers were not persuaded. They viewed the reform of theater as a chimera. A play, however much it rewarded virtue and punished vice, could never be "a mirror of Christian sentiments and morals."[44] Either the theater would disappear or religion and public morals would be corrupted. There was no middle ground. We should not forget, of course, that the rear guard of Protestant opinion that excoriated commercial theater was the evangelical ministers who made effective use of theatricality in revival meetings.

Rationalization probably is not the point. Religious leaders were all making adjustments. Churches interacted with, influenced, and were influenced by popular trends in commercial culture. Why on earth should that surprise us? Can we imagine any other possible scenario that would have provided religion with the same degree of public importance? As a historical exercise, we need to resist the temptation to hold churches to a standard of consistency that we do not expect of other institutions. Churches changed their practices, and many of them prospered. That does not make them guilty of selling out. Success is not proof of worldliness, nor flexibility proof of corruption. To say that churches survive by using the same strategies that other institutions use by no means exempts them from criticism. It does, however, allow us to see that churches play innovative roles in developing those strategies. They are not merely victims of secular forces that they have lost power to influence.

Whether religious leaders succeeded in raising the moral level of American theater is debatable. They unquestionably helped reform the behavior of the audience. They also forced people who defended the theater to speak in moral terms. Champions of drama in antebellum America did not talk about First Amendment freedoms. They did not speak out boldly for untrammeled artistic expression or promote a stage aesthetics that was indifferent to moral questions. They did not even talk usually about the rights of weary people to enjoy themselves, free of the Puritan worry that every moment of the day had to be devoted to some useful pursuit.

Defenders of the theater instead, in answering religious critics and in seeking religious allies whom they needed, filled page after page talking about the favorable didactic and moral influences of drama. A play was a sermon. Going to the theater was a useful and wholesome practice, not to be equated with gaming houses, brothels, or taverns.[45] In short, almost everyone who said anything at all about the theater made morality the measure of its social utility. Religious leaders had accomplished something. We can go farther. The collective cultural weight of American clerics was heavier than if it had been pressed upon American society by an established church. Constitutional disestablishment provided religion with a formula for market prosperity. Although many pious antebellum Americans, especially outside of cities, continued to act as if they had to choose between religion and the world, other Americans lived comfortably, as most people always had, with less Manichaean assumptions. The general religious and moral claims made in behalf of many kinds of commercially sponsored performance blurred their sense of having to face agonizing options. If a person was careful, he or she could go anywhere in the cultural marketplace and find some diversion stamped with a seal of virtue. The most broadly popular form of oral entertainment in fact—the public lecture—posed the fewest problems.

The Lyceum and Standards of Public Discourse

The lyceum, an institution that began in New England, brings us into another important area of oral performance in which religion and commercialization both played important roles. Lyceum organizations (and they became popular all over the United States except in the South) were formed to promote the spread of practical information among adults. Because their sponsors wished to avoid controversy, lyceums were ruled by a convention that banished from the podium any form of religious proselytizing that favored one sect or denomination over another. Such a consciously imposed rule of "non-sectarianism" would seem to indicate that people drew a clear line between religious and non-religious subjects and placed useful and practical information on the non-religious side. To the degree that that was so, we can speak of a cultural trend toward secularization.

Matters were not so distinct, however. The lyceum was itself a derivative cultural institution that encouraged lectures rooted stylistically in the colonial sermon. Initially, the influence of New England Calvinism steered the lecture style of lyceum speakers away from the emotionalism encouraged by the revivalists. Audiences were told to expect instruction, not oratorical fireworks. Not surprisingly, although men from all walks of life, and an occasional woman, served as lyceum speakers, the single most important category of speakers was ministers, usually either Unitarian or Congregational.[46] Put in that light, the early lyceum enterprise looks less like secularization and more like action by which New England religious elites sought to secure their cultural hegemony and also to find an attractive package for religion other than revivalism.[47]

By the 1840s, lyceum performances were becoming more commercialized and more dependent upon advertising buildup.[48] A national network gave a number of speakers a fame that commanded high fees. A virtual army of amateur and professional lecturers roamed the countryside speaking about a variety of subjects. The quality of the performances had taken on more significance. In some cases the nature of the act raised questions of fraud. We do not have to scan antebellum speaking rosters that listed mesmerists, phrenologists, and spiritualists to make this point. We can look instead at what should have been the most "respectable" and morally safe form of public address—the temperance lecture. Morality is never absolutely safe when there is money to be made, and people earned income from speaking out against the "demon rum."

With the rise of the Washingtonian Movement in the 1840s, temperance lecturers who had the greatest popular success were often ex-drunkards. None outdid John Bartholomew Gough, who in his drinking days had been an actor. Part of his crowd appeal, which could sometimes earn him a hundred seventy-five dollars for one lecture, was the curiosity that surrounded the question of whether he could stay on the wagon. His reported relapses, the accounts of his showing up at temperance meetings with breath that could burn the building down, were so important to his success that we may wonder whether Gough paid friendly newspaper editors to make up stories about his periodic drinking bouts. If there was sham, it worked. Gough promised, in advertising his speaking engagements, to mix entertainment into his calls for moral reform. One of his sponsors proclaimed: "He possesses, we believe, most of the elements of a popular speaker. He expresses his views in plain and intelligent language, without effort; and what he says comes warm from the heart. With good powers of mind, and a lively fancy, added to wit and humor, he cannot fail to please and amuse with his bright and glowing pictures of things as they exist, while he instructs the mind with sound views and principles, and warms up the heart with kind and generous feelings and sentiments." Gough told anecdotes, sang songs, and invited people to come forward and sign a pledge to swear off drinking. His style was a logical extension of the style of the early revival ministers. His hucksterism and his delight in show business may have been more blatant, but the logic about how to reach an audience was the same. Preach to people, improve them, and allow them to have a good time. They loved it in the countryside. And they loved it in the city.[49]

Although Gough's "enthusiastic" style of public lecturing copied the more exuberant forms of revivalism, lyceum-speaking in general retained its original preference for skilled but subdued presentation. Most of the lectures were well-constructed and delivered useful and practical information on top of inspirational homily. The career of Ralph Waldo Emerson, who in the 1840s and 1850s became a major figure on the lyceum circuit, tells us a great deal about the cultural significance of antebellum American oratory, its relation to print material, and its role in popularizing religious beliefs and values through the networks of commercial culture.

Despite the effort by many historians to turn Emerson into a representative American, we need to remember that his claim to philosophical fame lies in his religious radicalism. In 1832, he resigned his Unitarian pulpit in Boston, already a church more theologically "left" than the vast majority of American Protestant denominations, because he could not in conscience continue to administer the commemorative ritual of the Lord's Supper. In 1836 he published *Nature*, which is generally viewed as a manifesto of the decidedly non-orthodox transcendentalist movement. In 1838, he scandalized the small audience for his Harvard Divinity School Address by calling "Miracle, as pronounced by Christian churches . . . Monster." He tactlessly pressed his attack on organized Protestantism by saying: "Historical Christianity has fallen into the error that corrupts all attempts to communicate religion. . . . The prayers and even the dogmas of our church, are like the zodiac of Denderah, and the astronomical monuments of the Hindoos, wholly insulated from anything now extant in the life and business of the people." Sydney Ahlstrom, who before his untimely death left us an indispensable study of American religion, noted: "With the Divinity School Address, Emerson became America's first 'death-of-God' theologian, and it goes without saying that his efforts were not received with enthusiasm by the pillars of church and society."[50]

Emerson's radicalism, based as it was on formidable intellectual power, quickly established his fame in the environs of Harvard College. His leap into national prominence was less predictable. Prognosticators would have been hard-pressed to guess that Emerson's "death-of-God," almost pantheistic message would play well before churchgoing folk in Peoria and Cincinnati. Even in retrospect it is not obvious why Emerson succeeded on the lyceum lecture circuit and why shop owners shut down early when he came to town so that their employees might have a chance to listen to his words. There is an apparent gap between what intellectual historians have found in Emerson's philosophy, and perhaps what Emerson intended to say, and what audiences apparently made out of his words.[51] If we can judge anything from newspaper accounts of Emerson's lectures, the bourgeois mercantile audiences who attended his performances at "young men's" organizations in the 1850s heard very little of a fuzzy nature philosophy and absolutely nothing that sounded radical. Instead, they re-figured Emerson's addresses into a straightforward sanction for aggressive, economic expansion and an exhortation for young male clerks to improve themselves by working hard and laying up riches. It is not hard to find business metaphors in Emerson's writings. Strung together, they look like, well, grubby materialism.

Emerson was not guiltless in the transformation of his lectures into paeans to middle-class individualism and to capitalism as the sweetest form of mortal existence. True, American newspapers played their part by telling people to expect uplifting messages of good cheer. They trivialized popular lyceum figures like Emerson by turning them into celebrities whose private lives mattered more than their words. Even so, the papers were not necessarily distorting the message. Emerson resigned his ministry in large part to free himself from the restrictions of organized churches. Religious and moral instruction needed to became a popular mission, one that lifted itself above the sphere of sectarian religious controversy. To do that, however, Emerson and other successful lyceum speakers had to woo their audiences. Not incidentally, they made money from their travels. Their familiarity as orators helped sell their books. Emerson remained a religious philosopher and moralist when he expanded his audience beyond the institutional setting of Massachusetts Unitarianism to embrace paying customers. But a different context forges a different message.

The religious principles conveyed by Emerson the lecturer may seem bland, a necessary concession made to commercialization by a religious philosopher who sought prominent attention. In general, however, and what matters is that he was one of an important group of people who established religion as a standard form of performance speech outside the context of church. The lyceum was a perfect meeting ground for religion and commercial culture. What passed for non-sectarian under its sponsorship included a good bit of creed. Speakers who referred to a father god, a messiah son, Christian redemption, an afterlife where good and evil were punished, and the authority of the Bible were not likely to anger their audience. Emerson's religious remarks were of a different sort, but his hearers correctly understood that his advice for living fit comfortably within a Christian moral framework. The expansion of the lyceum network indicated how little distinction many Americans made between religious and secular teaching. It also indicated how they were conditioned by oral performance to think of instruction as entertainment, even when the instruction was moral and they were paying for it.

We should not understand from the relatively non-controversial nature of lyceum speaking that Americans were interested only in hearing those things that represented consensus values. The antebellum lecture circuit doubtlessly gave many Americans a sense that they shared ideals.[52] Religious moralists who applauded the self-improvement societies that sponsored lecturers certainly had that aim. The effort was only partially successful, however. Americans who attended lectures were fickle. If they collectively agreed with a speaker on one evening, they might collectively change their minds a week later under the influence of a different speaker. Or they might discover in conversation that they did not agree with one another about what a speaker had said.

Controversy, or at least the appearance of controversy, was what kept the system going. Well-established lyceum speakers, like Emerson, whose utterances tended to be reviewed as above criticism, had to compete with mesmerists, abolitionists, spiritualist mediums, watercure advocates, and traveling medicine men. The arguments stirred by Jacksonian forms of oral performance were often trumped-up, philosophically empty, and intellectually jejune. What they provided was energy, and American religion was a great benefactor. As was the case with a vast amount of popular print material, much controversy centered on the nature of "true religion." There were hundreds of topical subjects that lyceum speakers could avoid. Religion, the one topic that was ostensibly banned, was not among them.[53] It was ingrained in too many subjects. In antebellum America, religion as a vehicle to promote morality remained the best-selling commodity in the realm of oral performance.

In Search of the Purely Secular. American Education and What to Teach the Common Citizen

Something must be said about education, because an important aim of public education was to determine the taste of Americans and therefore the choices they made in the cultural marketplace. In the minds of educational leaders of antebellum America, the goal was only achievable by what most Americans today would regard as a flagrant violation of the separation of church and state. In the opening decades of the nineteenth century, primary and secondary education in the United States was a long way from the systematized public and private schools now familiar in American society. The idea of compulsory education scarcely existed in most places and applied, in any case, only to the first few grades. Public funds, when they were available for schools, went to charity schools, run mostly by religious denominations, and to private academies.

Once the apprentice system began to disappear and give way to wage labor, public authorities started paying more attention to how young workers were going to learn the rudiments of reading, writing, and arithmetic. Responses were initially sporadic and a long way from universal in their reach. Sunday schools, which first appeared in the United States in Philadelphia in the 1790s, were one way to fill gaps not covered by public expenditures. Originally they did not take as their primary task the indoctrination of young children into the ways of a particular religious sect. Although staffed by members of religious denominations, their more usual aim was to teach reading along with a general respect for religion.[54]

How children were taught was as important as what they were taught. We think of schools as having the task of teaching reading and writing rather than speaking, but oral instruction was then essential to the education process. Proper instruction required children to read aloud in a supervised environment that protected the intended meaning of a text and to pay close attention to elocution. They committed printed passages to memory and recited them again and again. Classroom drill was, above all, oral response. Discipline meant getting pupils to pay attention to what teachers said. A system of memorized oral drill, rote instruction, has a bad reputation in contemporary theories of education. Things were different in a society whose educational leaders were confident that they knew the right things to place in the minds of children. What children learned by rote stayed in their heads and could be called up years later and stated with a certain eloquence.

Instilling good taste in schoolchildren necessarily involved religion. There was no controversy about that. None of the early efforts at general education, *ad hoc* as they were, questioned the essentialness of religion to educational goals. The debates of those years featured no one who disputed the assumption that Christianity, good order, cleanliness, discipline, and morality had to be imparted to children as parts of a single intellectual construct. The view that religion belongs in the schools only became a questionable proposition, a controversy to clog court dockets, in the latter part of the twentieth century. The argument in the nineteenth century was over what sort of religion ought to be taught at public expense. The key issue soon became whether parochial schools that called attention to sectarian divisiveness should receive public money or whether public largesse should be restricted to schools that taught religion in a Protestant consensual style.

By the 1850s, in most school districts north of the Mason-Dixon Line public money no longer went directly to schools with denominational affiliations. The only exception thereafter was in American Indian communities where indifference to the plight of people displaced by European settlement put the hard work of education into the hands of whatever religious sectarians were willing to do it. Even so, in the putatively non-denominational public schools, children read the Protestant Bible, prayed, and recited lessons that took the Christian God for granted. The public school system in the nineteenth century, non-denominational though it was, brought more children into regular contact with Christian teachings than if schools had been left to church sponsors who could force no one to attend them.

Laicity in American public schools, then, was consistent with the aim of Christianizing students. Contemporary guardians of church–state separation sometimes cite Horace Mann, the secretary of the Massachusetts Board of Education from 1837 to 1848, as the author of secular schools. Indeed, he deserves considerable credit for wresting public education out of the hands of religious sectarians and for establishing classrooms in Massachusetts that followed the spirit and letter of religious disestablishment as it was understood by people of tolerant outlook (that is, Unitarians and Universalists) in the 1830s and 1840s. He spurned efforts to stock school libraries with books of a "decidedly religious character," and he faced down Frederick Packard, the corresponding secretary of the American Sunday School Union, who took Mann publicly to task for rejecting schoolbooks teaching doctrines of future punishment and of special providence. At the same time, for Mann non-sectarian was not the same as secular. He repeatedly affirmed his determination to "sacredly" include in the curriculum "all the practical and perceptive parts of the Gospel."[55]

True, Mann's opponents regarded his creedal minimalism as the equivalent of atheism. Most Protestant clergy only got around to full endorsement of his views after growing Catholic demands for a share of public education funds prompted them to close ranks around a Protestant view of non-sectarian religion. Yet they did get around to it, with the threat of Rome persuading them that Mann's plan for America's public schools did not permit religious indifference or neutrality. The books that schoolchildren were given to read emphasized God, general providence, and the supremacy of Jesus as humankind's greatest moral teacher. In the 1840s, when Mann was head of public education in Massachusetts, five of the eight members of the state's Board of Education were clergymen. Three of them were soundly orthodox in the ways of Protestant New England. The large majority of members of local school committees was clergy. None of them imagined, nor did Mann, that Protestant Christianity was itself sectarian. For them the moral discipline of schoolchildren and the encouragement of piety went together. Mann did not try to separate them. Quite literally, it was for him an unthinkable thought.

By the 1840s, public schools in the United States were more clearly distinguishable from the popular Sunday schools run by the various denominations. The latter gave up most of their responsibilities for teaching reading and writing and concentrated on teaching lessons that prepared children to assume full and responsible membership in a particular denomination. The mission of the two, however, was cast in complementary rather than competitive terms. They prospered together. Wherever public schools were strong and regularly attended, so were Sunday schools. What children learned in one about habits of decorum, and the recitative ways in which they mastered self-discipline, was reinforced by what they learned in the other. Schools of all kinds prepared children to assume responsible roles as citizens who would protect religion's sacred role in the nation's cultural life.

Horace Bushnell in 1853 argued that a "Christian nation" could go only so far in accommodating religious difference in the schools. Bushnell was prepared to set the limits more generously than most. He suggested that local school districts be allowed to adopt either the King James or the Douay version of the Bible. He further suggested that they might permit qualified teachers of the various religious groups to teach the children of their faith during set periods of the school day. But whatever they did, they had to ensure that Christian morality, somehow distinct from the doctrines of any particular Christian sect but also equally distinct from the teaching of paganism, atheism, or Muhammadanism, was taught to students.[56]

The most famous tools in this endeavor were the *McGuffey Readers*, an almost universal presence in antebellum classrooms. By 1850 at least seven million had been sold. McGuffey was a Presbyterian minister who regarded his primers as supplements to the Bible. Selections from the Bible were standard inclusions as well as many essays written by ministers. "The time has gone by," McGuffey said, "when any sensible man will be found to object to the Bible as a school book in a Christian country."[57] In his mind it was not a sectarian book; nor was it sectarian to teach young children to read in order to answer such questions as: Who is it that looks on all we do? Can God see us in the dark? What does God hate? and What must we remember to do if we have done wrong? God's providence was the underlying metaphysic of the *McGuffey's Readers*. Salvation and righteousness were the most frequently mentioned life goals. Piety, kindness, and patriotism were the praised interdependent modes of conduct.[58]

After 1857 McGuffey was no longer responsible for the readers bearing his name. Schoolbooks published later in the nineteenth century carried fewer passages from the Bible and far fewer selections written by ministers. Catholic pressures succeeded in getting many of the most obvious Protestant biases expunged from the daily rituals of school life. Jews and other non-Christians had to wait a long time for gains beyond that. For the rest of the nineteenth century and into the twentieth, the Christian God, the books of the New Testament, and a system of rewards and punishments in the afterlife based on divine judgment remained unexceptional references in the American classroom. An 1885 geography book, which contained specific definitions of prehistoric ages and the fossil record, used a frontispiece picturing a sunset in the mountains. The caption under it was the first verse of the book of Genesis.[59] It was an example of non-controversial religious presence in schoolrooms that our contemporary "creationists" can only dream about. It was that sort of religious presence that Protestant churchmen hoped would shape the taste of schoolchildren as they went out into the world. In that sense, schools carried more of the burden for what happened to commercial culture than churches did.

To Marginalize Religion: The Impossible Dream

We are a long way from being done with the subject of the ways in which religion infiltrated the oral and performative culture of the United States. Religious leaders did not immediately fall victim to secularization when they tried to exert a "non-sectarian" moral influence on popular lectures and the commercial theater. Most innovative avenues of religious influence involved religion in certain processes of commodification. The very effort to create a demand for religion committed revivalism to a market logic and ultimately to market strategies. In the early nineteenth century, clerical authority declined measurably vis-à-vis competing sources of authority. What we should learn from this multiplication of influential voices in Jacksonian America is that hegemony did not come easily for anyone. Precisely because clerics could not take their authority for granted, they embarked on a course of remarkable religious and cultural inventiveness.

Using the concept of power as a measure of how religion is faring in the world is arguably an odd bit of reasoning because it ties the importance of what is purportedly non-secular (religion) to an essentially secular standard (power in the world). However, we cannot avoid such worldly questions because there are no other answerable ones to pose. Instead, whether we believe in God or Michel Foucault, we should acknowledge that power works in mysterious ways, especially in all matters that touch upon culture. If the test of a society's religiosity is whether churches typically oppose and confront other kinds of vested power solely for reasons independent of self-interest, then we are not going to find a religious society anywhere in Western time. We might with as much luck go off in quest of a historical society that contained unicorns and real ghosts.

Either religion keeps up with other cultural aspects of national life, including the commercial forms, or it has no importance. That still leaves religion with many options. The United States is not yet a secular society, partly because of the cultural inventiveness of men like Parson Weems and Charles Finney. They help explain how it happened that many Americans in the nineteenth century continued to regard religion as performing vital work for their political and social democracy. Many people these days are convinced that much of this work was dirty, hypocritical work and that a prominent public role for religion is neither necessary nor desirable. That point of view concedes, of course, that religion, and no longer just Protestant religion, is deeply imbedded in the nation's cultural life, and also its political life.

CHAPTER THREE

The End of Religious Establishment and the Beginning of Religious Politics:

The Parallel Rise of Churches and Political Parties

> Politics are a part of religion in such a country as this, and Christians must do their duty to the country as a part of their duty to God.
>
> Charles Grandison Finney

> I claim that the pulpit has a right and a duty to discuss social questions, moral questions in politics, slavery, war, peace, and the intercourse of nations.
>
> Henry Ward Beecher

The relation between religion and politics is a perplexing subject.[1] Brief reflections about European history leave us dazed by the various patterns of conflict and accommodation that have marked the interaction between those who have ruled churches and those who have ruled states. The one thing that these historical figures have rarely done, although the formula has been prescribed often enough, is to leave one another alone. The United States was supposed to have learned something from the turmoil of the European past and to have written a Constitution that took politics out of religion and religion out of politics. That sundering proved impossible in the young republic. What emerged were new patterns of church/ state interaction that subsequently baffled just about everyone, not least the members of the nation's Supreme Court.[2] Although the First Amendment to the Constitution banned a national establishment of religion, although Thomas Jefferson recommended a wall between church and state, and although most states enforced a purported separation of church and state long before the Constitution's proscription was formally applied to them in the 1940s, religion and politics in America have remained closely related.[3]

In fact, their association might in some ways have been strengthened by the refusal in the beginning to give a state church a legally defined public role. Although England maintains a costly church establishment and assigns to a few bishops a privileged presence in the House of Lords, prime ministers and MPs can nod off during the occasions of ceremonial piety they are obligated to attend and otherwise ignore religion.[4] Not having the benefit of anointed state guardians who look after "the" church, American politicians frequently have to assume something close to that role as part of the image they must cultivate in order to get elected.

A state church does many things. Most relevant here, it relieves religion from market pressures, from the need to maintain its financial solvency through commercial self-promotion. An analogous observation might be made about our political parties that by and large are not publicly financed, not because of a constitutional ban but because the Constitution made no provision for them. The analysis of religion and politics in this chapter takes place outside the cultural marketplace we have been discussing. It is directly relevant, however. Political candidates have followed religious leaders into the world of commodification. For similar reasons they have taken on certain characteristics of public entertainers. They must curry favor with the popular media, seeking always of course to make their own distinctive impress on popular taste.

Some observers of the American scene noticed the paradoxical connections of religion and politics very early in the nation's history. The critical importance of religion to public life was already obvious by the time Alexis de Tocqueville visited the United States in 1831.[5] Echoing the Frenchman's more-or-less generous assessment, Francis Grund, an Austrian immigrant who became an American citizen, wrote in 1837: "The religious habits of the Americans form not only the basis of their private and public morals but have become so thoroughly interwoven with their whole course of legislation that it would be impossible to change them without affecting the very essence of their government." Predictably, Frances Trollope delivered a more jaundiced opinion about the same phenomenon: "My residence in the country [in Cincinnati from 1827 until 1831] has shown me that a religious tyranny may be exerted very effectually without the aid of the government, in a way much more oppressive than the paying of tithe, and without obtaining any of the salutary decorum which I presume no one will deny is the result of an established mode of worship. . . . Church and State hobble along, side by side, notwithstanding their boasted independence."[6]

And so it continues. Europeans may not encounter in America their own various patterns of church/state interaction, but they often remark on something more bizarre. They see a ubiquitous, sometimes flamboyant, presence of religion in political meetings, suggesting to them that ministers carry substantial influence over the ways in which American governments and politicians behave. Why else would an incumbent Republican president dare criticize the opposition party for failing to include "the three letter word God" in its platform?[7] Protestant evangelists have no monarchs to bless, but they are invited to sleep in the White House.[8] Catholic bishops get little public money for their schools, but the votes they can influence make congressmen in their districts extremely eager to please them.[9] Officials go to church and to prayer breakfasts and make certain that the press takes note. Women, African Americans, Jews, and virtually all other groups who feel congenitally excluded from the Oval Office may take comfort in knowing that one of their own will make it to the White House before an avowed atheist.

The commonplace intersections between religion and politics in the United States are multiple and diverse. Organized churches have acted in the past and in the present as political lobbies, taking stands on everything from the abolition of slavery to nuclear disarmament.[10] A catalogue of religious politics confined to the period before the Civil War has yielded material for dozens of historical monographs. The division between Federalists and Jeffersonians in the early republic followed fault lines that had been formed in contests between partisans of colonial religious establishments and religious dissenters. In Massachusetts and Connecticut, where religious establishment continued into the nineteenth century, no political issue was free of the church question.

Before half a century had passed, religion intruded into the controversy between Masons and Anti-Masons, between temperance men and drinkers, between abolitionists and their opponents, between immigrants and Know-Nothings. Religious people were not on one side of the line and freethinkers on the other. Partisans often talked as if that were so, as in the battle between Sabbatarians and anti-Sabbatarians over whether post offices should be open on Sunday. The dispute that lasted from 1810 until 1830 prompted one of the first effective efforts in American politics to mobilize mass opinion. Sabbatarians tried to claim the religious high ground for themselves. They were answered with furious scorn by anti-Sabbatarians, among them many Protestant evangelical voices, who saw a "Papist" trap in letting government dictate the terms of religious observance.[11] In the nineteenth century, religious people ranged themselves on both sides of every controversy in which organized religions claimed an interest. That fact was most glumly played out during the nation's Civil War when North and South threw themselves into their separate versions of a holy crusade.

Under present laws, churches can lose their tax-exempt status for engaging in too much political activity, but the threatened punishment has not frightened anyone. Religious lobbying in the twentieth century has been open and sophisticated. Sometimes churches have reconstituted themselves as ecumenical organizations in order to pursue political goals. The Federal (later National) Council of the Churches of Christ in the United States of America, which was founded in 1908, has spoken out on social issues in ways that have promoted specific and usually liberal pieces of legislation. Various white fundamentalist groups have recently worked the other side of the political divide.[12] Religious leaders have noisily linked themselves to political action groups, and they have sometimes run for and been elected to political office. Since they are constitutionally presumed not to form a religious establishment (such a thing is, after all, banned), they have in the name of religious liberty (the other half of the First Amendment's religious clause) enjoyed considerable leeway in the practice of religious politics.[13]

The many examples of overt linkage between churches and politics can easily be described in historical narrative. The formula that encouraged the links to become strong developed as religious leaders learned new techniques for maintaining their public influence. Without an established church, they could not depend upon the high social status that had formerly belonged to many of them as quasi public officials. Churches and clerics held their own in American life, however much their relative authority in public life declined, but they had to drum up business both among wealthy and influential lay people and among the general population. The general trend of American Protestantism toward Arminianism made individuals responsible for their own conversion. It also made churches responsible for their own growth and financial prosperity. They had to take steps to ensure expansion.

In the complicated interactions between religion and politics, what is cause and what is effect is never completely clear. The political stands that American clergy have often taken manifested rather than caused religious and political entanglement in the United States. Put another way, religion's importance to political attitudes and behavior was not the conscious and direct work of ecclesiastic institutions. Clerics did not in some heavy-handed way force religiosity into the speech of office-seekers. Neither did they dictate the political utterances that have made millennial hopes part of the American sense of national mission.[14] They did not have to. The blurring of secular and sacred in American political and religious rhetoric has served too many purposes.[15] American politicians learned early to trot out conceptions of American nationhood that blended the claim of popular origins with the claim of divine origins. They sounded good, and they won votes. Americans established no church, merely a nation under God, who sanctions with the same blessing its political system, its church system, and its economic system.

Doubtlessly, one of the most persuasive demonstrations of how religion has affected American politics has come from what we used to call the "new" political historians. Their quantified correlations between religious identification and political affiliation have passed from novel into standard interpretation. The attitude of a nineteenth-century American male toward Catholics was as important as his attitude toward slavery in determining his party affiliation on the eve of the Civil War. Perhaps, as some historians have suggested, the political breakdown that led to secession would never have happened had it not been for the Irish Potato Famine and the subsequent influx of many poor, Roman Catholic immigrants into the cities of the Northeast. The Whig party attracted the loyalty of far more than its fair share of evangelical Protestants; and antebellum Democrats, of Catholics.

The United States never developed religiously based political parties, just as it never developed class-based political parties. Nonetheless, religious affiliation was part of the equation determining how people distinguished their political allies from their political enemies. From the Civil War until Richard Nixon, most northern white Protestants voted for the Republican party, leaving white southern Protestants, black Protestants (after 1932), Catholics, and Jews to form an unstable and normally unsuccessful electoral base for the Democratic party.[16] Theological differences had little to do with the political differentiation. What mattered was the general cultural outlook of religious groups, as well as their place in the social hierarchy.

These various facts are generally well understood and certainly much discussed. Commonly the discussions carry the same overtones of judgment we can note in other sorts of controversy involving religion. Some deem the influence of religion on political life as a baleful one, an anachronism that somehow was never properly excised. Others see it as exactly what the founders wanted. From the first quarter, we hear calls for a higher and thicker wall of the sort proposed by Jefferson; from the second, we hear alarmed complaints about "the naked public square."[17] Whatever the wisdom now assigned or ever assigned to excluding religion from the political realm, we must recognize that religious and moral concerns have often been inseparable from the sorts of political issues that get a democratic people excited; maybe we should say a democratic, capitalist people. American citizens vote their pocketbooks, but appeals to greed are not the sole elements of successful campaigns. It has often taken something understood as a moral cause to get people to work for a candidate, to contribute money to someone's campaign, and even to vote. The issues surrounding slavery once excited political activism. So did the pros and cons of temperance. Contemporary American politics will not soon escape from the passions that are stirred when policy issues get tied to debates about divinity and national destiny, about the moral sanctity of the family, or about the teaching of religion in the public schools. For the moment, what presidential candidates say about God in the Pledge of Allegiance and about abortion may well be the most important stands that they take in an election because for many voters these serve as symbols of particular moral universes. Of course for many Americans, morality had more to do with economic issues than anything else. Their easily managed equation of church, politics, and business provides a much too predictable background for our main story.

The Party Spirit of the Antebellum Religious Revivals

The line of argument pursued in this chapter about how American religious denominationalism and political party spirit developed together in the antebellum period takes a major cue from the admonishment in George Washington's "Farewell Address": "Of all the dispositions and habits which lead to political prosperity, Religion and morality are indispensable supports." The insertion of that thought into American political rhetoric was extremely important, especially since an impersonal market system was destroying what was left of a rural moral economy.[18] Denominational religion and political parties were both reflections of the spread of *laissez-faire* attitudes in antebellum America. At the same time they were efforts to restore a public consensus that proponents of American republicanism had thought it vital to maintain. They were responses to worries about a crumbling social structure. Civic order that had once reliably depended upon the deference shown by people of lower sort to people of better sort now relied upon the fickle guidance of popular preference.

In responding to democratic pressures, religion and politics during the period before the Civil War developed almost identical ways of organizing, disciplining, and motivating people. Despite early battles fought between Federalists and Jeffersonians, permanent party organizations were solidly institutionalized in the United States only after the mid-1830s.[19] The first such parties in the world, they were in part the outcome of a unique political situation in which white males enjoyed close to universal suffrage. However, since most American males could vote well before they became strongly committed to party allegiances, and since the framers of the Constitution not only had made no provision for parties but also had viewed them with distaste, historians have noted additional factors that facilitated the appearance of national parties during the Jacksonian era. One set of factors owed to the transformations wrought by the tumultuous religious revivals of the early nineteenth century, especially those that shook communities all over the United States in the 1820s and 1830s. They were mass movements, large-scale efforts to try to control behavior by inventing new forms of publicity to stir people. What they accomplished was reiterated in political organization.

In a challenging interpretation made some years ago, the historian Donald Mathews suggested that the so-called Second Great Awakening, a label applied to the revival mania of the first part of the nineteenth century, contributed to the process of laying down a social structure. "In its social aspects" he wrote, it "was an organizing process that helped to give meaning and direction to people suffering in various degrees from the social strains of a nation on the move into new political, economic and geographical areas."[20] Putting people into churches had the consequence of providing them with a sense of responsibility for their rapidly growing and changing communities.

The association of the revivals with organization, or order, was a remarkably provocative argument that seemed to fly in the face of evidence of splintered churches and the widespread claim that revivalism, with its controversial "new measures" of soul-saving, divided and uprooted people. According to many opponents, revivals were a cause of social disruption, not a solution to it. Churches, without tax support and forced to cast about as best they could for voluntary contributions, entered into a destructive and disorderly competition for money. Revivals may have built church membership, but they also shattered authoritative interpretation of Scripture and inaugurated an age of religious hucksterism and charlatanism. Joseph Smith, William Miller, the Fox sisters, Andrew Jackson Davis, and John Humphrey Noyes were only some of the regrettable products of the contentious spirit fed by uncontrolled religious enthusiasm that had no way to control excess.

The three decades from 1820 to 1850 did constitute an antinomian moment for America's religious communities. To be sure, the surging number of religious people who followed new dispensations, new scriptures, new inward sources of prophetic power, and new laws were not all products of revival fever. Protestantism in general was responding to processes set going by democracy and *laissez-faire*.[21] Lay people seized control of their religious lives. In religious protest they flexed their muscles, cast off habits of deference, and felt the thrill of empowerment. The political movement we call Jacksonianism was fired by a spreading religious attitude exemplified but not confined to revivalism. Some of the ferment assumed an anti-clerical cast as people learned to treat ministers with the same fickleness they would later bestow on politicians. To the English visitor Frederick Marryat, the result was baleful: "It is the same here in religion as in politics: before the people will permit anyone to serve them in any office, he must prove his unfitness by submitting to what no man of honesty or conscientious rectitude would subscribe to."[22]

In religious terms, then, the revivals were only one manifestation of a more general quest for a firm basis of religious authority, something destroyed before the revivals had begun. Critics assigned special blame to them because they embodied the potentially anarchic side of the religious quest more dramatically and on a wider scale than anything else. They were made responsible for breakdowns in habits of deference because they encouraged a view that the spiritual lives of powerful people, including the lives of many who represented the learned ministry, were woefully impoverished. As we have seen, revival meetings could disrupt, even if only briefly, the normal hierarchies of respect based on age, social rank, and gender.[23]

We are faced with two broad interpretations of revivalism that seemingly compete with each other. One stresses order and organization; the other, chaos and fragmentation. In fact both notions are essential to an explanation of what happened. It helps to remember that we use both notions to explain a market economy. *Laissez-faire* is at one level a formula for anarchy because it makes possible an infinite number of individual choices. Thus, the First Amendment, in prohibiting a national religious establishment and in guaranteeing a legal legitimacy to virtually any religious claim, encouraged a multiplicity of sects. People with different social and economic rankings, with different attitudes toward moral codes, with different ethnic and historical memories, and with different plans for social advancement institutionalized and widened their differences in the churches they chose to create and join.

At some point, however, an invisible hand moves in to guide choices into an ordered and rational system. It transforms division in a complex society into an essential characteristic of organization. In the first several decades of the nineteenth century, churches, more than any other local institution and sometimes in the absence of other possibilities, served to encode people's sense of distinctiveness and to cover that distinctiveness with a plausible claim of respectability. Americans had to sort themselves out before they could live together. Religious splintering had to take place to bring order to America's heterogeneous population. If anything is surprising about this, it is the relatively low level of violence that went along with the differentiation. Not everything happened peacefully.[24] The destructive outrage that was directed against Mormons and Irish Catholics in the nineteenth century was one marked characteristic of American religious development. The price that any society pays for taking religious matters seriously is religious conflict. However, unlike what has happened in many other countries, religious division has not been a primary cause of American violence.

The publicity-fed revivals and the general democratization and expansion of religion that they encouraged worked simultaneously in two directions. They divided antebellum Americans and set them to quarreling. They encouraged attitudes that tempted women and men to cut ties with past loyalties, with friends, with communities, and sometimes with family. These severances dramatically affected authority and elevated individual will above community goals. They also accustomed Americans to think of their social encounters as anonymous interactions. At the same time, antebellum religious ferment softened and contained some of the very differences that they institutionalized. Churches of different denominations established codes of respectable behavior, relating both to private and to public conduct, that influenced not only members of newly emerging middle classes but also the "free" workers whom they hired for wages.[25] Men and women with different denominational loyalties settled into peaceful communities where moral discipline set norms and shaped behavior. The revivals by emphasizing conversion diluted many doctrinal differences that had split America's oldest Protestant denominations. The various denominations did not unite, and in most institutional ways they learned to multiply their differences. Yet the revivals helped to establish a national framework for religious controversies, normalizing and to some extent defusing quarrels by turning them into well-publicized "media" events.[26] For the most part, the nation's judicial structures had no role to play in mediating these controversies. Politics did.

Insofar as revivals were important to social organization, they were, broadly speaking, instruments of social control and discipline.[27] Although the enthusiastic religious seekers who attended revivals seized the responsibility for their own salvation, the headiness of that arrogant act against Calvin's God was subsequently weighted down by the self-imposed burden of proving that they were free of sin. The God of Calvin, hard taskmaster that he was, had at least not expected his creatures to demonstrate genuine worthiness. Although antebellum Americans proved to the satisfaction of their own and subsequent generations that they were not up to the challenge of moral perfection, the revivals, as a movement that was felt everywhere in the country, provided one set of symbols and standards to which Americans could rally. By the opposition they aroused, they also suggested other standards.

This formation of demarcation lines was essential to social organization—and to politics. The first enduring political party system in the United States, the one organized beginning in the 1830s, was influenced by divisions between those who were willing to use legislation to enforce Christian cultural norms and those who opposed Christian legislation. The collective weight of revivalism did not automatically fall on the legislative side. Too many Baptists and Methodists harbored historic fears of state sponsorship of religion. In the North, however, after 1840, the collective weight of Protestantism gravitated toward legislative enforcement.

The whole business of working up a revival, of inviting someone like Finney to come to town and preach, signified that many religious leaders in the United States no longer viewed their sole task as nurturing stable congregations of God's most easily visible saints. The law of American economic life has always been expansion and growth, and almost every American Christian denomination in the nineteenth century turned that law into gospel truth. Among Protestants, missionary work emerged as an important vocation that was encouraged by both the communications and the transportation revolution of the early nineteenth century. We have already seen some of the consequences for American publishing and for public speaking. The Congregational and Presbyterian ministers and laypersons who organized the American Bible Society and the American Tract Society were not always favorably disposed toward the "excessive" emotional behavior associated with Methodist and Baptist revivalists. They nonetheless all shared an imperative: evangelize people and attract them to the Word of God by whatever means works. The energy released as a result was impressive and made proselytizing a political act.

The work of the American Bible and Tract societies as it influenced commercial culture laid the groundwork for mass communications and for mass movements generally.[28] As a vast publicity campaign directed at dispersed, anonymous audiences, it had tremendous implications for political organization. A large success was claimed for the millions of morality tales that these societies distributed. Idle men picked up a stray tract thrown carelessly from the window of a stagecoach and found their way to Christ. Drunkards tippling in barrooms staggered home with a Bible that had been stuffed into their pockets and "chose" salvation after reading through it in the sober hours of the next morning. We may be certain that many of these published claims were spurious. No matter. The technology and the distribution networks that made possible the creation of larger and larger reading audiences stimulated alert entrepreneurs who concluded that personal contact was neither necessary nor even particularly useful in efforts to affect people's behavior. The trail opened by this discovery led eventually to Madison Avenue, but before that it led to the formation of modern politics.

Evangelical persuasive techniques had their perils, not the least of which was the loss of control over how the message was received. But what other choices were there in trying to discipline a society of free people who were daily scattering themselves over an ever expanding geographical territory? Evangelists glimpsed the troubling problems that might result in a pluralistic society of people who were forever on the road. They tried to render them "tractable" by relying on the "self-evident" moral appeal of a "practical" Christianity.[29] Revival preachers had the same problem as the tract societies. They did not necessarily want to abandon face-to-face persuasive techniques, but they recognized the need for performance skills that worked in impersonal situations. Revivalists adjusted to transience, both their own transience as they moved from community to community and that of their far-straying flocks. Because of the migratory habits of antebellum Americans, preachers had to reach out to many people who had no secure social moorings, strangers who did not belong to a church and who were on their way from one place to another.

In addressing an unsettled population, using unsettled credentials and unsettled methods, revival preachers were bound to gain a reputation from their critics as rabble-rousers. That was a misconception. They were as intensely concerned with the maintenance of order as any of their detractors. This attitude bound Protestant Americans together. Charles Grandison Finney calculated the effects of his preaching on crowd behavior. He employed novel methods, but made them systematic. He played to emotion, but in controlled ways.[30] In a literal sense, the advice books written to instruct revival preachers constituted a law-and-order litera-ture. Audiences had to be stirred because unless a preacher commanded their attention he had no way to control them. Specific techniques of "spontaneous" preaching aimed at achieving specific effects. Finney did not merely arrive in a town, announce a meeting for the same evening, and depend upon the force of his personality to arouse the confidence of strangers. Local churches advertised his visits, and what his audiences heard from Finney was in considerable part what they had been told to anticipate.[31]

The attention given to building expectations was especially important in organizing camp meetings. They quickly became regularized both in their occurrence and in their methods of procedure. We tend to remem-ber only the emotional extravagance. Many surviving engraved illustra-tions of camp meetings suggest a carnival out of control. Those who like to keep their history lively can be grateful that these parodied descrip-tions have a substantial basis in fact. However, there are other facts. Disruptive behavior is not the necessary consequence of spiritual rapture, not because the connection is unthinkable but because knowledge of the possibility results in cautionary practices. Reputable sponsors of camp meetings had so regularized their procedures by mid-century as to render disruptive and unauthorized behavior of any kind extremely difficult. Ac-cording to one defender of camp meetings, the first word in the motto of their organization was "order." "We can do nothing," he stated, "with-out order."[32] - from 1 Cor 12/or is of 14?)

The precautions that revivalists took were evident not merely in the way that they modulated their speech in order to play upon their audi-ence's emotions. All arrangements mattered. Organizers thought through details of spacial design. They laid out the many rows of seats before a central, prominently raised preacher's stand. Since camp meet-ings went on for as long as a week, staff workers paid careful attention to housing. People, usually family groups, lived in tents that were erected on "uniformly laid out lots." Activity schedules, including all preaching and prayer sessions, were worked out and announced in ad-vance. So were the rules of behavior. Manuals recommended leaving nothing to chance. They forbade late-night assemblies, any sort of unau-thorized socializing, and rowdy behavior. Boisterous persons whose con-duct could not be attributed to a conversion experience (and the literature prescribed ways to manage the emotional outbursts that went along with conversion) faced forcible expulsion from the meeting area. Organizers usually made arrangements with local police officials.

The illustrations that were drawn and published to depict the well-run camp meeting stressed the neatness and the regularity of the gathering.

In defending their practices, organizers of the meetings took the spiritual benefits of the revivals for granted. What they emphasized instead in the manuals was the social benefit that accrued to nearby towns—peace, quiet, and tranquillity. By the middle part of the nineteenth century, Methodists had more than earned a reputation for discipline. Already, many of their camp-meeting grounds had acquired the settled permanence of vacation resorts and real-estate ventures. Later in the century the annual reports of camp organizers dealt with railroad access, drainage, garbage, police, fire departments, boating and swimming facilities, and street grading.[33] Critics no longer complained about emotionalism but about the calculated commercialism that had replaced it. Nonetheless, the development had followed a consistent logic. Experiments that had begun with the aim of organizing people whose social moorings had been loosened had done exactly that—at least among one broad type of Americans who were white and aspiring to middle-class status. The success of order and organization made it hard to remember that the experiments had originated in the breakdown of older forms of social authority and deference. The antinomian impulse had been brought back within the law, though not without changes that had dramatically affected religious life in the United States.

Justifying Political Divisions: The Dangers and Opportunities Suggested by Religious Experience

The changes affected political life as well and forged the important complementarities between the world of religion and the world of politics that would come to characterize American life. From the early part of the nineteenth century, religious language riddled the development of party politics in the United States. Prayer was commonly a part of a political meeting, and the nominally secular activities of politicians sometimes acquired religious names. Political speakers were called itinerant preachers, and campaigning was labeled missionary work. The opposition party became "heathens," and winners referred to their electoral victory as "salvation." "Election" itself was a term that recalled Protestant theology.[34] In 1831 the Anti-Masons, who had created a hybrid organization that was in part an evangelical reform society and in part a political party, held America's first presidential nominating convention.

Observers persuasively likened the emotionalism of political rallies and demonstrations to the emotionalism of revivals. In doing so, they usually meant to extend criticism of the popular style of revivalism to party politics. Nathan Bangs, an influential Methodist leader in New York, complained about excess in Methodist worship: "I witnessed a spirit of pride, presumption, and bigotry, impatience of scriptural restraint and moderation, clapping of the hands, screaming, and even jumping, which marred and disgraced the work of God."[35] Anyone might have witnessed the same behavior in new styles of political campaigning that were developed in the 1840s. Whigs and Democrats worked to give their partisans the "thrill" of participating in mass rallies and processions. They charged their appeals to party loyalty with emotion and relied upon songs and theatrical devices as well as speeches.[36] Both revivals and political rallies qualified as what Michel Chevalier called "festivals of democracy." In an even more interesting observation, the French visitor said that a particular political parade he witnessed reminded him of a religious procession of Mexican Indians following the Eucharist.[37] Nineteenth-century elections became secular holy days that aped religious observance.[38]

To some historians, these commonalities have not meant anything of import. They may be right. Public affairs may simply have been replacing spiritual matters at the center of the white-male universe.[39] The overlap of language was perhaps a temporarily convenient transfer of familiar words and actions from one phenomenon to something that was displacing it. That does not seem likely, however. Why assume that religion was being displaced or replaced? Statistical evidence runs in the other direction. It is far more commonsensical to assume that religious and political concepts reinforced one another.[40] After all, national expansion required the same thing of politics and religion.

The invention of American government did not initially provide for political parties. Instead, the framers of the Constitution stated their explicit opposition to parties and tried to devise a system of checks and balances within the government that would discourage the formation of interest groups. The separation of governmental powers further undermined the ability of any organized group to control both legislative and executive action.[41] The opponents of a party system included Hamilton, Jefferson, and Madison—never mind that these were the very men who were most responsible for encouraging the first party polarities in the history of the young republic. They were adamant in their refusal to endorse the idea of a permanently organized opposition to elected officials. The word "party," which was often used as a synonym for "faction," stood for tumult, discord, and dissension. To promote a party spirit was to encourage selfishness. A man linked to a party was a man linked to selfish interests, frequently economic ones. He was therefore incapable of exercising disinterested judgment to promote the common good.

These seemed to be the clear lessons of eighteenth-century English politics. To be sure, in their own governments North American colonials had gained considerable experience with party-like groupings. Although nonexistent in some colonies, party activity was regularized in others. But nowhere did parties have much more than an *ad hoc* existence. In general, colonials retained the habit of deferring to the judgment of men who had been elected to office and concluded, even after their own experience with revolution, that organized opposition to seated authority quickly degenerated into lawless insurrection. Shays's Rebellion in 1786 showed how. It supplied those who worried about resistance with a strong reason to call the convention that produced the American Constitution.

Many of the political lessons were tied to the colonists' experience with religious discord, although the implications of possible analogies were not entirely clear. With the establishment of government under the Constitution, all elected national politicians were committed to some version of the principle of free religious practice. They associated any effort to enforce the practice of one form of Protestant worship with tyranny. At the state level, many extended that notion to protect the civil and religious freedom of Catholics and Jews. A certain amount of religious division represented in a multiplicity of sects was indicative of social health just as was a certain amount of political disagreement. By the end of the eighteenth century, and despite the Alien and Sedition Acts, toleration, a concept that had gained its strongest public meaning through the struggle for religious rights, was a model that worked to protect both religious and political opinion as well as one that rendered some organized dissent normative.[42]

But how much dissent was healthy? Memories of religious disputes suggested good reasons to hope for limits. A fierce spirit of religious sectarianism, even when shorn of state sponsorship, could itself multiply the forces of intolerance in a society, becoming as dangerous to the health of society as factionalized economic interests. What were competing religious denominations if not organized and permanent parties? In the 1790s, the Federalist clergy in New England opposed both political parties and dissenting sects for exactly the same reason.[43] The authority of those who had best demonstrated their capacity to lead could survive differences of opinion but not difference that was institutionally structured. Many historians of early America have underlined this argument as an example of the ideological distaste that revolutionary leaders held for what emerged as America's system of modern political liberalism. By the time Andrew Jackson was elected president in 1828, American politics had been transformed.

Religious dissenters in New England at the beginning of the nineteenth century, and their co-denominationalists elsewhere in the young republic, were not vying for state power, but history suggested that religious competition was rarely politically benign. Clerical figures picked from the European past served as leading examples of incendiary party intriguers. John Trenchard and Thomas Gordon, two English Whiggish writers well known to America's Revolutionary generation, consistently made the strongest case against "the many Mischiefs, which the Leaders and Deceivers of Parties and Factions in Religion did to the World, by throwing God's Judgments at one another, and impiously confining his Providence and Mercies to themselves; and by applying the common Phaenomena and Events of Nature to their own Advantage, and interpreting the same as Denunciations of his Wrath against their Enemies; by which unhallowed Presumption they have raised up and inflamed implacable Hatred, Animosities and Uncharitableness amongst Men of the same Nation, who are all Brethren."[44] Trenchard and Gordon were writing against intolerant church establishments, but "disestablishment" was no guarantee against the unpleasantness they described. Arguments cut both ways. In the young republic it sometimes proved useful to legitimate the role of political dissent by appealing to the hard-won rights of religious "dissenters." Liberty was in the first place religious liberty. With equal plausibility, however, those who deplored the appearance of political parties argued their case by citing the consequences of too much, and too firmly organized, religious discord. The issues were inextricably related.

The Constitution, arguably, had inadvertently opened up the dangerous possibility of a society rent by an infinite succession of party-like religious quarrels. No one had justified the religious clauses of the First Amendment in those terms. Rather, its proponents had argued that the government's sponsorship of religious tolerance would remove the dangers of religious contention and make public life more civil, less individualistic and self-centered. They believed that sectarian divisions were the unhealthy products of an established church, just as they imagined that political parties were the products of legally privileged wealth and class. Hence, Jefferson, who abhorred political parties, expected disestablishment and toleration to turn Americans into Unitarians who would put public interest above their private passions ("I trust that there is not a young man now living in the United States who will not die an Unitarian").[45]

As it turned out, these lessons drawn from the past were misleading about the future. The increasing number of quarreling religious sects in the United States confounded the Constitution's framers. And so did the insistence of free citizens on organizing political parties. Civic republicanism gave way to the competition of market liberalism. By mid-century,

Americans had to find rationales to justify two related developments that they had not initially anticipated but that had become central to the operation of their society.

A major text that guided discussions of factions, or parties, of any kind in America was Madison's Federalist Ten. Madison had reasoned that Americans could effectively nullify the dangers traditionally associated with factions by increasing the size of the nation and of representative districts. The geographical dispersion of collections of self-interested men thwarted their opportunities to gain a dominant voice in legislative assemblies. But Madison failed, at least in Federalist Ten, to consider one negative consequence of his proposal. "Extending the sphere," or weakening the possibility of one "faction" gaining a majority to enact "selfish" interests, risked stripping from voters a major motivation to become politically involved. The ability of a sizable political coalition to enact selfish interests, however much those interests harm the interests of other sizable coalitions, is a powerful political stimulant. Lacking that expectation, a democratic people will not easily be moved by appeals to act for the public good. Of all the fictions concocted by a democratic and very pluralistic people, the one about the "public good" remains the most abstract.[46]

Madison recognized that politics was in part driven by factional interests, and he did not expect factions to disappear. However, since he was concerned about their dangers, he could not assign to them any positive influence. The selfish interests that they represented had to be dissolved in deliberative assemblies in which goals that benefited the few gave way to goals that served the general welfare. Madison did not initially explore the possibility that a way might be found to join diverse factions in a private, national organization that diluted some of the worst dangers of single factions seeking power on their own. That coalition of factions could preserve a high level of commitment to political action, yet be forced in some measure to speak the language of general welfare. It would survive and gain power because the men who formed it recognized compromise and pragmatism as the highest forms of political wisdom. At the same time, such a coalition would accept the reasonable satisfaction of demands made by victorious factions as a legitimate function of government and the inescapable basis of political success.

What is summarized above describes what many came to view as the achievement of America's first permanent party system and its legitimation of an organized opposition to elected governments. During the 1830s, America's first generation of professional politicians decided that a national political party was not a faction. A party served diverse and competing interests and still made possible the organization and activation of the electorate. It was a way of overcoming the lack of power felt by men who counted for nothing as individual voters. A party respected the local interests of those who contributed to its national strength but also committed itself to sweeping statements of principle that encompassed divergent goals. Candidates of different parties found it possible to say most of the same things about most of the issues. What was done with political power had little to do with the publicized platforms of national parties, and somehow in this way political parties promoted political enthusiasm without strong ideological divisiveness. By the end of the 1830s, most Americans took parties for granted. Some, in fact, had concluded that the American constitutional government was impossible without a stable, two-party system.

As for religion's role in fomenting antebellum political developments, religious denominations inured Americans to the idea that party divisions, despite the catalogue of expressed fears, might actually serve the cause of social and political stability.[47] Indeed, at the grass-roots level, churches had provided crucial lessons in the mechanics of division. Not without cause had Tocqueville called New World forms of Protestant Christianity "democratic and republican religion." They "contributed powerfully to the establishment of a republic and a democracy in public affairs and from the beginning, politics and religion contracted an alliance which has never been dissolved."[48] When Catholics came in large numbers to the United States, they were accused of failing to observe this symbiotic relation between religion and democracy. In fact the Catholic Church recognized the political and religious requirements of a divided America better than many Protestants. In the course of the nineteenth century, they made, albeit by practice rather than doctrine, a franker acknowledgment of pluralism as it affected the operation of both the political and religious institutions of the nation.

These observations are all meant to suggest why the antebellum politicians' borrowing of religious language had more than a superficial significance, and why both languages had implications for America's rapidly developing commercial markets. When Jefferson spoke of his foes as "apostates," "political heretics," "bigots," and "votaries," when he cast himself as defender of the "true faith," he was reaching for analogies that made sense to his audience.[49] The terms that described the good and bad tendencies of religion also described the good and bad tendencies of politics. The easy interchangeability of reference made it possible in antebellum America for a church building to serve as a place for a political meeting. Political meetings in churches might occasion disapproval, but largely because of the particular political views being aired. Methodists and Baptists often said that politics and religion were separate activities, but candidates for office routinely visited their camp meetings in search of votes.[50] Before and after the Civil War, black churches in America demonstrated just how far formal associations between religion and politics could be pushed.[51] In black communities the preacher and the politician were the same person far more frequently than in white communities.

Throughout America, preacher and politician were bound by similar conventions affecting their public success. From what can be seen about the performance roles demanded of ministers, it is fairly clear how their oratory was to influence the work of politicians. Religious leaders had been pioneers in the field of popular speaking. Their manuals for attracting listeners had relevance beyond the churches. Moreover, the mechanisms of organization that were used in successful revivals, as well as in the various temperance crusades, provided models for political campaigns. Ministers recognized that dramatic effect was necessary to accomplish anything in large public assemblies. The image of the revival preacher was that of a man organized for practical activity. The ministers who were most prominent in conducting revivals cultivated an image of very masculine doers. They distributed "campaign" literature to promote their reputation as men of impressive physical size, men of endurance fit to lead military campaigns, resourceful men who knew how to speak the sociable language of common folk.[52] The importance of log-cabin origins attached both to successful politicians and to revival preachers.

The macho image, in part, grew in response to charges of effeminacy aimed at some elements of the "learned" clergy. Religion in the nineteenth century was clearly part of women's sphere. Women were by far the majority of church members in antebellum America, making churches extensions of their domestic space. Especially in the first part of the nineteenth century, men were reluctant joiners of churches, perhaps because they were reluctant to accept the discipline.[53] Only after churches had abdicated their power to control the moral behavior of their members (however much ministers might continue to talk about it) did men begin to appear in church on a scale even roughly comparable to women. We might conclude from this fact that antebellum men poured their meaningful enthusiasms into work and into politics.[54] Politics was their space, whereas women could not vote and had no role to play in the political process of party nomination and office-holding.

Such a conclusion is, in fact, too simple, with respect to both women and men. We are now beginning to recognize how clearly women regarded their work in voluntary church organizations, which excluded males, as political work. Through religious organizations women began the crusade for women's rights. In promoting religious and benevolent goals, they gained a forum for public address. They gained careers as missionaries and teachers. They did not until the twentieth century obtain the right to translate their church energies into votes. Interestingly, their experience rendered them more suspicious than men of the partisanship of party politics. Even so, their earlier political uses of religion were varied and brought them a critical form of social empowerment.[55] Religion was for many of them a way to advance causes.

As for men, they had pursued religion as a form of politics even before they identified with parties or showed much interest in joining churches. The historian Daniel Howe has made the intriguing suggestion that the men who became Whigs may have been slower to accept the legitimacy of political parties than the men who became Democrats because their work in religious benevolent societies gave them "an alternative mode of organizing in pursuit of their social objective."[56] Antebellum men who were not church members frequently worked for political and moral goals through lay-managed religious societies. These, in turn, gave money to support the various denominations that in rural America were overwhelmingly Protestant and evangelical.[57]

Middle-class men began to join churches in larger numbers at almost precisely the same time (in the 1830s and 1840s) that they began to join political parties. Their affiliation with the former may have signified that churches had been defanged as morally coercive agents, but it also signified the successful internalization of certain moral imperatives. Church membership suggests not that churches had ceased to care about the moral conduct of their members but rather that moral comportment had become important in many middle-class contexts. Men joined lodges— the Masons and the Odd Fellows, for example, for which temperance and steady habits were conditions of membership. Their reputations as businessmen often hinged upon the credit reports of R. G. Dun and Company that made moral behavior as well as past business dealings a condition of favorable ratings.[58] Church discipline was less essential in conditioning male behavior only because other institutions were acting like churches.

I am not trying to draw an equation between religion and politics. Political parties extended principles of organization that went beyond the patterns available to religious denominations. Political parties could legitimate the wisdom and necessity of permanently organized division more fulsomely than Protestant denominations. There was no consistently Christian way in the nineteenth century to argue that denominationalism, however important its competitive energies were to churching the American people, was a good thing. Religious leaders engineered one religious division after another, but they did not celebrate either division or competition as appropriate ideals when they were supposed to know what God wanted them to do. The most inventive sectarians in nineteenth-century America all justified their splinter movements as efforts to restore the one true church and to obliterate the need for multiple brand names.

In contrast, by mid-century political party builders proceeded in their work with a clear conscience, extending the principles of liberalism to argue the virtue of the institutionalized competition of self-interested *groups*. The bureaucratic apparatus of national party organizations along with their talent for promotion outgrew what most denominations managed. Somewhat inexplicably, the disputes that led to the Civil War provoked enduring rifts in many religious denominations that predated and in some cases outlasted sectional divisions in the major political parties. Although the same issues that divided the one divided the other, political parties responded to pressures to get back together in reorganized form.[59] Religious groups, once split, were less supple.

The legitimation of party organization was helped, of course, by a majoritarian political system that more or less forced political differences in the United States to stay gathered in two major coalitions. Religion in America lacked an analogous external pressure to resolve differences in this binary fashion. Some historical commentary has suggested that Catholics and Protestants in the nineteenth century formed two distinct church parties. That was scarcely true, if only because ethnic and racial divisions within those two groups doomed unified action. Religious Americans did on many occasions learn to form common causes across denominational lines; for example, with respect to missionary work and tract distribution. Antebellum temperance societies formed a sort of halfway house between political parties and religious organizations. However, most denominations hedged their participation in cooperative enterprises, and many refused. Paradoxically, the enduring ideal of a united Christian church made cooperation among different denominations somewhat suspect. Cooperation raised the uncomfortable suggestion that the reasons given to resist more formal merger were trivial and pigheaded. Interdenominational organizations were only partial imitations of political organizations because, lest we forget, churches did have other goals than political ones.

The Common Framework of Religious and Political Life

The most important accomplishment of religious arrangements in antebellum America, and also of political parties, was the energizing and the control of mass behavior in a society with an uncommon commitment to *laissez-faire* arrangements. The problems of social order were staggering. The American public was composed of very different sorts of people, and their cultural differences grew wider during the course of the nineteenth century rather than narrower. A religious badge of identification was a social marker. To those who wore it, often with vehement passion, it carried a whole set of connotations about who one was and who one was not. Both religious groups and political parties established comprehensible boundary markers without making the boundaries absolutely impenetrable. The institutions of division thus formed were also ways to bring people into some sort of common life—no mean achievement. Disagreements took ritualized forms that signified shared experience. This would never have happened if all religious groups had demanded a high level of theological sophistication and commitment or if political parties had demanded on all occasions a high level of ideological sophistication and commitment. The cost paid for a workable American democracy with a broad level of institutional commitment to religious and moral goals was a leveling down of political and religious concepts.

What remains striking is that the two agencies most necessary to the course of American democracy, religious denominations and political parties, were neither foreseen nor welcomed. The critics who were most worried about potential social breakdown viewed the mass activity encouraged by the religious revivals as symptoms of what they feared rather than its cure. They gave no credit to the revivals, or to aggressive evangelical activity generally, for providing some of the first successful experiments in ordering the national population; nor were they prepared to appreciate that the organizers of revivals and of political parties in the Jacksonian era were learning how to contain popular energy within a framework of discipline. The results were messy enough to allow mixed reviews. It is not an entirely objective assertion to say that American nationality, such as it is, resulted from the considerable success achieved by evangelists and party men in their risky undertakings. It is, however, a plausible proposition. Methods of generating crowd enthusiasm wound up serving the very cause of social order that conventional wisdom said they were bound to defeat.

Political parties and evangelical activities were experiments in mass persuasion in a world where people were free to choose. Working on the assumption that a democratic people would not by any natural habits strive for the common good, they sought to develop artificial means, "new measures," to stir commitment. The parades and the rallies that political parties sponsored, like religious revivals, sought to organize people who would never meet into unified armies for accomplishing social goals. Americans did not thereby banish disorder and violence from their mechanisms of democracy. They only stopped things from getting entirely out of hand. The orderliness of American politics at mid-century compares favorably with the boisterous drunken brawls that aroused election fever in Jefferson's home territory in the late eighteenth century.[60] American religion and American politics had by the middle of the nineteenth century achieved consequences desirable even to those who deplored the means of attaining them.

What, finally, about the question of displacement, the issue of whether religious activity and political activity go forward in their separate turns, the progress of one coming always at the expense of the other? The argument that they do is familiar even to non-Marxists, and it makes considerable sense. Religious and political identifications are strong forms of orientation, and it is difficult to imagine people who manage to give a full measure of loyalty and enthusiastic commitment to both. The plausible suggestion that people seek salvation, primarily, either through religious deliverance or through secular politics does seem to hold for many people. The absolute bar to political activity mandated by the Jehovah's Witnesses, for example, is a case in point. Another example is the Southern Baptists, whose heavy emphasis on conversion has at least historically acted to restrain political activism. Even under recent prodding from Jerry Falwell and Pat Robertson, Protestant fundamentalists and Pentecostals have not been easy to mobilize for sustained political campaigns. Highly educated agnostics vote in far greater numbers proportionately.

However, the history of nineteenth-century America yields as much evidence against the thesis of displacement as for it. The mere citation of numbers throws it into question. In contrast to many parts of Europe, where the rise of mass political parties came at a time when religious observance was lessening, organized religion and organized politics in the United States both continued on an upward rise throughout the whole of the century. The common underpinnings of religious and political enthusiasm in antebellum America made this possible. Acting religiously and acting politically arose out of the same need to give meaning and value to a collective view, thereby rendering a democratic society orderly. Most people, if we can conclude anything from silence, sensed no conflict between their religious roles and their political roles.

A different history in European countries that had formal religious parties gave prominence to more sharply articulated distinctions between "religious politics" and "secular politics." Political historians of the United States have noted that religious political activists have been more comfortable in the Whig/Republican tradition of party politics than in the Democratic tradition. That is true for white Protestant males, but they should not be the only focus. Regional, racial, and class differences, as well as particular issues, have kept both parties sensitive to religious issues. American Catholics, traditionally more Democratic than Whig/Republican, have often made religious demands on politics, a fact that Protestant political activists once used with an invincible lack of self-knowledge to challenge the American loyalties of Catholics. In the full range from populist to elitist politics, and in both political parties, religious resonances often shape campaign strategies. Given the way the nation was formed, it would be astonishing if they did not.

Questions of priority between denominational religion and party politics need not be posed. Since we are not dealing with a simple relation of cause and effect, it is not useful to insist that the religious revivals were the necessary prelude to the legitimation of permanent political parties in the United States. It is equally true to say that the highly charged political campaigns waged between Federalists and Jeffersonians in the 1890s created a hospitable environment for the revivals. The point is that both religion and politics were developing their principles of organization in the nineteenth century, not according to blueprints laid down in the American Constitution, but in tandem with the expansion and modifications of market-based liberalism.[61]

On the other hand, given the tendency of historians to give priority to whatever is political and the disposition of many contemporary observers to view religion as harmful to political debate, I am inclined to stress the centrality of religion in the formation of the nation's political life. The religious leaders of colonial America helped to regularize the habits that were also characteristic of colonial politicians. Those habits provided an important legacy for learning how to maintain authority in the young republic as older habits of deference were knocked down. Religious enthusiasm was prior to political enthusiasm, long prior. If the political philosopher Michael Walzer is correct, the very concept of a politically active citizen was formed by English Puritans long before the American political system was formed.[62] And even if he is partly wrong, ardent secularists in the United States find that they must still deal with a people who believe that American religion guarantees the success of its politics, rather than vice versa. Close to a majority of Americans is willing to say that religion is the most important thing in life. Almost no one makes the same claim about politics, not even smart politicians. The downside of some contemporary evidence that loyalty to particular religious denominations is lessening may be that religious and political loyalties are sliding downward together, their fortunes, as always, linked. Those who have wanted a politics without religion may get their wish, but at the cost of a politics without parties or voters.

Or, in the political realignment, will religion be on one side and areligion on the other?

CHAPTER FOUR

Americans Learn to Play and Religion Learns to Let Them

The truth is, the need of amusement is much less than people commonly apprehend, and, where it is not necessary, it must be sinful.

Reverend John Witherspoon, 1757

Let our readers, one and all, remember that we are sent into the world, not for sport and amusement, but for labor; not to enjoy and please ourselves, but to serve and glorify God and be useful to our fellow men. That is the great object and end of life.

The New Englander, a Congregationalist publication, 1851.

Religious leaders played innovative roles during the consolidation of America's market economy in the first half of the nineteenth century, especially in shaping the culture industry. The transformation of many cultural activities into commodity transactions meant that to improve themselves, to learn who they were, and especially to entertain themselves, Americans were given a large number of shopping options with respect to products and services.[1] Religion was itself rapidly taking on aspects of a commodity. It developed marketing strategies, ways of advertising itself, and distribution networks. Methodist circuit riders by themselves invented forms of religious proselytizing that could be adapted to the selling of virtually any product. They were not alone in their innovative cleverness, not in a land of fierce denominational competition. Religious entrepreneurs made aggressive use of technological changes in the media that were later copied by businessmen and politicians. Religion's systematic and expansive complicity in mechanisms of market exchange is surely the most important aspect of the particular kind of secularization that has characterized the nineteenth and twentieth centuries.[2]

The forces that drew everything in American society into the web of monetary exchange inevitably changed some essential aspects of religion. Among other things, they encouraged a "popularization" of religious messages. This does not mean that after a time every religious group aimed to do nothing more than pander to the tastes of unlettered masses. It only suggests that religious leaders could ill afford to take a disdainful stance toward what the market measured as the will of the people. In the antebellum world of religious democratization, clerics were no longer the guardians of high culture in quite the same way they once had been. Elitism became the pose of "serious" writers, "discriminating" literary people, who, once the antebellum book market began to return a substantial income to "scribbling women," assigned value to their work precisely because it did not sell well.[3] Religion had to sell. Although some American religious denominations developed high-toned services that reiterated the hierarchies discernible in other areas of culture, and although a few others survived by retreating altogether from the venues of technological and economic change, most religious leaders chose not to dismiss the great masses of ordinary citizens as unworthy of their message. Quite aside from the imperatives that tempt any organization in a competitive situation to seek growth, Christianity had doctrinal reasons not to desert the meek and humble. The more "degraded" the people were, the more they needed to be reached.

The changes in organized religion affected the rest of the nation's culture. The commercialization of divinity pushed religion into the public arenas of American life and made it central to American mythmaking, to its politics, and to its delineation of social and ethnic divisions. Americans learned to work and play, to read and write, to divide and unite by rules that were heavily influenced by religious messages. Measured by churchgoing habits, they became more and more a religiously observant people although that process did not exclusively or even mainly owe much to the work of particular churches. Many religious innovators were laypeople who argued that religion should not let itself be trapped within the bounded walls of church institutions. People who wanted religion to exert a powerful influence on public life needed to break through the spacial barriers erected by denominations and send religion abroad in whatever ways were effective.[4] They succeeded so well that we can call them major inventors of American popular commercial culture.

However, if religious leaders insinuated themselves fairly easily into many of the things that Americans purchased or patronized in the name of cultural enrichment, they found it more difficult to exert influence over the commercialized activities that Americans pursued in the name of pleasure. What many tried to do, and with a measure of success, was to turn the commercial forms of cultural enrichment and of pleasure into the same thing.

The Danger of Play

Americans, like people in any place, have always found ways to amuse themselves.[5] Social historians have virtually demolished the notion that a universal internalization of the Protestant work ethic explains the rise of the American nation. Colonial Virginians were too lazy to work even when their lives literally depended on more rigorously disciplined labor. Eighteenth- and nineteenth-century artisans, apparently everywhere, went to work as much to drink and to socialize as to get anything done. The fabled sobriety of New England Puritans policed, but did not eradicate their interest in sensual pleasures and in games.[6] We should not imagine that very many Americans ever regarded work as everything. The eerily self-controlled George Washington, if we can believe testimony collected by Parson Weems, made himself a leader among his peers through competition in youthful and "manly" sports. Benjamin Franklin managed to pursue his straitjacket prescriptions for self-improvement without spoiling himself for Paris.

Protestant leaders gradually recognized that they were in a dilemma. As was the case with their attitudes toward reading for pleasure and the theater, they had a tough time turning fun into something fully legitimate. The undisciplined, relatively rule-free, spontaneous uses of time, especially among young people, was to them (as it remains for us) a matter of serious social concern. For a time, they did not feel compelled to talk much about it. Most play fit into the natural rhythm of life without undue controversy. The rise of commercial culture, along with a compartmentalized structure of all uses of time, changed the nature of the issues. By the middle of the nineteenth century, religious leaders recognized that they had to give more attention to the way that people played. If they were to have any chance at all to shape the cultural practices of the nineteenth century, especially the commercialized ones, they had to learn to pronounce the word "leisure" without a grimace.

The debate in the early part of the nineteenth century is fascinating. In many ways the worried caution of those who were trying to find reasons to justify "safe" ways to play is more remote from contemporary attitudes than the tenacity of those who resisted placing any seal of approval upon pleasure. The consistency of people who find everything dangerous is at least easy to understand. It is the transition steps that seem prudish, the efforts to justify play by making play sound so strenuous that it might as well be work. Reverend John Witherspoon, the former president of Princeton, believed in the unnuanced proposition that all uses of time had to serve the purpose of religious devotion and self-improvement. That, in his mind, ruled out ball games. Later, many Protestant moralists wanted to turn ball games into an innocent pleasure. Yet they could not quite say it plainly. Innocent pleasures needed a justification.

The virulence of the exchanges on the subject of leisure suggests that many Americans were having their pleasures without offering the good reasons that the prescriptive literature said was their duty. What in fact is historically curious is that norms, the published ones anyway, seem more restrictive in the last years of the antebellum period than they had been in the supposedly stricter religious times of a hundred years earlier. The temperance crusade provides the most striking example of moral constriction. American colonials in the North and in the South had used, probably overused, rum and ale as lubricants of congeniality. They consumed liquor not only at what we might regard as purely social occasions but also at places of work, in conjunction with religious worship, and as part of democratic ritual on election days. By the second part of the nineteenth century, a sizable portion of the American electorate, people with influence in both political parties, but especially in the Whig party, were determined to make the consumption of even one drop of alcohol a mark of social depravity. In the main, this was not the work of twisted Puritans who delighted in images of infant sinners roasting in hell. It was the work of humanitarian reformers, abolitionists, utopian dreamers, vegetarians, protectors of the blind and the insane, who believed that human beings were physically and morally perfectible. Never did misanthropy have more generous-minded sponsors.

As soon as you think about it, the intensified volume attendant to the moral bans on idleness is not surprising. The Protestant ethic had its work cut out for it in an industrializing society. Americans had a lot to worry about with respect to the subject of public order. Their old safeguards were falling apart. A wide range of opinion, some of which we might even call liberal, had difficulty imagining pleasure apart from dangerous debauchery. It was a heritage as much of the American Revolution as of Calvinism. Republican ideology had sought to warn American colonials away from indulging in leisure.[7] To render England sufficiently odious to justify the severance of political ties, and to prepare themselves for the privations attendant to war, American patriots defined themselves as virtuous citizens who without political independence would succumb to the idled pleasures that had destroyed the character of Englishmen at both ends of the social scale. The English went in for fox-hunting, bear-baiting, gambling, street-brawling, drinking—activities that threatened not only the immortal soul but the moral fabric necessary to preserve a representative democracy. A virtuous people who hoped to launch an experiment in self-government had to be cautious about play.[8] Republican religion encouraged people to produce but not to consume.

Into the antebellum period, the theme of redemptive work continued to be stressed in a variety of ways. The northern states enlisted "Yankee" virtue during the antebellum period to serve their political aims against the South. The image of the southern cavalier signified that the most important difference between the two invented cultures of North and South was the extravagant uses of play made by slaveholders below the Mason-Dixon Line. Southern gentlemen raced horses. They gambled. They drank to excess. They valued elegant entertainments and financially imprudent hospitality as the marks of social status. Sizable measures of truth resided in the stereotypes, for sectional differences were, in fact, pronounced in the culture of work and play.[9] However, the South was not immune to creeping restrictiveness during the 1830s and 1840s. With the substantial inroads made by evangelical Baptists and Methodists into the lethargically run Episcopal religious culture, the leisured indulgences of the gentlemen cavaliers ran into more opposition than had previously been true. As in the North, the antebellum South witnessed an outburst of published agitation warning against unstructured uses of time.[10]

The stated goals of the prescriptive literature of the 1840s and 1850s to stamp out idle and disorderly recreations had little chance of success.

That does not mean that the literature had no significance and reflected nothing about life in the United States. Frances Trollope reported: "I never saw a population so totally divested of gaiety; there is no trace of this feeling from one end of the Union to the other." From her own background, she most missed the theater which seemed to be closed or poorly attended in every city that she visited. But she also observed "no fetes, no fairs, no merry-makings, no music in the streets, no 'Punch,' no puppet shows."[11] Her opinion on many subjects was challenged by American democrats who accused her of snobbery. But on this particular issue she found some unlikely support from Mike Walsh, a champion of the American working class. He complained at mid-century of the same deprivations: "The gloomy, churlish, money-worshipping, all-pervading spirit of the age has swept all the poetry of life out of the poor man's sphere. . . . Ballad singing, street dancing, tumbling, public games, all are either prohibited or discountenanced, so that Fourth of July and election sports alone remain."[12]

It is difficult to understand why traditional moralists poured so much energy into restraint if the only issue was the rigor of moral standards; nor can we understand the changing standards of what religious leaders tolerated by attributing the changes to lessened rigor. A comparison is instructive. Mormons emerged out of American Protestant culture of the 1830s and constructed a community that was second to none in the strictness of its moral discipline. The polygamy issue obscured that fact for contemporaries, but we can see it now. What is interesting is that Mormon leaders initially had a much easier conscience about leisure than the American culture from which they were exiled. They did not worry about play. They institutionalized it. The reasons why, which had nothing to do with lax moral standards, reveal a great deal.

The Mormon Way

On Christmas Day in 1850, a Mormon mother wrote in her diary: "On this day I went to Brigham's mill to a Christmas party. Stayed all night. We had a first-rate supper at midnight. I helped to get it on the table. They danced all night until five o'clock in the morning the party broke up."[13] Four years before that, the Reverend Henry Ward Beecher had rendered a typical list of amusements proscribed by Protestants in his popular *Lectures to Young Men:* No shooting matches; no taverns; no reading of novels, newspapers, and almanacs; no drinking, gambling, smoking, or swearing; no theater-going; no card-playing or dancing; no attendance at balls, race tracks, or circuses. As for anything suggesting the life of a sexual libertine, Beecher wrote severely that had he a son of such tendencies, he would wish him in his grave. "The plague is mercy, the cholera is love, the deadliest fever is refreshment to man's body, in comparison with this epitome and essence of moral disease."[14]

The constrast is both striking and puzzling. Given the reputation for strictness that Mormons have gained in the twentieth century and Beecher's later tastes for leisured pleasures, the juxtaposition suggests that at some time and for some reason a dramatic reversal occurred. "Gentiles" from the East Coast who now travel to Utah to ski do not associate Mormons with fun-loving qualities. They regard Mormons as dour people who shun alcohol, tobacco, caffeine, and sex outside of marriage and who belong directly in the line of everything that has been claimed about the moral seriousness of American Puritans. The ghosts of John Winthrop and Cotton Mather had pushed the hand carts from Nauvoo to the Great Salt Basin, carrying as baggage the Puritan emphasis on providential history, theocracy, the importance of a Christian calling, and a church of saints.[15] How did it happen that these Latter-day exemplars of Puritan piety managed to "legitimate" ideas of pleasurable entertainment in the first half of the nineteenth century, an era when many, perhaps most, other Christian ministers viewed fiction suspiciously, identified the theater with the brothel, and looked with horror at evening parties that included dancing? And why has this Mormon pioneering in the realm of popular culture been largely forgotten, even with the contemporary contributions of the Mormon Tabernacle Choir, the Osmond family singers, and J. Willard Marriott?

The beginnings were quite remarkable. While the Mormons were still gathered in Nauvoo, Illinois, Joseph Smith supported a theater as a medium of instruction and organized a dramatic company. Brigham Young, one of the original Mormon Thespians, went further. Already by 1850, he had mobilized the Salt Lake City Saints to build an amusement resort north of the city near warm springs. Also, a social hall was dedicated on the first day of the new year, 1853. This housed theatrical performances and musical programs. Friday night, especially, was for dancing. Most wonderously, Young ordered the construction of the famous Salt Lake Theater that was completed in 1862. It seated seven thousand people, was as well equipped as any theater in the United States, and mounted a set of serious and comic plays that was probably unmatched in its professionalism by any company west of the Mississippi. This was eight years before the railroad reached Utah and several months before the Temple was finished or the Tabernacle started.[16]

What is more, revelers and theatergoers in Salt Lake City did things that Brigham Young did not wholly endorse. Sponsors of parties occasionally permitted a set or two of "round dances," polkas and waltzes that brought young bodies into dangerously close proximity.[17] Young's orginal troupe of "amateur actors," a company that included one of his daughters, successfully wrested professional status from their reluctant leader who had resisted paying them. They also ignored, within reason, Young's dislike of tragedies and found ways around his ban against the depiction of violence on stage. Mormons did not view their entertainments as permissive; nor did they show much awareness that their attitudes were "advanced," as judged by the standards of most other churchgoing Protestants in mid-nineteenth-century America. Brigham Young had clearly developed what we might call an "ideology" of play at a time when many other American clerics still thought of play as the devil's invention.

Young, growing sensitive to his reputation as a man who liked to dance, did finally say something to his critics. Mormons, he admitted, liked amusements. They enjoyed themselves a great deal. It was wrong, however, to imagine that their pleasures got in the way of their worship. "Dancing and theatrical performance," Young insisted, "were no part of our religion." The Social Hall in Salt Lake City existed as a "fun hall," not as a place to administer the sacraments.[18] Actually, Young's disclaimer went too far. As he said in another context: "Our Work, our every-day labor, our whole lives are within the scope of our religion."[19] Mormons were permitted to have fun because their religion covered all activities. It supervised everything. Recreation was not temple ritual, but that was not the point. Since the Lord had made play essential to human happiness, it was a part of Mormon service to God. Mormons could safely go to the theater because the stage, in Young's words, "can be made to aid the pulpit in impressing upon the minds of the community an enlightened sense of a virtuous life, also a proper honor of the enormity of sin and a just dread of its consequences."[20] The confidence that lay behind that statement, the fact that not only the theater but a full range of entertainments had been incorporated into daily routines sponsored and encouraged by the Mormon hierarchy, remained in the 1860s a distinctive feature of the Mormon church.

Mormons had confidence in the moral purposes and security of their community. They did not confront the problem of disorder in the same way that many other Americans did. The moral imperatives stressed in middle-class prescriptive literature in the East were made urgent because no one, it seemed, had adequate power to enforce norms. That fact defined a world of difference between non-Mormon culture and what was being constructed in the Utah territory. The problem faced by Protestant clerics and other middle-class professionals who aspired to maintain the hegemony of their values in the cities of New York, Boston, and Philadelphia and in the smaller towns of New England and of upstate New York was largely unknown in Utah. Mormon men and women had not merged into nameless crowds. Joseph Smith and Brigham Young had much less to fear in the matter of leisure because they retained effective control over what happened when Mormons socialized with other Mormons. Commercial culture posed fewer problems because although Mormons proved to be shrewd businessmen, they did not allow profit to determine the nature of their cultural activities.

The rationale used by Young to justify dancing and theatergoing in Salt Lake City had some unabashed defenders among other American Protestants. By mid-century they were gaining ground. Frederick Sawyer, for example, in a book that he published in 1847, *A Plea for Amusements*, argued: "Our amusements can never be made as healthy, and as useful, as they are capable of being made, until the religious portion of the community assumes their true position toward them. . . . If libraries, and reading rooms, and gymnasiums, and galleries of art, and halls of science, and parties, and dancing, and museums and theatres, are to be made useful, it must be through the agency, and under the fostering care, and regulating hand, of the wise, the prudent, and the good. Religion must enter the common life and cease to be gloomy."[21] James Leonard Corning, a Presbyterian pastor in Buffalo, urged churches not to be paralyzed by their fears but to take an active role in separating "mirthful recreation" from "corrupting connections." "There are many christian men and women," he wrote, "worn out by dyspepsia and chronic melancholy, who could actually be trebled in value to the church and the world if they could be persuaded to devote an hour everyday to mirthful sport, just as scrupulously as they devote a given period to reflection and prayer."[22]

Horace Bushnell, a man whose opinion carried considerable weight among New England clergy, also weighed in on the subject. In an 1848 address to the Phi Beta Kappa Society he argued the superiority of play over exhausting work.[23] He defined work as an activity done *for* an end; play, an activity done *as* an end. To play was to enter a state free of "self-love, fear, contrivance, legal constraints, termagant passions"; to be spontaneous without the worry of pain and reward; to enter a state "where life is its own joy and end." "In short," he wrote in a fever of romantic ecstasy, "we are to conceive that the highest and complete state of man, that which his nature endeavors after and in which only it fulfills its sublime instinct, is the state of play."[24] Bushnell's determination to make play "sublime" points to some of the peculiarities of his and other religious leaders' defense of leisure. For Corning, mirthful recreation was "morally obligatory," "a great demand." Although Bushnell began his lecture by referring to a child playing with a cat on the floor, he had by the end of it moved play into the realm of genius where serious poets, writers, scientists, and religious thinkers had transcended the petty aims of working toward some end. Creativity and the highest forms of Christian worship—these were play. Not Bushnell or Corning or even Sawyer, who was by far the most permissive of this trio, was ready to accept play without first elevating it.

Even so, if their attitudes did not reflect a willingness to make peace with commercial culture (both Bushnell and Corning denigrated stage productions), they were at least prepared to deal with it and urged other Protestant leaders to do the same. They recognized the sources of anxiety about play in a society in which a growing market in leisure activities gave play an unaccustomed prominence among all social ranks. They were not themselves untroubled by the difficulties of maintaining decent communities, understood by Protestant norms, when churches had lost the means to exercise coercive moral discipline over the behavior of their members. Interestingly, the Catholic Church had less to worry about, not because the Church was indulgent toward immorality, as Protestants believed, but because urban, immigrant Catholics tended to live in closely bonded, ethnic neighborhoods. Proximity, the form of social control that worked in Mormon life, was less and less characteristic of the communicants of urban Protestant churches. Protestants had not had to concern themselves with drinking when church trials still intervened in the family life of communities and when masters and artisans had lived together under the same roof. Alcohol became a different sort of problem when privacy and anonymity weakened community surveillance. Effective influence had to come in other ways.

The Reformation of Wicked Assemblies

To the extent that the climate of religious opinion changed, it was because grounds emerged to justify cautious optimism about securing church influence over new forms of commercial leisure. Protestants were willing to talk about play in positive terms when they convinced themselves that they had some effective controls. The reading of novels crept gradually into the range of permitted activities because the content of many of them indicated the market could be made to respond to moral concerns. Unlike the saloon or the race track or any place where gambling was common, theatrical performances and balls also began to gain a significant number of moral-minded defenders in the second quarter of the nineteenth century. Partisans of the theater, in trying to clear away long-standing prejudices, pointed out correctly that the plots of nineteenth-century melodramas regularly punished vice and rewarded virtue. Arguing further that the literary genius of William Shakespeare, who was the most popular playwright among all social classes in antebellum America, resulted from his moral genius, they contended that the public benefits derived from viewing the right sort of plays were unlimited.[25] Somewhat less forcefully, people who liked to waltz insisted that the artistically patterned forms of dance that dominated social behavior at fancy balls posed no problems to conventional morality. Balls did not have to be, nor were they always, gaudy displays of extravagant taste. Men and women managed to dance and to socialize without any observable manifestations of sexual immodesty or lust.

Opposition to these arguments, of course, persisted. Some of it was mere habit. Throughout the colonial period, stage presentations were banned in New England. Even in supposedly more moderate cultural climates, the opposition had been serious. The Stamp Act riots of 1765 in New York were followed a year later by riots to protest the opening of a theater. In 1783 a rock-flinging crowd interrupted stage performances in Philadelphia. When in 1812 a theater burned in Richmond, Virginia, killing seventy-five people including the governor of the state, ministers rose to proclaim "one of the most distressing dispensations of Providence that our country ever witnessed."[26] As revival ministers had discovered early in the century, any association of their meetings with stage craft, the "play-house," opened them to criticism.

A prejudice of this strength does not simply disappear. What happens first is a shift in its terms and tone. When revivalists like Charles Finney began to boast of their theatricality, they made possible various compromises of religious morality with popular taste. Criticism tended to turn from criticism of the theater *per se* to the atmosphere in which plays were performed. What most bothered clerics about dances and the theater was the totality of a situation structured upon costume and deception. It was less the play or the performance than the rules of behavior encouraged by mostly male audiences and the prostitutes in the "third tier" that corrupted. Perversion lay not in the elegance of dance but in the unspoken understandings of the ballroom. In both theater and ballroom, the formal rules of propriety concealed the expectation of seduction. In such situations, order was precariously balanced. In the theater, in fact, it constantly broke down as expressions of disapproval broke into fights, even riots.

The path of accommodation lay in the reformation of the audience.[27] Theatrical entrepreneurs who sought a moral blessing for their efforts needed to regulate the actions of their patrons, to get rid of the prostitutes, and to create an ambience that was comfortable for husbands, wives, and sometimes children. Family entertainment was awaiting its commercial birth. The infamous Astor Place riot, which took place in New York City on May 10, 1849, proved to be something of a turning point. Partisans of the American actor Edwin Forrest tried to stop a production featuring his English rival William Macready. An ensuing melee resulted in the "sudden death or mutilation of more than fifty citizens."[28] It was an extreme example of the boisterous behavior that was common among audiences in New York's theaters up to that time. In this case, the extreme helped to consolidate a reaction that was already mounting. The very building of the Astor Place Opera House, whose high tone and high prices were partly responsible for the riot, indicated that many well-heeled theatergoers had determined to become patrons of the "legitimate" stage.

The term "legitimate" signified something about the nature of what was presented on stage. Legitimate meant that an evening would be devoted to a single play, uninterrupted by jugglers, comic songs, and dog acts. Of equal importance, it signified something about the manners and social composition of the audience. For a time, theatrical critics who supported efforts to transform overly participatory patrons of the stage into docile spectators were as apt to review the audience as the play. A writer for the New York *Evening Post* praising a performance of the popular melodrama *The Gladiator* tied its merits to the calming influence on the people who attended: "The play was listened to throughout with great attention and interest. . . . A more attentive and apparently a more engaged audience we never saw. Throughout the course of the whole entertainment, not a single sign of disapproval was given; and frequently applause, bursting out involuntarily from a part of the audience . . . was immediately checked and subdued by the rest, so that no line might be lost or the effect of no incident impaired."[29] This was prelude to a convention when schoolchildren would be taught to signal their approval of performance by applauding with two fingers on the palm of the hand.

True, the process of "censuring" theatrical audiences had the effect of driving many patrons out of the "opera house" toward pleasures that clerics had reason to regard as far worse. However, the reform was no less significant because of its incompleteness. The determination of many middle-class males to ride with their wives in carriages to respectable theaters farther and farther up Broadway marked a significant shift in the tenor of the most profitable forms of urban commercial culture. They

dressed well, drank moderately or not at all, and pretended to pay attention to the play or musical performance that unfolded before them. The
fare was still mostly melodramas. That did not matter. Theater owners
understood that it was atmosphere more than the play that enabled them
to charge higher ticket prices. They searched for vehicles morally suitable
for women and children, seeking to overcome the hesitations of women
by mounting matinee performances just for them. Some theaters stopped
selling alcohol, and all the "legitimate" houses banned the consumption
of alcohol in their auditoriums. The "third tier" was cleansed of its traffic
in sex and renamed the "family circle."[30]

None of this quite did what the "gathered" Mormons were able to do,
but it was sufficient to attract sympathetic interest in some clerical quarters. Many ministers dropped their unfashionable position that the stage
necessarily posed dangerous competition to religious worship. Formerly
they feared that a theatergoer might learn to value the Bible only "for
its fancied resemblance of style to his favorite play" and a sermon "only
by the degree of *stage effect* which accompanies its delivery."[31] Something like that may have happened, but maybe, just maybe, there was
some moral advantage to be gained from these connections. Clerics conceded first the value of reading virtuous plays. After all, how were they
to maintain their status as "learned" men if they set their faces against
masterpieces of the English language. Once ministers were confident that
audiences had reformed, some of them took the next logical step of attending the performance of a moral stage presentation. This activity was
not an idle pastime. The caveat was essential. It was an uplifting, edifying experience. As ministers modified their attitudes, the commercial advertisements for theater also changed. In 1870 Olive Logan, an actress,
advocated boycotts to keep the stage "free from the orgies of leg performers" and the "degrading influence of foul and immoral plays." Such
pressures did not always work, but she observed: "We seldom see on
our stage to-day any such absolute defiance of good morals as was exhibited by the dramatists of the Restoration. Even our blond burlesques
make a pretense of respecting public opinion, and offer 'appeals to the
public' in defence of their nude 'innocent amusements.' "[32]

These mutual adjustments that affected the world of commercial culture had many applications beyond the theater. Other important experiments in urban planning indirectly helped clerics find a way to voice full
approval of many commercial allurements that drew crowds together for
purposes other than work. Perhaps no single thing was more influential
in this respect than the design and construction of Central Park in New
York City.[33] It, in turn, encouraged the landscaping of countless green
acres in cities across the nation. The grand vision of Calvert Vaux and
Frederick Law Olmsted, which was accepted by New York City's govern-

ment in 1858, was, of course, not itself a commercial venture. Olmsted, especially, saw the natural beauty of his park as something entirely different from the popular pleasure gardens of New York City. The Palace Garden, Niblo's Garden, Jones Wood and other commercial "parks" made no effort to provide a consistent artistic whole. They contained fountains, gardens, and vistas of a sort, but they encompassed a full eclectic range of popular amusements. They sold beer, encouraged dancing, and ran circuses. Some of the rejected designs in the Central Park competition make concessions to popular urban amusements, but not Olmsted's. He viewed the commercial gardens as vulgar products of unreformed popular taste.[34]

To make sense of Central Park, we have to see it as a contested effort to control other popular pastimes and over the long run as an urban space where high moral ideals had to adjust to desires shaped by commercial culture. The intentions behind the advocates of Central Park, aside from those who stood to profit from skyrocketing land values on adjoining property, were to provide a pleasurable place for all social classes to mingle and to escape the hectic pace of the city that would one day enclose it. The park was a place of leisure, not of work. Its ideal was "rational" recreation, the passive enjoyment of a quiet, natural setting that, according to Reverend H. W. Bellows, induced orderly and contemplative habits. "It has been observed," he noted, "that rude, noisy fellows, after entering . . . the Park become hushed, moderate, and careful".[35] People rode in carriages or on horseback. They promenaded. They did not walk on most of the grass. They did not picnic. And except for cricket, they did not play team sports.

The idea of using architecture to control public pastimes, as a way of sacralizing leisure by conferring on it some purpose higher than mere enjoyment, was for the rest of the nineteenth century a standard way to judge the success or failure of any large public project. The idea carried over into the design of theaters and later of movie "palaces." Public parks, in the words of Andrew Jackson Downing, were conceived to "soften and humanize the rude, educate and enlighten the ignorant."[36] To Olmsted, the offspring of a prominent Congregationalist family, Central Park and landscape architecture generally were expressions of natural theology and a better way to remind people of God's presence in American cities than the fancy architecture of churches. About the democratic side of his virtuous aims he wrote: "It is one great purpose of the Park to supply to the hundreds of thousands of tired workers, who have no opportunity to spend their summers in the country a specimen of God's handiwork that shall be to them, inexpensively, what a month or two in the White Mountains or the Adirondacks is, at great cost to those in easier circumstances." Olmsted saw eye to eye with his good friend

Charles Loring Brace, whose Children's Aid Society laid the groundwork both for Fresh Air Camps and Settlement Houses.

For the first decade and a half of operation, Central Park was more a place for the middle and upper classes to display their manners than for poor immigrants to learn them. The latter stayed away. Use, however, gradually transformed the Park, as New Yorkers took over the grass, began to play baseball, and demanded concerts on Sundays. Severe moral codes with respect to park use gave way one by one, and already by the 1870s commercial culture was running many concessions on Central Park. As late as the 1890s, Sabbatarians were able to keep the Museum of Natural History and the Metropolitan Museum of Art, built on park land and opened respectively in 1877 and 1880, closed on Sundays. The point is that they finally lost.

However, if Olmsted's ideal was compromised, Central Park never became Jones Wood where minstrels, sword-swallowers, balloon ascensions, billiards saloons, and prizefighting exhibitions were part of the rotating fare. Boating, Sunday concerts, a carousel, a donkey ride, and candy stands were hard to depict as the end of the moral world. As the strict forms of censorship assayed by religious moralists gave way to accommodation, many decided that fun-loving crowds, even those drawn from the "dangerous" classes, responded to cues from well-designed environments. In any case, the changes in Central Park did increase its attraction to immigrant and working-class New Yorkers whose presence was essential to any proof that the Park was doing what it was supposed to do.

The modification of moral rules following conflicts with the behavior of real people in Central Park expanded the arena of legitimate leisure. That was not so different from what happened in the evolution of revival meetings. Central Park and a camp meeting both created a social context that blurred the boundaries between a pious use of non-work time and possibly dangerous frivolity. Steps were taken to control behavior at the same time that new forms of social relaxation intruded into the settings. Methodist camp meetings, certainly after 1830, looked less like emotional carnivals and more like the strictly supervised communities of Latter-day Saints. They also were more hospitable to the idea of leisure. The historian Ellen Weiss has described the transformation of a Methodist camp meeting that was founded on Martha's Vineyard in 1835.[37] Known as Wesleyan Grove, it grew from a campground laid out for the temporary erection of tents into a thirty-four-acre compound of five hundred permanent cottages, many of them architectural gems. The overall layout of the community was carefully plotted. Since the site happened to command a magnificent ocean view, it inevitably tied those who came to worship there into activities of recreation. By 1867, Wesleyan Grove was closely linked to a neighboring community that was developed quite explicitly as a summer resort. Oak Bluffs had a boardwalk and, until it burned to the ground in 1892, one of the best-equipped resort hotels in the country. Today Oak Bluffs is one of the two towns on the Vineyard that is not dry.   *of Ocean Grove*

Such a frank combining of religious revivalism with sea-bathing, vacations, and commercialism marked the direction of significant changes. When play could be controlled, morally strict Protestants could think of reasons not only to permit it but to promote it. The Reverend B. W. Gorham rattled off a religious justification of leisure as if there had never been a problem. The camp meetings, he said, were successful because they called "God's people away from their worldly business and cares for several successive days, thereby securing time for the mind to disentangle itself of worldly care, and rise to an undistracted contemplation of spiritual realities."[38] That is not yet copy for a travel agent's brochure, but it is an important step in that direction. Gorham found the divine justification he needed in the Jewish feasts of Passover, Pentecost, and Tabernacles—great festivals, he said, that proved "that there is an element in man which demands occasional excitement," a break from routine and, above all, a rest from labor.[39]

Interestingly, the entrenched opposition to many forms of popular entertainment came as often from elite observers who just did not like the ways that ordinary people had fun as from recalcitrant ministers who feared compromise. Andrew Dickson White, the first president of Cornell and a man whose stiffness had nothing to do with theological conservatism, wrote sneeringly of his visit to Oak Bluffs. He was repulsed by the sight of young people roller-skating with arms around each other to a waltz version of "Nearer, My God, to Thee." Charles Dudley Warner, an American writer who co-authored with Mark Twain *The Gilded Age*, judged what he saw of the bathing frolics of Wesleyan Grove residents as "the staid dissipation of a serious minded people. . . . Most of the faces are of a grave, severe type, plain and good, of the sort of people ready to die for a notion."[40]

Yet, criticism notwithstanding, the organization of a summer retreat that made conflict between religion and leisure a non-issue was an achievement that promoted a steady stream of inventive imitations. It even suggested a profitable formula for commercial culture that, to the degree it was followed, allowed religious moralists to accept some forms of commercialized fun as complementary to their organized church recreations. Methodists built another famous vacation retreat at Ocean Grove on the Jersey shore. Its annual reports covered all the concerns of a settled community—transportation, sewage disposal, parks, street repair, police and fire departments, and bathing houses.[41] It was a Protestant genius of sorts that discovered so close a parallel between the enhancement of property values and the reinforcement of religious values. In the 1850s, Henry Ward Beecher was counseling Americans to take vacations, to set aside indolent periods when one became "a passive recipient of all the impressions which the great out-of-doors can make upon you."[42] The regimen was not quite as idle as it sounded, and Beecher made sure to spell out the benefit. However, Protestant moralists were moving down a path where for the first time in industrializing America they tried to imagine a benefit accruing from doing absolutely nothing, from lying in the grass or on the beach and forgetting responsibilities.

Mirthful, Innocent Amusements: Ridiculous and Sublime

So there was a profitable formula to provide a basis of compromise between religious moralists and unabashed proponents of selling people the entertainments they liked. The compromise was in fact unstable, provoking more quarrels than agreement. We should expect that in a process of cultural negotiation. No one better exploited the formula, and set more controversy going as a result than the great American showman P. T. Barnum. He was, hands down, the most important innovative force in popular commercial culture in the middle part of the nineteenth century.

Barnum's story is part of the history of American museums, which also touches on the important subject of the commercialization of art. Before Barnum in the museum business there was Charles Willson Peale. Celebrated as an American painter, Peale gained equal fame in his time for the museum he opened to the public in Philadelphia in 1786. It was an effort to combine entertainment with high-minded purpose. For the next fifty years, Peale and his talented sons, Raphael, Rubens, Titian, and Rembrandt, sought to make a commercial go of an enterprise intended to reveal to a democratic citizenry the wonders and curiosities of nature as well as the artistic creations of human beings. Peale's personal religious convictions ran in the direction of Deism. His god was a first cause but not an ever-active presence. Toward Christianity he held roughly the same views as Benjamin Franklin. The dogmas associated with Christian denominations were on a par with animism and witchcraft, but the primary values of Christianity—charity, love, forbearance—provided an excellent code for moral behavior; therefore, he was willing to tolerate the dogmatic preoccupations of many Protestant leaders as necessary for maintaining a popular esteem for those values. Peale warned his sons "to keep clear of every offense to religious society," not only because the opposition of clerics was bad for business but because he imagined that his cause was only a more enlightened version of their cause.[43]

Peale's museum became well known for its archaeological and ethnographic displays, its cases of stuffed animals that sought to illustrate the Linnaean system of taxonomy, its mastodon skeleton, and its portrait gallery. Nature was assimilated to the category "a work of art," and both the displays drawn directly from nature and the products of human painterly skills used to imitate it testified to the benevolence of a Creator. Peale's Philadelphia Museum, housed until 1802 in the American Philosophical Society and then in Independence Hall, opened a branch in New York City in the 1820s.

This serious attempt to combine education, moral uplift, and amusement was something more than a purely philanthropic enterprise. It was a business venture that competed in the marketplace of culture. As the years passed, the Peale family found it necessary to stretch the idea of education to include somewhat "tawdry" attractions to sell tickets. By the 1840s, what was tawdry threatened to take over the museum business. The Peales faced a serious challenge in another type of public museum that more frankly turned the "curiosities" of nature into showmanship and live entertainment. Moses Kimball in Boston was perhaps the most successful of these entrepreneurs until P. T. Barnum purchased Scudder's American Museum in New York City in 1841.

Barnum not only picked up the Scudder collection but also the entire contents of Peale's New York Museum which had finally failed to keep up with public taste. When Peale's Philadelphia collection also went on the block in 1850, Kimball and Barnum split the lot. Peale's ideal of public instruction that was usefully entertaining fell into the hands of people who understood better than Peale the psychology of popular taste. A curious and fickle public, according to Barnum, demanded novel and constantly changing attractions. He contrived to satisfy their demands with trained dogs, educated fleas, jugglers, ventriloquists, fat men, giants, dwarfs, rope-dancers, dioramas of the Creation and of the Deluge, models of Niagara Falls and of Paris, and American Indians who enacted their "warlike and religious ceremonies on the stage." The American Museum displayed the fraudulent "Feejee Mermaid" and the diminutive Charles S. Stratton, renamed Tom Thumb for box-office appeal. The "lecture room" of Barnum's museum, which was in reality a theater that seated three thousand people, would have been recognizable to a later generation as a vaudeville establishment.[44]

Barnum embraced the possibilities of diversified entertainment with a greater talent for making quick profit than any entrepreneur of his time. In one crucial sense, however, Barnum did not abandon Peale's emphasis

on moral purpose. His formula for commercial culture was family entertainment—a strategy to provide men, women, and children with morally
wholesome entertainment in a morally safe environment. From a commercial perspective, it had the advantage of greatly increasing the number of paying customers. Hence, Barnum likened the theatrical performances in the museum "lecture room" to church services. Members of
the audience were his congregation, and they had to accept the rules
dictated by Barnum's ringing endorsement of "temperance." Barnum's
greatest financial success, the nationally sponsored tour of Jenny Lind,
was launched by an advertising campaign that couched the enterprise in
the language of the purest moral intentions. Along the tour route, Barnum made himself available to local churches to speak out against alcohol, his most successful lecture topic after "The Art of Making Money."
With as much honesty as is allowed to a public figure bent on self-
justification, Barnum stated: "My ambition will be sufficiently satisfied
in the anticipation that the great show, combining valuable instruction
with innocent amusement, shall become at once an institution worthy of
its originator and of the country which gave him birth."[45]

Barnum's aggressive showmanship crystallized the issues surrounding
leisure with precision. To Protestants who were not inclined to compromise, Barnum's efforts to moralize his entertainments were trivial,
harmful, and fraudulent. His spirited defense of the moral wholesomeness of his productions, his attacks on Sunday closing laws as efforts
by churches to monopolize the business of spiritual uplift, his concerted
projects to attract family groups—well, what else could people expect of
a Universalist? If everyone was eventually saved, then it mattered very
little how one lived. Serious people interested in their eternal salvation
found only the devil's work in humbug, even if the crowds at Barnum's
entertainments did behave themselves.

Barnum's clerical opponents were probably in the majority, but he set
moralists to thinking. His very considerable success in making the profits
of the popular pleasure palaces of cities dependent on a festive but sober
and ordered environment seemed to constitute progress in the realm of
commercial culture. The lesson reached beyond the designers of public
projects to affect men who began to construct a province of church recreation. Churchgoing Americans finished their specifically spiritual exercises by the early afternoon of a Sunday, and more and more of them
were not inclined to sit at home for the rest of the day in pious reflection.
Barnum was urging churches to stop wasting time trying to ban activities
that were not going to disappear whatever happened and to start working
seriously to influence the tone of those activities. They might even make
such activities part of their own social programs. In time, many did.

If religious moralists were having trouble making up their minds about

Barnum's inventiveness in providing popular entertainment, they were also having difficulty with what should have been an easier aspect of the emerging commercial culture—the fine arts. Viewing a painting was an activity that most everyone agreed was more rewarding than gawking at side-show attractions of the day like the Cardiff giant. Yet Protestants made nothing simple. They had to resolve their traditional worries about iconography and the misuses, as they saw it, of pictorial worship in the Roman Catholic Church. If American Protestants were to escape doubts about the moral purposes of painting and sculpture, the objects had to pass the aesthetic test of spiritual uplift. Justification was not easy because the most obviously uplifting subjects for the visual arts, scenes from the Bible and from the life of Christ, were, at least in the beginning of the nineteenth century, banned from Protestant churches. To consider displaying such subjects outside of churches, especially in places that sold tickets of admission, was worse. As a result, painting at the beginning of the nineteenth century, although more morally secure than novels or the theater, rested on more tenuous ground than poetry or music.

The problem was serious not only for American artists, many of whom found it less taxing to study and work in Europe, but also for those who wished to champion the cause of American art. They needed to think of ways to display art in an environment that would return financial rewards to the artist yet advertise a moral purpose. Many of the rising artists of the young republic were, in fact, Protestants who worried about the dangers of their métier. Was there a way for their art to be spiritually uplifting without becoming intoxicating in a Catholic or merely sensuous way? The least controversial subject matter was a portrait done from life. Portraits of real people, still alive, were the painterly equivalent of the "truthful tale." They were a mirror to reality that did not enflame the imagination. Dramatic scenes, on the other hand, even if they were historical, ran some of the risk of the playhouse.

Washington Allston, who married the sister of William Ellery Channing, was troubled by the dilemma. He sought to make his work a vehicle of religious expression that gave otherworldly spiritual power a tangible form on his canvas. The visual arts had to make themselves a part of "that mighty plan which the Infinite Wisdom has ordained for the evolution of the human spirit." Allston painted religious and scriptural subjects, but he did not depict the person of Christ. He proposed to paint as his contribution to the rotunda in Washington's Capitol the "three Marys at the tomb of the Savior." The subject was declined as too sectarian, although this consideration did not prevent the commission by other artists of paintings devoted to "The Baptism of Pocahontas" and "The Embarkation of the Pilgrims."

Samuel F. B. Morse, Allston's student and the son of the Calvinist loyalist Jedidiah Morse, was one of the most creative people in antebellum America. He, too, wrestled with the question of what to paint. Morse's vehement anti-Catholicism told him what he wanted to avoid. After visiting Italy, he condemned Catholicism as a "religion of the imagination. . . . Architecture, painting, sculpture, music have lent all the charm to enchant the senses and impose on the imagination by substituting for the solemn truths of God's word, which are addressed to the understanding, the fictions of poetry, and the delusion of feeling."[46] Of course, it was impossible to separate painting from imagination. If Morse had totally rejected the possibly sublime effects of feeling and sensual enchantment, he would have stuck with telegraphs. Like all talented artists who ever traveled to Italy, he found himself awed by the Renaissance. He painted in the shadow of Raphael and of Michelangelo, men who had labored, gloriously, for the Catholic Church. Morse needed an intellectual formula to get by this uncomfortable but incontestable fact, an aesthetic theory that condemned the iconic painting of religious subjects but justified a religious meaning for the work of Protestant artists. Unlike his mentor, Morse was never comfortable with biblical subjects.

For many American artists, the answer to the dilemma of what to paint lay in the American landscape. Already by the 1830s, a tourist industry was busy sacralizing the wonders of American geography. A visit to Niagara Falls was more than a trip. It was a pilgrimage that brought the visitor into the presence of divinity.[47] Natural beauty satisfied a devotional aesthetics without being too Catholic. To be awestruck before a mountain in the Catskills was Protestant American. To be awestruck in the interior of St. Peter's in Rome was European sensuousness. An editorial in *The Crayon* phrased one version of the needed formula: "The reverence of nature is the first step to the reverence of Nature's God, and the love which Art requires is the elder sister of that which Religion demands."[48] Americans may have lacked the traditions in which the art of Europe had flourished, but they did not lack scenery.

A number of American painters in mid-century clearly were influenced by Swedenborg's belief that the natural and supernatural worlds were joined in a system of visible correspondences. The natural world revealed God and reinforced the revelation of Scripture. Thomas Cole and Frederick Church sought painterly ways to sink the moral didacticism of Christianity into nature, to propel their viewers toward the "contemplation of eternal things." Their religious aims, which were very clear to their audiences, were not incidental to their commercial success. Cole belonged to and attended an Episcopal church and his intimate circle of friends included ministers. Religion explicitly informed his use of light and symbol so that he strove to "Christianize the sublime."[49] What mattered even more was Cole's belief in the "triumph of religion," a triumph guaranteed not by ecclesiastical activity (which was never the subject of Cole's painting) but by spiritual messages encoded in the physical geography of his nation. Cole often painted biblical subjects. He also used the Christian cross to ground the meaning of his allegorical work.

Cole's student Frederick Church found perhaps even greater financial reward in filling the American landscape with religious meaning. The display in May 1857 of his first great popular triumph, his giant painting of Niagara Falls, attracted a hundred thousand viewers in two weeks. The admission price of twenty-five cents was affordable and yielded a substantial return. Many Americans paid a higher price for commercially marketed reproductions of Church's work, engravings advertised as "silent, beautiful sermons, truly family pictures." As in most of Church's vast canvases of nature, viewers had no trouble finding biblical references. In the case of *Niagara* a rainbow, a sign of God's willingness to forgive his creatures, was placed over a natural wonder that had become almost a national symbol of the United States. Church, too, counted ministers among his most ardent admirers. Even if he had not expressed himself explicitly about religion, his fans among art critics framed the reception of his canvases. They saw in them lessons about divine providence. The language of antebellum criticism was dominated by evangelical and religious concerns.[50] Critics debated the question of whether artists who were immoral in their personal lives could produce great art, a debate that had long before been rehearsed in the issue of whether unsaved ministers could act as instruments of conversion. Moral criticism became by far the most important ingredient of American aestheticism. It was a clear and confident position that had the virtue of knowing what art was supposed to be and to do

The intricate ways in which these artistic issues could be manipulated in the commercial marketplace were marvelously exemplified in the late 1840s during the traveling display of Hiram Powers's sculpted *Greek Slave*. Powers learned to sculpt in Italy, working from classical models, but he learned his aesthetics from Swedenborg. In 1853 he wrote to Elizabeth Barrett Browning that "the legitimate aim of art should be spiritual and not animal." He worked to reveal the soul, not its sensuous covering. The disclaimer was useful since the highly praised *Greek Slave* was a realistic statue of a beautifully formed naked woman, in chains. What Powers and his friends were smart enough to do was to wrap the *Greek Slave* in a rhetorical cover of purity before she ever went on display. Like the tailors for the fabled emperor, the defenders of Powers's statue verbally clothed her with robes of modesty and nobility. These purportedly protected her from profane eyes. From her cast-off robe dangled a cross, another reassurance that she stood under a proper moral aegis. To allay all suspicions of salaciousness, Powers insisted that men and women be admitted together, although the afternoons were reserved for women and family groups.[51] Chaste advertising and safe environments would not make nudity a totally safe subject for art in America. This particular example is to demonstrate that the same formulas were at work up and down the scale of American commercial culture. Legitimating leisure was serious business. That much at least provoked substantial agreement.

The Discovery of Muscular Christianity

Possibly Protestant clerical accommodation to the proliferation of leisure or play opportunities, presuming that leisure could be made effectively Christian, might have happened sooner and with less anxiety had it not been for the accelerated arrival of German and Irish Catholics into northeastern cities beginning in the 1840s. The German newcomers, with the evident pleasure that they took in beer gardens and their enthusiasm for street festivals, posed a problem. The easy conscience that accompanied these pleasures struck many American-born Protestants as un-Christian; but since Germans often pursued leisure as a family enterprise, under general community supervision, it was hard to make out a clear case of unwholesomeness.

Fortunately for the Protestant conscience, the pleasures of the Irish were easier to condemn. Everything that the Irish did smacked of the unsavory. Their leisure activities seemed to revolve around rituals of drinking, especially dangerous in the Irish case because it was feared that becoming drunk was an end in itself rather than part of customary ways of socializing. Blaming Catholics for introducing permissiveness into American society, Protestant clergy in the 1850s redoubled their vigilance and in some cases renewed their opposition to most forms of commercial urban entertainment. It was a hard question for some Protestants to decide whether it was better to leave Catholic immigrants in their saloons or invite them to Central Park. The Irish came to symbolize the full range of disorderly threats that Protestants associated with industrializing society. There were safe ways to play, but Catholics introduced Protestants to new things to fear.

The commercial forms of leisure that enlivened nineteenth-century American cities depended upon the patronage of men and women who worked for wages. Recent studies of the urban working class have suggested that young single men and women, at least before the economic downturn of the late 1850s, had disposable money in their pockets. The B'Hoys of New York City, made famous on stage and in fiction as fast-talking, fast-fisted, street-smart workers, were better housed and better clothed than any comparable working class in Europe. They were incredibly better fed.[52] They sometimes spent their money on the same leisure activities as people of greater affluence, but more and more they did so in different areas of the city. When commercial entertainments began to sort people out by class, it was following other demographic trends that divided cities into distinct neighborhoods. By the 1850s in New York, Boston, and Philadelphia (and eventually everywhere), the residential geography of cities created demarcations in the use of leisure time. What the working classes did with their spare hours on their own city turf became almost by definition morally suspect. Much of it, by Christian evangelical standards, deserved the reputation.

Class would complicate all discussions of commercial culture in American cities for the rest of the nineteenth century. Already before the Civil War the complication was manifest in the very important Young Men's Christian Association (YMCA). This significant effort to legitimate leisure tried to maintain an equal distance from the lures of commercial entertainments and from denominational religious worship. Its sponsors took lessons from both but tried to extract from them only what was essential to the moral well-being and the pleasure needs of young men. Started in England, the YMCA organized its first American branches in Boston and New York City in the early 1850s.[53] The controlling or voting members of YMCA chapters formed in the nineteenth century were men who belonged to evangelical Protestant churches. In addition to Catholics, that rule excluded Unitarians, Universalists, and, of course, Mormons. Nonetheless, the YMCA movement wanted to serve all young men, including those who were not church members or regular attenders of any religious meeting.

By the end of the century, local Y chapters had tried any number of means to win adherents, almost all of them more successful among young men of the middle class than among factory workers or common laborers. In Chicago, the Y was dominated by one of its first members, Dwight Moody. As a young businessman who switched his trade to become a famous revival preacher, Moody tended to stick with the old notion that the best way to deal with sinners was to preach to them and to organize Bible-study programs. In other cities, such emphasis upon religious meetings was less pronounced. Financed and led by laypersons rather than clergy, many YMCA locals sought indirect ways to exert moral influence, ways that paid less attention to dramatic conversion experiences and more attention to a gradually acquired set of associations that Horace Bushnell, a major liberalizing influence in the Protestant clergy, had said were essential to successful "Christian Nurture." The goal was to attract young men into a Christian environment, an association that promoted affective ties among its members through Christian patterns of recreation.

More and more, the lure was sports that were at first cautiously and then enthusiastically promoted under the rubric of "Muscular Christianity." This was an idea with virtually limitless application. The sudden infusion of masculine toughness into Christ's persona was a reaction to institutionalized Protestantism's realization that women and "effete" ministers dominated the public's perception about what sort of people devoted their lives to church work. YMCAs effectively institutionalized the new gospel "that physical exercise in all forms can become a mighty factor in the development of the highest type of Christian character."[54] Insofar as athletics instilled obedience, self-discipline, self-sacrifice, honor, and truth, they were a useful surrogate for church attendance. Regular religious observance ought to be encouraged of course, but sports under YMCA auspices quite literally became a spiritual exercise. The cause of Christian sports benefited in the long run from plausible associations made between them and work. Both encouraged the same virtues and left the body too exhausted to cause trouble for the soul.

The most tangible problem that threatened the enthusiasm for muscular Christianity and the approval it gave to strenuous play was the commercially seedy aspects of many urban sports. Prizefighting and horse racing in the antebellum period were tainted by their associations with drinking, gambling, and violence. They could not be construed as forms of family entertainment, and there seemed to be no means either to reduce their popularity, especially among wage-earning men, or to reform them. The only available solution that had a chance of working was to construct sanitized alternatives and hope that the good forms of play would drive out the bad. The first YMCA gymnasiums were constructed in 1869 in New York City (the home base of the moral crusader Anthony Comstock who was an ardent Y supporter) and in San Francisco. They were not unique. Other interests had earlier championed gymnastic training as necessary to the proper formation of young men and women. Gyms were established in colleges and in elite boarding schools. Harvard, Yale, Dartmouth, and Williams were among the many American colleges that had constructed gymnasiums by the end of the 1850s. In ways that were more relevant to urban working classes, the German *Turnverein* pressed forward the cause of physical training. Dio Lewis had in 1861 in Boston opened the first normal school to train teachers of physical education.[55]

The gymnasiums associated with the YMCA movement, although part of a general trend, expanded the number of gymnastic and sports facilities that were available to young men of the general public. By 1900, there were approximately fifteen hundred local YMCA chapters in the United States. The association counted 507 gymnasiums and 294 paid directors. To train those directors, the YMCA in the 1880s founded a college in Springfield, Massachusetts, with an innovative Physical Education Department. The president of Springfield College, Laurence Doggett had connections to the evangelical world as well as to the arts. His father was a Shakespeare enthusiast, and his aunt was the mother of the American novelist Frank Norris. Her husband was a successful wholesale jeweler in Chicago who contributed generously to Dwight Moody's revivals. For Doggett, play was a fully legitimate concept. He likened the role of physical-education directors to "medical missionaries in foreign lands—to extend Christ's Kingdom among young men."[56] How many souls were eventually won by these athletic missionaries is uncertain. But their efforts resulted in the invention of two sports, basketball in 1891 and volleyball in 1895. The YMCA had its own "new" measures to supplement those that revival preachers had introduced in the first part of the nineteenth century.

"New" measures always have their critics, and the innovations sponsored by the YMCA movement were no exception. The ministers of many Protestant churches, whatever their attitudes toward the cause of muscled Christian men, wondered whether they should cooperate with a movement that so breezily seemed to imply that churches were not really the most effective centers of spiritual life. If sports were so good for the soul, then it followed that Protestant churches should look favorably on sporting events held on Sunday. And that, for a long time, most were not prepared to do. To play was one thing. Letting play crowd out everything that resembled religious devotion was another. It seemed fair to ask how local YMCA chapters could guarantee a Christian environment when their facilities were open to virtually anyone and when people passed in and out of their doors without hearing so much as a prayer. The national YMCA convention as late as 1913 reaffirmed that the association's supreme aim was to lead boys and men to become disciples of Christ, pointing them toward church membership. The association also, and this provision did not change until the 1930s, continued to limit voting rights to members who belonged to evangelical churches.

The YMCA did not quite manage to do what the Mormons had done. The critics were right in thinking that its unscreened clientele, upon whom no demands were made respecting faith, would ultimately secularize the institution. That may not be the point, however. What the founders of the YMCA wanted to demonstrate was that a clean ordered life was possible without dogmatic teachings. Play did not require a worship service to be made wholesome. It only required a proper atmosphere and activities that encouraged a spirit of fellowship. The failure of the YMCA in its initial stages was that its recreational facilities were not much used except by young men of the middle class. Because it did not affect the world of immigrant wage earners, because it proved to be a training ground for powerful men in the worlds of business and of organized religion, it reinforced class lines in moral evaluations of leisure. Still, whatever its limits, no other philanthropic venture commenced before the Civil War formulated a more effective means for religious leaders to make their peace with leisure. Its association of moral recreation with physical exertion was the most persuasive of all the formulas that sought to make fun and moral seriousness go together. Jogging really is a Protestant sport.

Conclusion: Sponsored Leisure versus the Market

By mid-century, Protestant clerical attitudes had progressed a good distance from the time when virtually all clerics had condemned novels, the theater, and any notion that diversion had a place in human affairs equal to work and religious worship. Without necessarily approving of particular activities, many ministers had decided that recreation was necessary, an essential part of the good life designed by God. Play was, in fact, virtuous. It had improper and dangerous forms. But could not the same be said about work and even worship?

The strong suspicion continued that play was the most easily corrupted of the three, a suspicion reinforced by the way in which play increasingly became an item of commercial consumption. It was one thing to countenance leisure when religious sponsors or trustworthy public philanthropists laid out and controlled the recreation environment. Mormons could sponsor dances and melodramas without thinking twice about it. Other Protestants could see the benefit of well-designed municipal parks and Christian-run gymnasiums. The serious problem started when one moved beyond the arenas established by people of unquestionable moral taste to pleasure palaces dependent for financial success on the desires of paying customers.

This was the battleground for Protestant moralists for the rest of the century. They had a series of options. They could condemn market culture as necessarily immoral because it had to pander to the basest instincts of human beings. Moreover it put religious people in close contact with non-religious people. As a second possibility, Protestant moralists could encourage their own version of the P. T. Barnum deployment of commercial culture, trusting that cultural entrepreneurs would learn to respect the connection between profit and wholesome family entertainment. Or, finally, they could study the appeal of commercial culture and try to duplicate it in their own "non-profit" institutions. In the last case, of course, they did not escape a market logic, since the success of what they did depended on attracting people to the enterprise. They had to give people something they liked, and that often meant cutting the line between market-driven and religious-sponsored leisure activities very thinly. It might even be said that religion in some cases wound up selling itself *as* recreation.

American religious leaders did all three of these things. One thing needs to be said about the reactionaries whose contempt for popular taste produced their steady insistence that all commercial culture was morally corrupt. It is odd in a way that these opponents of free-market recreations usually made no fuss about the market in its other operations. But then it is also odd that many academic opponents of free markets assert their populism by a dazzled admiration of the *laissez-faire* commercial culture of working classes in the nineteenth century. Attempted regulation of market culture produces a different set of alliances than attempted regulation of the stock market. Protestant reactionaries believed correctly that when religious people gained an easy conscience about play, the ways people played would slip out of the realm of godly determination and become a matter of politics.

What is very impressive is the earnestness of the ongoing debate. The acceptance of leisure did propel religious leaders into the marketplace of culture where they found themselves steadily revising their standards. They did so, however, in line with experience. Everyone changed—religious leaders, promoters of commercial culture, and audiences. A lot of the expanding options of commercial culture were not morally safe by anyone's standards. At the same time, the number of options that serious and sensible men and women could construe as moral choices did multiply. One important habit of the Protestant middle classes remained steady in the nineteenth century. They gave reasons for what they did. Merchants of leisure had to give them the right reasons to have fun. The most important aspect of the battle against prudishness was finally less a battle against morality than a battle to free recreation from the constant need to explain itself.

CHAPTER FIVE

The Market
for Religious
Controversy

At the hour designated I called with my
friends. Brigham Young was standing in
front of one of his houses—the "Bee
Hive," in which was his reception room.
He received us with a smile, and invited us
to enter. He was very sociable; asked us
many questions, and promptly answered
ours. Finally he said with a chuckle,
"Barnum what will you give to exhibit me
in New York and the Eastern cities?"

"Well, Mr. President," I replied, "I'll
give you half the receipts, which I will
guarantee shall be $200,000 per year, for I
consider you the best show in America."

P. T. Barnum, *Struggles and Triumphs*

Beginning early in the nineteenth century, religious leaders contributed to a process that made the organization of spiritual affairs in America congruent with an individualistic market-driven economy. Some of the results were intentional, leading some people to say in retrospect that ministers had struck a deal with wealthy capitalists. Alarmed at their shrinking significance, they agreed to preach a gospel of wealth in return for protection and financial assistance. Such a proposition makes history too deliberate. In the course of the nineteenth century, many ministers used their pulpits to legitimate capitalism, but just as many severely criticized greed, wealth, and untrammeled competition. Clerical complaints about commercial culture were, after all, complaints about the operation of a free market. The aim of American religious leaders in the early nineteenth century was to contribute to a spiritual awakening of Americans and, in so doing, to build up the moral energies that guided public life. What was pushing them was a determination to cleanse, not to sully.

If most American religions wound up running their operations like a business, it was because that was the way to get things done. Ministers were responsible participants in trying to exercise effective controls over the transformation of nineteenth-century American society. Believing that religion was crucial to whatever success the national experiment had, they adapted their tools of proselytizing to changing circumstances. No more than anyone else did they entirely foresee the sort of world they were helping to bring into being. What, in fact, is most obvious from their published statements are their worries about sinking moral standards and their resistance to change. American religious leaders did not set out to create a market system of competing denominations. They did not intend in trying to redeem Americans' commercial culture to become deeply implicated in commercial means of tapping popular enthusiasms. They did not want religion to become a commodity for consumption, advertised as something essential to a happy life, and to transform churches into institutions that supplied peace of mind to the rich and powerful. Yet in their roles as important cultural innovators, which they certainly were, they did all of these things.

Dare we call the result inevitable? Was there any way for religious leaders to avoid a market mentality—the imperative to expand, the association of growth with innovation, the reliance upon aggressive publicity, the assumed importance of building networks that linked the local to the national, the habit of thinking in tangible exchange terms that allowed a quick calculation of returns (converted souls or its measurable equivalent, moral behavior) for expended effort? Avoidable or not, these attitudes explain American religion's nineteenth-century organizational success that, in turn, helped sustain its public influence. Religious leaders criticized many of the consequences that went along with their prospering condition but not often in ways that showed a full awareness of what had happened and why. With respect to the ways that religious leaders found themselves cast as merchants in the realm of commercial culture, some things were clearly beyond their control.

The fact that antebellum America was a "spiritual hothouse" is usually set down in the narrative of religious history. It also deserves a place in the nation's economic history. Religious controversy became a species of paid amusement for Americans. Much of this story took place outside the boundaries of what many regarded as respectably constituted religion, but then, respectability was the very thing that controversy placed in question. The logic and dynamics of America's pluralistic system permitted no stable delineation of what was respectable. Although many clergy of America's oldest Protestant denominations said that controversy led to further religious splintering, that it fed the insatiable popular desire for sensationalism and threatened to make a mockery of the Christian ideal of religious unity, they could do nothing to stop it. Their anger only stoked the controversies and made the public eager to read all about them. Newspaper editors loved religious controversy.

Good Friends and Enemies

During her discomforting residence in the city of Cincinnati, Frances Trollope had occasion to hear an extended debate between her compatriot Robert Owen and the Scottish-born founder of the Disciples of Christ, Alexander Campbell. The subject of controversy was the truth of Christianity, with Owen taking the part of the village atheist. Trollope was amazed that in a city where the theater, balls, and other forms of public entertainment languished for want of patronage, these debates filled the Methodist meeting house, designed to accommodate a thousand people. It is one of the rare occasions recorded by Trollope of her stay in the United States when she heard Americans roaring together in laughter. Mostly, she encountered a population "totally divested of gaiety."[1] To her further surprise, Owen and Campbell, who ought to have been bitter ideological foes, seemed to enjoy their performance as a team. They applauded each other's jokes in public and dined together with apparent satisfaction in private. During a period of days punctuated by fifteen public encounters, the two had the best and close to the only show in town.

To Trollope, religion and entertainment in the United States were virtually synonymous, especially for women. Reflecting on "the triste little town" of Cincinnati, she noted that "a stranger from the continent of Europe would be inclined, on first reconnoitring the city, to suppose that the places of worship were the theatres and cafés of the place."[2] The cultural life of London had not prepared her to imagine that religion might be fun. The groanings and shrieks that she heard at camp meetings and revivals, which she interpreted as a form of debased theater, made her "sick with horror." "The coarsest comedy ever written would be a less detestable exhibition for the eyes of youth" than the sight of "violent hysterics and convulsions" seizing young girls who fell on their faces exclaiming " 'O Lord!,' 'O Lord Jesus!,' 'Help me, Jesus!' and the like." Religious enthusiasm was to her a terrible thing and no substitute for the street music and puppet shows that she remembered from England.[3]

Trollope's condescending comparative assessments of America's cultural offerings were not charitable, but her vision was clear. The orchestrated debates between Owen and Campbell aptly illustrated her point that religion had the double burden of making Americans behave while providing diverting entertainment. Disputes about religion and morals provided public stimulation and liveliness. In many communities they substituted for other forms of fun that were prohibited or treated by those who clamored to be recognized as guardians of taste as beneath contempt. To be sure, those same guardians regarded many of the publicized religious controversies contemptuously, placing them on the same level as arguments about the genuineness of Barnum's "Feejee Mermaid." To them, something had gone seriously awry when religion moved out of the church and became a form of exhibition exploited by writers and journalists who played up religious wrangling and especially any scandal attaching to it.

America's pluralistic system provoked controversies among existing denominations. That was only part of the story, however. The religious inventiveness of antebellum America also set people to quarreling about what qualified as religion and what did not. Disagreements about how God worked his will in a young nation with unsettled social conditions were seemingly endless. Many Americans believed that the creation of their republic marked a new divine dispensation. They were prepared to listen attentively to reports of providential manifestations that were altogether novel. Claims to spiritual power exploded many commonplace occurrences in antebellum communities into puzzle pieces to solve millennial prophecies. The controversy over revivals was part of a larger intellectual world that welcomed reports about strange spiritual gifts. The people who promoted the disputes claimed the role of spiritual teachers.

They sought to instruct Americans by keeping them religiously curious. As an important by-product, they provided forums for social mingling.

Nathaniel Hawthorne's *The Blithedale Romance* centers on one of the spiritual claims that excited antebellum Americans—the phenomenon of mesmerism. Priscilla, "the Veiled Lady," was a celebrity in the "mesmeric line," now forgotten because "her sisterhood have grown too numerous to attract much individual notice." She stood out, according to the narrator, for none of her successors had "ever come before the public under such skillfully contrived circumstances of stage-effect, as those which at once mystified and illuminated the remarkable performances of the lady in question." At a late point in the story, Priscilla performed in a homely village lyceum hall. The audience was "generally decent and respectable," farmers in Sunday black coats, the schoolmaster, lawyer, and shopkeeper, women of middle age, and pretty girls in "many-colored attire." Accustomed to a varied series of exhibitions in addition to the winter course of lectures, they had come to witness a display of what the narrator termed "mystic sensuality." Exchanging gossip beforehand and recalling similar demonstrations, they waited with "high-wrought" anticipation and hushed breathing another entertainment made common in the "epoch of rapping spirits." The thumping of their sticks and boots called forth Westervelt, the demonic character controlling Priscilla. His introduction was an "ingenious" and "plausible" discourse, "with a delusive show of spirituality." Then Priscilla herself appeared, wrapped in oriental robes, "as much like the actual presence of a disembodied spirit as anything that stage-trickery could devise."

These descriptions, illustrative of "the miraculous power of one human being over the will and passions of another," relied for their effect upon Hawthorne's readers knowing a great deal about mesmeric exhibitions. Hawthorne disapproved of mesmerism but also recognized the public's interest in it. He was deeply immersed in rural and urban people's popular culture, which among other things was filled with beliefs rooted in magic.[4] Hawthorne's tale played upon the dark association of mesmerism with the occult, with claims that mortals had made for centuries to see through the boundaries shrouded by death, claims touching on prophecy and revelation.

There was a lighter side that Hawthorne exposed in his depiction of the mood of casual gossip that permeated the audience. Mesmerism was a species of traveling theater. People attended the performance not necessarily because they were convinced by the explanations of the lecturer or by the genuineness of the phenomena but because the claims and counterclaims intrigued them. Here the analogy with the appeal of Barnum's "Feejee Mermaid" is exact. The controversy was deliberately wrapped in mystery at one extreme and attacked as fraud at the other. A lecture on one side or the other commanded the same fee.[5]

The Blithedale Romance was published in 1852. Mesmeric displays had been staged before American audiences at least since 1836 when a Frenchman, Charles Poyen who advertised himself as a Professor of Animal Magnetism (the alternate name for mesmerism), began a lecture tour in New England.[6] Poyen, who also supported abolitionism and was the author of a pamphlet on how to promote Christianity, claimed many benefits for mesmerism. It was the most important of the sciences and the foundation for human perfectibility. Mesmerized subjects, insensible to normal stimulants, were able to receive unspoken thoughts, locate lost objects, and describe events happening in faraway places. Their state of clairvoyance was, strictly speaking, a mere side effect of the passage of magnetic fluids through their bodies. Franz Mesmer's more important reason for placing subjects in a state of suspended animation was to heal them. His followers never quite forgot that purpose. Rheumatism, back trouble, and liver ailments routinely vanished from mesmerized patients. Mesmeric healers at least collected a lot of testimony to that effect. Even if the remedies did not work, they were less painful than the equally ineffectual ones prescribed by most doctors working in Jacksonian America.

Healing claims riveted popular attention in antebellum America in many religious guises other than mesmerism, but mesmerism was a special case because of its association with clairvoyance. "Miraculous" powers, rendered explicable and even ordinary by a fast-paced lecture, were worth paying money to see. People could gasp, gape, and share their astonished reactions with one another. It was for many people better, much better, than church but not something entirely removed from issues that they associated with church life. Poyen talked about science, but mesmerism, as discussed in the United States, was a science with hints of "Infinity and the Unknown." Some saw in it proof of God and eternity, of spirituality and immortality; and they were eternally prepared to argue with those who did not.

Mesmerism enjoyed a substantial popularity into the 1850s, entertaining people in public places and in private homes. Poyen returned to his native France in 1839, but his style as a hypnotist and lecturer was adapted to commercial uses by others. Among the more significant was Phineas Quimby whose perfected system of mesmeric healing was a key element in forming the ideas of Mary Baker Eddy. In broad terms, people read the religious implications of mesmerism as hostile to Calvinistic forms of Protestantism. The latter still stressed, albeit usually in weakened form, the inevitability of sin and inscrutable predestination. The "spirituality" available through mesmerism put God and humans on a more equal footing. It empowered women and men in the here and now, giving them control over their destinies and reducing the category "evil" to an illusion of "materialistic" thinking.

As a movement that blended religion with other features of popular culture, mesmerism attracted interest across denominational lines. Among the self-professed religious thinkers who made a living as itinerant champions of mesmerism, Universalists and Swedenborgians predominated. Universalists were naturally attracted to any doctrine that reinterpreted evil as something other than a permanent spiritual disability. The Swedenborgian mesmerists taught a complicated metaphysics.[7] They explored the Swedish thinker's notion of "spiritual matter," and his "doctrine of correspondences," for support of the possibility that changes in body chemistry, induced by mesmerist passes, freed human beings from the shadowy substance that they experienced as disease. Convincing demonstration of mesmeric healing was proof of the proposition that matter and spirit formed a continuum, allowing for the conscious manipulation and purification of matter. Healing also supported the view that the next world could be made tangible and visible.

Mesmerism appeared a relatively safe way to explore the realm of evil. Many antebellum Protestant Christians had been taught to regard human claims to exercise power over the invisible world as murky witchcraft or black magic. They were, consequently, wary of seeking spiritual illumination through forms that were not prescribed by their churches. The alternative forms of truth-seeking that flourished in antebellum America, however open and aboveboard they claimed to be, always carried a hint of Satanic influence, and sometimes considerably more than a hint. That frightened many people, but it also added allure to the claims. Exploring the dark side promised to produce greater light. Curiosity was a powerful magnet, and the duller the routines of daily life, the greater its force. So it happened that individuals who might never have attracted public attention in a culture that was more richly endowed with ways to pursue pleasure gained fame by making themselves the focus of religious argument.

It is hard to select the most unlikely case, but Andrew Jackson Davis makes a fair claim for that distinction. The interest that was taken in him was as remarkable as anything he professed to do. Through Davis, the popular enthusiasm for mesmerism diversified and expanded into public performances associated with phrenology, spiritualism, and a host of other divertissements advanced under the banner of "harmonial philosophy." The public discovered the talents of the "Poughkeepsie Seer" by a chance occurrence in 1843.[8] During a demonstration of animal magnetism, an itinerant lecturer asked for a volunteer from the audience. The seventeen-year-old Davis did a successful turn on the platform that launched him on his own lecture tour. Using his skills as a mind reader, Davis made an initial career for himself as a "clairvoyant healer." While in trance, he diagnosed disease and prescribed cures. By the late 1840s, Davis's trances allowed him to receive messages from departed spirits, messages so valuable that Davis and his friends undertook to publish them. *The Principles of Nature, Her Divine Revelations, and a Voice to Mankind* appeared in 1847. The first volume of a more massive opus, *The Great Harmonia*, came out three years later, in 1850. Davis's special talents gave him no reason to read books, but he went on writing them for the rest of the nineteenth century.

Since Davis's harmonial philosophy, at least in its original form, advertised itself as a species of new revelation, clerics who were conservative on the question of whether the *Bible* was, so to speak, a closed book, attacked Davis as a charlatan. But the unschooled Davis was not without "respectable" defenders. George Bush, a professor of Hebrew language and literature at New York University, certified that while in a mesmerized state, Davis could speak fluent Greek, Hebrew, Latin, and Sanskrit.[9] These language skills were put to no particular use, other than to provide evidence of the fact that Davis was something special. The Americans familiar with the significance of Pentecost had no trouble assigning importance to spontaneously acquired language skills.

By the early 1850s, Davis had dropped the trappings of mesmerism and presented himself as a spiritualist medium. He still considered himself a disciple of Swedenborg. The transition had as much to do with the repertory of performance as with substance. American spiritualism, which first captured widespread attention in 1850 after the Fox sisters took their "rapping" performances to New York City, vastly extended the stage possibilities for men and women who made entertainment out of the unseen world. The multiplication of "amazing" effects eventually repelled Davis, not because of their fakery but because, he thought, they provided only cheap thrills at the expense of enlightenment. His protest came too late.

Few cultural phenomena are as fascinating as the nineteenth-century proliferation of organized, commercial efforts to communicate with the dead. Great passion swelled the controversies about spiritualism, enough to hold the interest of audiences whose composition ranged from the bottom ranks of society to the top.[10] Séances and other spiritualist demonstrations (not to mention counter-demonstrations) became a national pastime that transcended class, gender, and ethnic barriers. The genius of popular culture lies in its varied repetitions of the same basic formula.

For many people of course, the formulaic quality of the products of popular culture is precisely what makes them worthless. Critics of spiritualism regarded its claims, despite the assorted ways they were packaged, as monothematic and dull. The written accounts of raucous spirit concerts, mysterious messages delivered in sealed slates, and gauzy materializations of human forms might leave us wondering why people went back for more, except when we remember what people heard in church on a Sunday morning; people develop a tolerance, even a relish, for repetition.

When we speak of the commercial marketing of spiritualism, we are talking about commerce on a small scale. No one made a fortune exploiting public interest in spiritualism. The Fox sisters, Kate and Margaret, were as successful as any professional mediums, and their financial returns were modest. Their various detractors who arranged demonstrations to "prove" that the Fox sisters achieved their raps by the conscious cracking of their knee joints did no better. By some accounts, as many as one hundred mediums were doing business in the vicinity of Auburn, New York, by the summer of 1850. Even allowing for exaggeration, that is a formidable competitive environment. Inventiveness was clearly requisite to any success at all. Audiences grew tired of raps and switched their loyalties to mediums who raised tables, levitated bodies, and produced spirit photographs. These dubious phenomena, and many more, gathered crowds in American towns and cities throughout the nineteenth century, but no one medium was versatile enough or credible enough to rise to steady fame and fortune.

As commercial entertainment, spiritualism "worked" for the same reasons that mesmerism had worked. It depended upon clever stage effects to arouse public curiosity. Equally important, spiritualism advertised the gravity of its claims. Spiritualism's popularity required a controversy that people could invest with moral and religious seriousness. It was not an idle pastime; nor was it simply a way for bereaved parents and spouses to find consolation after the loss of a loved one. Spiritualism proposed a challenge to received wisdom. What else but the importance of its implications can explain why a team of Harvard scientists investigated spiritualism in 1857, why William James did the same thing for a longer period of time and with more sympathy at the end of the century? Nineteenth-century mediums were always actors and sometimes straight-out frauds. The successful ones were also something else. To the extent that they acted and dissembled to gain their audience, they did what many contemporary evangelical preachers and temperance lecturers did. Spirit mediums and their customers no less than Protestant ministers and their parishioners carried the heavy burden of sincere belief in their power.

Serious entertainment gained high-class sponsors. Belief in the reality of spirit manifestations was common in the high echelons of American reform movements, especially abolitionism and women's rights.[11] Spirits carried a democratic message. They released people from the dead weight of dogmas. Spiritualist entertainments survived in the marketplace of culture for as long as they did because the controversies they provoked were important to nineteenth-century Americans who were religious but who believed that many religious issues remained open to debate. Like mesmerism, spiritualism was a means to start wide-ranging discussions of issues that served many Americans as their popular philosophy. Was spiritualism one of the signs of a "new dispensation"? Was it demonology, the masterwork of Satan? Was it the instrument of God trying once and for all to make clear to human beings what life meant? The antebellum Americans who quarreled about these questions enjoyed the debate because they agreed that is was possible to come to definitive answers. The fun might be in the argument, but the justification lay in getting to the bottom of it all.

The Religious Dimensions of Sexual Controversy

Although mesmerism and spiritualism affected the way that antebellum Americans talked about religion by associating it with controversial publicity, neither movement itself became an alternative religion, at least not for very many people. A small number of spiritualist churches were formed as a sort of populist outburst of American Swedenborgianism. But it was left to other religious innovators to exploit the atmosphere in which controversy flourished and to use the public attention they called to themselves to construct enduring, financially sound church organizations. In these respects, no groups in the first half of the nineteenth century outdid the Mormons, who gathered around the visionary dreams of Joseph Smith, and the Seventh-day Adventists, whose church started in the end-of-the-world preachments of William Miller. It is impossible to imagine either of these new religions succeeding in the way that they did without the national publicity that was focused on them.

Most of the publicity was, as was true in the cases of mesmerism and spiritualism, negative. Excoriating condemnations that appeared in print victimized all new religions founded in the United States during the nineteenth century. At the same time, condemnation provided a collective ego boost to a new movement. It was a sign that it was taken seriously. Sensational "exposés" functioned as a backhanded aid to religious proselytizing. The amount of publicity given to new religions indicated a shift in the interest of audiences. Popular writing about religion turned away from the devotional and the exegetical to embrace the gossipy and the scandalous. Educated elites in the nineteenth century may have been narrowing their definition of what counted as a plausible transcendental claim, dismissing anything bearing traces of the magical, the mystical, and the occult. If so, their efforts did not seem to affect popular opinion. Many Americans, who were excited by science, seized the banner of empiricism in order to validate religious beliefs that most Protestant church leaders were eager to bury.[12] Claims and movements that might have remained marginal and ephemeral in the seventeenth and eighteenth centuries, centuries conventionally seen as more hospitable to superstition and folk belief than the nineteenth, attracted in antebellum America steady attention. Mormonism was not merely a new religion. It was a new religion that owed its success to cheap newspapers and their aggressive editors who relied upon controversy to stimulate public demand for their product.[13]

Mormonism served from the 1840s until the end of the nineteenth century as a serialized best-seller for American readers, a story tantalizingly released over several decades in a multiplicity of ephemeral and diverse texts. Pamphlets, especially those written by apostates, promised "startling disclosures," an "exposé" of "mysteries and crimes," the "unveiling" (a double-entendre reference to the despised Islam) of the "prophet's harem." Fanny Stenhouse, the former wife of a Mormon elder, entitled her memoir *Tell It All*. Ann Young, with a similar past, called her true story *Wife No. 19, or The Story of a Life in Bondage*. Mormonism was the subject of some fifty nineteenth-century "truthful" novels, the most successful being Maria Ward's *Female Life Among the Mormons*. Published in 1855, it very quickly sold in excess of forty thousand copies. As a small, eccentric, and little-noticed faith, Mormonism might have dwindled away to nothing. As a "national menace," "Uncle Sam's abscess," it commanded sufficient attention to attract a stream of converts in the United States and in England.[14]

The Latter-day Saints, under Joseph Smith and then Brigham Young, did a number of things to mark their distinctive beliefs and rituals. The innovation that really caught the eye of the non-Mormon public was their practice of "plural wives." This gained enormous publicity and became the focus of the struggles of Mormons against the federal government. As a bonus, Mormon marital practices gave Americans a rare opportunity to talk openly and publicly about sex. When sex could be joined to religious controversy, it became part of the news fit to print. Newspaper editors and pamphlet journalists pushed the formula as far as they could. Luckily for them, sex and religion almost always provided material for "sensational" disclosure.

Protestant ministers deserve most of the blame for popularizing the formula. Even before they had Joseph Smith to kick around, they had exploited the subject of sexual misconduct as a means to attack Catholicism. According to them, the authoritarian power given to the Catholic priesthood, combined with the sexual deprivation required of those who took holy orders, created a situation that was bound to result in depravity. Among the predictable consequences were homosexual activity among monks, sexual assaults upon nuns by priests, and the murder and secret burial of infants born within the walls of convents. As if these crimes internal to religious orders were not enough, bands of holy fathers reportedly kidnapped young Protestant virgins and carried them forcibly to the monastery, using them sexually and killing them.

These charges appeared in perhaps the most sensational of all publications of the antebellum period, the "awful" disclosures of Maria Monk regarding the Hotel Dieu convent in Montreal.[15] A firm closely tied to Harper and Brothers first published the book in 1836. A fraud from beginning to end, it was successfully peddled in part because a group of prominent ministers was willing to sponsor it. They apparently found no story about the sexual aberrations of Catholics too incredible to swallow or too salacious to sell to the American public. An account of nuns who were subjected to humiliating questions in the confessional and then raped was a "respectable" use of scandal. So successful was Maria Monk that a rival convent escapee, with equally horrific tales, appeared on the scene to scramble for a share of the market. The theme of depraved Catholic sexuality became a staple of American popular fiction that continued through the rest of the nineteenth century and into the twentieth.[16]

Protestant ministers soon enough had reasons to regret the reckless ways in which they exploited anti-Catholicism. What sold well in the fight against Rome also sold when Protestants turned the same charges of clerical misconduct against one another. Revival ministers, because of the emotional atmosphere they sometimes encouraged and the deliberate attention they called to themselves as dynamic conveyors of divine power, were easy targets. One example was the murder trial of Ephraim K. Avery, a Methodist "exhorter" who was accused of seducing a woman who fell under his spell and then killing her when she became pregnant. Catharine Read Williams thinly fictionalized the story in *Fall River* published in 1833. A year before her "truthful tale" appeared, newspaper editors in states far distant from Rhode Island, the scene of the crime, had publicized the story. According to one historian, songs and plays about Avery became popular, and partisan pamphlets either defending or condemning the minister "flooded the country." The largest room in Newport's courthouse was not big enough to hold the would-be spectators of the trial. Many followed the proceedings by waiting in the street for news to be passed out.[17]

Revival ministers were not the only targets. Accusations of sexual misconduct reached everywhere in clerical ranks. The *Police Gazette* treated clerical scandal in a regular "religious" feature section of the journal. Most of it dealt with cases of seduction. Many readers apparently could not get their fill of stories about the "reverend rake." Hawthorne had many contemporary models for Arthur Dimmesdale.[18] So did George Lippard in portraying the figure of Reverend F. A. T. Pyne, the odious Calvinist lecher who figured in his best-seller of 1845, *The Quaker City*. Benjamin T. Onderdonk, the Episcopal bishop of New York was accused in 1844 of trying to seduce several of his female parishioners, usually while he was under the influence of alcohol.

Onderdonk's case, which led to his suspension by the Episcopal church, garnered quite a bit of attention, unhappily for the bishop increased by the fact that his brother, the Right Reverend Henry U. Onderdonk of Pennsylvania, was undergoing clerical censure at the same time for a drinking problem.[19] Onderdonk had supporters as well as detractors, and they all put their case into "sensational" pamphlets. One of them began: "To look at the reports of the newspaper press, a stranger would set down the American clergy as the most depraved class of mortals on the face of the earth. Not a mail arrives, not a newspaper do we open, but our eyes light upon some malefaction committed by a clergyman."[20] We get a sense of the likely readership of the pamphlet by noting that its front inside cover carried an advertisement for J. H. Ingraham's "romance of the Blue Sea," *Forrestal, or the Light of the Reef*. Exaggeration in the Onderdonk case was as requisite as it was in an adventure tale. Some urban newspapers with large readerships did what they could to make the saga of the New York bishop a matter of "increasing public excitement."

No New York newspaper outdid James Gordon Bennett's *Herald*. The "Onderdonk Excitement" remained on the front page, in one issue taking up all of it, and on the editorial page through the entire month of January 1845 and into February. The breathless words of its coverage did not change much over this time period. The editor simply repeated what he wrote on January 8: "The public excitement is increasing every day. Not only in this city and throughout this diocese, but in the surrounding

cities, as far indeed as the intelligence has gone, the excitement is spreading with the greatest rapidity and attaining the highest intensity."
Whether the published pamphlets "outstrip Eugène Sue's works in circulation and knock Bulwer's novels into a cocked hat," whether they were
passed around during intermissions at Niblo's Garden, or whether "there
never has been such a sensation produced in the literary and reading
world" is open to question.[21] What provides insight into antebellum culture is the fact such claims generated public interest.

The crusading Bennett, who enjoyed warring with the clerics of the
city, managed to take sides against Onderdonk and also the bishops who
defrocked him. He reserved a gallant defense only for the offended
women of the stories. For him, the trial provided an occasion to celebrate
"the role of the press in spreading . . . the greatness of Christianity,"
despite the machinations of "ecclesiastical intolerance and darkness."[22]
Fighting for a proper system of religion and morals in this way was
also a good marketing decision for Bennett. Sound morals promoted high
circulation and vice versa. Such was Bennett's maxim. Any trick to promote sales was permissible because profits that accrued to the *Herald*
translated into disciplined citizens for America. Bennett slyly stationed
one of his staff writers in Philadelphia to report: "Your interesting
sketches of evidence in the Onderdonk case have been read by the pious
ones amongst us with an avidity absolutely indescribable. No sooner has
the New York mail arrived, than crowds appear among the several agencies of your widely circulated journal in this city, in anxious anticipation
of the further developments in the serio-comic drama."[23] Bennett complained that Onderdonk's Episcopal judges made money from the books
they wrote defending their actions. In doing that, he called attention to
the cheaper way the public could get the information in the *Herald.*

The danger lurking in Protestant religion that threatened sexual probity was the inner voice, resistant to all external authority. Antinomianism was the specter that haunted the descendants of Calvin and Luther
who feared that some among them might suddenly decide that they alone
understood the Word of God. These enthusiasts, and history provided
examples, then rose above the "moral law" to announce a new dispensation. Their attendant claims of purity had sometimes resulted in spectacular overturnings of prevailing norms regarding sexual behavior, marriage, and gender roles. The collective memory of churchgoing Calvinists
in antebellum America remembered cases of false Protestant saints who
tried to make public nakedness and unrestrained fornication signs of spiritual rebirth. Most of them had lived in England during the period of
that country's Civil War and Interregnum. A tamer case was Anne
Hutchinson, who had rudely disturbed the patriarchs of the Massachu-

setts Bay Colony. However satisfactory her end had been (she was mas-
sacred by Indians), many who worried about the weakness of moral standards in nineteenth-century America saw formidable competition
developing to the era in English history that had spawned the early
Quakers, the Diggers, and the Seekers.[24]

In the antebellum period, the developing ideology of domesticity
helped to stimulate the public's interest in the sexual misconduct of ministers. It consigned middle class women to the home sphere, but it, in
effect, also made churches (and all their female-dominated social activities) into extensions of the home. The champions of domesticity presumed that women could move safely from home parlor to church parlor,
for in both places they served as moral guardians of their husbands and
children. There was an unforeseen problem. In changing the setting of
their activities, they changed authority figures. The male head who ruled
women in church competed with the male head who ruled women at
home. It just might happen that the intimate contact a woman had with
her spiritual pastor would become more satisfying than what she enjoyed
with her husband.

The inordinate attention given to the Onderdonk case becomes more
explicable when we note some puzzling details of the situation. Virtually
all of the bishop's reported attempts at seduction took place under the
very nose of the husband or a brother, often in the home itself. In the
case of Mrs. Charlotte E. Beale, the husband was driving the bishop
home after dinner in a single-horse barouche, while the bishop, seated
with the wife on the back seat, thrust his palm "into her bare bosom,"
and having it thrust away, "immediately put it on the lower part of her
person." The "hand of consecration" slid along the lady's leg past her
knee and hip to the "centre of her person." To the puzzlement of the
other ecclesiastical people who had to pass judgment on Onderdonk, the
bishop was invited again to dinner and greeted by both husband and wife
"in a friendly manner."[25]

One way to defuse the potentially explosive issue of clerical influence
over women, aside from insisting on married clergy, was to effeminize
the pastor. Antebellum New England produced a number of ministers
known for physical weakness and poor health.[26] They took upon themselves the "feminine" traits of sweetness, meekness, gentleness, sensitiv-
ity, and delicacy. However, this conveniently frail clerical specimen was
not the only type of stereotypical pastor. Itinerant preachers who rode
horses over long distances day after day to save souls cultivated a more
virile image of themselves. Under their sway women swooned. We do
not have to dig very deeply in the autobiographies of revivalist ministers
to find themes of the love triangle.

Most of the stories had a successful spiritual resolution, else they would not have been told. The Methodist itinerant Peter Cartwright boasted of a meeting he conducted near Hopkinsville, Tennessee. His conversion of the wife and two daughters in a "fashionable, wealthy" family "enraged the husband and father of these interesting females very much." The offended patriarch, according to Cartwright, threatened to whip and kill him, charging that "I must be a very bad man, for all the women in the country were falling in love with me." Over her father's protests, Cartwright offered to take the eldest daughter, "a fine, beautiful, intelligent young lady," in his carriage to the camp meeting. The disgruntled father finally determined to attend himself in order to prove Cartwright's evil intentions. On the way, the daughter warned Cartwright to protect himself from her father's rage, but he assured her that he had not the least fear. "Seeing me so bold and confident she wept." The rest was predictable. Cartwright had the satisfaction of converting the father who fell suddenly "powerless . . . as if a rifle ball had been shot through his heart." The domestic circle was left intact despite the powerful admiration of its female members for Cartwright.[27]

The autobiographical narrative of Charles Finney records a comparable episode. We learn of a woman who came to his meetings over the bitter opposition of her husband. The husband, in fact, "forbade his wife attending meetings any more." The wife, whose "first obligation was to God," heeded Finney's advice to attend anyway. The husband next flew into a rage, broke up the furniture in the house, drew a dagger on his wife, and chased her from room to room. Happily, just before he plunged the dagger in her heart, God struck him down and converted him. God was Finney's surrogate in restoring domestic bliss, and Finney was thus saved from charges that he had grossly intruded into a domestic covenant. Finney went on to note that the husband became a pretty good preacher, though not so good as Finney himself.[28] What is remarkable about these narratives is how plainly the sexual tension appears even under the cover of religious conventions.

The public interest generated by Mormon sexuality becomes more understandable in this context. The controversy was an unusually unhampered opportunity to put the question of sexual promiscuity before the public and to allow a good bit of frank talk about sex in general. The oddity of the situation was that none of the new American religions, including that of the Latter-day Saints, encouraged sexual promiscuity. However novel their teachings about marriage and the equality of sexes (and most of them taught nothing novel at all), their aim was to carefully restrict sexual conduct and to codify with obsessive attention to detail different roles for men and women. Publications overlooked those facts.

What people wanted was less the truth about the Mormons and other groups than a way to imagine sexual misconduct without feeling guilty about it. Instead of blaming themselves for impure thoughts, they blamed what they had misportrayed. The Shakers abstained from sexual intercourse altogether, and still had to live with reports that their communal living arrangements were cesspools of free love. Somehow their strict standards of commitment encouraged husbands to cast off wives and wives to run away with lovers.

Aside from the Mormons, the Perfectionist community founded by John Humphrey Noyes at Oneida, New York, received the most attention. Interestingly, the Oneida community suffered less hostility for most of its existence than the Mormons, even though it was geographically much closer to where other Americans lived. Upstate New York was isolated, but Utah was remote. Moreover, the arrangements at Oneida combined economic communism with a more radical rejection of the bourgeois family than Joseph Smith proposed. It is true that the ill-defined term "free love" is a poor label to describe Noyes's system of complex marriage. Oneida was an experiment in rigid self-control. People had more than one sexual partner, but not at the same time and not out of whim. The community monitored sexual liaisons with an eye toward breeding better people. The famous system of birth control at Oneida depended upon men learning how to cool down without ejaculation, not *coitus interruptus* but *coitus reservatus*. Nevertheless, Noyes based complex marriage on his notion that "the marriage supper of the lamb was a feast where every dish is free to every guest."[29] That phrasing might have made a Mormon man with twenty wives blush and was, on the face of it, more than sufficient to stimulate gossip and condemnation.

The relative lack of persecution directed at Oneida owed much to the economic peace that it made with its neighbors. Oneida hired people from the outside to work in its enterprises and gained a reputation for treating them fairly. These workers provided reliable testimony to the fact that community life in the Mansion House did not resemble a Roman orgy. Noyes, in contrast with the Mormon leaders, followed a deliberate policy to improve community relations. Earlier, he and his adherents had been driven out of Putney, Vermont. He did not want a repetition of that unpleasantness. Oneida put on a show for visitors and turned itself into a tourist attraction.[30] In 1866, four thousand people signed the Visitors' Book. Tourism increased with the completion of a branch railway line in 1869 that stopped a few hundred yards from the Mansion House. Day trips to Oneida became an "entertainment." Visitors were escorted through the community and often fed and lodged.

According to a writer for the *New York Tribune*, "Rarely have I eaten meals so well-cooked, so neat and so good. They equal, to my taste they excel, those at the best hotels."[31]

The self-control practiced at Oneida resulted in something that American capitalists approved—first-class manufactured products. Oneida in the most literal way transmuted its religious perfectionism into commodities—first, animal traps and later, silverware. By the end of the nineteenth century, the radical meaning of Noyes's venture had been lost amid commercial associations. Much the same thing happened at the Community of True Inspiration founded in Amana, Iowa. Americans have forgotten that the Amana Society, now an incorporated cooperative, was originally a German pietist cluster of villages committed to economic sharing. In the modern world, Amana stands for refrigerators. *cf Shakers + furniture*

Mormons were equally successful in their economic arrangements. Even while the attacks upon Mormons continued, fueling strong reactions in the American Congress and causing a virtual state of warfare between the national government and the Latter-day Saints, Mormons engaged in effective proselytizing endeavors and built a church institution and a community of considerable wealth. In the Mormon case, the wealth was jealously resented by non-Mormons in the Utah territory who felt deliberately excluded. When the federal government moved strongly and decisively against the Mormon church in the 1880s, it outlawed polygamy. Since most Mormon men did not practice it, the ban drove only the leaders underground and left open the possibility of an adjustment that did not totally overturn Mormon society. More seriously, the government seized church property and held it in receivership for eight years. The Mormon church could survive in the twentieth century without plural marriage; its wealth it needed back.

The controversy about Mormon sexuality had a lighter side that provoked general amusement. In addition to the exposés written by Mormon apostates, which promised in unfailingly hyperbolic language to reveal Mormonism as "the most dangerous practice," "the greatest threat," and "the most infamous perfidy and treachery," other writers used the Mormons as the butt of their jokes. The perambulatory figure of Brigham Young in pajamas was an easy image to manipulate in order to get laughs. Two of America's best-known humorists, Mark Twain (Samuel L. Clemens) and Artemus Ward (Charles F. Browne), found in the Mormons a profitable subject. Twain, who characterized the *Book of Mormon* as "chloroform in print," professed to give up trying to effect a great reform in Salt Lake City once he laid eyes on Mormon women: "the man that marries one of them has done an act of Christian charity which entitles him to the kindly applause of mankind, not their harsh censure—and the man that marries sixty of them has done a deed of open-handed generosity so sublime that the nations should stand uncovered in his presence and worship in silence."

Like Twain, Ward took the trouble to travel to the Great Salt Lake and meet with the "profit" Brigham Young. What he found there became the subject of several humorous articles and of one of his most successful lectures. The latter he presented with slides. Ward's comments about Young were, indeed, funny. "In a private conversashun with Brigham I learnt the follerin fax: It takes him six weeks to kiss his wives. He don't do it only onct a yere and sez it is wuss nor cleanin house." His observation that Young "loves not wisely—but two hundred well" drew predictable laughs as did his description of the funeral of another Mormon husband whose wives marched "twenty abreast" behind the bier so that none would seem to have been the preferred spouse. Ward's humorous deprecations of polygamy were tempered by an evident liking for Young and respect for the fundamentally decent society he found in Utah. For an accurate portrait of Mormon life, especially for Mormons at play, people could have done worse than attend Ward's lecture.[32]

Mormons wrote in their own self-defense, for they recognized the benefits of keeping themselves a subject of lively controversy. Finally controversy brought down the full force of federal authority upon them. But before that happened, Brigham Young welcomed media attention and enjoyed interviews that he handled with the skills of the actor that he was. Counting the bedroom gables on his house became a tourist activity once the transcontinental railroad was complete.[33] Afterwards, "Gentile" American tourists continued to write home about the scenic wonders of Utah and also to reflect about the Mormons who first built stable families and communities in that environment. What was once discussed as the sexual outrageousness of Mormon men was not forgotten. It continued to serve as a way for other Americans to think about what was wrong and unsatisfying about their own sexual practices. Well into the twentieth century, the subject of sexual maladjustment searched for commercial formulas to get by censors. In the nineteenth century, religious controversy was by far the most useful framing context.

Marketing New American Religions as a Quest for Health

The media play that attended the vogue of Millerism was briefer than what attended the rise of the Latter-day Saints. In the late 1830s and early 1840s, however, it was intense. The apocalyptic fervor of William

Miller's followers was a natural subject for writers skilled at exploiting public taste for sensationalism. Millerism itself died down in late 1844, after several predicted dates for the end of the world passed without the slightest quaver in the orbital course of the earth. Memories of the fuss did not immediately fade, however. They kept the way open for the permanent institutionalizing of Millerism in the Seventh-day Adventist church. It was especially the attention given to the prophecies of Ellen White that renewed Adventist purpose and led in time to the church's incorporation in 1863.

Leon Festinger, in a famous psychological study of failed prophecies, concluded that people who are disappointed when an ordinary summer morn follows their projected doomsday aggressively track down the media to talk about what happened. Rather than retreat in embarrassment, they seek to call attention to themselves. Rather than concede defeat, they reinterpret the nature of the event that was supposed to transpire and increase their fervor.[34] This counter-intuitive proposition helps explain why Millerism survived its errant prophecies. In fact, Millerites began an aggressive media campaign before any of their disappointments. It took concerted efforts of publicity to make William Miller, an uncharismatic lay preacher, known beyond a small circle of rural New Englanders and New Yorkers. In the early 1830s, his was not a household name that started arguments. The person who deserves much of the credit for a successful selling campaign was Joshua V. Himes. One historian has termed his efforts in behalf of Miller an "unprecedented communications crusade."[35] Whether the crusade was unprecedented does not matter. What matters is that it was deliberate.

Himes was born in Rhode Island in 1805. The ambitions of a wealthy father, had they been fulfilled, would have propelled Himes into the pastorate of a socially prominent Episcopal church. Instead, his father lost his money, and the young Himes found his religious moorings in the latitudinarian "Christian Connection," an important movement of religious populists eventually dominated by Barton Stone and Alexander Campbell.[36] The denominational outcome was the Disciples of Christ. "Christian" churches sought an end to "corpse-cold" human creeds and tried, not for the first or last time, to recall Protestants back to their primary duty of searching for truth in their own, clerically unmediated, readings of Scripture. The enterprise, when taken seriously, trained those who undertook it in the art of dispute. Himes took it seriously and reaped his reward. In the 1830s, he turned his own Christian church, the Chardon Street Chapel in Boston, into a center of social and political contention. Himes was a bold champion of abolitionism (William Lloyd Garrison remained a lifelong friend) and of women's rights.

Thus, when Himes met Miller in 1839, he was no stranger to public controversy and unpopular causes. The latter, he sensed, often attracted fervent supporters in some rough proportion to the number of their fervent detractors. When he took it upon himself to "publicize" Miller's views and to raise money for the cause, he thought in bold terms about conquering an audience. His tactics were, broadly speaking, indistinguishable from those of successful revivalist preachers. In scale, he outdid most everyone. The tent that he carted along for his speaking engagements was said to be the largest used by anyone for any enterprise, seating between four thousand and five thousand people.

Himes built a publishing empire as well. It flourished on his guiding principles of cheapness and aggressive distribution. In 1840, Himes claimed fifty thousand readers for the first Millerite publication, the *Signs of the Times*. *The Midnight Cry*, a daily two-cent newspaper, had a weekly circulation of ten thousand in early 1842. Himes estimated that it had a casual readership ten times that number. These and later publications were sent to postmasters throughout the country, carrying news of the spreading Millerite excitement as well as advertisements for the many books, pamphlets, and tracts written by partisans of Miller's prophecies. Himes did not overlook the utility of visual aids, and he published large, illustrated historical charts to indicate the important dates prefiguring God's nearing judgment. Understandably, the opponents of Millerism accused Himes of cynically profiteering from these enterprises. The accusations were unfair, especially in the implication that Himes did not believe in Miller's predictions. They do usefully remind us, however, that Himes ran a show that covered costs and a bit more.

Financial chicanery was the least serious of the charges against Millerism. The movement's detractors cited it as a symptom for virtually everything that was wrong with the times. It bore the blame for all phenomena that resulted in public anxiety in the antebellum period. Were social disruption and a possible sectional rift matters of widespread alarm? Millerism was the cause. Were popular enthusiasms for madcap movements a reason for people neglecting their vocational and professional responsibilities? Millerism seemed to provide ample affirmation. Was the United States in danger of losing confidence in the future of the national experiment and being drawn back under the influence of reactionary European powers? Millerism was responsible because it turned America figuratively into the beast of the apocalypse and spoke about the nearness of Armageddon. Did Americans have insufficiently firm moorings in a stable social structure? The passing fad of Millerism with its socially useless passions was evidence of the fact.

The often repeated stories about the excesses of Millerism made good copy, for they were, in the first place, amusing. A merchant in New York scattered his stock of goods on the street, claiming that profits from their sale were no longer of use to him. A man in New Hampshire, enrobed in a long white dress, climbed a tree and tried to "ascend." Believers dressed in similar ascension robes, huddled together in the cold of a winter night, and wept at dawn when the sun rose on schedule. Something more troubling was being argued in these repetitive tellings of doubtful anecdotes. Many of them ended in grizzly death. The New York merchant later committed suicide in an asylum. The man who tried to ascend fell from the tree and broke his neck. The huddled campers perished from exposure to the elements, including two little children reportedly found in a Millerite gathering place "perfectly cold, stiff, and dead."[37]

Mormonism gave Americans an opportunity to talk about their sexual practices. Millerism and Adventism provided occasions for them to talk about their health, physical and mental. Often, in fact, religious controversy joined the issues of sex and health. The pejorative literature directed at the Millerites reflected real anguish about reported rises in the rates of madness and suicide. Many critics of American institutions blamed these troubles on the formlessness of the nation and its lack of sufficient centers of authority. It was easier to blame Millerism. People cited statistics from asylum directors who, for the most part, were happy to attack any form of what they could construe as religious fanaticism.

The United States was not a notably unhealthy environment in the early nineteenth century. People who lived in its larger cities on average probably enjoyed a more substantial diet and a cleaner living environment than urban dwellers elsewhere.[38] Americans lived and died in a shorter span of time than is common at the end of the twentieth century, but they were in no worse shape than people in European countries where scientific and medical knowledge was still presumed to be greater. Even so, they worried a great deal about health. The expectation of good health was part of the confident and optimistic mood that American mythmakers wanted to project. When, against that expectation, infant mortality remained high, when mothers commonly died in childbirth or of illnesses attributable to child bearing, when plagues of cholera and yellow fever ran unchecked through cities, and when men and women died rapidly of complications from seemingly slight wounds, people began to wonder whether more, much more, might be done to minister to the sick and dying. What seemed very certain to some was that medicine, whose professional practitioners sought to distinguish its methods from the traditions of folk healers, as often made illnesses worse as better. Medicine had not advanced much beyond the theories and the practices of the sixteenth century. Doctors knew nothing of infection or germs. They had no medicines whose curative principles were understood in "modern" scientific terms. They could amputate, but they could not operate. What they prescribed to critically ill people—bleedings, blisterings and purgatives—almost always caused pain and further weakness. It rarely healed.[39]

Out of the perceived failures of medical doctors arose a proliferation of various systems of "unorthodox" or "alternative" medicines. The practitioners of the alternative paths to healing did not regard their prescriptions as a return to the folkways of the past. In tones as confident as those of "regular" doctors, they boasted of their originality. They advertised their theories as up-to-date, scientific, and totally in the spirit of intellectual liberation associated with the eighteenth-century enlightenment. Despite some obvious parallels with practices carried through centuries of oral tradition, they for the most part refused to acknowledge links to occult curative principles. Unconventional they were. That was the trait that drew them into association with unconventional religious leaders who were also struggling with ways to make their own attention-seeking claims saleable.

Mesmerism was one important case of unorthodox medicine that merged health claims with religious claims. There were many others.[40] In the first decade of the nineteenth century, Samuel Thomson carried along the same routes that revivalist preachers traveled a message of medical self-help using botanical remedies. He was for a time associated with Elias Smith, an innovative character in the history of religious publishing who also befriended and instructed Joshua Himes.[41] A few years after Thomson began his career, the homeopathic system created by Samuel Hahnemann made its way to the United States. Homeopathy encouraged people to think about the spiritual dimension in medical healing, as did hydropathy, the water-cure movement that became a familiar product of commercial medicine during the 1840s. Supported by Russell Trall, Orson Fowler, Mary Gove, and Thomas Nichols, hydropathy became associated with a variety of reform causes that aimed to challenge status-quo hierarchies based on gender and class.[42]

All of the alternative medical systems, whatever they were supposed to be alternative to, advertised themselves in democratic terms. Their practitioners studied popular styles. They appealed to crowds in ways that were almost identical to the procedures of revivalist ministers, temperance lecturers, and millennial-inspired antebellum reformers. Efforts to rid human beings of sickness were part of the broad movement to bring down the new heaven to the new earth. Nothing had greater vogue on the lecture circuits in antebellum America than claims to demonstrate, in a supposedly scientific way, that what human beings regarded as their spiritual nature interacted with their material self. Proper interaction produced health. To be in tune with God meant to feel good. That attitude was to have a long commercial ascent, one that some promoters would translate into the proposition that monetary wealth followed quickly from the spiritual recovery of health.

That was later. The man who in the antebellum period most strikingly brought the elements of spiritual and physical health together was Sylvester Graham, the inventor of the Graham cracker. Graham's dietary reform was part of an entire program that sought to release human beings from unhealthy and unnatural passions that debilitated their physical vigor. Like his father and grandfather before him, Graham was trained for the ministry. Licensed by the Presbyterian church in 1826, he expanded his pulpit repertory to include temperance lecturing.[43] Convincing himself that disease sprang from the violation of God's moral laws, he founded the Christian Health Movement. Those who joined were enthusiastic. One of his followers exclaimed: "It is our solemn and deliberate conviction, after faithfully studying the book much of the past year that, next to the Bible, Graham's Lectures on the Science of Human Life should be read and studied by every family and especially every minister and medical man." Salvation, or the attainment of human perfection that prevented a backsliding into sin, resulted from both a spiritual and a physical regimen.[44] "We pervert the intentions of Divine benevolence by misusing our bodies," he declared. Perversion for Graham meant, above all, too much sex, even within marriage. He prohibited meat-eating because of his belief that animal flesh stimulated sexual desire: "We need a proper diet—then we will lose the propensity to sexual overindulgence which is not natural."[45]

Movements that joined physical healing to spiritual regeneration encountered opposition and a predictable barrage of ridicule. Despite that, they have lasted down to the present. Some, like homeopathy, that stress a holistic approach to healing are undergoing a renaissance. D. D. Palmer, who with his son established chiropractic medicine in the United States, was well versed in the Bible as well as in many varieties of esoteric philosophy; he filled his writings with spiritual references. Andrew Taylor Still, the founder of osteopathy, was the son of a Methodist minister, a spiritualist, and a man who linked bonesetting to harmonial philosophy.[46] All of these movements owed their initial success to the public display of "marvels" and the religious arguments they caused. The debate over healing drew attention both to the challenge that science posed to spirituality and to the hope that they were intimately connected. However a person stood on those issues, most middle-class Americans

141

were predisposed to believe that to be a healthy people they had to be religious.

In the case of healing religions, and the publicly controversial claims attendant to them, women were uncommonly important. Ellen White emerged as the leader of the Seventh-day Adventist church. Prominence in health/religious movements was a way for women to reclaim a role that had been taken from them. The practice of "orthodox" medicine in the nineteenth century was almost entirely restricted to men, even though women historically were strongly associated with healing. The antebellum cult of domesticity gave some women an idea about how to use their reputed moral and religious nature to gain power over health.

Later in the nineteenth century, Mary Baker Eddy did exactly that. In a different way, so did Lydia Pinkham. Her vegetable compound was perhaps the most famous of the nineteenth-century patent medicines and possibly the most cleverly advertised product of the century. Pinkham sprang from a family of radical Quaker abolitionists. Although she had little use for organized religion in her adult life, she persevered in her attachment to the doctrines of Swedenborg and remained a committed spiritualist to the end of her days.[47] Both Eddy and Pinkham owed a debt to White. Earlier in the century, she grounded the appeal of her church and its financial success in a commercial venture into health care.

White's inspirations were various. A multitude of antebellum health reformers taught her to warn Americans away from alcohol, tobacco, caffeine, and meat. White added dress reform for women as a particular feature of her religious crusade for hygiene. In a more important institutional ploy, she gathered many of her followers at Battle Creek, Michigan, where she built a sanatorium/hospital that was the first of the many Adventist medical facilities that now operate in the United States and around the world. Her partner in this venture was John Harvey Kellogg, a respected doctor whose associates later included the Mayo brothers, who built a famous medical complex in Rochester, Minnesota.

Kellogg invented granola and also a flaked wheat cereal that he patented and offered to White as a way to finance the church. Sensing too great a contradiction between preparing church members for eternity and a heavy investment in food processing, White turned down wheat flakes and the later proffered corn flakes.[48] It was, therefore, Kellogg's brother, W. K., who constructed the commercial empire of the Battle Creek cereal industry. White's church never reaped any of the financial benefits of the Kellogg Company or of the C. W. Post Company that was founded in Battle Creek by another health reformer. John Kellogg, in fact, finally broke with the church, and Adventists spread to other places in the United States.

The church did not entirely forgo its commercial opportunities. It marketed Battle Creek Sanitarium Foods in the nineteenth century and a line of health and dietary products under the name of its California base in Loma Linda in the twentieth. The ventures were not modest ones. In Australia and New Zealand, the church-owned Sanitarium Health Foods Company manufactures Weet-Bix, perhaps the best-selling breakfast cereal "down under."[49] In addition to its health foods, medical care became a product closely associated with Adventism. A movement originally tied to the worldly pessimism of a premillennial prophet declaring the near end of the world succeeded because of its ability to help people live longer. Adventism is a church. It is also a medical establishment.

It is more than a footnote to observe that the medicalization of morality, the linking of health to religious faith and virtue, has remained an important aspect of twentieth-century American life with a wide range of commercial applications. The media success of faith healers, the New Age ideologies of many health-food advocates, the public controversy over AIDS, the typically Protestant excesses in crusades against smoking and in commitments to achieve self-mastery through running—all of these recall the spiritual exercises of many antebellum Americans. Type A personalities, the high-risk category for heart attacks, are supposed to find ways to relax. Little about the intense market of health reform promotes relaxation, at least not in the slovenly old ways of traditional societies that did not have stop watches, diet books, exercise videos, and stores filled with nothing but athletic shoes. Clearly, the issue now is not merely health and spiritual peace. It is the internalization of a disciplined way of life that promises to allow people, men and women, to live long enough to make a financial killing.

Commercial Culture and the Web of Market

The experiences of four-score and seven years split the American nation. The ferocious Civil War that ensued was a rupture in the nation's history, but it by no means eradicated all the patterns of communal life that had formed in the early period of the republic. A century and a half beyond the Civil War, the sheer scale of American institutions would leave much of its heritage distorted almost beyond recognition. Even so, contemporary America still owes much to the first generations who struggled to find ways to make the nation work.

The basic rules of American religious life are among the surviving relics. Religious leaders had started national life aware that they had to deal with competition. They said so in many forums, and in one way or another they declared it a problem. All procedures were in the beginning *ad hoc.* Innovation was a forced option. One locus of competition was between denominations, but in some ways that was the easy part of it. The unexpected proliferation and prosperity of new religious groups aided church leaders generally. Looming as a bigger problem was competition with non-religious enterprises on the cultural landscape that attracted people's attention and energies. Many of those enterprises were changing the nature of leisure in the United States. Increasingly, they turned casual pastimes into organized businesses.

Religious leaders entered a long struggle to try to control the direction that commercial culture took. In many ways, religion's determined intrusion into the marketplace of culture made that arena the central moral battleground of American life. What religious leaders did early in national history, they continued to do later. They opposed many new forms of commercial culture as they came along. They tried to set up attractive, alternative diversions under church sponsorship. They fought with cultural entrepreneurs who resisted the idea of running their businesses according to guidelines dictated by a Protestant moral economy.

These efforts gave American religious life a distinctive quality that was radically different from what it had been in the colonial era. For one thing, almost all of them committed religious leaders to a process of popularization. They had to attract people to what they were doing. Whether they were trying to clamp controls on the marketplace of culture or not, they found themselves using the language of selling and commodification. Religious controversy spilled out of churches and theological centers to become a form of American entertainment. Sometimes people paid money to hear the debate; sometimes it was free. In either case, religious spectacle changed the meaning of religion in American life. Religion politicized the moral issues of public life by running the risk of becoming part of the problem of omnipresent commercialization.

The market impulses that shaped the nature of religious proselytizing in the United States were not purely economic in nature. Ties between religion and wealth are part of the historical record we must consider along with the charge that religion was a way to hog-tie the working classes in humble submission to capitalist oppression. However wealth, or its near proximity, had little to do with the religious initiatives I have been describing. Many Protestant evangelicals, who in fact led the way in religious marketing, betrayed their rural origins for many years after their political alliance with Jeffersonians had led them to oppose banks, taxation for internal improvements, and the national promotion of manufacturing.[50] Their perspective was shaped more by agricultural subsistence than by wealth and luxurious consumption. Besides, women, who are key players in our story, were deliberately excluded from the sort of indoctrination that would lead to thinking about markets in cold economic terms. Supposedly, there had to be a moral point.

Inevitably and for good reasons, we assign to abstract market forces a power over all cultural products. That is not quite to say that the market conquered religion, forcing religion to walk the streets, to make its spiritual mission a cash transaction, to surrender its power and influence to the secular. Whatever compromises religious leaders made were matched by those who negotiated on the other side of the bargains that were struck. Religion's position in the marketplace of culture always managed to retain some of its regulatory intent. To play a role in a national market system, people did not have to advocate the accumulation of wealth or banks or the judicial doctrines of John Marshall. Innovation and participation happened in a variety of ways, some of them aptly labeled democratic and populist and even spiritual.

Reinhold Niebuhr described the American national past as a massive tangle of ironies.[51] It is hard to resist his characterization. When considering the story of religion down to the present, one might conclude that religious leaders have a great deal to regret. They assumed so many voices that they possibly lost one that is clearly distinctive. What they set out to do often led them to wind up embracing what they had set out to oppose or at least to modify. One thing we need to remember. The word "spiritual" is a culturally constructed, highly problematic concept. Whatever its subjective import, its visible manifestations change over time. If what people call the spiritual is to have any worldly or public importance, it has to be recognizable in something tangible, some institution, some set of legal privileges, some specially anointed group of officials. In the United States, the tangible form of the spiritual was in the proselytizing that made churches resemble non-religious offerings in the marketplace of culture. Spirituality lay in hard-sell church campaigns and the efforts of religious leaders to say with respect to certain commercial activities how culture was marketed, in what formats, with what claims, and to which audiences. Without those campaigns, we might not be talking about spirit at all in these days. In American life, religion had to become a commodity, but that did not make it peanut butter.

CHAPTER SIX

Chautauqua and Its Protective Canopy:

Religion, Entertainment, and Small-Town Protestants

How many beautiful values can be made to live for all mankind by gaily marching children, by youths contending in athletic games, by maidens winding round the Maypole, by lively music quickening and dissolving the quaint formations of the folk dances, by free families released to wander with romping children through the parks or over the green of the countryside?

Richard Henry Edwards (1922)

The United States emerged from its Civil War with the victors intent upon industrial development. The need to connect the expanding country by a transportation network drove national politics. The great railroad empires of E. H. Harriman, J. J. Hill, and Collis P. Huntington, in turn, set forth innovative models for capitalist organization and created a large demand for steel, machine technology, imported labor, and finance capital. To many observers, powerful financial interests in the postwar American nation finally succeeded in making materialism supreme over all other values. The religious moralists who had previously worried about rampant hedonism in the nation's cities found new reasons for alarm. Endless pleasure-seeking appeared to be the only demand to which commercial culture responded. The grim conclusion that money had debased church life, like everything else, took on an axiomatic ring. According to Jonathan Baxter Harrison, "the real religion" of Americans was a "decorous worldliness." Churchgoing was just another social activity that kept life varied. "For a very large class . . . all the barriers and distinctions between the church and the world have been removed." Religion had been reduced to a "kind of sacred amusement," "an aesthetic entertainment."[1]

Mark Twain put it differently. Americans, he said in 1871, no longer got their religion from the "drowsy pulpit." Christianity came "filtered down" through plays and the "despised novel."[2] A nation that measured taste by its dollar value made it hard to distinguish the patrons of religion from the patrons of commercial culture. Others had made similar observations. Harrison and Twain simply reflected a sharpened perception that the efforts of America's religious leaders to establish moral boundaries for American popular culture had, by degrees, turned their own creeds into competing products in the marketplace of culture. A market that dealt mainly in leisure commodities forced churches and religious organizations to come up with schemes to put "high-minded" pleasures in head-to-head competition with the morally unthinkable.

In his excellent book about working-class people in antebellum New York City, the historian Richard Stott noted the untroubled ease with which diary writers complained on one page about the city's lack of saloon seating and a few lines later recorded their baptisms. In the same paragraph covering one day, workers recorded going to a minstrel show and attending church.[3] The emphasis was equal. Such a blurring of subjects grew more common in the late nineteenth century and affected everyone. Tourists in New York City flocked to the spectacular stage sensation *The Black Crook*, which opened at Niblo's Garden on September 12, 1866, and then headed downtown to climb the spire at Trinity Church. Mindful of the "forest of female legs" on display at the former, a reporter for the *New York Tribune* coyly suggested that they would "see a good deal in both places."[4] The ability to move easily among such seemingly disparate activities was one result of religious leaders' efforts to have their churches keep up with other attractions.

Few patterns applied everywhere in America. The United States was never more plural in its social composition than in the last half of the nineteenth century. In this chapter, the lives of Americans who lived outside the nation's biggest cities are the focus. Given the speed of industrialization in the last quarter of the nineteenth century, it is easy to forget that in 1890 almost three-quarters of the American population lived in rural areas or in towns with fewer than eight thousand people. The Americans who farmed, who settled in small hamlets, who were part of the population bustle of middling-sized cities were not isolated from the momentous economic upheavals that were turning America into a leading industrial nation. The island communities of these mostly white and mostly Protestant people were not yet closely tied together by transportation and by communications networks.[5] Even so, they had moved beyond self-sufficiency. Trade regularly introduced them to the pleasures of consumerism and the desire for goods manufactured a long way from home. They knew what sorts of entertainment were available to people in New York City and Chicago.

Out in America's heartland, religion seemed healthy by all external signs. The largest Protestant denominations were growing, a fact evinced in swelling membership rosters, the size of church buildings, and the expansion of missionary activities. The religious prosperity was partly a continuation and consolidation of the evangelical surge of the early nineteenth century. Churches were also benefiting from new methods of institutional management adapted from business models. Protestant churches that had had a reputation for wild emotional manners earlier in the century were adjusting to stability and a respectability that several brief decades had rendered timeless. American memory was short. The processes that turned American communities into societies in which most people claimed church membership were in the most common-sense way processes that moved churches closer to the world. More men came to church after churches stopped trying their members for moral lapses.[6] People signed their names on denominational rosters often with no greater outward fervor than when they joined other organizations that promised fellowship and economic advantage.

The culture industry and religion learned from and adjusted to each other. Protestant religious leaders and their allies renewed their determination in the post–Civil War period to restrain the proliferation of morally dangerous activities. They worked hard and with considerable effectiveness to keep professional "entertainments" under moral surveillance.

What was permitted or not permitted on Sundays reminded people that rules bound play time and work time. Merchants in the culture industry had to respect them. In turn, religious leaders recognized that successful moral regulation required them to devote more and more energy to thinking about how to provide adequate equivalents for pleasures they deplored.

Religious leaders in small towns had to contend with a narrower range of commercial entertainments than was found in cities, but that did not stop them from worrying. They feared contagion. They knew that in the end the market would supply people with what they wanted. The trick was to stay ahead of the market so that when it arrived, it had to respect entrenched local standards. The religious leaders of some denominations were better prepared than others for the challenge. For sheer inventiveness, nobody outdid American Methodists. Their bans on drinking, dancing, gambling, and almost all types of commercial entertainment might seem to have disqualified them for any role in teaching Americans how to have fun. In fact, they were geniuses in manipulating popular culture. They were also close to the center of Protestant America. Methodism did not reach everyone, not by a long shot. Its field of influence was large, however, and acted persuasively on other American Protestants in the matter of emphasizing the church's responsibility to provide Christian leisure. Vacation Bible School is a quintessential Methodist idea. Methodists had their camp meetings on Martha's Vineyard and on the Jersey Shore and also developed one of the most familiar institutions on the American cultural landscape of the late nineteenth and early twentieth centuries: the Chautauqua Association.

A Moral Vacation

The rural camp meeting had succeeded as an institution because it satisfied the competing desires of piety and play. Tennis, ocean-bathing, and salvation under proper sponsorship worked together. Not all Protestants yet believed that. Conservatives even within the broad Methodist persuasion feared that sponsored recreation within a revival camp setting threatened to shove any spiritual mission so far into the background that it virtually disappeared. Many disapproving Methodists joined the Holiness Revival, a great surge of perfectionist zeal that swept through their denominations beginning in the 1860s. To the Holiness people, who sought to revitalize the Wesleyan movement by emphasizing charismatic gifts, camp sites by the sea were part of a shameful decline. When "families secured their tenting-ground, put up swings for their children, arranged for the favorite croquet-game, and, in short, prepared for a week or ten days' relaxation in the grove," they forgot the spirit. Holiness reformers reported that within or just outside many Methodist camp grounds were concessions selling candy, ice cream, and tobacco.[7]

Actually, all the Holiness critics managed to demonstrate was that selling religion, whatever the purported spiritual format, entailed compromises. From its inception, Protestant revivalism had functioned as a form of entertainment. Holiness meetings were no less staged theatrical events than any others. Whenever people rush down aisles, fling themselves in the straw, and cry for salvation with mighty sighs and groans, other people become spectators. By the 1860s, religious recreation was far too deeply imbedded in popular Protestant church habits to permit a reversal. The Holiness people might convince themselves that they knew when religion had gone too far and had crossed a line that made it indistinguishable from entertainment. They were kidding themselves. Out of the Holiness movement came Pentecostalism and out of Pentecostalism came Oral Roberts, Jimmy Swaggart, Pat Robertson and Jim Bakker.

The founding of the Chautauqua Association in 1873 was a major event in the history of Protestant labors in the marketplace of culture. Its original purpose was to provide a program of mental training for Sunday-school teachers of all denominations. The key sponsors were John Vincent, who was later to become a bishop in the Methodist church, and Lewis Miller, a wealthy Methodist layman. Chautauqua quickly moved beyond its origins to find a mass audience. A major portion of white Protestant Americans embraced it. Chautauqua was so wholesome that almost no one objected to its subversion of older and stricter ideas. It popularized more than ever before the idea that churches owed their members some good times.

Out of a splendid natural setting in western New York, Vincent carved a human space where people would feel no separation between the religious and the worldly. The organization of time at Chautauqua did not distinguish the sacred and the secular. "Every day," Vincent said, "should be sacred. . . . There should be no break between sabbaths. The cable of divine motion should stretch through seven days, touching with its sanctifying power every hour of every day. Kitchen work, farm work, shop work, as well as school work, are divine."[8] Vincent sought to re-affirm what he believed was the core idea of Protestantism that distinguished it from Catholicism. Catholicism, according to Protestants, restricted sacred activity to what took place within the sacramental system controlled by the Church. It made the Church the repository of God's grace and linked salvation to ritual practices that sustained the Church financially. Not only did Catholicism thereby permit a lax set of moral rules to govern what was nominally secular activity. It actually encouraged sin, for without a dependable line of penitents outside the confessional, the Church had no reason to exist. Without sharing all of these misapprehensions, Vincent justified Chautauqua by the Protestant view that God's steady judgment applied to everything people did, wherever they did it. The same rules governed activities at home, at work, at play, and at church.

In fact, Protestant theory poorly described practice. Protestants made all kinds of distinctions between how they acted at church and how they acted elsewhere. They were every bit as skilled in the psychology of compartmentalization as the most devout Catholic. Vincent knew this. That is why he viewed Chautauqua as a necessary corrective. It was an effort to prove that in an appropriate setting people did not have to segment their lives. Protestant leaders who stressed obviously pious activities and who let their fears about the world turn their churches into defensive fortresses were not providing solutions. Being a good Christian in church was easy. The hard part was to make Christian conscience relevant to other life activities. Multiplying the episodes of formal religious observance got the Christian community nowhere. It was an unbalanced discipline. Trying to make certain that people were busily at work whenever they were not in church was equally misguided. A proper Protestantism sought to provide men and women with Christian ways to carry on all life activities.

The original Chautauqua Sunday School Institutes lasted for two weeks and were organized around lessons, sermons, devotional meetings, *plus* concerts, fireworks, bonfires, humorous lectures, and music in both light and serious forms. The "Department of Entertainment" was a central element. Vincent insisted: "Away with the heresy that man is stepping aside from his legitimate work as a Christian minister when he is trying to turn all secular nature into an altar for the glory of God." Chautauqua, in his mind, expanded the opportunities and occasions for Christian behavior. Programs generated more programs. The Chautauqua Literary and Scientific Circle, which started in 1878, aimed to promote valuable reading. "All knowledge," Vincent argued, "religious or secular, is sacred to him who reverently surrenders himself to God."[9] Every year, people who had in their homes stuck with a correspondence course of assigned books, journeyed to the now famous lake in western New York for "Recognition Day," "the great day of the annual gathering." The ceremony to honor them took place in the "Hall in the Grove," an open-sided structure that permitted the participants to look beyond the busts of Plato, Socrates, Homer, Virgil, Goethe, and Shakespeare, which lined the space, to the splendor of their wooded setting.[10]

By the turn of the century, those who visited Chautauqua to hear lectures by distinguished preachers, college presidents, authors and editors, leaders in social reform, politicians, and distinguished foreigners (as well as to play golf and tennis) were no longer primarily Sunday-school teachers. Six American presidents spoke at Chautauqua.[11] Chautauqua had become a non-profit business that marketed Christianity and other great ideas. It offered a cultural commodity that high-toned people purchased in almost the same way that they purchased the furnishings for their middle-class Victorian homes. To make the transaction easier, Chautauqua distributed its product to local markets. Imitative institutions formed in towns and in attractive vacation spots across the Northeast and Midwest. A good part of the operation's monthly newspaper, *The Chautauquan*, was given over to "organization hints" for how to run a local circle. Chautauqua, as a chain store of Protestant values, succeeded in shaping important aspects of American taste. Its strategy was comparable to that of the mail-order catalogues of Richard Sears and A. C. Roebuck.

These references to retail trade are not meant as metaphors. They apply literally. The people who kept Chautauqua going knew the value of advertising. They published testimonials from pleased consumers of their product who came from all over the country, in fact the world, and from all walks of life. These make interesting reading, particularly for the evidence they furnish of how easily many Americans mixed the ambition to rise up the economic ladder with religious exertion. Thus, a dry-goods clerk, who followed the course of the Literary and Scientific Circle, testified that its influence "has opened up to me a future of glorious possibilities and has aroused my ambition." Endeavoring "to rise above my present circumstances, and to gain a place of influence and usefulness in the world," he said that "many of the young men associated with me in the church have experienced the same benefit." A graduate of the University of Michigan credited the course with helping him pass a four-year college program in three years: "for this I am deeply grateful to you, and above all to our Heavenly Father who has crowned each effort with success." A Methodist Episcopal minister said of the course: "It gives me a leverage upon the younger members of my congregation, and the more intelligent part of the community, which as a pastor I desire to hold." Cultural capital gave evidence of God's blessing and was as useful as money—so went the testimony of women, seamen, mill workers, railroad conductors, mothers, students, and businessmen.[12]

Chautauqua, as it outgrew its Methodist camp-meeting roots, eased the way for Protestant ministers to change their minds as more of them in the late nineteenth century shifted from being negative to positive about leisure.[13] Some announced their new attitudes almost as if they were unveiling a revelation. They turned on the disciplinary practices of their parents, recalling with dismay harsh prohibitions that had made them miserable as children. No longer did Protestants have to bear the "antagonism" that historically had existed between Christianity and "popular amusements." Washington Gladden, whose career became synonymous with the Social Gospel movement, recited an all-American painful moment from his youth. When he was twelve and considering the state of his immortal soul, he struggled with his belief that salvation "involved the sacrifice of baseball." This spiritual dilemma lacked something of the depths we associate with the torments of Saint Augustine. Still, Gladden faced a crossroads. To him it was a sweet vision indeed that convinced him of the moral probity of holding a ball and bat in his hands. However, he asked, did Christians ever manage to believe "that the only enjoyment deemed strictly legitimate for the eminent saint was religious rapture."[14]

As it turned out, Gladden's break with the past was hedged all round with doubts and reservations. Such are the crab-like movements of progress. Like most other Protestant ministers, Gladden showed little enthusiasm for moving beyond his spirited defense of having fun into energetic efforts to make an honorable truce with the world of commercial entertainment. His Protestant conscience saw too many problems with the ways that even churched people chose to play. Baseball was one thing. Spectator sports associated with gambling were another. The fact that lectures ought to be amusing did not justify "coarse" comedies. At his boldest, Gladden questioned "casuistic efforts" to draw up firm categories of "clean" and "unclean" amusements. Expansively, he listed "wholesome" diversions. Christians could skate, boat, attend reading circles, play tennis, sing in group chorals, run, swim, do gymnastics, camp, ride, picnic, fish, act in private theatricals, garden, and do woodcraft.[15] When the list ran out, however, Gladden returned to conventional moralizing.

The conservative drag on Gladden's attitudes was evident in the way he framed the need for pleasure. Amusements had to have a purpose. Even recreations without an overtly serious side to them, like lying on a beach, aimed "to increase the power and readiness for work." Idleness was preparation to endeavor. With Gladden, moral sponsorship remained all important. Churches, he recognized, could not supply the greater part of people's recreational needs. That left many unsafe zones where, in the absence of intervention, people might go astray. Whenever Gladden talked about entertainments not controlled by churches or their close affiliates, his upbeat mood swung very far down. Since commercial amusements rested "wholly on a pecuniary basis," they could not be trusted to reinforce the right attitudes. The quickest profits pandered to perverse taste. Gladden's self-styled progressive spirit was consistent with a firm belief in censorship, the official censorship of Christian men and women acting politically in their communities. They had a duty to close down debauchery, to publicize the moral inadequacies of commercial leisure, and to call upon government and philanthropic organizations to set up alternate forms of amusement.[16]

Prudishness was in some ways more pronounced in a liberal-minded clergyman than in one who thought that any mention of fun was essentially un-Christian. The former's debt to his severe upbringing was evident in the anguish he spent debating fine points. He argued with like-minded colleagues about whether a professional sport like baseball could be morally uplifting on Wednesday but damnable on Sunday. Together, they worried about "guilt-by-association" questions. If an activity might in certain circumstances encourage drinking and gambling, then was the activity evil *per se*? "What-it-might-lead-to" arguments produced equal heat. Dancing and card-playing, some said, might seem innocent, but they stimulated the wrong appetites. Gladden's religious prescriptions about what people ought to be doing by way of diversion continued to favor what was "educational."

His favorite example of an innovative non-church institution that successfully housed piety and play under the same roof was Cleveland's People's Tabernacle, a public enterprise that exposed large audiences "composed mainly of workingmen and their families," "clad in Sunday clothes," neat, bright, and decorous, to two and a half hours of interpretation of "the masterpieces of English poetry." How much better this, "an incarnate Gospel," than the cheap theater, "where they would often have their prejudices roused and their hearts inflamed against their more prosperous neighbors; for the cheap theatre is one of the mouthpieces of the communist." The People's Tabernacle was applied Christianity, "wisely-managed Christianity."[17]

Chautauqua's sponsors, for all their untroubled endorsement of various recreational activities, also illustrated the unconscious need to pull back a step with every two steps forward. For example, Chautauqua showed a bit of daring by maintaining a novelist in residence. Mrs. G. R. Alden ("Pansy") spent summers at Chautauqua from 1873 to 1895 and wrote about a hundred twenty books.[18] The publications of Chautauqua recognized fiction as an important part of literature. Yet caution followed the apparent boldness. Almost instantly in any discussion of books, an editorial note reminded Chautauquans that "information reading" was superior to made-up stories. According to the movement's journal, "there are plenty of good novels; but one a month is a very large supply, probably an overdose for a well-organized mind. One a year would probably be a safer prescription."[19] The prescribed reading for people pursuing one of Chautauqua's courses included history, geography, science, and literature. Chautauqua students read about the works of famous writers and dramatists. They were given plot summaries to study. The novels themselves stayed off the course lists.

That is difficult logic to follow, yet for all its tortuous course, it was a step forward. If we are not witnessing a clean break with the past, we are marking the point at which the number of Protestant endorsements of leisure made many of the reservations irrelevant. Compared to what attitudes had been seventy years earlier, most Protestant ministers had moved a considerable distance. Victorian they remained. Play was best when it sounded like hard work. The difference was that a Protestant day was not complete without a period specifically devoted to leisure. Leisure no longer belonged in a category of things to avoid. It was now an onerous duty.

Like the YMCA, Chautauqua appealed mainly to people who were already safely and securely Protestant. They were the ones who most readily accepted as entertainment five illustrated lectures on the art of cooking, prefaced by prayer and reminders that religion was essential to education. On the other hand, the built-in security of Chautauqua allowed organizers to take certain things for granted. They did not have to mention religion all the time. They could rely upon a morality that was diffused through a light-hearted atmosphere. Consistent with their belief that it was wrong to divide the day into "times for religion" and "times for something else," they did not find it necessary to remind people that everything they did was equivalent to worship. The best proof of a religious environment was when the formal symbols of religion could be left in the background. Saying that placed many of the activities of commercial culture within the reach of redemption.

A Social Organization for Moral Work

The Women's Christian Temperance Union maintained its offices and held its national meetings in cities, but it was an institution rooted in small-town Protestant America. Founded with John Vincent's aid within the precincts of Chautauqua in 1874, it became one of the largest organizations of privately mobilized citizens in late nineteenth-century America. It was the largest and most important organization of American women. Its first national convention in Cleveland in November 1874 elected Annie Wittenmyer as president.[20] Prior to assuming the leadership of the WCTU, she had been the founder of the Methodist Home Missionary Society, the editor of the *Christian Woman* (a Methodist newspaper), and a former member of the Sanitary Commission. Like their president, the original members of the organization were steeped in the culture of Sunday schools, evangelical mass meetings, prayer services, and missionary societies. They were Protestant to the core, and they were determined to influence public life in the United States.

The WCTU might as well have been the political arm of Chautauqua. It was a multipurpose organization that blended its religious aims with legislative goals and the need to provide women with a useful and satisfying social life. As a social organization, the WCTU's leadership recognized that leisure posed special problems for middle-class women. Since most of them did not have jobs or careers, and since many of them had servants to help with domestic duties, they had time on their hands. Boredom was a chronic problem. Nervous breakdowns seemed almost part of the female life cycle. Alcoholism and suicide were possibilities. These unpleasant consequences of middle-class domesticity made the issue of providing women with proper leisure activities urgent. This was doubly so since a woman's choice among leisure options reflected on her character. A man's pleasures were more or less expected to be errant now and then. So long as he behaved himself most of the week, his lapses did not destroy his reputation. A woman's leisure had to be unambiguously moral, all the time. Men entertained themselves by going to saloons. The women in the WCTU found their amusement in closing them down.

The fame of the WCTU is most closely tied to Frances Willard, who served as president of the organization from 1879 until her death in 1898. Willard poses an interesting case of leadership. In her challenges to the status quo, she strictly observed conservative form. Willard pushed the WCTU beyond temperance. She prodded it to embrace women's suffrage and to explore ways to advance the rights of trade unionists. Determined to make the WCTU more than a debating society for wives of businessmen, she befriended leaders of the Knights of Labor. At the same time, she kept the WCTU away from confrontational tactics and anything that might bring upon it a reputation for sympathy with "foreign" radicalism. The social agenda of the WCTU focused on the home. Willard justified her legislative goals as "home protection" measures. Temperance controlled a husband's brutality; trade unions won better wages for those responsible for the economic support of families; women's suffrage provided a political voice for mothers.

As for leisure, Willard's views and practices also mixed innovation and caution. She did not countenance frivolity. As late as 1886, she was warning women not to read novels. A historical "story" was an acceptable and useful pastime, whereas fiction placed readers in "an artificial relation to life." It filled them with "evanescent and unreal" pleasure. Willard summed up the practice of novel-reading as "a sort of spiritual hasheesh eating . . . , a fevered and fantastic vision of utter unreality."

Women needed always to cultivate time, not kill it.[21] In other writing, Willard exhibited an implacable hostility toward commercial entertainment that made Gladden's standards seem permissive by comparison. So where was the fun? How did the WCTU help bring religion into a closer association with commercial culture?

Actually the main formula that Willard followed in promoting leisure for women repeated the rationale of the Chautauqua Society: make leisure sound serious, give it an underlying moral purpose, and then let people relax. The formula was not a ploy. Willard was a serious woman whose plans to liberate women involved calling them to fame on a world stage. The books that she wrote for women had such aggressive and daunting titles as *How to Win* and *Do Everything*. She was not worried about women being led by their imputed weaknesses into sin. Her fears for women were about their passiveness. They let opportunities slip by. The problem with novels was not their reputed appeal to overheated female passions; it was rather their diverting ability to tempt women into neglecting serious ambition. "I am a wrestler for the laurel in life's Olympian games. I can make history, why should I maunder in a hammock and read the endless repetitions of romance?"[22]

Having made her claim to serious purpose, Willard saw to it that meetings of the WCTU provided diversion. The members of the organization were an audience, her audience. Willard, a talented platform orator, had developed a taste for performance while working at temperance camp meetings and for Chicago's master revivalist Dwight Moody. She understood theater. In arranging a convention, she lingered over the details of stage-setting. She wanted neither the ambience of a "funeral" nor the "forlorn aspect of a Lyceum stage." Her assistants "thought that if Henry Irving, the greatest of English actors, had built up not a little of his reputation by the unrivalled, artistic skill with which his plays were put upon the stage, they could well afford, for the splendid real drama of the 'Home Protection' Cause, to arrange such a picture as should remind each person present of home itself!" Willard "beautified" her platforms with plants and vines, easy chairs, warm rugs, an easel, a Bible, and a hymn book. The scene was not quite like home since homes were not festooned with flags and brightly colored silk banners or filled with marching and singing children. Willard wanted spectacle. She added a choir of three hundred voices that burst forth not with "doleful ditties" but with "choruses that could but key the audience to concert pitch and put the speaker's soul in tune." The purpose of all this was to enable good speakers to "bring down the house."[23] Members and spectators who purchased reserved seats and filled meetings at New York City's Metropolitan Opera House expected to enjoy themselves.

Frances Willard, then, along with America's most effective religious leaders, was taking cues from commercial culture even as she criticized it. She demonstrated a considerable talent for encouraging and exploiting the media. Her enthusiasm for the press was especially warm. Journalism, she said, held great opportunities for women. Women reporters would do "for journalism what they long ago accomplished for literature—to drive out the Fieldings and the Smolletts from its temple; to replace sentimentality by sentiment; to frown upon coarse jests, debasing innuendoes, and irreverent witticisms. . . . " They would carry perfumes rather than tobacco fumes into the "editorial and reportorial sanctums" and bring to reporting the concerns of the home.[24] To contemporary feminist sensibilities, gender stereotypes take on an alarmingly upbeat resonance in Willard's prose. Gender stereotypes were part of her conservative form. She believed in them and saw no reason why they could not be used to support her ambitions for women: "The daily press, which has already become the people's university, is to be the pulpit and the forum of the future. Here woman has a place to stand, a pulpit ready from which no ecclesiastic edict can exclude her."

Willard relied extensively on journalism and other forms of publishing to advance the work of the WCTU. Its robust financial health, which had been anemic until the 1880s, resulted from the print empire that Willard built. She merged a string of temperance newspapers to begin publishing the *Union Signal* in Chicago on the first day of 1883. A year later it had fourteen thousand subscribers, and by 1900 it was the largest women's paper in the world, with a circulation close to a hundred thousand. It carried stories, poems, and other "diverting" features and made enough money through subscriptions and advertising to pay a dividend to the stockholders. In addition to the *Union Signal*, the Women's Temperance Publishing Association published two periodicals for children, a German-language newspaper, books, and two million pamphlets a year. With annual receipts of over a hundred eighty thousand dollars it employed over a hundred persons, most of them women.[25] Willard aimed to appoint in every town in the United States a press superintendent whose job was to influence the editor of the local paper. "There is to my mind," she said, "nothing secular but everything sacred in the contemplation of the press department through which we have as White Ribbon women, spread the pure light of a pure life over nations fast and far."[26] Summed up, the WCTU became a business that mixed diversion with high purpose and provided jobs. It pioneered a variety of Christian advertising and marketing methods that became extremely important to churches in the late nineteenth and twentieth centuries.

The WCTU recognized and applauded people's need for sociability. Its formula for rescuing sociability from moral debasement supplied a strong pattern for life in many small Protestant communities. Like Chautauqua and the YMCA, the goal was to bring people together in social settings where a Christian ethos prevailed without a need for the heavy hand of prayer and theological sermons. Meetings of the WCTU were caricatured but not well characterized by the many cartoon pictures of Carrie Nation wielding her hatchet against the saloon door. In fact, those who formed the WCTU no longer believed that unsmiling people who lived and died for religious meetings could build a Christian culture in America. Although the official delegates to WCTU conventions proudly declared themselves Sunday-school teachers, although Willard regarded the WCTU as "part and parcel of the Church," the organization embraced a range of activities that sought to make religion an intrusive but pleasure-giving influence on everyday life.[27] Its members were not prepared to privatize religion; nor were they prepared to concede that the market-place of culture was an arena where religious values had no importance. As a non-profit operation, the WCTU adopted relevant techniques from profit-making enterprises to sell Americans the moral standards that religious leaders were determined to force upon them in one way or another.

The Uses and Misuses of Thomas Edison's Inventions

The sorts of entertainment promoted by Chautauqua and the WCTU led occasionally to direct cooperation between their leaders and the merchants of American show business. Neither side had any reason to discourage cooperation so long as a moral canopy erected in the marketplace allowed room for profit. Many promoters of commercial amusements who operated in modest-sized towns and in rural areas sought out religious leaders as useful allies. In turn, religious leaders learned to value skilled showmen who stayed within their moral guidelines and at the same time taught them new ways to find audiences. When P. T. Barnum died in 1891, most of his clerical opponents had died, shut up, or changed their tune. Most successful men are honored if they live long enough. In Barnum's case, the honor owed something to the belated but general recognition that the word "wholesome" really did apply to his enterprises.

Movies were to cause a lot of problems for religious leaders. In the early days, there were promising signs of a congenial relationship. Most of our historical attention has focused on the urban nickelodeon craze that in the first years of the twentieth century set off moral protests in places as diverse as New York City, Chicago, Houston, and Worcester. But in some locales, the first movie entertainments were closer to what

Thomas Edison had said he wanted them to be.[28] The "Wizard of Menlo Park," who became the son-in-law of Lewis Miller (one of Chautauqua's founders), contributed not only to the technology of film projection but also invented two other things that revolutionized mass culture in the early twentieth century—the electric light and the phonograph. Edison cultivated an image of himself as a practical man of simple pleasures. He wanted his inventions to educate as well as entertain. Although he had no faith in Christianity or the dogmas of any organized religion, he did believe in an orderly universe overseen by a "Supreme Intelligence" who rewarded moral behavior.[29]

The man behind the myth was a complex figure. Edison ruthlessly pursued financial gains from his inventions. As a powerful figure in the early film-production industry, he was not especially vigilant in holding his product to high moral standards. Yet in 1907, when movies ran into serious censorship trouble, Edison declared that "nothing is of greater importance to the success of the motion picture interests than films of good moral tone."[30] The statement was in part a business calculation. It was also in part a resurgence of conviction. Edison's long life allowed him to witness many commercial applications of his inventions that troubled him. He had not foreseen the neoned illumination of Times Square, the recording of "Negro-inspired," "lascivious" dance music, or Hollywood films about adulterous relationships. About some of these developments, he harbored reservations, especially ones he no longer controlled or profited from. Religious moralists were more outspoken. The controversies they started made it hard to recall a period when churches had welcomed commercial phonograph and movie exhibitors in their places of worship.

Once upon a time, it had happened. Charles Musser has rescued this chapter of entertainment history in a fascinating biography of Lyman H. Howe, the most successful of a band of traveling exhibitors who in the 1890s applied recordings and film to commercial amusement. Unlike the people who profited from urban nickelodeons, Howe trimmed his exhibitions to fit the moral norms of Protestant America.[31] Into the first decade of the twentieth century, he put before small-town audiences a "sanitized alternative" to urban commercial culture. A resident of Wilkes-Barre, Pennsylvania, Howe moved with his shows around his home state and in parts of New York. He avoided the largest cities. The communities that he worked in ranged in size from five thousand to seventy-five thousand people.

Howe built his first entertainments totally around phonographic concerts. Typically they consisted of band music, interspersed with selections of church chimes, the recitation of a biblical parable, and perhaps a brief sermon. Although little of the recorded music was specifically sacred,

Howe avoided ballads and love songs that were the staples of "nickel-in-the-slot-phonographs" found in urban saloons. In 1896 Howe began to add motion pictures to his programs. His film "concerts," lasting up to two hours, quickly achieved a popularity that retired the phonograph from the concert stage into home use. As before, variety was the key to his success. Howe did not try to stick to a single subject. He appealed to people's wandering curiosity. His shows consisted mostly of travelogue and newsreel material—a ride on the Black Diamond Express, a view of President McKinley at the Pan-American Exhibition where he was assassinated, scenes of firemen at work, incidents of the Spanish-American War. Whatever the fare, Howe enticed people to crowd into his "concerts" by promising them a thrill. Illustrated, broadside advertisements pictured attentive audiences watching an onrushing train or a great steam vessel at sea. They were the first movie trailers, promising "Life! Motion! Realism!" Howe, who billed himself as "the Barnum of them All," ran together the adjectives "Astonishing! Thrilling! Refined!"

Howe managed the oxymoron "refined thrill" because he carefully nurtured his reputation as a "high-class" exhibitor. To do that, he did not have to make his programs religious. Except for a filmed version of the Oberammergau Passion Play (produced by the Eden Musee in New York City and screened by various exhibitors in 1898), few of the short selections that he exhibited had anything to do with religious subjects.[32] He billed them as moral entertainment all the same and won the endorsement of religious leaders. It was not difficult. Mostly, he avoided showing films that he knew would arouse moral objections—the Corbett–Fitzsimmons fight for example. For the rest, he simply courted religious sponsorship and arranged to hold many of his shows in churches and in YMCAs (which often had more seats than any other building in town, sometimes seating over a thousand people). The religious sponsors received a benefit in return since part of the proceeds went to the sponsoring organizations. Howe's exhibits were a way for churches to raise money. In the 1896–97 and 1897–98 seasons, Howe exhibited in thirteen opera houses or theaters, thirteen churches, and thirteen halls, mostly YMCAs. Of the twenty-five religious groups that sponsored him, Methodists were the most numerous, followed closely by Baptists, and then Congregationalists, Lutherans, and Presbyterians. During the off-season summer months, Howe found eager sponsors on the Chautauqua circuit.

The General Conference of Methodist churches went on banning the commercial entertainments of the city, while small-town Methodists were sitting in church basements watching a film showing people enjoying themselves in Luna Park at Coney Island. The citizens of Wilkes-Barre and Allentown and Owego who went to Howe's exhibitions reaped the full benefits of the logic made popular by Chautauqua. They enjoyed morally secure entertainment that did not bombard them with explicit religious and moral instruction. They could have their thrills with a pastor present who did not utter so much as a single "amen." Possibly, we should recognize a good bit of hypocrisy in these arrangements, at the very least some moral evasions. Yet what was going on is better described as a process of cultural negotiation that was important to both sides. Leaders in many American communities, and not just the ministers, placed a concern for virtue at the top of their social and political agenda. Religiously grounded morality was as much a public concern as it ever had been. What was needed were new public programs to meet this goal. Popular commercial culture was inventive, seductive, and not finally avoidable. The church officials who invited Howe into their sanctuaries recognized that Protestant churches were in no position to attack commercial culture on the grounds of profit-seeking alone. Howe's religious sponsors also wanted money. It was necessary to build more churches and to sustain charitable and missionary endeavors. What ministers hoped to find was a way to make a profit for themselves by promoting cultural activities that served the moral standards they wanted to normalize in American communities.

The logic was consistent with the innovations begun by religious leaders in the first part of the nineteenth century. Chautauqua and other innovations led to bolder and more ambitious steps. So long as commercial entertainments bowed to community insistence on sobriety and orderly behavior, almost any kind of gaiety and fantasy and spectacle became, in theory, permissible. At some point, Protestant religious moralists stopped worrying about imagination, the quality of the human mind that earlier had rendered so many forms of commercial culture suspect. By the last decade of the nineteenth century, the grand traveling circuses of Ringling Brothers Barnum and Bailey passed in some quarters as the epitome of wholesome entertainment. To say that troops of elephants and high-wire acrobats instructed and edified was a long stretch or a definite break from religious and moral attitudes that prevailed in 1800. It is, nonetheless, possible to see that the earlier attitudes were both flexible, permitting the changes that happened, and stubbornly persistent, reappearing in all the justifications that accompanied the changes.

Southern Male Honor and the Evangelical Spirit

Northern white Protestant leaders who surveyed the country at the end of the nineteenth century found reasons to judge it the best of times and the worst of times. Much of the earlier foundation for a secure moral order had vanished. Clergymen were keenly aware that they had lost their preeminent position in many areas of public life they formerly had dominated. Still, one of the first things that Americans did as they moved across the country was to build churches. Northern moralists always took comfort in looking at the South. The region reminded them that matters could be worse.

Their view of the South was not entirely accurate. In fact, after the Civil War the prospects for Protestant hegemony were greater below the Mason-Dixon Line than above it. There were fewer cities there to corrupt behavior. The region was relatively untouched by the new immigration that before and after the Civil War dramatically changed the ethnic and religious makeup of northern cities. That meant that the South had few Catholics. New Orleans was the New York City of Dixie, but in both economic and cultural terms its influence did not extend very far through the South. The rural South had its own labor problems, complicated enormously by racial divisions. White Southerners took a mixed comfort, however, in knowing that the region's poorest people, the newly freed African Americans, were securely churched in a Protestant fashion. After the Civil War, church growth in the South was even more impressive than in the North.

On the other hand, history pressed a heavy weight on southern life. Much of it did not favor Protestant morality. In the first part of the nineteenth century, the privileged white males of the future Confederate states had internalized a set of values that had little to do with evangelical Christianity's restrictions on drinking, swearing, and brawling. The contrast with the North was striking. There, the internalization of a Christian conscience was the essence of middle-classness.[33] It was at the core of the process of class formation. The southern male code of honor instead emphasized aggression, revenge, and swagger. Southern gentlemen learned polite rules of courtliness, but these rules served romance, family ties, and paternalism, not Christian charity. Ministers did not count for much unless they had personal connections to landed wealth.[34]

The Second Great Awakening of the early nineteenth century was a southern as well as a northern phenomenon. Baptists and Methodists became the largest church denominations in the South, sweeping up many of the unchurched common people. For various reasons, however, antebellum evangelical fervor in the South had fewer visible moral consequences on white society than in the North. For one thing, the slave system needed defending. Evangelical religion learned not to do anything that disturbed the South's peculiar institution even as it worked to teach Christianity to the slaves. Efforts by churches to intrude morally into public life bore the taint of northern fanaticism, especially the fanaticism of William Lloyd Garrison. As a result, white male behavior in the ante-bellum South did not much change. At all social levels, males learned a careless, self-indulgent sort of enjoyment that was immune to clerical criticism. The church of the gentry class, the Episcopal church, was not inclined toward the moral discipline of its members in any case. Good Episcopals hunted and fished and rode horses. The streets and squares of southern towns were male preserves where single and married men swore, loafed, drank, and gambled. Cock fights were popular along with games that allowed men to pit their strength against one another.[35]

Northern religious moralists looking at the traditional pleasures of the South might have found reason to reconsider the suspicious and negative way they judged the rise of commercial culture in their own territory. Popular theater, cheap romances and adventure tales, museums featuring nature's oddities, pleasure gardens, lectures on modern miracles—none of these things that worried northern ministers were especially wide-spread in the South. That was because of the South's rural character. In southern cities like Charleston and Savannah, people supported concerts and stage plays. Indeed, they held few biases against the theater.[36] Yet in southern towns and farm areas, popular culture remained much closer to rites of socializing that belonged to a past without a strong market economy. Little of it, by Protestant moral standards, was reassuring.

In contrast, the sort of orderly rules that people were learning in the North by exposure to commercial amusements constituted an impressive achievement as judged by Protestant norms. The rise of family entertain-ment was a sign of acquired moral comportment. Much of the North's pulp fiction was a veritable schoolhouse in teaching people to respect a sentimental humanitarianism. Although the moral comparisons that northern Protestant clerics drew between North and South ran heavily in the North's favor, it took them a long time to see that part of the North's advantage might lie in the operation of its commercial culture. They eventually got the point, but slowly.

Evangelicals in the South had to rely mostly on their own church insti-tutions to reform behavior. With the spread of revivals, they made prog-ress. Revivals provided the occasion for a good time, a festive meal, the exchange of gossip, and the courting rituals of the young. For the major-ity of Southerners, this was better than the liturgical worship offered by Episcopal churches. The latter was theatrical but cold and evocative of the ties that existed between religious and social privilege. Baptist and Methodist meetings were lively. Considered severe in their moral stan-dards, they offered their converts surrogates for many of the pleasures they were supposed to renounce.[37] In their own way, which in the South had only sporadic help from the region's elite, southern evangelicals began to war against the South's traditional forms of amusement. Concerns about moral order grew stronger in the postwar South because of fears about the collapse of the South's social structure. For many whites, the end of the slave system destroyed the region's most important means of social control. Suddenly it mattered much more how the white population conducted itself. Proper conduct extended to the uses of leisure time.

Postwar southern Protestant leaders still had few of the institutional aids that their northern counterparts had developed to influence popular culture. There were no tract and temperance societies, no thriving lyceum organizations, no traces of the YMCA or Chautauqua. Under these circumstances, the religious achievement was, in fact, astonishing. One minister claimed of the southern states that "there is no part of the world in which ministers of the Gospel are more respected." According to another: "The controlling sentiment of the Southern people in city and hamlet, in camp and field, among the white and the black, has been religious."[38] Membership in southern Methodist churches doubled in the fifteen years following the war. Among whites, they along with Baptist churches established a virtual stranglehold on church members, accounting for 94 percent of them in Mississippi and Alabama and 81 percent in Virginia where the Episcopals might have been expected to be more formidable rivals. Nationwide, Baptists and Methodists accounted for about 47 percent of Protestant church membership. According to Edwin A. Alderman, the president of the University of Virginia, "The fancied home of the cavalier is the home of the nearest approach to puritanism and to the most vital protestant evangelicalism in the world to-day."[39]

Southern aversion to moral legislation that was associated with northern abolitionists faded dramatically. Southerners were latecomers to the temperance movement, but by the 1870s they were ready to make up for lost time. The results of local-option legislation passed by most southern states created broad and long-lasting bans on the sale of alcoholic beverages. When national prohibition arrived following World War I, there was not much commercial liquor business left to outlaw in the South. Southern evangelical churches continued to discipline their members for moral offenses after most of the northern churches had given up the effort. Southern Protestants turned enthusiastically to Blue Laws. Legislation against swearing, against cock-fighting and gambling, and against sporting events on the Sabbath suddenly made the South the stronghold of Protestant power to set moral norms. Legislative wars that northern evangelicals had largely lost by the middle of the nineteenth century were just warming up in the South. Religion was an independent force that had not yet had to strike many bargains with commercial culture. The latter was growing in the South but not on a scale to match northern innovations. Bereft of traditional pleasures and not yet introduced to modern ones, the postwar South had a leisure problem to match its lack-of-work problem.[40]

Actually the Protestant South was never in danger of overtaking Boston's reputation for censorship. Aside from alcohol and Sunday sports, legislation did not succeed in banning much. A great deal went on outside the law. The South was too tangled up in trying to deal with its racial divisions to worry about every fistfight and backwoods still. By the 1890s, it had ruinously overextended its political and economic resources to police a program of racial segregation. The white southern male showed a strong resistance to prudery. Southern evangelicalism doubtlessly did something to corral male immorality. It even expanded the public influence of women. There remained a long way to go. Organized religion did almost nothing to extirpate the violent side of male behavior that was forever complicated by racial scapegoating. The white Protestant mind envisioned Providence as something that manifested itself in "just" lynchings. Southern evangelical preachers were often themselves just a step away from a morally disordered past. A territory of dry counties, of divorceless families, of Bible-reading Baptist and Pentecostal churches, the American South was also uncommonly murderous. The number of crimes of violence against people was much higher in the South than in the North; crimes against property, much lower.[41] People clung to religion and its moral restrictiveness out of desperate social need, but their grip kept slipping.

The most obvious success of evangelical religion in the South was the conversion of African Americans to Christianity. Slaves became Christians and remained Christian after emancipation. It is impossible to find a consensus about just what this mass conversion meant to the collective psychology of American blacks—especially in relation to the implications for political action.[42] The Christianity of white southern Protestants, which was supposed to be what blacks had learned, was a religion of social hierarchy that put African Americans at the bottom. The only thing that whites expected Christianity to do for the slave population was to make it meek and subservient. In the white mind, Christian humility meant that blacks ought to accept low status and discrimination. The African-American understanding of Christianity was, of course, something else. Slave and emancipated blacks never accepted the meanings of their religion placed upon it by white Christians. Their Christianity shielded them in various ways from the oppressive abuses of southern white racism. Within it were the seeds to overturn southern society.

The military defeat and consequent impoverishment of great sections of the South made the Old Testament message of unjust suffering followed by deliverance, adapted with such force in African-American Christianity, relevant to many southern whites. Christianity in Dixie was a way to rescue hope from a situation of deeply felt powerlessness. The need for economic redemption was about the only thing in southern life that settled equally on its segregated parts. That did not prove to be a sufficient basis for common cause. Although southern white evangelical churches were in the same gospel boat as African-American churches, the shared plight worked to sharpen the racial divisions. Economic insecurities prompted whites to strengthen their social hierarchy based on race. The Christianity of southern whites at its very best did no more than transmute racism into benevolent paternalism. It regarded the emotionalism of African-American Christianity as a sign of backwardness, of an innate, ineradicable primitiveness. The more emotion in black religion, the more assured southern white Protestants became that they were taking care of an inferior race that accepted its subordination.

Meanwhile, African Americans used their religious resources to create a cultural life for themselves separate from that of white Protestants. Free blacks in the North formed the first African-American churches in the early nineteenth century. The prejudice of white Christians who would not permit African Americans to kneel in common prayer beside them led Richard Allen, Absalom Jones, and others to create their own churches. The Abyssinian Baptist Church in New York City, the First African Baptist Church in Philadelphia, the African Methodist Episcopal Church, and the African Methodist Episcopal Zion Church were some of the results. The example of assertive independence was crucial. When freedom came to the southern slaves some decades later, the emancipated African Americans discovered that their options for economic and social advancement were almost as restricted as they had been under slavery. They had some important choices to make, however. One of the first was the decision to keep their religious life separate.

Much, really too much, was demanded of the southern black churches that were formed in the late nineteenth century. Within the African-American community there were no other institutions of comparable importance. Black churches had to teach children and adults how to read. They were the locus of political activity. They served as banks, insurance companies, and providers of shelter.[43] The financial resources they possessed to deal with these expectations were simply not adequate. African-American churches were poor. They carried the burden of racist stereotypes heaped upon them by mocking whites. The one thing they had, which stood out on a Protestant church landscape where money was becoming a major determinant of religious prestige, was an unabashed spiritual expressiveness.

W. E. B. Du Bois wrote in *The Souls of Black Folk:* "The Methodists and Baptists of America owe much of their condition to the silent but potent influence of their millions of Negro converts. Especially is this noticeable in the South, where theology and religious philosophy are on this account a long way behind the North, and where the religion of the poor whites is a plain copy of Negro thought and methods. The mass of 'gospel' hymns which has swept through American churches and well-nigh ruined our sense of song consists largely of debased imitations of Negro melodies made by ears that caught the jingle but not the music, the body but not the soul, of the Jubilee songs. It is thus clear that the study of Negro religion is not only a vital part of the history of the Negro in America, but no uninteresting part of American history."[44]

In a few words, Du Bois made a number of points worth pursuing. One is that the soul of the African-American church lay in its music. Other Americans could hear the powerful feeling even if they heard it badly and refused to recognize the creative inventiveness of it. "Debasements" of the slave spiritual opened the way for the commercialization of African-American music.[45] Black church music has not been the only religious musical tradition in the United States that has been commercialized. The late nineteenth-century revivals of Dwight Moody turned the gospel singing of Ira Sankey into a marketable commodity. We have today the Mormon Tabernacle Choir. The African-American case had the most important consequences, however, for the music went on influencing American popular music right down to rock 'n' roll. Also, to pick up a second point from Du Bois, this particular example of commercialization raised significant questions about exploitation and corruption.

Already in the late nineteenth century, the Fisk Jubilee Singers, the creators of the Jubilee songs mentioned by Du Bois, were traveling around the United States, to England, to Holland, to Switzerland, and to Germany, raising money to transform their Nashville school into a university "dedicated to the Christian education and training of the emancipated slaves of America." The group, drawn from the larger Fisk Choir in 1871, cautiously built up a repertoire of black slave music. The Jubilee Singers were cautious because they worried about the effects of singing a music that might be labeled "unsophisticated." Spirituals had not been transcribed into written scores. The popularity of minstrel shows illustrated the dangers of providing white audiences with cultural material to reinforce racially demeaning stereotypes. Originally the Fisk Choir was drilled to sing "operatic music," "the more difficult and popular music of the day, composed by our best native and foreign artists."[46] The Jubilee Singers switched to the folk music of slaves because it was popular with the white audiences that were, for better and worse, their patrons.

Twenty of the first twenty-four singers to perform with the Jubilee group had been born into slavery. According to the carefully calculated press releases, all were Christian, and none used tobacco or drank. "Inspirational" books written to publicize the group picked up the well-worn formulas used in other cases when a religiously sponsored entertainment played to a paying public. The Jubilee Singers "furnished a refined and wholesome entertainment, which Christian people who did not care to visit the theatre and kindred places of amusement could attend and enjoy."[47] The churches and religious organizations who sponsored the Jubilee Singers also applied principles of shrewd business. They worked in cooperation with other institutions. Education, business, and the church—these three entities were becoming a sort of sacred American Trinity, separate and distinct and yet one. A promoter of the group wrote: "Nothing will make a market for the things produced in factories so surely as the school-house and the church. Nothing has made New England what she is to-day but her educational institutions—the church and the school."[48] This was the message that preceded the first northern performances of the Jubilee Singers; immediately followed by the singing of "What Shall the Harvest Be," it successfully opened pocketbooks.

The triumphs of the Jubilee Singers were not automatic. They had no audience of wealthy sponsors in the South, and the white audiences they depended on in the North were no freer of racial prejudice than any assemblage of the Ku Klux Klan. If they were more charitable toward "unfortunate" African Americans, it was only because their charity helped get the Fisk singers safely and distantly established back in Nashville. The first appearances of the Jubilee Singers, in Protestant churches and in town halls of the midwest, were for the most part financial disappointments. The cold consolation of the group was that it did not have to cover the costs of lodging. Few hotels would accept the singers as guests. Only when the group reached New York City and Boston did a financial harvest begin. By that time it had the important backing of Henry Ward Beecher, who opened his large Brooklyn Church to them. Also, the managers of the group, who worked for the American Missionary Society, had mastered better the principles of marketing, especially the need to give a key role to an advance agent. According to G. D. Pike, the group's business manager, as much as a hundred dollars was put aside for advertising a concert.

Although the programs of the Jubilee Singers contained mostly religious songs, Pike (like Lyman Howe) had learned something from Chautauqua: do not constantly hit people in the snout with piety. He calculated that the concerts, if they were going to make a substantial profit, had to attract a "general" audience. Therefore, he billed the concerts not as religious but as a "healthful pleasure." He was pleased with the results. People purchased concert tickets in the same spirit that they purchased "tropical fruit or a mountain excursion."[49] The early published accounts of the Jubilee Singers' tours read at one level like financial ledgers, a running diary of profits and losses—with good reason. The group earned at least a hundred thousand dollars for Fisk in its first three years of touring, a sum that was vital to the financial solvency of that institution.[50]

How much racial prejudice the concerts cleared away is another matter. Not much changed in Kentucky. The ever-exultant Pike recorded that when the group returned home from its first tour through Louisville a "hot-headed young man," who was protesting the group's attempt to purchase a first-class rail ticket, was silenced when he learned that the Jubilee Singers had just given a concert that grossed more than a thousand dollars. Pike did not mention the "applause of a cursing mob of one or two thousand people" when officials ejected the Jubilee Singers from the first-class waiting room.[51] He was not insensitive to the constant mistreatment of the group. He simply believed that money guaranteed moral triumph.

In one sense, Pike's enthusiasm was well-placed. The financial success of the Jubilee Singers proved a contagious example. They were soon rivaled by groups formed at Hampton and other African-American college-level institutions in the South. "Negro spirituals," what Du Bois called "sorrow songs," had found an audience. There was a downside to the popularity. In the nineteenth century, even the most well-intentioned white appropriators of African-American music were condescending. In an article published by the *Atlantic Monthly* in 1867, before the founding of the Fisk singers, Thomas Wentworth Higginson, unrepentant friend of John Brown and promoter of racial justice, recorded the words of "Negro Spirituals." He had heard them in South Carolina, Georgia, and Florida when he "approached some glimmering fire, round which the dusky figures moved in the rhythmical barbaric dance the negroes call a 'shout,' chanting, often harshly, but always in the most perfect time, some monotonous refrain."[52] Appreciative Higginson was, but the adjectives "simple," "elementary," and "barbaric" that he used in his article detracted from what he otherwise understood about the music and the words.

After the great success that the Jubilee Singers won in New York City, the press dubbed them "Beecher's Nigger Minstrels." In retrospect, it appears that white promoters and interpreters robbed African Americans of their own traditions. Beginning with Du Bois, many people have expressed regret about the commercialization of African-American slave music or, for that matter, any of the other ways that white promoters have marketed the rhythmic patterns of black culture. White revivalists, including Moody and Sankey, introduced African-American spirituals into their largely white meetings. White audiences equated African-American music with the songs of Stephen Foster. Fisk and Hampton singing groups sometimes included Foster's music in their programs, although it had first become popular in black-face minstrel shows.[53] To many whites, it all sounded the same anyway. White coloration of African-American "spirituals" was inevitable since whites first recorded the words and music in written form.

African-American commercial music in the United States originated in two places—their churches and the urban saloon cum brothel. In the first venue, there was religion; in the second, everything that the religious mind regarded as morally unsafe and crime-ridden.[54] The juxtaposition is interesting and perhaps not unique to the African-American case. American commercial culture in many other instances had the task of trying to build some sort of bridge between the sacred and the very profane. Religious leaders demanded morals, and popular taste leaned toward naughtier forms of fun. Soul music came from what was sung on Sunday morning in a black Baptist church or played on Saturday night in a Basin Street bordello. African-American religion is as impressive a testimony to the power of spiritual invention as anything we can locate in America's national past. It offered important consolations, kept alive perceptions of self-worth, and permitted people not merely to endure but to enjoy their lives. What its power could not for a long time transcend or seriously dent was a system that structurally ordained poverty for the vast majority of African Americans.

When the financial resources of the church failed, commercialization provided an avenue of assistance and an income for many black entertainers. The religious meaning of the music was not entirely lost, but it certainly operated in a different way. African-American society protected its spirit or soul or whatever you want to call what lies behind those rare and ineffable moments in religious experience when even non-believers recognize an emotional depth that is transforming. Not that that fact should be adequate compensation. As with so much else about African-American experience, white Americans claimed most of the profits when black religion became entertainment. They owned and operated the means of distribution. They provided the customers. If religious commercialization is something to be condemned, it is this sobering reality more than other that explains why.

CHAPTER SEVEN

Selling Religion in the Workplace:

Wage Earners and the Pressures of Marketed Morality

It is the culmination of Christianity—the City of God on earth, with its walls of jasper and its gates of pearl! It is the reign of the Prince of Peace!

Henry George on the effects of the single tax

In the 1860s, Philadelphia artisans organized the Knights of Labor. The ideological direction of this secret society, which became the first mass trade union in the United States, recalled the ideals of civic republicanism, ideals that independent craftsmen had emphasized earlier in the century to argue the dignity of skilled, self-directed work. The articulate and intensely political leaders of the Knights still stressed values and behavior that they associated with self-improvement. The most important of these were education, stable families, and temperance.[1] Fearing that common laborers wasted too much time on trashy amusements, the early leaders of the Knights, mostly Protestants, sponsored reading rooms, lecture series, dramatic presentations, and a didactic press. This was not imitation of bourgeois mores. Criticizing an unregulated free market that robbed workers of their job security and their moral fiber, they sought to create not a society governed by the principles of *laissez-faire* but an economy in which cooperative groups of productive workers exercised control.

Civic republicanism, adapted to the collective interests of workers, was the invention of skilled Protestant craftsmen who had resisted the translation of labor value into a fluctuating wage determined by demand. The resistance was doomed for many reasons, among the most important being the influx into the United States of large numbers of immigrants who needed work at any price. By the 1880s, the decade when the Knights of Labor gained its greatest national strength, the demographic base of American working-class movements had changed dramatically from what it had been fifty years earlier. Somewhere around 40 percent of the wage earners engaged in manufacturing and mining were immigrants. Along with those who were the children of immigrants or of African-American parentage, they constituted the vast majority of the country's industrial workers. Culturally, the balance had shifted from Protestant to Catholic; and among Catholics the English-speaking Irish were challenged in numerical terms by immigrants from Germany, Italy, and Poland. At the end of the century, Yiddish-speaking Jews from eastern Europe and Russia also constituted a significant minority of wage earners in important urban labor markets. The United States had always been culturally pluralistic, but its pluralism in rapidly growing cities burst through the Protestant boundaries that had contained it earlier.

What role did religion play in this situation, especially in accommodating "free" wage earners to a capitalist system that arguably had taken from them everything they formerly had had in the way of power and security? The classic Marxist argument against religion, battered but far from dead, asserts that most Catholic and Protestant religious leaders in the nineteenth century promoted reactionary social policies. The goal of clerics was either to lead workers to internalize the very values that oppressed them or, failing in that, to sucker them into an ineffectual and socially withdrawn piety. The only important question left by this interpretation is whether organized religion so managed to alienate workers that they found the strength to abandon it and seek secular sources of resistance in working-class politics and trade unionism. An important modification of the Marxist position argues that workers turned religion to the cause of social protest. They did not abandon their religious traditions but instead read them in ways that placed justice on the side of oppressed trade unionists.[2]

The case of the Knights of Labor suggests just how complex these issues are. Terence Powderly, the man who led the Knights through its headiest days and into decline, was of Irish parentage and a practicing Catholic. He clearly had to do some creative balancing between conflicting pressures. Despite the fabled reactionary posture of Roman Catholicism under Pope Pius IX (1846–78) and with somewhat less rigidity under Leo XIII (1878–1903), Powderly in fighting to improve the precarious position of labor in a market system was not without some support from his church. After all, Catholicism's illiberal and non-progressive attitudes in the nineteenth century, for all the Church's commercial traffic in candles, icons, and saints' medallions, carried the weight of pre-capitalist values. Among the targets of Church leaders were the more absurd claims to benevolence advanced by free-market zealots.

However, if the common breed of capitalism's running-dog ministers was Protestant, Rome was not friendly to most forms of collective labor action. In the early 1880s, all labor organizations fell under suspicion—they were guilty by generic association with the condemned Molly Maguires, or they gave purported encouragement to anti-clerical socialists, or they tried to bring Catholics and Protestants together in friendly associations that were presumptively dangerous to Catholic identity. A further complication in the case of the Knights of Labor was its oath of secrecy. The Knights, like any number of other labor societies, established initiation rituals adapted from Masonic practices, occult rituals that in the eyes of the Church compromised the obligations of Catholics to bring to confession an open and fully disclosing conscience.

Powderly struggled to rid the Knights of its features that were most objectionable to the Church, although he was also determined not to truckle under to what he saw as unjustified clerical hostility or unwarranted Church interference. In refusing advice to take his defense of the Knights directly to a skeptical Vatican, he said: "I have made every honorable proposition to the clergy of this country to make changes in our laws, and they either do not want to suggest any thing or else they do not *know enough* and I am as positive that God gave me a soul to save that I know more about the condition of the laboring people and their wants than the Pope." Since his cause was just, he was "willing to face hell in defense of it." If the Church opposed him, "I will array myself where I now stand, on the side of God's poor, along side of those for whom God died."[3]

For a surprisingly long time, Powderly was able to keep both his faith and his independence. For most of the 1880s, Powderly lectured for Catholic causes and maintained cordial relations with Cardinal James Gibbons, who gave cautious support to the Knights and was genuinely sympathetic to the difficulties of working people. The faithful carted off Powderly's portrait from Church fairs and prized them in much the same way they did the portraits of saints.[4] Yet one day he ran out of compromises. Powderly found himself caught between Catholic officials who thought that he was dangerous and Protestant critics within the union who accused him of attending mass three times a day, "of confessing all the secrets to the priests, and of pledging to bind the Order to the will of the clergy."[5] Despite Gibbons's help in winning "conditional toleration" for the Knights, the Church never encouraged membership in the union. Important Church officials, including Archbishop Michael Corrigan of New York City, were aggressively hostile and used the Knights' friendliness to Father Edward McGlynn, an outspoken Single Taxer whom the Church silenced in 1887, as an excuse to press their attacks. Henry George himself, whose works were condemned by the Church, albeit *sub secreto*, was a hero to the Knights for his opposition to injustices caused by unearned increments in land value that a free market permitted.

In bottom-line calculations, Powderly's struggles suggest that organized Christianity in the late nineteenth century was a net loss for the fortunes of union-organizing. Despite their majority in urban workplaces, Catholics were never more than about 15 percent of the membership of the Knights. Church opposition has to be counted as one of the reasons why more Catholic workers did not enlist. Powderly's faithful Catholicism placed limits on his radicalism, and the Knights found no effective way to avoid the religious divisions that slowed the organization of American workers. Opponents ousted a frustrated Powderly from the leadership of the Knights in 1893. In 1901, as if to concede the futility of what he had attempted, he gave up Catholicism and joined the Masons. The tense union between religion and labor activism that he had worked to uphold had failed him.

Religion as Opiate and as Resistance

To frame the class issues in terms of my general argument, I might say that nineteenth-century capitalists manufactured an ideology (product) that they called benevolent capitalism. They wanted to sell it to wage earners, potentially resistant consumers, so they sought an attractive package. Religion was the perfect device. They appropriated its language of moral striving and applied it to their own activities. Religion taught meekness and docility. Best of all, its ministers were cheap to hire. Most capitalists would have sympathized with the following and not uncommon exhortation: "Now if your mill owners want to make a good dividend, let them see to it that they have plenty of good orthodox preaching, a good minister well-housed, and [take] my word for it, it will prove to be the best part of their investment; for godliness is profitable to all things, having the promise of this life and that which is to come."[6] We know that nineteenth-century manufacturers entered church contributions into their books as a business expense, a practice that modern tax laws countenance by permitting people to deduct their church pledges. Their self-serving biases added to the processes that were commodifying religion.

Obviously, this sort of market model is simplistic. It is useful, but only if we recognize that wage earners did not have to buy the product. Markets have at least the virtue of encouraging diverse brands. Working-class people at times cut their religious views along lines that only marginally fit the pattern of expansive capitalism. The resulting attitudes had latent power to encourage opposition to the logic of individualism and free enterprise, saving religion from its bourgeois forms of commodification and wage earners from cultural, if not economic, co-optation. Historial scenarios that make American workers more rebellious than is suggested by the spotty record of their collective resistances are important correctives to older narratives, although workers had restricted choices. By the last half of the nineteenth century, a market economy was a reality in the United States, and religion was part of it. The practical issue that faced most American workers was not the acceptance or rejection of wage labor but acceptance on what terms and with what qualifications. This fact left ample room for choices; among them, ones that affected how they became consumers of religion and of activities that organized religion tried to influence.

The development of urban commercial culture was in many ways more important to the working classes than to any other segment of the population. As significant consumers in the market for leisure and pleasure, they made their own standards of taste bear on what was offered them.

They were not immune to religious appeals that affected their options, but reactions varied. In the late nineteenth century, conflicts that delineated class affected both religion and the development of commercial culture. In the end, although the mass culture of the twentieth century bore marks of middle-class restrictiveness, cultural tastes that the working classes had made commercially viable were its primary component. We can make many good arguments to demonstrate bourgeois cultural hegemony and the effectiveness of instruments of social control used by the American middle class. However, neither working-class religion nor popular mass culture turned out to be what middle-class moral leaders had wanted.

To provide an understanding of working-class religion at the end of the nineteenth century, the ways that it appealed to wage earners and its effect upon their commodity choices in the cultural marketplace, I will need to say something about what the middle classes were trying to sell and to review class issues that were already evident in the first half of the nineteenth century. A good place to begin is with the consensus scholarly view that Arminian theology, the free-will replacement of Calvinism that was at the core of antebellum revivalism, encouraged the drive toward free-market individualism.[7] Economic ideology and religious ideology reinforced each other. According to one important historical account, the famous religious crusades of Charles Finney in Rochester in 1830 were popular in the first instance "among entrepreneurs who bore direct responsibility for disordered relations between classes." Their unusual preoccupation with church prompted them to promote a workingman's revival, the most "powerful source" of which was "the simple coercive fact that wage earners worked for men who insisted on seeing them in church." Workingmen who went to church got something for their trouble. They advanced economically. However, those who employed wage labor got a good bit more. They won a social order that they had prescribed and that first and foremost served their needs.[8]

Some of these points are beyond dispute. The evangelical fervor that spread among common people in America, spurring the astonishing growth of Baptist and Methodist churches, was a democratic challenge that was incomplete. It shook up authority only to rearrange it, and older elite groups as well as newer commercial and manufacturing powers were not left out in the cold. Evangelicalism was adaptable to other than populist uses.[9] Episcopal, Presbyterian, and Unitarian congregations were early front-runners in the contest to drive self-conscious middle-classness into the hearts and minds of their members. Other Protestants were not far behind in seeing that the success of their churches depended on an outlook tied to mannered politeness and a determination to get ahead.[10]

Middle-class women and men tailored a religion designed to validate values that ensured their preeminence and their economic security. Initially, the behavior they changed was mostly their own, but the effects spread. Either by the force of rational persuasion or by the system of economic rewards that they controlled, they convinced many of their servants and their employees that the path to success lay in the adoption of similar behavior.

The aim of middle-class religion was cultural homogeneity and social control. Its champions saw only nobleness in those aims. What else could idealistic social reform hope to accomplish? However, since middle-class versions of Protestant triumphalism were doomed from the start, many middle-class churchgoers, in effect, used their standards of Protestant moral homogeneity to mark social divisions between the "us" and the "them." The people they could not change they abandoned to the invidious cultural warping of economic disadvantage. What the "abandoned" made of these processes is another story. They did not necessarily stop going to church or assume the sort of "low" moral behavior that many in the middle class expected of them. Wage earners often found their own reasons to appropriate the ethical demands of evangelical religion. After all, Protestant discipline could lead to economic gain for reasons quite other than the promise of favors meted out by paternalistic employers. There is a curious sort of inverted class bias in the judgment that only middle-class people have something to gain from sobriety, piety, and moral rigor. In any case, wage earners during the antebellum period often used their religion to advance collective interests against their employers. The rapid churching of many people of low economic station did not automatically and everywhere produce a population of gulled workers who failed to understand their own self-interests.

Many recent studies of antebellum labor movements have credited religion a positive role. Just outside of Philadelphia, for example, working men and women who had been converted at revival meetings in 1832 led strikes in textile mills in 1833.[11] In Pawtucket, Rhode Island, mill workers, although they shunned the churches of their employers along with Sunday schools, moral reform societies, and temperance associations, pursued their separate interests in Methodist and Free-will Baptist churches. For them, Protestant moral discipline led to protest and resistance.[12] Forty two percent of the members of the Workingmen's Association in Fitchburg, Massachusetts, belonged to churches; the same figure as for all adults in the town. The large number of wage earners in Fall River who belonged to evangelical churches made demands in the language of millennial Christian perfectionism, and ignored, equally, anti-clerical freethinkers and Protestant ministers hostile to labor activism.[13] Moral reform movements were especially popular in burgeoning manufacturing centers; for example, in Lynn, Massachusetts, where after 1830 workers and employers used moral reform in different ways and under different religious sponsorship.[14]

The emotional investment that wage earners made in religion and the importance of religion to labor demands seem to have lessened in large urban areas, despite the efforts of many revivalists, including Finney. The soaring, Gothic-inspired urban churches that Episcopals built in the 1840s and 1850s were not congenial retreats for workers. Unintentionally but inevitably because of the elite sponsorship, they became testaments to wealth rather than to the spirit that their builders had wanted to capture. New York's Trinity Church, finished in 1846, appropriately stood at the top of Wall Street.[15] One exhaustive study of New York City's workers uncovered little evidence to suggest that wage earners were excited by revival crusades during the 1830s. Even before the War of 1812 and despite the efforts of colorful preachers with genuine commitments to the poor, most artisans remained indifferent to organized religion. During a period of aggressive proselytizing in the 1830s, Methodists failed to improve their standing as a percentage of the population, and every Baptist church founded on the Bowery in that period was no longer there at the end of the decade. Urban religion among the working classes often fed on chiliastic despair and did little to encourage robust hope in the power of collective resistance.[16]

Figures on organized religion are important, but they can mislead. What may have been happening among workers in New York City during the antebellum period was not so much a disgust with religion, or even the crowding out of religion by other urban attractions, but a period of independent-minded waiting. Workers attended to religious controversy but avoided middle-class churches. Controversy did not always have happy consequences. The entrance of large numbers of Catholic immigrants into the work force in the 1830s reinforced religious loyalties among urban industrial workers and in the process led to violence.[17] Working-class Protestants burned Catholic churches and convents, and Catholic immigrants responded with threats to level New York and Philadelphia. As we know from many far worse situations in the world, ugly religious rivalry works powerfully against religious indifference. We should not wonder that less than 50 percent of New York's Catholics went to mass on any sort of regular basis in the 1850s. What is striking is that the percentage of observants increased, not decreased, for the remainder of the nineteenth century.[18]

Among Roman Catholics, the Irish were the most observant, and their reward was control of the Church; the Germans were the least. The Italians were devout, but anti-clericalism was part of their inherited Catholic practice. In all cases, Catholic women went to church more frequently than men and much more frequently than young Catholic working men. The effects of this far-from-uniform devotion on working-class militance were both negative and positive, with many issues hanging somewhere in the middle. The main point is that religious allegiances were inescapably a major factor in working-class culture and in patterns of behavior. We get nowhere if we ignore them and seize every statistic of sporadic church attendance, every hint of anti-clerical feeling, as proof that religion had ceased to matter. American Catholics, even in their secular organizations and their secular activities, found themselves surrounded by a heavily confessional atmosphere, if only because whatever they did was done in the company of other Catholics. Religion was part of the folk life and social identity of each immigrant. It gave meaning to moral values. It was how immigrants defined themselves. It made their communities cohere.[19]

The close association of religion with general cultural practices perhaps did not apply with the same force to working-class Protestants, but much of the shape of their secular world also revolved around religious loyalties. Religious allegiance certainly affected politics. To be Protestant, which signified above all not to be Catholic, weighed on judgments about Sabbatarianism, about temperance proposals, and about public schools. These particular issues did not always bear directly on working-class militance since they were not fought exclusively, even in the case of temperance, along class lines. But religion was a way of asserting difference, and not merely the differences of a divided working class where Catholics and Protestants joined separate volunteer fire companies, frequented different saloons, and lived in separate neighborhoods. To be different, and to have a moral and religious basis for asserting difference, was potentially a useful component in the psychology of resistance.

In statistical terms, we are stuck with some guesswork. However, the census material that we have, rather than giving evidence of declining church participation by urban wage earners in the last half of the nineteenth century, suggests that it increased significantly. In the period between 1890 and 1906, church membership across the nation increased 60 percent. In cities alone, it increased 87 percent. In 1906, 46 percent of American city dwellers belonged to some church against a figure of 39 percent of all Americans. Much of that differential may be attributed to the influx into urban areas of Catholic immigrants who in 1906 outnumbered Protestants in America's 117 principal cities by 5,824,663 to 3,487,516.[20] The Catholic Church counted members in a less stringent way than most Protestant denominations, so it is difficult to keep a base line for comparison. Even so, the swelling of urban church membership, coming at a time when many affluent Americans were discovering the suburbs, could not have happened without working-class participation.[21]

What the Middle Classes Tried to Sell

In the latter half of the nineteenth century, middle-class religious leaders were clearly thinking harder than ever before about how to reform the behavior of working classes through religion. Part of their problem lay in their Protestantism. They found it difficult to accept Catholicism as a proper religion. From their perspective a Catholic worker was almost as bad as a worker who had no religion at all. Quite aside from this bias, middle-class religious reformers correctly perceived that a good bit of working-class behavior, whatever it owed to religion, deviated sharply from their own norms. Efforts were made to reach urban working-class young men through the important experiment of the YMCA. The Y was part of a broader benevolent effort to repackage religion in a way that combined its restrictive duties with fun. In particularly exuberant cases, this effort entailed recasting Jesus as a "radiant personality" who led his followers in round after round of "wholesome merry-making." Richard Henry Edwards, a fellow of the YMCA, asked his readers to imagine "his [Jesus'] spontaneity and sense of humor," "his relish for the out-of-doors," "his high mood of fellowship in the bridegrooms' joy."[22] This broad middle-class initiative, which in many ways sought to bypass the organized efforts of evangelical denominations, focused on recreation, on parades of "gaily marching children," of "youths contending in athletic games," of the "lively music" of folk dances. The sermon, already reduced to a crowd-pleasing performance, gave way to the social hour.[23]

The economic sponsorship of these movements is not in doubt. The money came from successful, churchgoing businessmen who believed in reform and also in the proposition that Christianizing the social order was too important a task to be left solely to churches, at least to churches that failed to understand the principles of operating in a competitive environment. These highly creative participants in national life never adopted the language of despair that was habitual in some quarters of the

Protestant clergy. High tone and confidence rather than fear and dismay distinguished their voices. For the last two decades of the nineteenth century and for at least three decades afterwards, their enterprising spirit was everywhere.

Their concerns, as had been true since the antebellum period, centered as much on the proper uses of leisure time as on the workplace. They harbored special fears about the commercial forms of urban leisure. On the one hand, they tried to restrict leisure by insisting on moral content; on the other, they sponsored any number of activities whose sum effect was to make the idea of leisure attractive, so attractive that the norms of middle-class morality had to keep stretching in order to remain relevant to new leisure opportunities. In 1901, a committee of fifty distinguished and open-minded men, men of generous and liberal principles, issued what they regarded as a no-nonsense report entitled *Substitutes for the Saloon.*[24] Applauding the intentions behind the YMCA, they nonetheless announced that its scale was inadequate. Baltimore, the report noted, had a population of at least 75,000 young men but enrolled in the YMCA a scant 2,398. In New York City, the proportion was 4,479 YMCA members out of a possible constituency of 550,000. In the entire nation, the estimated population of men between the ages of sixteen and forty-four was 6,119,646. YMCA membership in five hundred towns and cities was only 169,299, most of it drawn from the "better class of workingmen," tradesmen, clerks, or professionals. Few were strangers to the city. The majority were native born, came from religious homes, and attended a Protestant evangelical church. The YMCA, the report concluded, was, despite its leads in the right direction, little more than a church annex, a safe recreational haven for young men who were already Christian but not a means to influence people who otherwise had no association with organized Christianity.[25]

It was time, once again, for privileged men and women, who cared deeply about religion, to push their liberal ideas several steps forward. Gymnasiums were not enough. What else was there to do? What opportunities and initiatives were being overlooked? The cornerstone of their progressive pronouncements, an insight that the committee urged upon skeptical churchmen, assumed that middle-class ethical standards had intrinsic appeal. Wage earners who succumbed to "immoral" entertainments did not do so because they preferred immorality. They merely sought an atmosphere of conviviality. Men drank in saloons, but liquor was not the essential attraction of the barroom. Rather, the saloon was "the most democratic of institutions," "the poor man's club." Workers needed places that provided them with occasions for relaxed sociability, comfort, and pleasure. If religious-minded people provided "decent" surrogates for the saloon, they would destroy the social context that permitted immorality to infect what was a natural and healthy desire in human beings. But to do that, they needed to construct something more than conventionally nice-sounding gathering places like gyms, kindergartens, parish houses, and reading rooms. They had to provide smoking rooms, salons for card-playing, and billiards rooms. The report singled out St. Bartholomew's Church, an Episcopal church in New York City, for praise in providing the latter.

In most ways, the report simply expanded a conclusion already reached by many earlier religious reformers: it was the atmosphere in which an activity took place, not the activity itself, that determined moral content. The Committee of Fifty had not changed its mind about the need for an educational aim in entertainment (always the high tone), but "the popular lecture with educational aims . . . must be pleasing" so that "the audience is able thoroughly to enjoy it." In its most controversial advice, the report repeatedly emphasized that "the religious atmosphere should not intrude." Saloon substitutes had to be rooms "in which the religious element makes no appearance."[26] Even that was not a new idea to people who had long been urging churches to regard play as part of God's regimen. They were prepared to agree that for religion to be effective, it had to address "the temporal concerns of the people." It needed to encourage "diverting" activities that clerics had once despised as unwholesome competition to spiritual exercises.[27] In particular, the committee praised melodrama with nostalgic relish: "It sets things morally in their right relations. . . . Evil is never so black, good so alluring." What the committee endorsed, well before Madison Avenue heralded the idea for different purposes, was subliminal conversion.

Chautauqua and the YMCA had taken their own steps to disguise religion. The Committee of Fifty lent to the effort a far more paternalistic tone. Nothing better symbolized the commodification of religion than the committee's recommendation to repackage it using attractive but deliberately misleading labels. The men of the Committee of Fifty were definitely thinking in terms of a spiritual economy even if they did not believe that a capitalist market by itself could supply society with what it needed in the way of leisure commodities. They thought in conventional ways about popular taste and commercial culture. The market offerings of commercial culture pandered to popular tastes that they despised. They were hopeful that in the long run they could reform taste even if they could not quite explain how it got to be so bad in the first place. If people innately preferred middle-class morality, why had immorality ever become part of commercial culture?

Metaphysical questions did not haunt the progressive minds of middle-class religious reformers. They looked to the future, paying as little attention to intractable puzzles from the past as possible. It was enough to seek government money at the local level to sponsor cultural facilities that people would never ask for if left to themselves. Wherever the wholesome forms of pleasure did not immediately drive out the unwholesome forms, they were prepared to use censorship. They were more than ready to close down immoral pleasure palaces once society had put the approved substitutes in place. As reform ideology, what the Committee of Fifty proposed embodied the Republican party's version of market exchange. People could be left to pick products from the marketplace freely unless prosperous white Protestants construed their selection as involving a moral choice. Then they needed guidance.

In fact, this sort of thinking had a tangible impact on the development of popular culture. It did not carry everything before it, however. As a direct influence on the behavior of workers, the surrogate-pleasure movement largely miscarried. The battle to ensure moral choices had to be won or lost squarely in the market of commercial culture, not in sanitized social arenas set off and protected from the creative energies produced by urban diversity. Those special arenas were important to people who already belonged to middle-class churches. The ones set up by the middle class for the working class foundered. Ironically, the Protestant churches that had the most appeal to white working classes tended to be more severe on matters of moral discipline than was evident in the Committee of Fifty's latitudinarian ideas of moral reform. Many working-class people liked their religion up-front and lively. The charitable services of the Committee of Fifty, and much else that passed under the rubric of the Social Gospel, modified the presence of religion so drastically that any well-meaning secular organization might provide them without dependence on, reference to, or memory of any religious tradition. Most American religious leaders pulled back when they saw the special features of their product being eradicated.

Old Time Religion and Urban Revivals

The effort of the Committee of Fifty to bring the right sort of religion surreptitiously to urban working classes proved to be less significant than the enduring, ardent populism of revivalism. Dwight Moody, the chief figure in late nineteenth-century revivalism, was content to slug it out in the cultural marketplace with all comers. He did not seek government sponsorship or aid. As a shaper of popular/commercial culture he was as important a figure as P. T. Barnum. No one understood better than he did that religion had become a business in the nineteenth century and that success in religion depended on sound and innovative business practices. Moody did not imitate the methods of the businessmen who supported his revivals—John Wanamaker, Jay Cooke, and George Stuart in Philadelphia; Marshall Field, Cyrus McCormick, and George Pullman in Chicago. He had his own methods of selling. These men met on equal terms, all of them convinced that businesses and churches alike should be forms of organized piety. Religious enterprise depended in part upon secular genius; commercial success depended in part upon religious dedication. Moody was not the tool of his business sponsors, but he was their ideological companion.

Moody, a New Englander, joined one of Boston's Congregational churches as well as its YMCA. When he moved to Chicago in 1856, he was a salesman for a boot-and-shoe operation. He aggressively pursued worldly success, distributed religious tracts, became the president of Chicago's Y, and started an urban mission Sunday school. The tenor of his later religious work was conveyed in what he wrote home about his attendance at revival meetings: "Oh, how I do enjoy it."[28] In 1858 his career paralleled that of John Wanamaker who started as a clerk in a clothing store at the age of nineteen, became the first paid secretary of Philadelphia's YMCA, and devoted himself to the Methodist church. Wanamaker, using the money that he saved from his work at the Y, went on to build department stores. Moody, in contrast, gave up business in 1860, teamed with the gospel singer Ira Sankey in 1873 to begin full-time revival work, and constructed a religious empire that centered on the Moody Bible Institute in Chicago. Despite the divergence, it is not difficult to see why the two men found cooperation so easy or why Moody was able to tap resources so effectively from a large network of manufacturers and merchants.[29]

Moody knew how to move his commodity. His large urban revivals between 1875 and 1880 were carefully organized and extensively advertised. To know the time and place of Moody's meeting, people turned to the amusement pages of their newspapers. He trained his choir, his ushers, and his "inquiry-room" workers in the same way that Wanamaker trained employees in his department stores. Above all, his campaigns went forward with a solid capital base. To conduct his first revival campaign in Chicago, consuming three months in 1876, Moody successfully solicited funds to build a brick structure seating eight thousand people. Overall, he spent thirty thousand dollars. In Philadelphia a year earlier,

Moody preached in a large depot-tabernacle owned by Wanamaker that seated ten thousand people and amply accommodated the press. Wanamaker converted his capital when Moody was done. He turned the tabernacle into a department store. Moody's revivalism boldly and with no sense of impropriety interlocked religion with business, epitomizing what Wanamaker called for in an article "Bringing Business Efficiency into Christian Service."[30]

Moody, a strict Sabbatarian and an uncompromising temperance man, provided a surrogate for other forms of urban amusement in a spirit quite unlike what motivated the Committee of Fifty. Close himself to popular taste, he sought to compete with the offerings of commercial culture, to undersell them, to drive them out of business. The scale was large, even extravagant. His choirs of five hundred people, Sankey's attractive singing voice, Moody's largely anecdotal style of preaching and his talent for story telling—these provided entertainment and ensured the enjoyment of Moody's audiences. He did not forget the need for good order and disciplined spectators. He began his meetings on time and instructed his workers not to seat latecomers. People could laugh when it was appropriate, but they were expected to sit absolutely still while listening to the testimony of the distinguished and powerful men whom Moody invited to sit on the stage with him. Moody's world fit comfortably in the market of commercial culture, right down to the religious items, really souvenirs, that were offered for sale.

America's next great revivalist, Billy Sunday, provided more of the same, gaining national prominence in the first decade of the twentieth century with a slightly more populist version of the religion-as-business formula that had propelled Moody's career. Sunday made his first money in professional baseball, the American sport that at the end of the century cut across as many class and ethnic lines as any other form of commercial entertainment. A chance encounter with a gospel wagon—an institution in Chicago that carried coffee, rolls, and salvation to neighborhoods oversupplied with saloons, gambling houses, and brothels—changed Sunday's life.[31] Called to a different kind of performance, he quit baseball, enlisted with the YMCA, and worked as a preacher on the small-town "kerosene circuit" during the 1890s. After 1908 his revivals began to make money. The amount of the offering was never kept secret. With his encouragement, newspapers emblazoned the figures in headlines and used them to estimate the success of meetings. Everything that mattered in Sunday's religion could be counted and inventoried. Sunday marketed his biography as well as picture postcards of himself, his family, and his evangelical team. On souvenir tables in clearly designated concession areas of the revival meetings, Sunday displayed his sermons and hymn books. They sold well, as did his book *Love Stories of the Bible*. Sunday courted the press and sought to keep himself front-page news. John Rockefeller backed him—so did John Wanamaker, Elbert Gary, Louis Swift, J. Ogden Armour, H. J. Heinz, John M. Studebaker, and S. S. Kresge.

Sunday made politics a part of his preaching. He did not, any more than Moody, rise from established wealth. Both were self-made men who had tremendous rapport with ordinary Americans. Sunday's experience turned him into a lifetime Republican who excoriated greed but carried the gospel of the good capitalist to America's meek and humble. The difficult question about his work is not whether workers were part of his audience. They were. What our evidence does not clearly answer is whether Sunday's social messages had any large effect in discouraging trade unionism and protest in working-class politics. It is crystal clear, despite the scriptural allusions attacking greed and wealth, that the economic implications of Moody's and Sunday's sermons pleased powerful capitalists. The two revivalists spoke against strikes and unions; they praised middle-class values; and they placed order along with cleanliness next to godliness. According to one Chicago journal, "If Moody and Sankey have the success which good men pray for, the Democratic vote in Chicago will be next to nothing in November."

One of the best pieces of evidence attesting to Sunday's "repressive" effect had to do with the Labor Forward Movement that rose and fell between 1912 and 1916. It was especially strong in Philadelphia.[32] Inspired by the Social Gospel and largely sponsored by craft unions, the movement for several years effectively joined Christian appeals for social justice with efforts to energize the labor movement. The Labor Forward Movement organized a parade of a hundred thousand marchers in Philadelphia in November 1914. It coincided with a promising upsurge in labor activism and the annual convention of the American Federation of Labor. At this point, Sunday entered the picture. Accepting an invitation from Philadelphia's industrialists and bankers, he arrived in town carrying a different religious message to Philadelphia's workers that "wreaked havoc within the labor movement." Under pressure from the same people, Philadelphia's YMCA closed its facilities to trade-union meetings and more generally to any organization influenced by the Social Gospel.[33]

At the same time, it is clear that the influence of Moody and Sunday did not spread evenly through the complex layers of the American working classes. They were far from reaching everyone whom their business sponsors wanted them to reach. It was not for want of trying. They sometimes went to inordinate lengths to seek out the poor. Both provided financial support for the charity work of urban missions.[34] Doubtlessly, their work contributed to an increase in the number of American Baptists and Methodists, an achievement they welcomed since evangelical churches often were less favorably inclined toward trade unionism than more socially elite Presbyterian and Episcopal churches. However, if the hope had ever been for Moody and Sunday to convert much of America's immigrant, working-class populations, Catholic and Jewish, they clearly failed. Mostly they spoke to the lower end of the middle class, extending down to clerks and bookkeepers. The majority of people in their audiences were already churched. Many, predictably, were women.[35] The violent labor strife that was more or less constant in American life from 1877 into the new century suggests that capitalist sponsors of religion got a great deal but not everything that they had bargained for.

The Class Politics of Leisure

The purification intentions of the YMCA movement reached a parodic extreme in the person of Anthony Comstock. The self-anointed knight of Victorian prudery devoted his lifetime to cleansing the American nation of impure thoughts and any opportunity to discuss human sexuality in frank and open terms. From secretary of the New York Society for the Suppression of Vice to a special agent for the United States Postal Service, Comstock went after abortionists, purveyors of information about contraception, smutty literature, naked statuary, gamblers, drinkers, and dance-hall denizens. He was a powerful nuisance who, in fact, inflicted serious damage on women of all social classes. But in the effort to make middle-class religion an influence on the commercial pleasures of working people, his activities met with only scattered success.

Chicago's splendid Columbian Exposition of 1893 represented a different tactic. Its planners called upon Frederick Law Olmsted to repeat his Central Park accomplishment. Chicago's commercial and professional elite allied with America's leading architects wanted to demonstrate how a carefully planned urban environment could join together joy and moral uplift in the interest of public order. After a struggle with Sabbatarians, the backers of the exposition threw open its portals on Sunday and closely observed the behavior of the working classes, whose numbers were presumed to be numerous on that day. Moody chose the occasion to hold one of his revivals, although in this case he was asked to operate outside the boundaries of the exposition.

Moody's exclusion did not mean that Chicago's business leaders no longer looked kindly on his efforts. The economically troubled year of 1893 saw Chicago's elite busy on many fronts trying to hold together a vision of public order that required the systematic cooperation of business and religion.[36] Ten years before George Pullman was applauding the Columbian Exposition, he had erected a controversial community for his workers that in his mind would improve the material and spiritual quality of their lives and make them better employees. Pullman tried to fix culture for his workers in the same way that he fixed commodity prices in the community stores. He banned "vicious" amusements, constructed a library, sponsored a wholesome theater, and welcomed Moody. Nearby Pullman's town, the lumber magnate Turlington Harvey built his own "dry" Chicago suburb in cooperation with Moody and with Moody's brother-in-law, Fleming H. Revell. Revell was an extremely successful religious publisher who correctly saw a large market for cheap evangelical books tailored to popular taste.

Economic hard times undid these urban experiments. As efforts to bring all Americans into the culture of the Protestant middle classes, they were doomed anyway. Pullman saw his effort to impose upon workers a moralized commercial culture dissolve into a bitter strike in 1894, one of the most publicized and ugly labor disputes in American history. The cultural paternalism of business and religion failed in a colossal way, and Pullman fell back on the non-progressive solution of repressive and brutal force. He won the strike, but he could scarcely have been happy about the shambles of his town. He could pay workers low wages, but he had not taken away their "coarser" pleasures. In the meantime, Harvey's economic empire had tumbled in 1893, and the people of his suburb voted-in liquor.

The trouble with the schemes of most middle-class reformers is that they did not understand either the religion or the moral norms of working-class people. When working-class religion encouraged protest, they decried it as foreign radicalism. They far overestimated the threat to democratic social order when labor leaders from William Sylvis to Eugene Debs made a habit of calling upon scriptural passages to decry the injustices of economic power and monopoly. Catholics, Protestants, and Jews rose to leadership in the American labor movement. But as happened in England where activists in reformed faiths shaped the politics of the Labour Party, middle-class reformers found it difficult to appreciate collective protest as a sign of "true" religion. True religion might encourage sympathy for the victims of social injustice, but it stopped short of justifying confrontation along class lines.

American middle-class religious leaders had even more difficulty understanding working-class religious faith when they turned to consider the ambiguous ways it could influence moral norms. Believing that ethical standards were invariant, they misconstrued and then deplored the way that many wage earners applied moral principles to the contested area of commercial culture. In matters of leisure, middle-class reformers were constantly expecting people to show moral qualms when in fact they only seemed to be interested in having a good time. Different traditions opened up possibilities of massive misunderstanding. The crucial issue of whether middle-class religious aims worked to deprive working-class people of their traditional pleasures is open to mixed assessment. The issue is important not merely for assessing the nature of working-class religion; it also relates to questions about labor militance and resistance.[37] If, for example, American workers over the course of the nineteenth century persisted in class-based pleasures that worried the middle class, thus stimulating an oppositional mentality useful for collective action, they may have accomplished something affecting cultural autonomy that was as important as any economic gains they won in the sporadic victories of nineteenth-century trade unionism. If, on the other hand, a trickled-down morality robbed working-class pleasures of their dangerous side and workers of their capacity to make independent moral assessments, leading to a tractable, passive behavior that many critics attribute to the mass culture of the twentieth century, then the capitalist promoters of a religiously tamed commercial culture had largely gotten what they wanted.

Class sharply differentiated urban commercial entertainments after the Civil War, both with respect to what people did and in what parts of the city they did it.[38] Recent studies of working-class leisure that resulted from this differentiation point in two directions. They argue both a cultural autonomy sustained over much of the late nineteenth century, the first possibility suggested above, and an inevitable trend toward accommodation to the pressures of middle-class moral propriety, a second possibility that presumably undercut the first. Perhaps we should make room for a third possibility with less clear-cut implications; that is, a religiously influenced commercial culture serving working-class interests not always well but at least in ways that its sponsors had not foreseen. We should not assume that the Moodys and Comstocks of the world whose souls had been purchased by capitalist overlords crammed propriety down working-class throats. In fact, the moral sanitation of leisure often reflected the independent moral and religious values of working-class people, let the middle class be damned.

To illustrate the point, let us consider four examples of urban commercial culture that the taste of working-class men and women deeply affected: boxing, the saloon, vaudeville, and dime novels.[39] Although middle-class religious reformers, as well as the clergy of Protestant working-class churches, would have outlawed all of them if they had been given the power, the specter of disapproval and the threat of censorship did nothing to impede their popularity. If anything, strong moral condemnation made them more attractive. However, each of these cultural offerings underwent changes, both in terms of their content and what we might call their ritual practice, that reflected the virtually indistinguishable pressures of commerce and religion. Profit followed a morally cleaned-up product.

During the 1840s, bare-knuckle fighting replaced horse racing as the professional sport that drew the biggest crowds. Although sparring began as a gentlemen's sport in England, working-class men shaped its commercial destiny in the United States. Boxing as a spectator sport was unthinkable without the ethnic and, to some extent, racial rivalries that became part of urban working-class culture by mid-century. In bare-knuckle fighting, moralists had plenty to worry about. Its popularity was tied to heavy drinking, heavy betting, and a whetted appetite for violence. Its male sponsors deliberately made boxing unfit for women and children. Few rules governed the sport. Fighters bloodied themselves, if not to death (there were deaths in the ring), then to early physical wreckage. To be a spectator was sometimes as dangerous as to be in the ring. Fierce partisanship led to fights not only among the crowds of people who attended the event but also in saloons where the match was previewed for days before it took place and relived for days after it was over. Fighters and their champions celebrated a life of dissipation and intemperance that set working-class male culture against effeminacy, against softness, against politeness, against deferred gratification, and against good order. In brief, boxing stood for subaltern autonomy.[40]

By the 1870s, however, prizefighting as a spectator sport was badly in need of reform, not because its partisans had been softened by the constant moral criticism directed at their pastime but because corruption was destroying its commercial potential. The prospects of easy money took boxing out of the hands of working-class sponsors and made the sport part of an unregulated underworld. The saloon owners' handling of purses and betting arrangements grew lax. Fixed fights, mismatched fighters, and indifferent attention to rules lessened the interest in bouts, especially in the gambling that was a part of boxing ritual and seemed essential to its commercial expansion. By the last quarter of the nineteenth century, a specialized network of fight promoters was in the mood for reform, reform that would provide a reliable set of rules, that would permit boxing to become a legal sport, and that would even enact compromises with the sport's moral and religious critics.

In the last endeavor, the middle classes undeniably had an impact. Around mid-century, many Christian ministers had for their own reasons decided that it was time to pump some virility into the image of Christ. The ideology of muscular Christianity encouraged participation in sports and at the same time sanctioned the activity of watching sports. Although bare-knuckle fighting in the working-class style remained well outside the range of leisure activities that got a nod of moral approval, males of the middle class began to praise the manly art of self-defense as something that built discipline and character. In 1878 the socially exclusive New York Athletic Club sponsored the first national amateur boxing championship. By the turn of the century, one of the country's most inveterate amateur boxers, the man who had led American troops up San Juan Hill in Cuba, was in the White House.

The financial calculations of promoters and the model of gentlemen sparring worked to change the nature of American boxing. So did moral condemnations that were in large part middle-class intrusions. Yet did the end result unambiguously represent a victory of middle-class cultural designs over working-class desires? Or did moral reform also suit working-class needs? These are the class issues in moral/religious reform, and they are difficult to unravel. In fact, commercial boxing was never to exemplify very well Theodore Roosevelt's notion that sparring was valuable because it taught men to internalize habits of steady discipline. Rather, popular boxers continued to fight as a way to make money, enough money to turn their lives between bouts into an extravagant binge. The most famous American fighter in the 1880s and 1890s was appropriately, given the roots of professional fighting in working-class culture, an Irish American. John L. Sullivan's singular version of the American rags-to-riches story, following formulas not imagined by Benjamin Franklin or Horatio Alger, was a strong indication of how popular culture had changed in fifty years. Sullivan was the most celebrated American sportsman of his time, really the country's first sports celebrity, albeit a Catholic, a rowdy, a heavy drinker, and a womanizer.

True, the market made it financially prudent to do some middle-class moral work on Sullivan's image. Sullivan's career benefited from efforts to reform the sport. Although he started his long series of ring victories during the bare-knuckle era, he also led the transition into the more orderly boxing behavior dictated by the Marquis of Queensberry rules. Under the latter, fighters wore gloves and fought uniform three-minute rounds. They also stopped fighting after a fixed number of rounds or after one of the fighters had been counted out. Boxing remained violent, but the new rules favored skill. The next step was to bring forth a champion who was tailored to counter the idea that professional fighters were of necessity uncouth bullies. Gentleman Jim Corbett (a.k.a. "Handsome Jim" and "Pompadour Jim") had attended college and worked as a bank clerk before taking his talents to the ring. In the most publicized pugilistic contest of the century, in New Orleans in 1892, Corbett knocked out Sullivan in twenty-one rounds.

The fight in New Orleans took place two years after its city council had authorized Queensberry fights, so long as the spectacle was without liquor concessions and never on Sunday. The law required those who received profits from promoting a match to contribute fifty dollars to charity. Fight promoters viewed these restrictions as reasonable, for in order to increase the commercial rewards of the sport they needed to expand the audience beyond the working class. Journalists who covered boxing began to review the spectators as closely as the matches. In anticipation of the Sullivan/Corbett fight the Chicago *Daily Tribune* noted the change in audience: "Now men travel to great boxing contests in vestibule limited trains; they sleep at the best hotels."[41] Even women appeared seated at ringside.

The moral reframing of boxing added a middle-class component to its audience and in a short time made it thinkable that respected members of middle-class churches could become ardent enthusiasts. A boxing match became less a ritual in which working-class groups placed their champions in the ring and more a gladiatorial contest in which the greedy rich watched with pleasure as their social inferiors destroyed themselves. The transformation was far from complete. Boxing never gained the patina of the "great American pastime" that was reserved for baseball; nor did it find the respectability of American football whose origins among privileged college males did not keep it from being every bit as bloody. No minister ever offered a prayer at a prizefight, a practice that until recently was routine in college football contests. Corbett's fame did not last long. The training of boxers continued in the twentieth century to reflect how close the sport was to street brawling and to the ethnic and racial rivalries of working-class males. Whatever professional boxing has become in the United States, it was not, is not, and never will be a middle-class invention.

A second point is also important. Bare-knuckle fighting was a bloody and macho sport that had destructive consequences not merely for the fighters, not merely for wage earners who overinvested in the sport by gambling, but also for working-class women and children. Therefore, any suggestion that the reform of boxing by rules of the English nobility undercut one base of subaltern cultural autonomy overlooks the fact that, from the standpoint of workers, reform had become necessary. In the 1830s and 1840s, bare-knuckle fighting was a ritualized way to validate lives that otherwise could not easily have borne the weight of middle-class moral disapproval. But when boxing changed, it was in part because many workers had changed. They had decided that some moral reordering in their marketplace of culture suited their best interests. Middle-class Protestant moralists had not forced them to renounce pleasures they enjoyed. Their own social needs, and their own religious views, dictated the application of relevant moral norms.

The history of male saloon life prompts analogous observations. The institution ran a course that took it from a despised moral cesspool and turned it into a profitable commercial establishment where middle-class men and even women were physically and perhaps even morally safe. That was later.[42] In the middle part of the nineteenth century, the saloon served male working-class culture in the same way that boxing had. The arrangement of fights in taverns was no coincidence.[43] Many trade-union leaders worried about excessive drinking and encouraged temperance, an encouragement that took hold of German Lutheran workers. At the same time, wage earners viewed the politics of temperance as an effort made by middle-class moralists to control their behavior. In response, many of them resolved to keep the saloon the focus of their community life. Most saloons not only were working-class institutions, but also had a distinct ethnic character. Situated between work and home, they were centers of easy and relaxed sociability among men who shared common values. Along with heavy drinking, the boisterous life of the saloon revolved around story-telling, singing, card-playing, and gambling. Temperance leaders correctly said that some working men threw away their chances to get ahead by squandering their wages on drink. Yet in an important sense, the point of communal drinking was to challenge the idea of "getting ahead" and to champion the solidarity of poor but honest men. Drinking was not a political act *per se*, but in struggling to preserve their right to drink, working-class men built a distinct kind of political consciousness expressly directed at middle-class effeminacy.

By the end of the nineteenth century, a moral economy was at work in the minds of working-class saloon owners. They discovered that more people crowded into saloons when they spruced up the interiors and made serious efforts to ensure orderly behavior. Working-class toughness remained part of the saloon world, but in relative terms there was less fighting. The most popular urban saloons competed with the social clubs of wealthy professionals. Some old-timers regretted the lost ethnic character of many urban drinking places. Even so, we should not imagine that wage earners gained nothing from the changes and had nothing to do with them. To do so is to assume that religious and moral values were not important in working-class communities. Moral didacticism was a prominent element in the American labor press of the late nineteenth century—recall the Knights of Labor. Merely on functional grounds, the adoption of more morally self-conscious drinking habits was not a bad idea. Besides, if there was value to working-class morale in giving affront to middle-class clerics and moralists, the efforts to gentrify the saloon did not eliminate the affront. The ratification of the Eighteenth Amendment to the American Constitution in 1919 made that fact clear.

A third example of contested cultural terrain is vaudeville. We have already seen how urban theater in the antebellum period changed from an activity that included in the same space men of all social ranks into an activity that pushed urban classes spacially apart.[44] Theaters in New York City that catered to upscale, well-behaved audiences moved uptown while those that catered to the working classes, which used rotten eggs and vegetables to make their opinions known, remained located along the lower Bowery. In these despised reaches where rowdy attendance to melodrama remained standard practice, wage earners acted out their social and psychic grievances, sometimes carrying those feelings into antebellum urban riots against high prices.[45]

The social separation of audiences in urban theaters was never complete. In New York City, an area of middle Broadway perpetuated theatrical spectacles that drew audiences from all levels of society.[46] The fare was mixed—melodrama, equestrian dramas, musical spectacle, and the variety shows of pleasure gardens and "concert saloons." It was here that minstrel companies performed and where vaudeville was born. In its heyday, at the end of the nineteenth century and for almost two decades after the turn of the century, vaudeville was the least class specific of any form of American theatrical entertainment. The working classes attended. Many of its stars grew up in immigrant neighborhoods. Some were Italian, many were Jewish. The Yiddish theater that flourished in New York City after the arrival of Jewish immigrants from eastern Europe and Russia was perhaps vaudeville's most important training ground. Vaudeville theaters were places where people were supposed to have a good time, to laugh uproariously, to weep, to express feelings openly. Protestant restraint had no place in vaudeville. A mild sexual naughtiness did, which of course subjected vaudeville to a moral censure that gave working-class spectators an appreciation for their own independent moral standards.

Vaudeville came too late in the day for priggish moral judgments to drive away the urban middle class. Besides, as with boxing and the saloon, the story of vaudeville repeats the tale of how business and religion cooperated to promote moral regulation. The career of Tony Pastor illustrates one way this happened.[47] Pastor, an Italian American and devout Catholic, went through several phases of American show business before he became a successful promoter of vaudeville. During the 1840s, he performed on the temperance circuit, both as a singer and a lecturer. From there he moved on to minstrelsy, worked in P. T. Barnum's museum, and sang as a variety entertainer in New York City's concert saloons. By the 1860s, he was putting on his own variety shows in his own theater with the determination to find "first-class" patronage. In his mind, he could only accomplish that goal by ridding his theater of smoking, swearing, and drinking. During the mid-1870s, when he had moved his theater from the Bowery to Broadway, he advertised that "Mr. Pastor never permits a word on his stage that can offend the ladies." His vaudeville amusement was "innocent" and did in fact draw women in large numbers both to matinees, which they attended in the company of other women and their children, and to evening performances. Press reports suggested that "it was decidedly a 'family' audience, a large number of ladies, many of them coming in twos and threes, without escort, showing that it is politic to manage an establishment of this description in such a manner that no gentleman need fear to bring his wife, sister, or mother to see the show, or even to allow them to go by themselves."[48]

Politic, and profitable. Pastor kept a crucifix on his office wall. He placed a "poor box" in the theater lobby for religious charities. Backstage he posted a placard warning against anyone taking the Lord's name in vain. He also balanced his books and provided well for his family. Other kinds of theatrical/concert fare persisted in ethnic and working-class neighborhoods, for what Pastor did required a substantial capital investment. Even so, the future belonged to family-style vaudeville. It reached the largest audiences. B. F. Keith and Edward F. Albee, two of the most skilled financial operators in the history of American vaudeville, ran what became known with affectionate sneering as "the Sunday school circuit." Keith traced his attitude about morally suitable entertainment to his churchgoing boyhood. He and his partner understood that effective control of the audience was a vital element, as important as what happened onstage, in making popular theater moral.[49] They posted strict rules of audience behavior, leading the *Independent* to say in 1901 that "vaudeville manners are now on a par with those of the parlor."[50] In some circles, vaudeville gained a reputation for moral healthfulness exceeding that of "legitimate" theater. American performances of the plays of Strindberg, Ibsen, and various morally ambiguous French comedies suddenly made "serious" theater *the* moral problem.

The point is simple. If there were invidious class designs underlying the moral improvement of vaudeville, morality did not drive away working-class patronage, not by itself. Insofar as that happened, it was because of higher ticket prices, a better guarantor of moral comportment than a Bible laid on every seat in the house, and because of the newer and cheaper fare offered in urban nickelodeons. The entrepreneurs of commercial culture had nothing to gain by suppressing opportunities for the working classes to enjoy themselves. By the turn of the century, most forms of commercially successful vaudeville provided lessons in normative behavior.[51] This was not because of a concerted effort to make commercial culture middle-class. Rather, market considerations prompted vaudeville's sponsors to make the entertainment as little class specific as possible. Large amusement halls in class-neutral areas of the city challenged the popularity of the variety theaters and concert saloons in working-class neighborhoods. Times Square in New York became the most famous of these new urban centers of commercial culture. There, people of all social ranks had to learn new rules of conduct. Architecturally, the emphasis in vaudeville turned to building opulent interiors. Critics indicted this trend as a puerile effort to sacralize commercial entertainments by housing them in the modern equivalents of medieval cathedrals.[52] What infuriated the critics, of course, was that the formula worked to a very impressive degree.

The effort to make commercial culture as mass-based as invention allowed is also apparent in one last example, the story formulas of the dime novel. In Chapter 1, I indicated that many of the worried arguments about the reading habits of Americans were grounded in fears about an unsupervised work force, the composition of which was radically different in 1850 than it had been in 1800. In the late nineteenth century some of the fear abated, but by no means all of it since a good bit of cheap fiction circulated among working-class women and men, especially the young and single people in that class. The most heralded form of this fiction was the "dime novel" (four-inch by six-inch paperback books of about a hundred pages), which forged a big business for the publishing firm of Beadle and Adams. The success of Beadle and Adams had precursors in the giant story papers of the 1840s (sheets measuring as large as four feet by ten feet) and the pamphlet novels marketed by Park Benjamin in the 1850s. After the Civil War dozens of houses devoted to cheap products published a wide range of costume romances, detective stories, mysteries of the cities, outlaw and western stories, and inspirational fiction.[53]

Without doubt, many of the readers of cheap fiction in the late nineteenth century were industrial workers, female and male, rather than businessmen, professionals, and middle-class housewives. They gravitated to dime-novel plots that revolved around outlaw and bandit tales. These allowed working-class readers to make out allegorical stories about the conflict between labor and capital. Many of them, in fact, had working-class characters. Michael Denning, the most provocative student of the genre, has argued that middle-class morality and Christian piety played little role in the pulp fiction of the late nineteenth century.[54] Even if moral ideas appeared in the text, they missed their mark or were re-accented to suit the moral outlook of wage earners. In the creative imaginative zone of readers' responses, workers established an autonomous cultural world.

The argument that working-class readers had little patience with the Christian piety of domestic novels assumes in a refreshing way that the bourgeois moral critics of the dime novel knew a danger to their interests when they saw one. Many historians of the genre have suggested that middle-class fears about moral subversion in cheap "escapist" fiction were but the stirrings of a tempest in a teapot. The reading of a dime novel was perhaps a waste of useful time but otherwise harmless. The contrasting argument suggests that young wage earners brought a serious attitude to their reading and that the commercial formulas of the dime novel only worked for them because their moral values, not middle-class moral values, could determine the meaning of a story. Their interpretation of struggles between Molly Maguires and Pinkerton detectives or between the James brothers and a federal marshall encouraged them to identify with oppressed groups.

What is interesting about cheap reading material, a factor that makes the case somewhat different from the previous cases, is that the authors and publishers of cheap print defended the moral quality of their product from the beginning. Things were much the same in the book market in the last part of the nineteenth century as they had been in the first part, with moral claims and counter-claims—made in preponderant numbers by clergy—being a constant factor. We can be suspicious of the moral claims of dime-novel promoters in the late nineteenth century. We can also read with a grain of salt the nostalgic accounts of twentieth-century grandparents who, dismayed at the cheap reading material of subsequent generations of young people, looked back on dime-novels as moral primers. We might make a law of this phenomenon: The material of commercial culture despised by moralists in one generation is recovered as exemplary by the next generation of moralists who think they have found far worse matter to fear.

At the same time, we cannot be entirely dismissive. It is hard to imagine that working-class readers managed to make their way through the "Ragged Dick" stories of Horatio Alger, the various books of the "Luck and Pluck" series, and the "Tattered Tom" tales without feeling the weight of moral instruction. The reader's imagination cannot re-figure everything, nor does it want to. Morality inhabited the dime novels, not all of them but many of the popular ones. Authors made explicit interventions in the story to underline moral points. Even without the author's direct voice, moral concerns were manifest in the codes of sentimental and melodramatic plots that pitted good against evil. In fact, most of the dime novels of the late nineteenth century were tamer than the pre–Civil War novels of George Lippard and Ned Buntline who much more explicitly attempted to excite the outrage of wage earners against the moral and religious bankruptcy of capitalists and clerics. The disappearance of their sort of angry, sensationalized moralizing reflected a trend to the still tamer formulas that after 1900 dismissed working-class men and women along with tramps and outlaws altogether from plots. Publishers of cheap fiction replaced them with middle-class moral heroes like Nick Carter and Frank Merriwell.

Several things are equally true. Middle-class religious moralists could record some success in influencing popular fiction. To the extent their efforts worked, they took away from young working-class readers a cultural resource that had been important to their sense of fighting back. At the same time, the taste of those readers was as responsible for what happened as any purported middle-class conspiracy. The case parallels that of vaudeville. Changes resulted from successful experiments in mass culture that made issues of class largely irrelevant to an audience. There may be good reasons to regret the development of formulas that banished rebel figures from cheap fiction. The more blanket the indictment, however, the more we leave oxen gored all through the social spectrum. If pulp novels of the early twentieth century left young workers with less to rebel against in their imagination, the same can be said about young middle-class readers who needed the stimulation much more. Readers, in any case, got something they apparently liked.

Does Anyone Win?

Theodor Adorno and Max Horkheimer have made the most powerful indictment of the blandness of mass culture. They call it the "culture industry," so as to exclude any interpretation that it arose from the people, and label it a twentieth-century disaster for everybody. What was on their minds primarily was the conflation of high and low art through the imposition of the "profit motive onto cultural forms." The conflation damaged them both. High art was deprived of its seriousness because it was tailored for consumption. Low art "perishes with the civilizational constraints imposed on the rebellious resistance inherent within it as long as social control was not yet total."[55] On their terms, the middle classes lost evenly with the working classes in the moral transformation of traditional working-class pleasures. Although the middle classes succeeded in imposing some of their moral standards on production of mass culture, they capitulated to the profit base of cultural activity, accepting in the process forms of cultural entertainment that made them all in one way or another clones of Sinclair Lewis's famous character George Babbitt.

To say that the working classes had more of their way than the middle classes in the creation of twentieth-century commercial culture is in Adorno's and Horkheimer's terms not merely wrong but an insult. It would imply that working classes knowingly exchanged the oppositional base of their traditions for the cultural equivalent of a mess of pottage. However, a great deal of truth resides in the statement. We should think about urban commercial culture at the turn of the century as a compromise of class-based moral perspectives. With good reason, the most conservative voices of middle-class morality and religion were a long way from satisfied with the offerings of commercial culture. Most pleasure-seeking Americans, including the ones who went to church, no longer paid much attention to a rule against diversions that "can not be used in the name of Jesus Christ."[56] On the other hand, they were not necessarily keen on doing things that, when pressed, they could not square with moral principles. The promoters of secular commercial entertainments needed the blessing of religious leaders and made steady effort to get it. Baseball promoters at the turn of the century forbade the sale of liquor at games, acquiesced in bans on Sunday ball (lasting in Boston until 1929 and in Philadelphia until 1934), and saw to it that clergymen got season passes in every league town.[57] Clerics for a good part of the twentieth century were able to lead a "vigorous patrol" over most forms of mass entertainment that, in spite of themselves, they had done so much to create.[58]

To the extent that these successes had only middle-class sponsorship, and brought profit only to middle-class promoters, they translated into losses for the working classes. City and state licensing requirements drove many working-class pleasures out of existence. They forced others to become more prim. In the worst cases the result was to drive up the price of what had been cheap or free, leaving the bottom ranks of society with truly destructive pleasures sustained by organized crime. Moral accommodation often represented unwanted intrusion. Nineteenth-century police surveillance destroyed the spontaneity of parades and the vitality of street theater enjoyed, above all, by industrial workers.[59] Working-class young women resented protective restrictions on their movements, especially efforts to ban commercial dance halls that permitted the unchaperoned mixing of the sexes. These became a favorite target of the many vice investigations that were Progressive America's favorite public enterprise.[60]

For all that, from one end of the nineteenth century to the other the most popular forms of urban entertainment—melodrama, minstrel shows, vaudeville, amusement parks, saloons, the movies—prospered first among working-class and immigrant audiences. The creation of popular culture as it moved into the new century was a trickle-up not a trickle-down operation. In Pittsburgh as late as 1890, the theater and other forms of commercial culture depended entirely for their survival upon working-class patronage.[61] Working-class taste in cities across the nation placed an indelible imprint upon most forms of commercial entertainment, allowing commercial culture to develop in the twentieth century without the constant burden to proclaim, as P. T. Barnum had once done, that it was doing the same work as churches. In 1911, Mark M. Davis, who had developed a scale to measure the morality of any entertainment, figured vaudeville as three-quarters "not objectionable," one-fifth "lowering," and one-twentieth "positive." That was scarcely the balance that middle-class moralists had sought for an acceptable entertainment, but eventually the judgment "not objectionable" became a sufficient standard to pass most boards of censorship.[62] What really had happened was that other standards of religious morality, ones that had never found anything objectionable in theater or fiction, had gained an ascendancy in American life equal to those that censorious Protestants proclaimed.

This was not just a working-class accomplishment. It was more specifically a non-Protestant and ethnic working-class accomplishment. Immigrant Catholics, whether Irish, German, Italian, Polish, or Hispanic, carried to the United States a great variety of street entertainments, a zest for holiday and carnival rooted in folk traditions. Not only could these specific things be commercialized but they also reflected an untroubled acceptance of gaiety that made possible an enormous range of other commercial pastimes.[63] In the case of immigrant Jews, especially in the traditions of Yiddish-speaking orthodox Jews who began to arrive in American cities in significant numbers in the last quarter of the nineteenth century, the contribution was equally dramatic. So like American middle-class Protestants in their work habits, they introduced into American culture an expressive exuberance that made clearer than any other religious tradition yet present on American territory that work, play, and religion had natural, untroubled connections. The mass commercial culture of the twentieth century, whether in publishing, movies, radio, or television, was unthinkable without the Jewish contribution.

The Protestant response took some bizarre forms. Many working-class Protestants at the end of the nineteenth century renewed a flesh-denying moral vigilance and squeezed into the tight mold of Holiness sects and the Jehovah's Witnesses who perpetuated the narrowest of views condemning leisure outside of church programs. The Catholic and Jewish cases continued to illustrate other ways to look at the moral possibilities of mass entertainment. Their non-religious forms of enjoyment had always been woven into their religious life. The Church often sponsored the lodges and clubs of ethnic immigrant Catholics. Catholics held religious meetings in lodge halls that were proximate to a saloon or beer garden. Jewish men who met to discuss the Talmud might share the same space with a Jewish trade union and a Yiddish theater. This was not merely the result of the cramped living conditions of an overpopulated neighborhood. It was reflective of a way of life in which joyous religious worship included dancing, spectacle, and expressive emotion.

When folk traditions entered into the relatively expensive territory of commercial expression, there was, inevitably, corruption. This is more of the story of religious commodification that can lead us into judgments similar to those that Adorno and Horkheimer made. On the other hand, the transformations had a creative side and indicated innovative ways that religion could operate in the marketplace of culture in forms other than whining complaint. Protestants had been important shapers of popular culture in the early part of the nineteenth century. They still had means to control the direction it took, and they had only begun to explore the possibilities for placing their own product before a consuming public. But in the matter of how religion moved in the cultural marketplace beyond attempted censorship and beyond the means used to sell the religion itself, imaginative leadership had passed to other religious traditions.

CHAPTER EIGHT

Religious Advertising and Progressive Protestant Approaches to Mass Media

"Now, as to hearing a sermon today, if you wish to do so, you can either go to church to hear it or stay at home."

"How am I to hear it if I stay at home?"

"Simply by accompanying us to the music room at the proper hour and selecting an easy chair. There are some who still prefer to hear sermons in church, but most of our preaching, like our musical performances, is not in public, but delivered in acoustically prepared chambers, connected by wire with subscribers' houses. . . . I see by the paper that Mr. Barton is to preach this morning, and he preaches only by telephone, and to audiences often reaching 150,000."

Conversation between Dr. Leete and Julian West in Edward Bellamy's *Looking Backward*

A book about religion's role in commercial culture must eventually get to the subject of Christmas. The pagan origins of this holiday linked to the winter solstice is not in doubt. When the Catholic Church in the fourth century singled out December 25 as the birth date of Christ, it tried to stamp out the saturnalia common to the solstice season. Yet various local festivities continued to precede and follow it. Since these never were and never would be wholly Christian, they provoked controversy. Luther did not make Christmas a target of reformed practice, but Calvin did. The attitude of the latter determined the stance of English Puritans, and among their first acts when they rose to power under Oliver Cromwell was to ban not merely the festive celebration of Christmas but any special observance of the day. Across the Atlantic, their ban spread to colonial New England but little affected what happened south of Connecticut. Anglicans in colonial Virginia, grateful for the Restoration of the Stuarts in 1660, made Christmas a time of feasts, hunts, and fancy balls.[1]

Local patterns persisted in the early republic. Presbyterians, Congregationalists, Quakers, and most Baptists ignored Christmas. Episcopalians, Lutherans, Catholics, and the Dutch Reformed did not, although their celebrations in the early nineteenth century went forward without Santa Claus, toy stores, exchanged Christmas cards, and (except among Germans) Christmas trees. By the end of the nineteenth century, Christmas was a legal holiday in all states (Alabama was the first to make it so in 1836). Virtually all Christian denominations observed it, no longer much concerned that it prompted a broad range of eagerly pursued secular diversions. Christmas was becoming the season, a longer and longer season, when American merchants did their biggest business. The cries that churches carried to the Protestant-founded department stores of Macy's, Wanamaker's, and Marshall Field's to "put Christ back in Christmas" only served to stir up a market for manufactured crèches, cards with religious messages, and recorded sacred music. Merchandising in the twentieth century gave Christ a more visible role in Christmas than he ever had before, even if the same could be said for Bing Crosby and Rudolph.

The major changes took most of the nineteenth century. Washington Irving in 1819 described a "traditional" English Christmas for Americans in *The Sketchbook of Geoffrey Crayon, Gent*. Clement Clarke Moore, a wealthy, conservative, Episcopal professor of Hebrew who lived in New York City, set the stage for Santa Claus by writing a poem about a toy-giving St. Nicholas who rode around the world in a sleigh pulled by flying reindeer.[2] Published in 1823, it remained popular thereafter. Charles Dickens made Christmas a stock item of the book trade with "A

205

Christmas Carol," a wonderful tale that sentimentalized the holiday as a special occasion to remember the poor and unfortunate. Advertisements for Christmas gifts appeared in the United States as early as the 1820s, and denominational resistance to the holiday began to fade. Christmas became a holiday in Connecticut in 1845 and in Massachusetts in 1855. In 1851 an enterprising merchant hauled loads of fir trees into New York to sell to the middle class.[3] Christmas cards made a surging appearance in the 1870s. The cartoonist Thomas Nast, remembered for his depiction of Boss Tweed with his vulture cronies, provided American audiences with a more lasting image when, beginning in 1863 in the pages of *Harper's Weekly*, he drew Santa Claus. By the early twentieth century, a huge toy industry, bank-sponsored "Christmas clubs" to enable parents to save for the season, and Thanksgiving parades to bring Santa and his helpers to the stores were securely part of an American Christmas.[4]

A certain canard surfaces every holiday season, sometimes politely disguised as humor, that Jewish department-store owners, with a little help from Irving Berlin, were responsible for the commercialization of Christmas. The elegant displays that have graced the windows of Saks Fifth Avenue and Bloomingdale's along with the seasonal catalogues of Nieman-Marcus compose the evidence. The claim is nonsense. The inventors of the commercial possibilities of Christmas, which more than anything else in American culture present religion as a product promising pleasure and sentimental self-mastery, were earnest Protestants who saw nothing awkward about promoting their faith with a boost in profits. Merchants who turned Christmas into a consuming celebration worked with clerical allies. Skilled advertising required that the "miracle" of Santa Claus and his reindeer refer back to the "miracle" at Bethlehem and the gifts that the three kings carried to the Christ child. Liberal Protestant leaders had their own agenda in looking benignly upon such associations, although what they wanted also encouraged the consumerism that encouraged seasonal sales. With a clear sense of how they wanted to build a just and good society, they began in the late nineteenth and early twentieth centuries to invest heavily in advertising and in the techniques of efficient business management. Those investments, which set the context for the commercialization of Christmas, made possible much else besides.

The Meaning of Henry Ward Beecher

If Benjamin Franklin is the best example of Max Weber's point about the Protestant work ethic and its refusal of the spontaneous enjoyment of life, Henry Ward Beecher may very well best illustrate how the ardent Protestant became the consummate consumer, endlessly "striving after stimulative pleasures, the gratification of each new want."[5] Born in 1813 into a host of what would become famous siblings, Beecher had to contend with the reputation of an eminent father who fought some of the last losing battles of Connecticut's Calvinist standing order. Lyman Beecher repositioned his views on original sin and predestination; and once removed from New England to Cincinnati, he conceded that religion to stay in favor needed to cultivate more resources than sound, orthodox preaching. The son went a good bit farther, leaving behind all familial feeling for Calvinism to embrace what one of his biographers calls "Romantic Christianity."[6] The change seemed striking and sudden. In 1843 in his *Lectures to Young Men*, Beecher had outlined with unusual force the full array of Puritan warnings against pleasure. Shortly after being called to the Plymouth Church in Brooklyn in 1847, he became a regular and avid visitor to New York City's jewelry and department stores, buying books, semiprecious stones, and art. He attended the theater. And partly to pay the debts incurred from his consuming habits, he joined the lecture circuit and wrote a novel. His lecture fees set a new market high, providing evidence for one historian that intellectual life in America was itself becoming "wholly fungible."[7]

The change in Beecher's attitude, far from astonishing, was a natural progression. His Protestant imagination had always tended toward romantic feeling. His success as a preacher owed to his ability to make his middle-class congregation luxuriate in their emotions, to weep and to take pleasure in the many ways they could imagine themselves as good-deed doers, as loving and as loved agents. The inexhaustible stock of these images was part of God's abundant love. The abundance had a material payoff. In 1850 Beecher oversaw the construction of a new church structure seating three thousand people. By the end of the 1860s, he had established a communications network that made his name familiar across the nation. He wrote for newspapers; he edited a religious journal (that by 1872 had 132,000 subscribers); and he published numerous volumes of his sermons and lectures. The embarrassing scandal of 1874, in which Theodore Tilton accused him of having an adulterous relationship with his wife, did little to rock the fame. Acquitted in the trial, he emerged a celebrity, mobbed and cheered and applauded during a lecture tour he undertook in 1876 to cover his legal debts. Commanding a fee of a thousand dollars per talk, he played to "sold out" houses across twenty-seven thousand miles in eighteen states.

Beecher gave tangible proof of the profits of religion—about sixty thousand dollars from the 1876 lectures. He also justified in explicit terms the developing mania of America's wealthy elite to collect art, to build expensive mansions, and to purchase precious antiques and furniture. Luxury and extravagance were not only respectable but also the proper tendencies of pious men.[8] The well-heeled Christian, by selecting for consumption what reflected refinement and good taste, made a contribution to the public welfare. Good taste was the equivalent of sound moral judgment (a wastrel could not by definition buy well), and both were premised on a consumer's holding to the Christian sentiments of love and benevolence. Once Beecher had worried that Protestant imaginative power, which it took a Puritan to recognize, had to be sharply restricted. That worry disappeared. The good Christian could be trusted with his attachments, spiritual and material.

Most of the people who fell under the power of Beecher's preaching were women. This could be expected both from the gender composition of Protestant churches and from the socially constructed traits that defined Victorian womanhood. Emotion, not reason, was the essence of femininity. Ann Douglas was the first scholar to argue the connection between the Protestant clergy, their sentimental female listeners, and the growth of consumerism that depended on the style-consciousness of female shoppers.[9] The sensibilities apparent in sentimental fiction, which was written and read by women, reflected vast pleasure in the ownership of material things, even if these authors criticized crass materialism. Materialism did not mean the wanting of worldly goods. It meant buying without feeling or taste. Elizabeth Stuart Phelps's much maligned *The Gates Ajar*, first published in 1868, offered a concrete heaven where people enjoyed market desires in full and refined plentitude. What Phelps's book commends is not luxury consumption (the most expensive item in her heaven is a piano) but the imaginative freedom to wander over the endless possibilities of humanly scaled pleasures.

Attacks on the consumptive mentality of Americans have become a cottage industry of recent social criticism. Under these circumstances it is hard to remember that consumerism once served a reformist perspective. The message of material abundance preached by Beecher and in a hundred forums by women was not conservative. It was essential to the utopian designs of many nineteenth-century American writers and to what became in the early twentieth century the "Progressive Movement." Moral reform, which led many women out of their homes and local church circles into political activism, meant, above all, learning to make moral choices in the marketplace. Under the guise of what Frances Willard called "home protection" legislation or what the General Federation of Women's Clubs in the 1890s embraced as "municipal housekeeping," women discovered more and more public ways to play out the moral and religious responsibilities that they had been given in the home.[10]

To be sure, the morality that sought to give everyone the wherewithal to become an intelligent consumer often sought legislation to restrain choices, temperance being the prime example. The effort, however, was to reform capitalism so that wealth and moral choices acted as mutual reinforcements. In Charles Sheldon's best-selling novel *In His Steps* (1896), a work frequently cited by Progressive reformers, readers followed the progress of a middle-class congregation, the members of which had taken a vow not to do anything that they could not imagine Christ doing. As a result, a newspaper editor decides not to report boxing matches or to carry advertisements from liquor dealers or to publish a Sunday edition. A railroad executive can no longer abide the corrupt practices in his industry and resigns. A talented soprano abandons her career on the world's stage and sings instead for a local slum mission. Although these Christ-imitating characters initially sacrifice money and social position, Sheldon's book was no more an indictment of material comfort than Edward Bellamy's famous fictional vision of a collective state, *Looking Backward*. None of the characters who take up Christ's burden starves. None, in fact, loses anything worth having. Sheldon's reform message was not aimed at material denial. Rather, the measure of successful social reform became how adequately it made middle-class commodities generally available. The progressive Social Gospel ministers wanted to demonstrate that God's material abundance, if managed in the right way, left everyone in *private* possession of a comfortable share of the world's goods.

In this context, we can begin to understand how the reforming concerns of Social Gospel ministers in the late nineteenth century went hand in glove with a concern over the financial profile of their churches. The imperative urged upon churches to learn business methods was not a conservative reaction to a reformist program aiming to moralize commercial practices. It was an essential part of the reformist program. Liberal Protestants who were convinced that Christ preached a practical social message relevant to modern America entered the twentieth century jubilant about signs of their impending triumph. Organized churches were doing well, expanding their membership roles faster than the rate of population growth. Between 1880 and 1900, the Disciples of Christ increased in number from 473,00 to 1,025,000. Episcopalians and Methodists doubled their rosters. Southern Baptist membership shot up from 960,000 to 1,658,000.

To manage the social responsibilities that went with these numbers, responsibilities that extended beyond organized religious bodies to embrace the country's general material and spiritual welfare, churches needed to run themselves with business efficiency. They needed to adopt aggressive techniques for growth, to budget their resources, and to run campaigns that raised "millions for the Master." The commodification of religion in these ways, which ignored distinctions between consumerism and social uplift, may well be the most important accomplishment of liberal Christianity. Dwight Moody and Billy Sunday had used business techniques with different political intentions, but liberal Christians made them part of everyday denominational activity. Henry Ward Beecher never quite made it into the Social Gospel camp, but his booster successor at the Plymouth Church, Lyman Abbott, most certainly did. The modern Christ required well-managed and well-spent wealth.

The Social Gospel and the Business of American Progressive Reform

Many historians have just about given up trying to define the Progressive movement of the early twentieth century. Wherein was its essence? In Jane Addams's Hull House? In Theodore Roosevelt's 1912 promise to battle for the Lord at Armageddon? In the reports of urban vice commissions that urged "civilized" outlets for men's debased passions? In Jacob Riis's photographs of praying children rescued from the squalor of urban tenements? Without insisting that Progressive reform was one thing, we may make a fair beginning at characterization by saying that Progressive reform was an effort to actualize moral and religious values by building an economy of abundance using the knowledge of a new science of efficiency. For its most typical expression, we could do worse than settle on the Federal Council of the Churches of Christ in the United States of America, founded in Philadelphia in 1908. The Federal Council was above all an optimistic effort to put Protestant unity in the service of social reform.[11]

The Protestant fraternity of the Federal Council lopped off Unitarians at the liberal end of the spectrum and Southern Baptists, a far larger group, and most Lutherans at the other. Even so, the ecumenical impulse among Protestants had never seemed stronger. In the early twentieth century, religious leaders of the white Protestant middle class thought that they were close to inaugurating God's plan to secure their hegemony at home and ultimately in the world. Evangelical conversion remained on the agenda of Social Gospel ministers, but the Federal Council translated that aim into the need to "promote the application of the law of Christ in every relation of human life." A report on the "Church and Modern Industry," presented by the Methodist minister Frank Mason North at the council's first meeting, advocated trade unions, collective bargaining, legislation providing for safe workplaces, and the right of wage earners to leisure. Adopted by the council as the "Social Creed of the Churches," it made the Federal Council "a sort of official keeper of the Social Gospel."[12]

The positions taken by the Federal Council were as close to the middle of the spectrum of Progressive reform as it was possible to be, a long way from socialism but to the left of those who believed that the creation of a moral society depended on individual action entirely without recourse to regulatory legislation. Its interest in political lobbying began to offend some of its original Protestant affiliates as early as 1913, but middle-class enthusiasm for reform was sufficiently strong before America got entangled in World War I to protect the Federal Council from the leftist reputation it later battled. The Federal Council, far from seeking to overthrow capitalism, concerned itself with adapting business methods to its own operations. The alacrity with which Social Gospelers embraced the slogans and tools of advertising, financial growth, and efficient scientific management assumed almost apocalyptic significance.[13] Church leaders had to make themselves ready to lead the coming social transformations.

Soon enough, the conservative political implications of their actions became manifest. They were clear, for example, by the time Bruce Barton published *The Man Nobody Knows* in 1925. In its popularized debasement of Christ into a glad-handing host, Rotarian, speculative promoter, and canny businessman, Barton's volume is in a class by itself. Where else is it stated with such unabashed enthusiasm that "Christ picked up twelve men from the bottom ranks of business and forged them into an organization that conquered the world?" No "pale young man with flabby forearms and sad expression," Jesus loved the outdoors, had a great body steeled with hard muscles, and was the most sought-after bachelor dinner guest in Jerusalem. Barton, like Mary Baker Eddy, fancied Christ in his own image. The son of a Protestant minister, he was voted "most likely to succeed" by his class at Amherst. He wrote for magazines, invented slogans to sell the "Five-Foot Shelf of Harvard Classics," raised money for war work, and in 1919 joined Roy Durstine and Alex Osborn to form one of America's largest ad agencies. Barton's successful book, which remained on the best-seller list for two years, betokened a reckless booster spirit that viewed untrammeled corporate expansion as itself the remedy to any social problems that might be caused by growth.

What is sobering of course is that the Republican Barton's model for the corporate-minded Christ lay in the books of Social Gospel ministers whom Barton had once admired.[14] They had embraced the cause of muscular Christianity and sought during the Progressive Era to alter the symbols of their faith so that Christianity became synonymous with effective public action.[15] Consider Harry Emerson Fosdick's *The Manhood of the Master*, a virility-promoting study published in 1913. Fosdick was perhaps, after Walter Rauschenbusch, America's best-known preacher to arise from the Social Gospel tradition, and his influence extended long after the conventionally designated death of Progressive reform in 1919. His most famous stint as a pastor was at New York City's Riverside Church, an interdenominational Protestant church built largely with a benefaction from John D. Rockefeller, Jr., and completed in 1931. Fosdick established his fame through his pulpit performances, his pronouncements in major, general-circulation periodicals, and a long list of best-selling books.

Like Barton, Fosdick rejected all portraits of Christ as a man with a "wan, sad face." Christ enjoyed nature, friendship, social life, good health, and joys that were "fine and high." Fosdick did not claim that Christ was the first modern businessman, but his Christ was someone who knew how to get "benevolent" wealthy men on his side. Such men were "the masters not the slaves of their possessions." They were Christ's favorite "examples of right living." Fosdick's images favored the military—Christ as the great general, the "spiritual Garibaldi." Christ was no dreamer, no failure, no starry-eyed optimist. He was a man of "prodigious power," persevering, self-confident, and loyal to a clear plan of action that changed the world. The mystery of divinity was as absent in Fosdick's tale as it was in Barton's. Christ was the all-American male who saw how to solve problems and did whatever was necessary to sell his message.[16]

The main difference between Fosdick and Barton, aside from Fosdick's effort to remember the spiritual aspects of faith, was that Fosdick's religion was intended to make business operations just. Barton had it almost the other way round. Fosdick's Social Gospel fit snugly with Progressive ideals in trying to make Christian values felt everywhere in American life, reforming the workplace, the schools, the armed forces, urban missions, all levels of government, and the home. To further this effort, churches had to drop petty dogmatic concerns, pay close attention to new forms of organization, and adopt aggressive styles of management copied from America's fastest-growing corporations. Expansion was everything. What enterprise, the Social Gospelers asked, had ever grown faster than Christianity itself? To control the tremendous resources at their command in the modern world, Christian churches had to follow the principles of scientific management.[17]

Frederick Winslow Taylor's *Principles of Scientific Management* sank deeply into the consciousness of the men who organized and ran the Federal Council. In 1911, the same year that Taylor published his famous study, Shailer Mathews, a prominent modernist theologian and dean of the University of Chicago's divinity school, promoted scientific management in addressing the Sagamore Beach Sociological Conference. In the book that followed, Mathews urged church leaders to make use of "the experience of successful businessmen."[18] Mathews feared that too many church workers were like Taylor's industrial laborers. Their amateur enthusiasms and rule-of-thumb strategies led to waste and needed to "be restrained within well-conceived plans and a proper division of labor." Ministers could manage this restraint only if they received a different sort of education than most of them were getting, one that turned them from pulpit exhorters into leaders "of a social group with a definitely religious and moral function." Divinity-school training had to concern itself with "the needs of our social order, the psychology of religion, the methods of organizing church agencies from Bible Clubs to Sunday schools, and the best means of conducting studies of neighborhoods and the concrete problems of a pastorate."[19]

Although Mathews insisted on a vital distinction between business and church activities, the urgent part of his message was the need to make "the church something of a business establishment."[20] If there was tension between the principles of church and corporate organization, Mathews did not stretch it very tightly. Francis H. Case, who saw eye to eye with Mathews on the need for better organization, was even blunter in his *Handbook of Church Advertising*, published in 1921: "The objection will be raised that we are mixing faith with business, and that they won't mix. Too long has the world labored under this delusion. They must mix if civilization is to endure." Case added the caveat that "we need to remind ourselves over and over again, and in as many ways as possible, that church advertising is an aid to, not a substitute for religion."[21] In truth, Case's mnemonic devices customarily let him down. The modern Jesus was not spending much time on his cross. He had too much to do. If he was not the first businessman, he was, according to Albert F. McGarrah, the "first efficiency expert."[22] Case, who was then working for the Young People's League of the northern Presbyterian church, went on to enter Republican politics in South Dakota, serving for many years in the House of Representatives and later in the Senate.

The subject of church advertising and publicity filled a disproportionate amount of the church manuals that emphasized efficiency and business-like management. Given the success of the evangelical drive in the nineteenth century, that is understandable. The fastest growing Protestant denominations in the United States had kept abreast of media opportunities from the beginning of the nineteenth century. Advertising as a professional science to move products through the market was a new opportunity that progressive religious leaders quickly endorsed. Had not Christ done whatever was necessary to spread the word to people who had not heard it? Subtlety was not his way. When Christ performed miracles, he was deliberately making news. It followed logically that religious leaders in the twentieth century had to learn how to capture headlines.

Charles Stelzle was among the first Social Gospel ministers to get an advertising manual into print. His *Principles of Successful Church Advertising*, published in 1908, was cited as a standard reference for two decades. Stelzle had a closer view of the competition that faced churches than many of his colleagues. Growing up on the Lower East Side of Manhattan, Stelzle knew the attractions along the Bowery and Grand Street that appealed to ethnic workers. He retained a keen taste for vaudeville himself; and although he became a champion of prohibition, he recalled in his memoirs that saloon owners were often charitable, well-meaning people.[23] He embarked on a career to minister to America's working class, speaking out for a non-radical, non-socialist trade unionism. In 1910 he founded and managed to fill on most days of the week New York's Labor Temple, a brownstone church on the corner of 14th Street and 2nd Avenue.[24] To compete with the lighted marquees of nearby movie houses, Stelzle emblazoned the name of the Labor Temple on an electric sign with letters two feet square. To provide information about his programs, he erected on the exterior sides of the church four large bulletin boards "studded with electric lights." Inside, on Sundays, he ran a continuous "bill" with no interruptions between attractions that included a "carefully censored motion picture." His favorite was "Kelly the Cop." He did not want to give his audiences a chance to escape. He boasted: "I had carefully studied the methods of motion-picture houses and vaudeville theaters to discover means for introducing life and snappiness into the programs."[25] Stelzle was called upon to raise money to win the war in Europe as well as to battle for prohibition. When he left the ministry, he became an advertising agent.

Practical information filled the advertising handbooks for churches. It ranged from suggested slogans, to ways to get church news in the papers, to information about how to lay out a church bulletin with maximum eye-catching effect. Case's *Handbook of Church Advertising* compiled suggestions from ministers as well as from people working in the advertising business. These first of all provided a thorough justification of publicity. Christians had the best product in the world with potentially a universal set of buyers. They could not sit back and wait for consumers to come to them. They had to reach out to the many people who had not yet heard about Christian salvation. "What would become of theater, if that institution advertised itself only within its own walls and by half-inch advertisements once a week?"[26] The crucial thing was to get people's attention, to spark their curiosity so that they would try church, like a brand of soap. How? With slogans: "Know the handshake of St. Paul's"; with a colored poster showing the moon falling behind a lit church named the "House of Happiness"; with commercial placards in streetcars: "A MAN NEEDS GOD. In times like these, Go to Church Sunday"; with advertisements in newspapers emphasizing the "red-blooded manliness" of Jesus, John the Baptist, and Paul; with outdoor billboards using colored letters and large visuals. One of the visuals cited in Case's manual was a circle graph entitled "Your World Market." The circle which represented the 1,640,000,000 people in the world was divided into two sectors, a smaller one to depict those who had heard the word of Christ and a larger one to represent the 1,000,000,000 "Heathens" who were "Destructive to Civilization and Progress." Under the graph was printed the bold proclamation: "Christianity Makes People Healthy, Happy, and Prosperous."

Publicity meant telling people what the church had "for sale." The contributors to Case's manual emphasized companionship, community uplift, and comfort in distress equally with salvation from sin, Bible study, and inspiration to higher ideals.[27] The primary goal was growth, presumably in the number of right-living Christians, but more measurably in the size of church buildings, the range of church facilities, the variety of sponsored programs, and the amount of money in the collection plates. Church advertising stressed churchgoing as a popular thing to do. According to the manuals, posters should show crowded churches with standing room only. People, it was noted, loved to be with crowds. If they came to church attracted as much by an advertised bag-pipe band as by the sermon, nothing had been compromised. Next week they might listen to the sermon.

Perhaps the most troublesome aspect of this trend in church progressivism was that it gave explicit approval to the advertising industry that was already under attack for creating phony desires and elevating lying to a science. Protestant liberals ignored the criticism. The advertiser's claim to professional standards swept up Social Gospelers in a wave of enthusiastic support. The tricks used in advertising to get people's attention were not the same as lying. Ministers convinced themselves that no positive claim made in behalf of Christianity could mislead. Customer satisfaction was guaranteed. Constructing a good society required catchy publicity to ensure that people made the best choices in product selection. Christianity was a sound choice. Ivory Soap, Campbell's soups, Pond's beauty lotion, and Aunt Jemima's pancake mix were others.

Liberal clerics were at least right in believing that advertising worked. The organizational achievements of the Protestant liberals, allied with progressive businessmen, were remarkable. The efforts provided opportunities for some remarkable individuals as well. The career of John R. Mott is exemplary. As a young Methodist student at Cornell University, he threw himself into campus YMCA endeavors and played a major role in raising fifty million dollars to construct a home for campus religious work.[28] Barnes Hall (Alfred S. Barnes was the principal donor) now houses a post office, a center for international students, assorted non-religious agencies, and a concert hall; but when it was constructed, religious work at the non-denominational Cornell had the full endorsement of the university president and the faculty. For many years Mott worked for the YMCA, expanding its domestic and foreign missionary work. He stayed in constant motion around the world. His success depended on generous support from businessmen—Cleveland E. Dodge, Chicago's McCormick family, and John Rockefeller, Jr. They became his companions. Mott's disciplined Christian activism and strong organizational skills complemented the aim of businessmen to open world markets to American trade. Trade and missionary work were both ways to effect world Protestant outreach and to achieve what Mott had called for in 1900, "the evangelization of the world in this generation."

Mott's mission work thrust him into the company of world leaders, and the idealism he preached was sufficiently credible to win him the Nobel Peace Prize in 1946. He provided a model of American diplomacy that had considerable influence. John Foster Dulles, Eisenhower's "brink-of-war" Secretary of State, emerged from a network of men who took for granted that a moral world depended on the Christian cooperation of expansive-minded businessmen and expansive-minded clergy. Dulles abandoned plans to become a Presbyterian minister and set to work for international peace believing that Christianity taught the values necessary to a secure world order. After Pearl Harbor he chaired the Commission on a Just and Durable Peace sponsored by the Federal Council.

The Social Gospelers' endeavor to make the world Christian using the patronage and many of the methods of corporate sponsors reached its apogee (or nadir) during the decade of the 1920s. Church newspapers of many Protestant denominations in all sections of the country beamed editorial praise on enlightened men of wealth.[29] Following up the success of his best-selling *In His Steps*, Charles Sheldon edited the *Christian Herald* which during America's "Jazz Age" ran an investment column as a regular feature for readers and carried advertisements from banks, trust companies, and investment houses. Journal after journal in the 1920s praised religion for the foundation it laid for a successful business career. *A Journal of Church Management* appeared in 1923 along with books bearing the titles *The Technique of a Minister, Business Methods for the Clergy, Church Administration,* and *How to Make the Church Go.* Religion's inclusion within the market economy was explicit: "The minister is a salesman. His success or failure depend upon the skill with which he persuades people to accept that which he has to offer."[30] A Baptist minister ran a newspaper ad billing his church as a "representative for the following articles": clothing (stays clean, the robe of righteousness), food (one loaf will last a lifetime, never gets stale, the bread of eternal life), and drinks (fresh from the FOUNTAIN the only drink that lasts a lifetime). The ad ended with an invitation "to look over our stock of goods" from the "oldest business in the world. . . . Every article and package bears the trademark-JESUS One price to all."[31]

Perhaps the best illustration of how the messengers of the Social Gospel had unwittingly joined in a celebration of benevolent capitalist expansion was the enterprising ministry of Christian F. Reisner. From the first decade of the century, Reisner had dedicated himself to strenuous social service. The church, he said, had to address the problem of "dirty faces, bare backs, and empty stomachs." Successful social service, as he explained in his books *Workable Plans for Wide-Awake Churches* (1906) and *Church Publicity* (1913), depended upon service that entertained as well as instructed. He remained committed to the Social Gospel when he became president of the Church Advertising Department of the Associated Advertising Clubs.

Called to a Methodist congregation in New York City after achieving national prominence in Denver, Reisner turned his talents in the 1920s toward rebuilding the Broadway Temple in Washington Heights. He wanted a four-million-dollar "skyscraper" church. The prospectus called for a twenty-four-story tower housing offices and apartments to rise over the sanctuary, this amalgam of religion and commerce to be crowned by a thirty-four-foot lighted cross. Reisner's associates marketed bonds to finance the construction with the slogan "Buy a Bond and Let God Have an Office Building on Broadway—a Bond Between You and God." Churches in Chicago, San Francisco, Minneapolis, and Detroit quickly copied the concept of making religion dramatically visible on the urban landscape as a diversified investment.[32] Reisner combined his real-estate sense with show biz. His services included performances by magicians, acrobats, and bird-call imitators. Every July he preached his "snow sermon" atop a mound of ice built in the sanctuary.[33]

By the middle of the 1920s, church publicity and the use of business imagery was no longer the exclusive property of the Social Gospel. Political and religious conservatives put their own mark on the uses of advertising to build mega-churches. As the Barton volume indicated, the difference between liberal and conservative appropriations of business methods seemed to lie more in tone than in substance. Social Gospel liberals suffered embarrassment from satirical attacks on religious "enterprise." Thorstein Veblen was the most savage. In *Absentee Ownership and Business Enterprise,* he described in his skilled ironical way how religious leaders had blazed the way in bringing the world to modern sales techniques. "The Propaganda of the Faith," he wrote, "is quite the largest, oldest, most magnificent, most unabashed, and most lucrative enterprise in sales-publicity in all Christendom." "Secular" salesmen were by comparison no better than "upstarts, raw recruits." When the latter peddled their "soap powders, yeast-cakes, lip-sticks, rubber tires, chewing-gum and restoratives of lost manhood," they appealed to "the same ubiquitously human ground of unreasoning fear, aspiration and credulity" as salesmen of the "sacred verities." What they had not quite mastered was the final untroubled skill with which religious merchants promised much and delivered nothing. Secular advertisers handicapped themselves by feeling it necessary to pass a visible product over the counter.[34]

Liberal Protestants did not abandon their strategies, although their words tried to correct a balance that had been lost. They filled their sermons with allusions to the need for economic altruism, for men of wealth to exercise their Christian stewardship in a more serious way, and for regulations to halt the injustice of unrestrained economic competition. What Protestant liberals could not do was abdicate their faith in "Modern Times" or throw out their proudly kept roster of Christian businessmen who gave generously. To the names that have already appeared in this chapter can be added J. C. Penney, John J. Eagan, Howard Heinz, John E. Edgerton, and William P. Hapgood. By one historian's count, most of the fifteen thousand annual business conventions in the 1920s held sessions devoted to religious inspiration. The language of Christian service flowed freely everywhere that businessmen came together—in meetings of chambers of commerce, in newly formed service clubs like Rotary and Kiwanis, in the Associated Advertising Clubs, and in better business bureaus. Never before (or since) had earnest Protestant rhetoric spread so widely beyond the churches into sessions conducted by America's most powerful men.

It was a very seductive bandwagon. To leap from it was tantamount to a denial of progress. Such an act would suggest that America's business civilization was immune to moral suasion. It would admit that Protestant ecumenical efforts to instill Christian values deeply into the conscience of Americans had gotten nowhere. It would raise the possibility that the only way to do anything to alleviate social injustice was to junk the entire American system and start afresh with something else. Most Social Gospel ministers, whatever their worries about whether they had sold out, remained wedded to progressive assumptions about the complementary flowering of scientific management and moral behavior.

In their defense we should remember that their attitudes were not timid pieties limited to religious sentimentalists. No less a hard-headed secularist than Walter Lippmann had announced in 1914 a "rebellion against the profit motive" led by new business professionals. He imagined a human psychology that rendered obsolete "private commercialism" and that created servants of civilization like Henry Ford "with his generous profit sharing."[35] If Lippmann could believe in businessmen who were not profiteers, then liberal Protestants might be excused for their hopes. In fact, only when we realize what a generous proposition they held, how sincerely leading American capitalists spoke about Christian stewardship, and how reasonable it was to envision a spreading Christian power of loving persuasion that would triumph over coercive force and violence can we appreciate why the challenge to the Social Gospel thrown down by Reinhold Niebuhr was so startling.

Niebuhr had gotten his fill of the paeans sung to honor Christianized business practices in 1926 while still a pastor in Detroit. The American Federation of Labor met in America's automobile capital that year. Following a tradition encouraged by the Federal Council, a few of Detroit's ministers along with the YMCA extended invitations to labor leaders to speak. An industry determined to maintain an open-shop policy went on the attack, prompting laymen to put pressure on their ministers to stay clear of the union. Three of the five invitations to labor leaders to speak in pulpits were withdrawn; and the YMCA, whose building program depended upon the largesse of the city's business community, also bowed to pressure. The fiasco convinced Niebuhr that churchmen who cared about social justice wasted time in mastering the techniques of publicity, budgets, and administration. Instead, they needed to study the operations of power and learn why their efforts to extend Christian influence throughout America had served only those who wielded power.

In *Moral Man and Immoral Society*, published in 1932, Niebuhr criticized the cultural and economic nostrums of the Social Gospelers for wrongly assuming the possibility of overcoming human selfishness. What they offered was a dreamy utopianism that had lost its passion. Niebuhr in 1932 laid down a program of passionate Christian realism. Human society, he insisted, was imperfectable and Christians had to abandon their hopes of achieving social justice by applying the gospel remedies of love and forgiveness. Economic power was not gentle, and only force could overturn it. Utopian ideals were not irrelevant to Niebuhr. He turned a vision of perfect justice realizable only in Christ's eternal kingdom into an exacting measure to expose the wretchedness of social conditions in the United States. What was wrong with the liberal Social Gospelers was not that they were blind to business corruption, or that they lacked ideas for social legislation, or even that they imagined that social perfection was easy and lay just around the corner. The problem was that they had exchanged the emotional fervor of Christianity, its deep and moving feeling for the terrible burden of human depravity, for a breezy faith in efficiency. Niebuhr turned social reform again into something that was urgent and radical.

Niebuhr's fire blazed most convincingly during the economic crisis of the 1930s. After the Depression and after World War II, the anti-utopian emphasis in his writing overtook his angry apocalyptic conviction that something had to be done now. It all but swamped the nation's political speech. Liberals and conservatives both talked of gradual change because, after all, human society really did not progress. It only rearranged its imperfections to maintain in a competitive world the most believably fair balance between the haves and have-nots. In that climate it became clear that the cheerful, accommodating Progressivism of the liberal Social Gospelers was a long way from dead. Despite the insurgence of Niebuhr's Protestant realism in America's leading divinity schools, and despite a more numerically significant challenge from Protestant fundamentalists who had their own list of sugar-daddy businessmen, Protestant liberals held their own. But successful influence had come at a price. We need to consider their dilemma as it developed on another twentieth-century front where religion ran up against the market. The arena shifts our attention again to the cultural marketplace.

Protestant Liberals and Mass Media: The Movies and Radio

By the second decade of the twentieth century, liberal Protestants had grown comfortable with a Christian theology predicated on the need to keep up with advances in knowledge. That meant staying abreast of science. The pace was fast. Change was worrisome, but, according to liberals, the Christian drama of redemption had always been subject to rephrasing. The message had to fit particular historical times. The same adjustments applied to notions about what God required in the behavior of a good Christian. Although liberal theology did not follow the American pragmatists in asserting the cultural and historical relativeness of moral values, what it taught came close to the same thing. If moral values were to set the norms of social life successfully, those who were privileged by birth and education to recognize moral truth and to live by its dictates had to bend when confronting the duller moral sensibilities of those less fortunate. They had to suit their strategies of influence to popular desires and understanding.

Following convictions formed in the nineteenth century, Protestant liberals believed that a great deal was at stake in how the institutions of commercial culture developed. The battle over movies that was joined even before the new century began almost immediately dwarfed in importance previous cultural struggles over sensational reading material, the theater, sports, and vaudeville. The number of nickelodeons swelled into the thousands in some cities and lined entire blocks in working-class neighborhoods. Moralists worried about the content of the early movies that they feared featured an endless sequence of boxing matches, girlie shows, and adulterous liaisons. They worried even more about the atmosphere of movie houses and its effect upon the audience. In the Protestant mind, the location of nickelodeons was morally proximate to saloons, brothels, and ragtime music. Nickelodeons were dark. Open seating drew young men and unescorted women together. Continuous shows invited casual dropping-in. Quite aside from the encouragement that these arrangements gave to illicit courting and lovemaking, films multiplied the dangers that the theater posed to uninstructed, unprepared imaginations. Screen images were larger than life. The magnified lips that touched in a screen kiss magnified the passion. The silent images with no didactic script to frame the action allowed the audience to daydream in morally dangerous ways. The perils of reading novels paled in comparison. Readers might daydream. Movie daydreams, according to early critics, evoked primitive passions that psychology was just developing a language to describe.

What differentiated the battle over movies from earlier cultural struggles was scale. As movies grew in popularity, it became clear that they were going to reach the majority of Americans on a weekly basis. No other form of commercial leisure had yet done that. Although the number of active readers had multiplied in the nineteenth century, the regular reading of fiction, even cheap fiction, was the practice of a minority. Most Americans had only intermittent experience with the theater or even with vaudeville. Attendance at professional sporting events was geographically restricted, and few American communities boasted a Coney

Island. Church leaders at the end of the nineteenth century could claim that more Americans attended church each week than paid for any kind of commercial entertainment. Movies changed that. Easily portable, they required no skills or educational attainments to watch. Many had equal appeal to all ages, all social classes, and both men and women. They were cheap, yet the profits that accrued from them made possible the construction of huge and comfortable movie houses. By the 1920s, most Americans attended a movie at least once a week, with the largest movie box office collected on Sundays. In 1937, despite the Depression, weekly attendance at the movies was estimated at eighty-eight million—more than three times the estimated weekly attendance at all places of worship by Protestants, Catholics, and Jews.[36]

How was liberal Protestantism to make an impression on this commercial giant? Clearly the days of a "high-class" traveling exhibitor like Lyman Howe were numbered. Legal suppression was one possibility that Protestant moralists explored. On Christmas Day in 1908, New York City's reform mayor George B. McClellan ordered his police force to close down five hundred fifty movie houses and nickelodeons. Behind him stood the city's leading Protestant ministers who had the year before won an important legal victory in their demand to close Sunday vaudeville. In his opinion, Justice Thomas A. O'Gorman had written: "The Christian Sabbath is one of the civil institutions of the state and that for the purpose of protecting the moral and physical well-being of the people and preserving the peace, quiet, and good order of society the Legislature has authority to regulate its observance."[37]

McClellan's action was a triumph for the Reverend Charles Parkhurst, the pastor of the Madison Square Presbyterian Church who had been leading the pulpit's charge against Tammany Hall since the 1890s. Some ministers who supported the closings made no attempt to conceal their anti-Catholic and anti-Semitic feelings when large numbers of New York Italians and Jews rose in protest. One dimension in the cultural conflict over movies was new. For the first time, Protestants witnessed a major form of commercial entertainment coming under the dominance of a non-Christian group. Actually, Protestants had been losing their grip on theater and vaudeville, but movies accelerated a shift. Edison lost his hold over the production and exhibition of movies, and they became the property of men who did not claim, as P. T. Barnum once had claimed, to be faithful Christians. They were Marcus Loew, Adolph Zukor, Carl Laemmle, William Fox, and Samuel L. Rothafel. The latter made the name "Roxy" synonymous with sumptuous, well-run, and spotlessly clean theaters. These were some of the men who created the great Hollywood studios of the 1920s and 1930s. They were all Jewish. Most of them were immigrants.[38]

Given the potential for cultural warfare inherent in this situation, the animosity remained relatively submerged for a variety of reasons. Protestants knew that they could not hope to close down a profitable industry permanently. Interestingly, movies in New York City were exempt from the Sunday closing laws that affected vaudeville and from state censorship laws that regulated the theater. The legislators who had written statutes to keep stage productions clean had not used language applicable to film.[39] A more permanent Progressive tactic to deal with movie houses was to force new rules on the exhibitors. New York City's Motion Picture Ordinance of 1913 gave the police power to inspect movie houses and to report on immoral operations. The licensing fee for motion-picture-house operators was increased from twenty-five to five hundred dollars on the sound calculation that operators who paid the higher fee would seek to expand their clientele into the middle class. The ordinance outlined safety requirements. Children under sixteen had to be chaperoned. Most operators fell in with the spirit of the ordinance and took precautions to protect women from unwanted advances. The Women's Municipal League and the Children's Aid Society refused to be satisfied with an industry that provided entertainment in dark rooms that seated both sexes. The Reverend F. M. Foster denied the right of men to "profit from the corruption of the minds of children."[40] Other moralists, however, stepped forward to defend movies as "family entertainment."

John Collier, who was part of the staff of the People's Institute, worked toward another solution that he hoped would allow business innovators and religious moralists to find common cause. He proposed self-censorship for the industry, and the idea had a promising start. In March 1909, the Moving Picture Exhibitors Association asked the People's Institute to organize a board of review to judge the suitability of all films shown in New York. Wealthy Protestants and a few German Jews, not the ones who went to Hollywood, dominated the executive committee of the National Board of Censorship (renamed the National Board of Review in 1915). Movie exhibitors and producers funded the operation, although volunteers drawn from such organizations as the Federal Council, the YMCA, and Reverend Charles Parkhurst's Society for the Prevention of Crime, did the actual reviewing. They worked hard and reviewed about six hundred films a month. The board gained subscribers from all over the country and by 1914 claimed that it passed on 95 percent of the nation's films.

In the period between 1912 and 1920, liberal Protestant moralists had other reasons to think that their business sense and their confidence in correcting commercial culture through friendly persuasion were paying off. Most important, the first director genius of the industry used Christian symbols in his narrative epic films to present conflicts between good and evil.[41] D. W. Griffith grew up in a strict Methodist environment, and he was buried in the graveyard of the same Methodist church he attended as a child. Images of Christ or the cross appeared in most of his movies, including the celebrated and controversial *Birth of a Nation* that set box office records in 1915. Griffith developed screen lighting techniques to differentiate his "pure" characters, mostly women protected in a halo glow, from the villainous. His favorite actress, Lillian Gish, was portrayed on screen and off as "the very essence of virginity." Griffith made sure that Gish, who had considered becoming a nun, and her sister Dorothy were supervised by their mother during projects. Moral propriety ruled his sets.

Ironically, Griffith's greatest popular triumph, *Birth of a Nation*, destroyed the semblance of Protestant consensus. Some members of the National Board of Review, offended by the film's racism, or at least its favorable depiction of the Ku Klux Klan, resigned rather than be party to a vote of approval. The board never recovered its power to exercise effective censorship; nor did Griffith fully recover his authority despite his role in forming United Artists.[42] His subsequent epic *Intolerance* (1916) attempted to answer the charge that he was a prejudiced man. Although later regarded as a masterpiece that included sequences telling the story of Christ, the film failed to make money. Foreshadowing the moral tone to be associated with Hollywood, the actor who portrayed Christ was arrested on a charge of sexual misconduct.

Cecil B. DeMille had credentials that might have made him a successor to Griffith as the screen's protector of Christian morals. His father had been for a time an Episcopal priest, and his mother, a converted German Jew, read the Bible to her children every night. DeMille directed in 1923 his famous epic *The Ten Commandments*, a spectacle advertised by a gigantic billboard over Times Square. A hundred thousand volts of bluish flame streaked down every few minutes as divine lightning to strike the tablets held by a colossal Moses. DeMille also gained fame in the 1920s for *King of Kings*, but most of his films were not biblical. His silent comedies leaned toward a modern morality that many liberal Protestants found a bit loose. Marriage is an ideal, but unions dissolve anyway. The scripts punished adultery, but also depicted it.[43] Douglas Fairbanks and Mary Pickford, divorced from other spouses before they married and eventually divorced from each other, set the glamorous tone for life in Beverly Hills. Other stars of the 1920s, Theda Bara, Rudolph Valentino,

Greta Garbo, Gloria Swanson, suggested the importance of sex to American box office.

In 1921 when murder charges put the popular Mack Sennett comedian Fatty Arbuckle behind bars, Hollywood had its first major sex scandal. Protestants moved to exercise the influence they still retained to regulate commercial culture. Some localities disappointed with voluntary review took measures to bring movies within the range of official censorship that applied to literature and the theater. In 1921 New York followed action already taken in Pennsylvania, Ohio, Kansas, Maryland, and Virginia and set up a movie censorship board. These state agencies had the authority to demand changes and cuts in movies before they could be shown. Other states and cities were considering similar laws.[44] The executives of the eight major Hollywood studios, men who for the next almost three decades would control the movie industry from production to distribution to exhibition, decided to try to quell the rising moral protests by forming a trade association. In 1921 they launched the Motion Picture Producers and Distributors of America as a lobbying agency for the film industry to improve its image, to sell its products at home and abroad, and to defeat state and national legislation unfavorable to its interests. Unfavorable, above all, meant official censorship bureaus with the power to cut profits. What the industry had to make believable to the American public was that it could morally regulate itself.[45]

With the effective demise of the National Board of Review, this was not an easy trick to pull off. In 1922 in one of the best casting decisions that Hollywood executives ever made, they called William Harrison Hays, known as Will, to run their trade association. Two identifying marks intended to reassure Protestant liberals and the Federal Council stamped Hays's character. He was Presbyterian, a prominent elder of his church, and Republican, formerly chairman of the Republican National Committee and at the time of his call from Hollywood Warren Harding's Postmaster General. Hays maintained his office in New York City, in part to establish his independence, and from there worked to persuade Protestant activists that movie producers wanted to provide Americans with wholesome fare and to prevent salacious advertising of their coming attractions. His best weapon in this endeavor was money. He hired as advisors people who belonged to organizations most likely to mount effective attacks on the industry. These included Mrs. Thomas G. Winter, president of the General Federation of Women's Clubs, and Charles S. Macfarland, the secretary of the Federal Council. Without the knowledge of the other leaders of the Federal Council, Hays paid the latter a monthly salary of a hundred fifty dollars from January 1928 to August 1929.[46]

How well Hays delivered on his promise to clean up the movies in the 1920s has been a matter of debate. Most have concluded that the things Hays did—his list of "Do's and Don'ts" and the moral clause written into actors contracts—were largely symbolic. American film-goers saw a lot of female nudity and explicit sexuality in films during the latter part of the silent-screen era. Hays was a compromiser. He believed in "passionate but pure" films that gave "the public all the sex it wants with compensating values for all those church and women's groups."[47] Whatever he thought, his office in its first ten years of operation had little power to get between producers and their own judgment of what audiences would pay to see. His job was to keep people outside the industry from interfering, not to interfere from within. At the end of the 1920s, the producers were not even sending him the majority of their projects to review. What is surprising, given the lax enforcement of moral restrictions in movie production, was Hays's general success in protecting the industry during the 1920s from hostile legislation. Monopolistic control amassed in those years by the large studios reduced independent exhibitors and producers to marginal status.

Trouble was brewing, however. The General Conference of the Methodist church and the Northern Baptists expressed little confidence in Hays's actions. Under the aegis of the General Assembly of the Presbyterian church, fourteen religious and civic organizations participated in three national conferences on motion pictures in Washington, D.C., in 1922, 1924, and 1925. The upshot was the formation in 1925 of the Federal Motion Picture Council. Named as its head was Charles Scanlon, the general director of the Department of Moral Welfare of the U.S. Presbyterian Church.[48] Later, the leadership passed to Reverend William Sheafe Chase, Maude M. Aldrich (the National Motion Picture Chairman of the WCTU), Mrs. Robbins Gilman (of the Women's Cooperative Alliance of Minneapolis), and the Reverend Clifford B. Twombly.

The council was a relentless critic of Hays's office, charging it with conducting public relations by putting Hollywood's critics on the payroll. In the early 1930s, the Payne Fund gave a two-hundred-thousand-dollar grant to Reverend William H. Short of the council to study the effects of film. Published in 1933, the Payne Fund studies blasted the moral influence of motion pictures from every conceivable angle. The Federal Motion Picture Council also lobbied hard for legislation that would end Hollywood producers' practice of block-booking, a monopolistic practice that forced film exhibitors, whose theaters in many cases were owned by the studios, to order films in blocks. They could not select individual titles (in many cases they had no knowledge of content anyway) and had little leeway to return films that they did not want to show from a particular block.

In 1930 the council picked up a valuable ally among liberal Protestants when the *Christian Century* threw its weight behind its proposals and opened a decade of editorial war against the idea that Hollywood could police itself. The opening cry, from Maxwell S. Stewart, stated: "There can be no doubt but that the movies with their sentimentalism, their false standards, their pornography, and their open exhibition of moral laxity and lawlessness are influencing our young people today far more than the church."[49] The editors disavowed any wish to become censors or to legislate morality. No one in his right mind, they said in apparent forgetfulness of their support for the Eighteenth Amendment, would attempt that. Rather, they wanted to build moral responsibility into film production in a way that would make review of the finished product unnecessary. Until that happened, they saw fit, starting in 1932, to run each week capsule film reviews issued by the independent National Film Estimate Service.

The position of the *Christian Century* contained a contradiction. On the one hand, it criticized the industry for responding only to profit, even when profit required it to pander to prurient public taste. Mae West's *She Done Him Wrong* and *I'm No Angel* were the favorite examples. On the other hand, the argument against block-booking actually trusted the free market to provide effective censorship. Exhibitors, especially the independent ones who were necessarily sensitive to local outcries of morally outraged citizens, would select films fit for family viewing if liberated from the strong-arm tactics of the producers. That was a long way from clear. To support their premise, the editors of the *Christian Century* tried to argue that the biggest box-office films were also the films selected as the year's best by the review board they trusted. A skeptic might ask why, if this were true, Hollywood producers, no financial fools, chose consistently to issue so many films, 70 percent of the output by the *Christian Century*'s estimate, that were morally damaging junk.

Flawed or not, the campaign of the *Christian Century* came at a propitious moment. The advent of sound in movie production increased the worries of moralists. With scripts, sex and crime became bolder. Between 1930 and 1932, with the onset of economic hard times and a downturn in movie-going, Hollywood sought to keep its audience by throwing moral caution to the winds. However, producers ran into unexpectedly stiff resistance. State censorship boards grew vigilant and blocked the showing of some films in prime commercial markets or had them so cut up that they were virtually incomprehensible. Hays's office was acutely aware of growing pressure for legislation, and the producers had to listen.

From a Protestant perspective, the story at this juncture took a very Catholic turn. Martin Quigley, the Catholic publisher of the *Motion Picture Herald*, decided that it was time to move Hollywood toward enforcement of a tougher moral code. Quigley began to talk to friends in the Catholic hierarchy, a network that reached up to Cardinal Mundelein of Chicago. He also talked to Joseph I. Breen, another Catholic whom Will Hays had installed in Hollywood in the early 1930s to pressure producers to clean up scripts. Breen brought an unaccustomed adamance to the job, and the producers had a new reason to take him seriously. In 1933 the Catholic hierarchy started to organize its famous Legion of Decency, an organization with the purported power to convince American Catholics, a sizable audience in any calculation of profits, to boycott movies until something was done. The Legion inaugurated a system of ratings—A for morally unobjectionable, B for morally objectionable in part, and C for condemned—that for the first time since the early days of the National Board of Review had economic significance.

In part to make sure that films did not receive a C rating, Hays's office in 1934 established the Production Code Administration headed by Breen, a review council with authority to enforce a production code that had, in fact, been written and adopted in 1930. After 1934 any picture that did not carry the Production Code Seal was doomed to limited distribution. The production code was an extremely interesting document. Drafted at Quigley's instigation by Father Daniel Lord, a professor at Catholic St. Louis University, it set forth guidelines for how films should treat such morally difficult subjects as divorce, adultery, prostitution, violence, and crime. It also enumerated subjects that films could not treat at all. That list, with subsequent additions, included abortion, impotence, incest, miscegenation, venereal disease, homosexuality, birth control, and anything demeaning religion or the clergy.

Of most significance, the production code contained a long and rather thoughtful justification that spelled out in explicit terms the moral responsibilities of the movie industry. Moviemakers, it said, could not use the words "art" or "entertainment" to escape a moral burden. "The MORAL IMPORTANCE of entertainment is something which has been universally recognized. It enters intimately into the lives of men and women and affects them closely. . . . Correct entertainment raises the whole standard of a nation. Wrong entertainment lowers the whole living conditions and moral ideals of a race." The code discussed films as mass entertainment, explaining why they ought to have more restricted latitude in their subject matter than printed material: "The motion picture, because of its importance as entertainment and because of the trust placed in it by the peoples of the world, has special MORAL OBLIGA-TIONS"[50] Never before in the history of American commercial culture, despite the steady efforts of Protestant moralists, had the entrepreneurs of an entertainment industry accepted such a formal declaration of moral obligation or bowed to pressure to encode explicit restrictions. The docu-ment was written by a Catholic theologian. And those who pledged com-pliance were Jewish.

The editors of the *Christian Century* were clearly queasy with this turn of events. The Catholics and Jews in Hollywood got on too well together. Moreover, Protestants feared that Catholic moral objections be-gan and ended with unfavorable movie depictions of the Church. Even so, liberal Protestants initially praised the Legion of Decency. A 1934 editorial in the *Christian Century* criticized the Federal Council not only for its inability to organize equally strong pressure but for releasing a statement asserting that 75 percent of motion pictures were wholesome. One misguided Federal Council representative had even referred to the "consummate artistry" of Mae West.[51] The honeymoon between Protes-tant movie critics and the Legion of Decency was not to last. Throughout the 1930s, the *Christian Century* steadfastly maintained that little in the industry had changed. It never gave any credit to the Catholic Breen and viewed the Production Code Seal as a farce.

The Legion of Decency was more sanguine. When the Pope in 1936 suggested that American films were getting better, the *Christian Century* had had enough of its united moral front with Rome. It used the occasion to blast the Legion of Decency's refusal to join its crusade against block-booking or to otherwise look to state authority to regulate Hollywood. The Legion's argument was reasonable. Breaking up the studio's monop-olistic practices would encourage independent filmmakers and exhibitors who would be free to operate outside the production code. They were not likely to do anything positive for the moral standards of the indus-try. Never mind that argument; the *Christian Century* detected conspir-acy: "The Big Eight, apparently, will produce nothing offensive to the Roman Catholic Church provided the Roman Catholic Church keeps hands off the Big Eight's monopoly. . . . What happens to the whole democratic principle of free enterprise and the right of community choice in the selection of films seems of no consequence to the legion."[52]

The "religious outsiders" were having their revenge. Yet the Protes-tant liberals represented by the *Christian Century* had more to worry about than a "foreign" conspiracy to defeat the moral wisdom of ordi-nary Americans. If they were being hoist by a petard, it was one of their own design, crafted from a problematic strategy to base a claim for hegemony on their intellectually up-to-date beliefs. It is somewhat surprising to turn from the consistent editorial denunciations of Hollywood that appeared in the *Christian Century* during the 1930s to the list of films that were accorded high praise in its capsule summaries. In 1936 these included *Alias Bulldog Drummond, The Man Who Broke the Bank at Monte Carlo, Captain Blood, Magnificent Obsession, A Tale of Two Cities, Ah, Wilderness, Modern Times, Follow the Fleet, The Petrified Forest, Louis Pasteur, The Great Ziegfield, Mr. Deeds Goes to Town, Showboat, The Ex-Mrs. Bradford, Girl's Dormitory, Dodsworth, Charge of the Light Brigade, Born to Dance,* and *Winterset*. Aside from reminding us of just how brilliant the old Hollywood studio system could be, the list indicates that the liberal Protestant definition of "wholesome" was not especially prudish and not narrowly confined to Shirley Temple vehicles (most of which were panned) or films conveying unambiguous moral lessons. Adult readers of the *Christian Century* could find ample recommendations to more than sustain a weekly habit of movie-going. Snippets of admiration accompanied appraisals of films when we might have expected only condemnation. *Scarface* was "finely made, photographed, and acted." *It Happened One Night* was "mostly amusing, engaging . . . innocent yet carefully suggestive." And *Gone with the Wind*, with its celebrated "damn" and scene of marital rape, was heartily recommended to adult viewers.

Protestant liberals, for all their complaints about the moral affront of Hollywood productions, were wrestling with the problems of moral relativism. What really annoyed them about the Legion of Decency was that Catholics were so damned sure. The determination of Protestant liberals not to seem ridiculous in modern cultural circles bound them to a dilemma. They had fought for and gotten rigorous enforcement of moral codes in the 1930s. But by the end of the 1940s, they found themselves running the risk of seeming naive, of saying that serious fiction and serious theater ought to stick to the clearly demarcated universe of good and evil that melodrama had portrayed. Who now could dispute that fine drama involved the presentation of social problems and that artistic integrity required complexity in exploring moral issues? Protestant liberals discovered that their moral codes might actually impede the production of movies that treated significant social issues.

A number of events signaled a need for reassessment; for example, in 1949 and 1950 a storm raged over efforts to distribute in the United States Vittorio De Sica's *The Bicycle Thief*, which had collected a number of prizes in Europe.[53] Finally denied a Production Code Seal because of a urination scene and a scene in a bordello, both brief and neither revealing anything to excite prurient eyes, the film was released anyway, was acclaimed a masterpiece, and won an Oscar for best foreign film. Did liberal Protestants want to stand in the way of such "art"? At the end of 1950, a bitter controversy erupted over another acclaimed Italian film, Roberto Rossellini's *The Miracle*, in which a retarded woman believes she is pregnant with the Christ child. The trouble came not only from abroad. In the 1950s, Hollywood was having difficulty turning important pieces of American theater into credible film because of code restrictions, restrictions that liberal Protestants had once said did not go far enough. For a time the *Christian Century* found itself stymied, literally with nothing to say. It stopped its practice of carrying film reviews in 1953 and in that year ran not a single article or editorial about movies.

The National Council made pronouncements about the moral offenses of various films throughout the 1950s, but by the end of the decade, the production code was on its way out. In addition, the Warren Supreme Court was striking down old state censorship laws and leaving little room to enact new ones. Liberal Protestants showed only modest interest in turning back the clock. There was little to do except accept the movie rating system that replaced the production code. Protestant liberals had failed in their goal to make movies moral. If there was consolation to be found, it was in persuading themselves that, all things considered, movie-going in America was not morally corrupting. Like other forms of commercial entertainment, most movies stayed within broad formulas of "family entertainment." If that was not completely true, it was not completely false either.

The encounter of liberal Protestants with the other major force of mass culture in the twentieth century prior to television—the radio—was different in significant ways, even if it also ended in disappointment. In the case of radio, the story began much more happily for Protestant moralists. The primary reason for this optimism was obvious. Unlike earlier innovations in the marketplace of culture, whose origins had been tainted by unruly consumers and the taste of the socially low-down, the first commercial experiments with the wireless appealed to the enthusiasms of the affluent. Wireless equipment was not necessarily expensive, but its use required a certain style of educated inventiveness and access to information. Radio enthusiasts immediately pooled information through specialized, relatively costly journals—one of them, *The Wireless Age*, quite handsome by the high standards of commercial magazines in the 1920s.

In any case, the first non-experimental, regular radio broadcasts emanated from station KDKA in Pittsburgh. Two months later on January 2, 1921, KDKA started its first broadcasts of church services from the Calvary Episcopal Church. Of the six hundred stations operating in 1925, none yet joined to a national network, perhaps sixty-three were owned by churches.[54] It took almost a decade after the first KDKA broadcast before entrepreneurs transformed radio into a form of mass entertainment with large commercial possibilities realizable through program sponsors. For much of the 1920s, programming consisted of the sort of fare now broadcast over National Public Radio; that is, classical music, political addresses, and news, uninterrupted by commercial messages. Program content aroused few worries. Despite the early popularity of sports reporting, including the occasional live broadcast of a boxing match, most of what went out on the airwaves was squeaky clean in a moral sense.

The religious potential of radio seemed immense. What especially pleased Protestant liberals was the fact that most of the ministers who gained airtime in the early days of radio were of the right sort and background. They included Dr. Ernest M. Stires of St. Thomas Church on New York's Fifth Avenue (the "wealthiest of American churches"), the Reverend Warren L. Rogers, dean of St. Paul's Episcopal Church, Detroit, Dr. S. Parkes Cadman of Brooklyn, and Harry Emerson Fosdick. Early in the 1920s, the Federal Council was actively engaged in interdenominational efforts to secure broadcast time for the "best" representatives of the pulpit on local stations. They were God's most effective salesmen. The only controversy that surfaced in the 1920s over the religious uses of radio was whether the live broadcasts of church services on a Sunday morning, with sermons delivered by some of America's most gifted pulpit orators, would encourage people to stay at home tuned to the dial rather than take the trouble to dress and go to church. That fear was particularly bruited with respect to rural churches where, it was condescendingly assumed, only the most meagerly talented of the profession held sway. Why, it was asked, would people choose to attend a service presided over by a parson who delivered a boring sermon in a monotone when they could tune in to the persusive, educated voice of a Stires or a Fosdick?

Some radio programming was rescheduled to Sunday afternoons to dispel the threat of emptied churches. But the fear gave way to the heady notion that effective radio preaching stimulated interest in religion. It made people want to attend church and to give money. Dr. Stires reported from Fifth Avenue that because of his broadcasts, he was seeing people on Sunday mornings whom he had not seen in years. Even on New Year's eve, when almost no one before had come to special services, the sanctuary was packed with people in resplendent evening clothes either coming from or on their way to attending parties or the theater. Radio made church glamorous. Stires boasted that his message, thanks to radio, reached beyond the walls of the church and covered "hundreds of square miles over which the ether waves roll." The poor became part of his congregation, as did people in hospitals and convalescent homes.[55] Fosdick was more realistic in assessing the usefulness of radio in reaching people who were not likely to come to church: "I understand that my sermons are heard in many parts of the campus of Princeton, for instance, by students who enjoy their pipes at the same time."[56]

Very little dissent made itself heard over the euphoria. According to Warren Rogers, radio "has enabled us here in the cathedral to embark upon a great missionary enterprise in the broadcasting of the Gospel of Jesus Christ, on a scale that would have astonished the old-time Apostles of our Lord. By it we have been able to reach and help many thousands of non-churchgoers, and it has, therefore, opened the way for the greatest missionary achievements since the time of Christ."[57] In fact, radio was Protestantism's dream medium of advertising. The message was direct, not dependent on the uncertain reader reception of print material that had worried Protestants since the early nineteenth century. It represented the perfect blend of the public and private. The notion of a public church service carried into the home was wonderfully compatible with ideals of domesticity they had championed.

Radio was going to change, especially after the first network airing of *Amos 'n' Andy* in August 1929 (on NBC). Radio had before that experimented with drama, comedy programs, and variety shows, but the success of *Amos 'n' Andy* signaled that radio would thereafter belong to the sponsor who purchased time on the airwaves. By this time, the federal government with the creation of the Federal Radio Commission had begun to regulate the airwaves, and national networks (NBC in 1926, CBS in 1927, ABC and MBC in the 1930s) organized much of the programming. Within this new market democracy where popular taste finally determined what was aired, the "right" sort of religion retained its privileges. NBC under David Sarnoff broadcast religious services gratis as part of its public service obligation. As a result, "only the recognized outstanding leaders of the several faiths" got on the air.[58] "Outstanding" was judged by the advice of the Honorable Morgan J. O'Brien for Catholics, Mr. Julius Rosenwald for Jews, and the Reverend Charles S. Macfarland for Protestants. The latter was already drawing a salary from Will Hays to render advice about movies.[59]

The other networks experimented a bit with religious programming. William Paley's CBS initially gave half an hour of free time on Sundays each to Protestant, Jewish, Catholic, Christian Science, Mormon, and Dutch Reformed bodies; a generous policy, but not one that really covered America's diverse religious population. Only MBC was willing to follow what was arguably the only democratic and fully capitalistic policy, to sell airtime to religious groups. That made possible the success of Charles Fuller's *The Old-Fashioned Revival Hour* in the 1940s. The Federal Council resisted such a frank involvement of the market. For the most part, until the networks and the government changed course deep into the days of television, the use of free airtime on networks restricted the range of religious opinion and barred much of it altogether from access to a national radio audience. Controversial ministers like Father Coughlin or Bob Shuler either had to set up their own stations or buy time from local stations wherever permitted.

Interestingly, the *Christian Century* at the same time it was attacking movies led a fight to give "non-approved" ministers easier access to the airwaves.[60] It need not have worried, for the future belonged to fundamentalist preachers who broadcast from their own stations and turned their listeners into paying sponsors. In the case of radio, liberal Protestants might better have followed their acquired business instincts more aggressively. Roger W. Babson, a statistician devoted to the joint interests of business and religion, urged large churches with access to radio to organize smaller churches within their hearing range along the model of "chain stores." "I look forward," he wrote, "to the day when the Federation of Churches of our different cities can combine and purchase the time for all day Sunday from our great broadcasting chains, and thus outbid secular competitors with their jazz contests."[61] That proved to be too crass an idea for Protestant liberals, although based on their earlier behavior, it is not clear why. Protestant liberals were to pay a price of a different sort in trying to sell religion on the air without paying for the time. They vowed to keep their free programming non-controversial. Radio religion was supposed to be ecumenical. According to the Reverend William Hanzsche, "no man can preach a narrow denominationalism to a congregation which listens to the radio during the week. It [radio] has released those enmities between denominations; it has done more to bring the great Army of Christ together . . . than anything I can recall, certainly in modern history."[62]

Hanzsche was dead wrong. Radio ecumenism was an impossible ideal in America. The claim only stirred strong opposition within the "forces of Christendom." The effort to remain non-controversial was sincere enough, but that too produced a serious problem. The effort not to antagonize an audience (listeners after all only had to turn the dial) seemed a strange extrapolation from the life of a crucified Christ. After several decades, liberal Protestants had to wonder whether their broad messages were worth anyone's attention. Because of the directive not to give offense, they could raise no social issues over the radio or otherwise disturb the rich and the powerful. One manual for religious radio unwittingly summed up the dilemma with this advice: "Don't alarm listeners with long lists of what is wrong with the world. Don't speak dogmatically. Remember it's normality we're all striving for."[63] Warren Harding could not have said it better.

In the case of the movies, Protestant liberals in the interests of morality had wound up complicit in a code of restrictions that made it difficult to speak in frank ways about socially difficult issues—abortion and birth control being prime examples. Their less troubled endorsement of radio had produced the same problem in a different way. What they were not paying for reduced them to the same level of non-controversial entertainment that governed the rest of radio programming. Radio rarely raised moral concerns despite a hilarious Mae West/Don Ameche "Adam and Eve" radio skit that was aired on the Edgar Bergen show in 1937 (Eve to Adam: "Take me outta this dismal dump and give me a chance to develop my personality").[64] That was precisely the difficulty. A 1947 poll found that Protestant churches were content with radio sit-coms—*Ozzie and Harriet*, *The Aldrich Family*, *A Date with Judy*—as well as with soap operas. They believed that serials supported family values. Weekly westerns and detective stories sustained social morality. This was a moral victory premised more on silence than positive teaching. What did not offend morality was moral. Any further struggle over values had ceased to matter.

Conclusion

In many ways the record that Protestant liberals could review was not that bad. Despite a vastly overextended optimism that had swelled with the growth of well-funded churches and other religious organizations, liberal Protestant influence had reached just about every cultural niche where it could reasonably have been expected to go. "Hegemony" is not the right word to describe the situation. Liberal Protestants had underestimated all along the reality and the enduring strength of religious pluralism. But their problem as they entered the post–World War II era was not so much the inadequacy of their past achievements but what to do next. What future actions congruent with their past actions might solve problems they had not anticipated? Was Christianity condemned to blandness, complicity with consumerism, and an inability to make religion change the way people lived? In perhaps the unkindest cut, liberal Protestants watched their religious opponents pick up their business and commercial strategies and prove that they had a stronger stomach for them. Fundamentalists were principled market men who asked for no subsidies from the government or from media. They sold religion the old-fashioned way, except that they took full advantage of technology.

The high point of liberal Protestant influence in the twentieth century had been Prohibition. Prohibition was major-league cultural politics that affected not only the way people drank but also many forms of urban commercial entertainment. It takes an effort to recapture the reasons why Prohibition could ever have seemed to anyone a way to bring the moral resources of the country into full flower. The mood behind crusades of any kind are the most ephemeral of historical memories. After a time, liberal Protestants recognized the failure of Prohibition, but that made it all the harder to pull back from it. It was a last chance. With the repeal of the Eighteenth Amendment, Protestant liberals uneasily recognized they had changed with the world. To them, leisure was no longer a worry *per se*. Protestant leaders were more relaxed with the institutions of commercial culture after World War II than they had been at any time since they had first tried to set rules for the market. They were prepared to believe that family participation had rendered most forms of once worrisome commercial play morally harmless. Although evils associated with drink, gambling, violence, prostitution, and pornography remained, "wholesome" entertainment was big business. The unsavory had been contained, localized, and subjected to some sort of regulation. In that sense, the rapid growth of Las Vegas in the 1950s was a Protestant victory.

So why didn't it feel better? For one thing, moral wholesomeness too often meant trivial. More truly disappointing was the fact that when liberal Protestant moralists gave up battling, they ceased to be creative innovators in the marketplace of culture. In the early nineteenth century, their influence had set trends. As authors and critics of popular fiction, as journalists, as the leading voices in educational reform, they had played a major role in the reading revolution. As performers, they had shaped public appreciation for theatricality and affected the standards for political oratory. Moral inoffensiveness had once not been enough to placate them. They had not merely nodded their heads acquiescently when some form of wholesome leisure came along by happenstance. They provided it. And when they could not sponsor it themselves, they tried to find ways to make wholesomeness part of commercial culture. Beyond their stridency, censorious intolerance, and defensiveness, they were sometimes impressively creative.

Over the course of the twentieth century, the inventiveness dissipated. The ambition receded and ended in the tasteful packaging of a religious product that still sold but did not arouse much consumer enthusiasm.

Before retreating, they had prepared the way for the world of televangelism in which everything is for sale, including an assortment of Armageddons seeming to exceed in number all the varieties of dog foods, canned soups, and ribbed condoms in an upstate New York grocery store. Protestant liberals showed a certain grace in retreat. They were at least honest enough to recognize that their efforts to homogenize the moral taste of Americans have served whatever legitimate purposes they had. To pursue them further would totally demolish aims that already had gone badly off the track. If they are out of ideas about how to create a middle-class moral society that has solved the problems of avarice and violence and ethnic hatred and poverty, they are not the only ones.

CHAPTER NINE

Recent Market Entries:

Contemporary Evangelicals
and Purveyors of the New Age

To get anywhere with faith, learn to pray
big prayers. God will rate you according to
the size of your prayers.

> Norman Vincent Peale, *The Power of
> Positive Thinking*

Following World War II, religiously inspired commodities saturated the American cultural landscape. It was as if a hundred fifty years of history had worked with determined persistence to produce the purported spiritual awakening of the late 1940s and the 1950s. The mass media tallied the evidence. In 1949, *Newsweek* reported an increasing number of religious books on the non-fiction best-seller lists. These included Thomas Merton's *Seven Storey Mountain*, Fulton J. Sheen's *Peace of Soul*, and Norman Vincent Peale's *A Guide to Confident Living*. Sheen and Peale were already known to Americans because of their radio preaching, and Sheen would shortly make himself a master of television. Another Catholic, Fulton Oursler, scored big with his 1949 retelling of the life of Christ, *The Greatest Story Ever Told*. Two years later his narrative version of the Old Testament, *The Greatest Book Ever Written*, found almost as many readers. When the paperback boom started in the mid-1950s, religious titles were a strong part of the market.[1]

Hollywood cashed in on the Bible. Religious epics were nothing new in film. Cinematic pioneers had recorded a version of the "Passion Play of Oberammergau" in 1897, and a nine-reel version of *Quo Vadis* (1912) had been one of the early successes of feature-length, narrative film. Cecil B. DeMille produced in spectacular fashion *The Ten Commandments* in 1923 and *The King of Kings* in 1927. In the former, DeMille used the story of Moses as prelude to a cautionary modern tale in which all the commandments got broken. The 1920s also saw lavish film treatment of *Ben Hur* (1926) and *Noah's Ark* (1929).[2] However, screened biblical drama went into decline during the financially tight 1930s. Hollywood religion during the 1940s surfaced usually in contemporary dress, as in Bing Crosby's priestly portrayals in *Going My Way* (1944) and *The Bells of St. Mary's* (1945).

Then, with *Samson and Delilah*, a DeMille production with Hedy Lamarr and Victor Mature, sex and the Bible surged forward to set a trend for the coming decade. *David and Bathsheba* and a new version of *Quo Vadis* followed in 1951. When Hollywood introduced the massive screen techniques of Cinemascope and Todd-A-O to fend off the competition from television, film investment in biblical extravaganza became substantial. Twentieth-Century Fox sank four and a half million dollars into *The Robe* (1953) and three and a half million into its sequel, *Demetrius and the Gladiators* (1954). Producers collected star casts and big budgets for *Salome* (1953), *The Silver Chalice* (1954), *The Big Fisherman* (1959), *Solomon and Sheba* (1959), *Ben Hur* (1959), and *Spartacus* (1960).

DeMille predictably made the most impressive use of special effects with his 1956 remake of *The Ten Commandments* starring Charlton Heston as Moses and Yul Brynner as Rameses. Not all of these films brought major box-office returns; plans to cash in on filmed treatments of Jezebel and Sodom and Gomorrah produced disappointment. Nonetheless, the potential profits were sufficiently dazzling to keep the genre going into the 1960s. *Newsweek* noted in 1961 that four lives of Christ, the lives of several saints, and a ten-hour version of the Bible were either in production or pre-production stages. That movie audiences were ready to move on to something else became apparent with the release of *King of Kings* (1961), *The Greatest Story Ever Told* (1965), and John Huston's *The Bible* (1965).[3] The cinematic Bible bubble had burst.

While it lasted, many observers took the audience that Hollywood found for religious spectacle as evidence of a spiritual revival in the nation. When Jane Russell, the big-busted star who was advertised in the 1940s in ways that affronted the production code, referred to God as a "livin' doll," she made instant news. Mae West had never tried to join sexiness to Christianity. Russell's phrase suggested that God ("the man upstairs" in the words of a popular song) had a sense of humor and liked to cuddle. She was telling moralists to relax because even at its naughtiest, popular commercial culture was clean. What was there to fear in a nation where 60 percent of Americans belonged to a church and almost as many attended on a regular basis?

Figures about religious observance were, in fact, at a historic high after World War II, and many people believed that churches would soon claim as members the entire 97 percent of Americans who professed belief in God. The publications of Henry Luce, *Time* and *Life,* turned the spotlight on a young revival preacher named Billy Graham who spent the 1950s conducting well-attended revivals in the major cities of the United States and Europe. His 1957 crusade in New York City's Madison Square Garden was a major media event. Other religious "stars" were on the rise as well. *Life* devoted a photographic essay to the meetings of Oral Roberts, a Pentecostal faith healer who could fill a tent seating ten thousand people almost anywhere in the nation.[4]

Not all of the stirrings of religious interest reflected in the world of entertainment amounted to bread and circuses for the uncouth masses. The two high priests of commercialized religion in the 1950s were Bishop Fulton J. Sheen and Norman Vincent Peale. They may have been slick, but their audiences were educated. Clad in his bright scarlet clerical robes, Sheen constructed a TV personality based on urbaneness, sophisticated wit, and literateness. His only prop was a blackboard. The image that he projected was in a generic sense liberal and broad-minded. So was Peale's. The latter, who was pastor of the Marble Collegiate Church of New York City, linked religion to successful living.[5] Considering his spacious Fifth Avenue apartment, he had reason to know.

None of Peale's best-selling books (the most successful being his 1952 *The Power of Positive Thinking*) evinced much interest in old-fashioned conversion. The world that Peale addressed was already Christian. He did not have to warn his readers in some quaint nineteenth-century fashion about the dangers of drink, the temptations of sex, or the evils of Gotham's night life. They suffered not from sin, for they were good, earnest people, but from unawareness of the practical power of their faith. They believed in Christ, but they did not know how to use him to construct prosperous lives for themselves and their families. Faith, prayer, and Scripture, Peale said, existed for one thing—to help individuals overcome their feelings of insecurity and inferiority.

Peale's spiritual mission lay in collecting anecdotes, almost all of them having to do with businessmen who overcame despair. His books were virtually nothing else. In his chatty illustrations, the despair of the Christian grew from something other than the consciousness of unrighteousness. It mounted from the salesman's fear that he could not close the big deal. What Willy Loman had needed when he went on the road was Peale's advice to repeat over and over to himself : "I can do all things through Christ which strengtheneth me." Peale guaranteed results. He told his readers who practiced his principles that "your relations with other people will improve. You will become a more popular, esteemed, and well-liked individual. . . . You will become a person of greater usefulness and will wield an expanded influence."[6] Peale did not mention riches directly, but most of his stories ended with financial dividends as well.

The reported signs of religious interest during the 1950s powerfully suggested that American religion had settled comfortably into the marketplace of culture. Churches prospered. The various forms of commercial leisure that clerics had once feared seemed under reasonable control. Much of it bore the explicit imprimatur of agencies representing the Judeo-Christian tradition. Religion accepted its responsibility to provide entertainment but at the same time acknowledged that entertainment could be delivered in various ways and by various sponsors. For many Americans the spiritual help available in churches or in movie houses or on television or in a best-selling book or at a businessman's prayer breakfast tended to become equivalent. Organized religion had not made a full peace with popular culture, and some small denominations remained at war with it. From one perspective, however, it was becoming hard to view religion as something distinct from popular culture.

America, as it happened, had not seen anything yet. From 1960 to 1990, religious entertainment grew with the economy. That fact gives poignancy to the warnings of religious leaders in the 1950s who were deeply skeptical of the claim that religion had triumphed in postwar America simply because some representation of it sold books or movie tickets. Few of the doubters wished to throw cold water on the long-held belief that Americans were somehow especially religious. Who, after all, could dispute the facts that more Americans went to church than Europeans and that no strong political element in America promoted anticlericalism? However, if Jane Russell, Cecil DeMille, and Norman Vincent Peale were the registers of America's spiritual pulse, then something was wrong.

Writing in the *Christian Century*, A. Roy Eckardt made his doubts public. Insofar as Christianity inside and outside of churches had endorsed a salable peace-of-mind philosophy, it was nothing more than an extension of American nationalism tied to the monied interests of socially reactionary men. A soothing anodyne that envisioned God as a chum was not a religious revival. Americans might go to church, but most of them could not name the first four books of the Bible. Most thought that Matthew, Mark, Luke, and John were four of Christ's disciples. Eckardt did not write in despair. After all, the National Council was still in operation. He sought to deflate the hullabaloo about a religious resurgence tracked through popular culture by calling attention to the health of the citadels of true faith. Eckardt's fears might have been more troubled had he ventured a historical look to determine whether American religion and its citadels had ever been entirely resistant to the tendencies he deplored in the 1950s.[7]

The tough-minded Reinhold Niebuhr was also critical, but he hedged his bets in questioning whether the religious revival announced in the postwar years was bogus. He dismissed Peale with something near contempt. He was marginally kinder to Graham who, although a theological cretin, at least understood that the "good news" of the gospel was not written on a check. American Christianity in the postwar period, according to Niebuhr, was almost as complacent as it was when he had written *Moral Man and Immoral Society* in 1932; except for one important thing. Religious interest, he argued, was growing at American colleges and universities. The horrors of World War II and the sober realities of the Cold War had finally chastened the intellectuals. They had lost confidence in their secular securities—art, political ideology, and a make-do pragmatism. Transcendentally grounded truth re-emerged as a respectable philosophical option. America's leading universities formed departments of religious studies staffed by scholars who believed that research on religious phenomena was consistent with strong religious faith.[8]

That Niebuhr, the proponent of Christian realism, should see evidence of a religious revival on American campuses is, in retrospect, astonishing. He latched onto an epiphenomenon, a call to put God back in Yale's curriculum, and missed the pedigree and the permanence of what he hoped was transient; that is, the interpenetration of American religion and commercial popular culture. Peale was a superficial man, but the vein he tapped in American culture ran deep. American intellectuals after the war were hungry for complexity, and the theologies of Maritain, Tillich, Bultmann, and Perry Miller's Puritans qualified. Niebuhr did see something. But a hunger for complex ideas, if it made some academics sympathetic to the ambiguities and ironies explored by twentieth-century theologians, also explained campus interest in Sartre, Nietzsche, and the prematurely buried Marx. The sort of theology that interested Niebuhr was not part of the "end of ideology" mentality that the sociologist Daniel Bell used to identify Western intellectuals at the end of the 1950s.

Will Herberg, who admired Niebuhr, became the country's best-known sociologist of religion during the 1950s, despite his lack of any college degrees and the lies he told to the contrary. His influential assessment of the American religious landscape that appeared in *Protestant, Catholic, Jew* (1955) was perhaps the bleakest of the decade, although he, too, saw hopeful stirrings of religious interest on college campuses. Herberg, a Jew who had contemplated conversion, had no personal stake in whether there was a Christian revival in America. What bothered him was the clear evidence that a watered-down Protestantism was diluting everybody else's religion. A faith with few traditions, it had influenced other faiths to abandon theirs.

According to Herberg, Catholics and Jews in America had melted down their own internal ethnic pluralisms. Italian Catholics married Irish Catholics, and Jews of German descent married Jews of Russian descent. That was not a bad thing in itself, but in the context of American society, it signified a lost will to remain truly distinctive. The essential forms of Catholicism and Judaism had collapsed under the pressures of accommodation. What was left in the United States was three faiths distinct in name but not in meaningful practice. All three had merged with the general culture. American religion in the 1950s was a serious form of identification, but the identification was with "the American way of life." "It is only too evident," Herberg wrote, "that the religiousness characteristic of America today is very often a religiousness without religion, a religiousness with almost any kind of content or none, a way of sociability or 'belonging' rather than a way of reorienting life to God." The reported signs of religious revival in the 1950s indicated "a religiousness without serious commitment, without real conviction, without genuine existential decision."[9]

Herberg underestimated the persistence of American pluralism. Moreover, the positive reception of his book was in itself evidence that not all Americans interested in religion had endorsed the feel-good versions of it. Many people thought that Hollywood's mixture of the Bible and bubble baths was blasphemous and tried to resist the temptation to place the terrible moral burdens of the nation on movie stars. Yet popular culture was what it was, and religious leaders of all persuasions had created the conditions that allowed religion and popular culture so breezily to intermingle. Protestant liberals in the 1950s had reason to feel acute discomfort. Much of what seemed shallow in the cultural marketing of religion had grown from strategies of their own devising. Worse, what they had invented was being taken over by fundamentalists. In the 1950s, liberal Protestants could not have known that the denominations where they enjoyed the greatest strength would enter a period of numerical decline. That would only become clear in the 1970s.[10] But already in the popular expressions of religion in the 1950s, there was evidence that others were gaining the upper hand.

This is not to suggest that Protestant fundamentalists should be blamed for whatever was vulgar in the ways that popular commercial culture appropriated religion. They were not Peale's readers. They did not watch Sheen. And they did not much go to movies. What is true is that postwar Christian conservatives looked out on America's culture industry and did not see their mark upon it. They awakened in the 1950s furious at the way religious liberals had used their influence in the national media to suppress their voices. It was time to outflank the enemy with their superior numbers and beat the liberals at their own game. What was surprising was how quickly they mastered the organizational and technological skills that liberal Protestants had used to build big churches and to control the press and airtime. People waiting to be caught up any second in the Rapture, leaving cars driverless and pot pies abandoned in ovens, were not supposed to do that. They did, however. It was their turn to adopt the techniques of aggressive religious advertising and to float religious empires on a sea of debt.

The Electronic Church Turns Right

Recent journalistic comment has recorded the obvious. These days, religious broadcasting on radio and television belongs to theologically conservative Protestants. Terminology causes problems. The word evangelical in the nineteenth century applied to Protestant churches that stressed

the need for a deeply felt personal conversion experience, valued preaching over religious ritual, and commanded Christians to win other souls
to Christ. Protestant evangelicalism still expresses these tendencies in the
twentieth century, but what was once the dynamic center of growing
Protestant churches now looks more defensive. Many people these days
divide Protestant evangelicals into fundamentalists (especially Southern
and independent Baptists) and Pentecostals. They stand for anti-
modernism; in fact, anti-intellectualism, political conservatism, and quar-
relsome factionalism.

Problems with this usage are readily apparent. Many Christians who
are evangelical are neither fundamentalist nor Pentecostal.[11] Many others are not politically conservative; for example, most African-American
churches. Some fundamentalists, the Missouri Synod Lutherans for example, are not in the classic mold of evangelicals. Neither perhaps are
Pentecostals whose preaching style and church services are a bit different
from the evangelical revivals of the early nineteenth century.[12] These
problems notwithstanding, we do sufficient justice to the current phenomenon of televangelism if we associate it with conservative evangelicals, both in a political and theological sense, whose major split is, in
fact, between fundamentalist and Pentecostal camps.

An equally important initial issue, besides keeping the terminology
clear, is recognizing that the current state of religious broadcasting,
though different than it once was, reflects changes that started before
World War II. Televangelism was not a product of the Reagan years;
nor did conservative evangelical broadcasting begin when Pat Robertson
founded the Christian Broadcasting Network (CBN) in 1960. That was
the same year in which the FCC made the important ruling that radio
and television stations did not have to "give" time to religious groups in
order to meet their public-service responsibilities. The decision hurt the
National Council which had monopolized most of the free airtime
awarded to religion. Conservative evangelicals benefited because they
were already practiced in buying time on radio and had found ways to
get their message on television before the FCC ruling.

The evangelical route to radio success had required constant redirec-
tion. Fundamentalist and Pentecostal Christians had been on the airwaves
since the beginning.[13] In the 1920s, Paul Rader and Aimee Semple Mc-
Pherson had their own stations. (Rader's station was WJBT—Where Jesus Blesses Thousands.) So did the Moody Bible Institute after it received
a license for Chicago's WMBI in 1927. R. R. Brown actually founded a
radio church and sent his listeners certificates of membership in exchange
for donations. The formation of radio networks put conservative Protestant denominations that were not joined to the Federal Council at a dis-

advantage. That was because NBC refused to sell airtime to religious groups and established its Protestant religious programming in consultation with the Federal Council. This strict policy lasted until 1956. CBS was initially more flexible and permitted Donald Grey Barnhouse to become the first religious broadcaster to purchase network time. Until 1931 when CBS adopted a policy similar to NBC's, the newer network also sold time to *The Lutheran Hour* and to Father Coughlin.

Fundamentalists made more headway with MBC, the last of the national networks to be founded. In the late 1930s, it sold large blocks of prime Sunday-evening time to religious broadcasters, producing the first national religious hit in Charles E. Fuller's *The Old-Fashioned Revival Hour*. But MBC's policy had more to do with financial necessity than with conviction. During its first years of competitive struggle when it had trouble finding sponsors, it got around 25 percent of its revenue from religion. When secular sponsors began to appear, MBC changed the rules. In 1943 it rescheduled religious programs to Sunday mornings and limited them to half an hour. So much for the *Revival Hour*. To keep a national audience, Fuller had to leave MBC and work out a plan of sending recordings of his programs to independent stations.

In fact, religious broadcasters could build sizable audiences by buying time from an *ad hoc* network of independent and local stations. The best-known religious programs of the 1930s that aired outside the Federal Council's charmed circle of sponsorship included Herbert W. Armstrong's *Radio Church of God*, M. R. DeHaan's *Radio Bible Class*, and the Christian Reformed Church's *Back to God Hour*. Independent secular stations were happy to cooperate. They could plug in recordings of religious programs where they best fit their schedules (that is, during hours when they could not sell time to regular sponsors). They did not have to worry about finding advertisers or whether a preacher's audience was large or small or non-existent. Fundamentalists also built powerful religious transmitters in foreign countries to advance missionary work. Across the border in Mexico, they could produce signals much stronger than American regulation permitted and could beam programs over a large geographical area back in the United States.

The Federal Council stuck with the networks and acted as a media trade-association group for its member churches. When the Federal Council in 1950 changed its name to the National Council, it formally organized a Broadcast and Film Commission. To secure its existing privileges, the National Council acted as a lobby to thwart paid-for religious programming on the networks, an action that predictably generated resentment and set in motion strong counter-actions. In large part because of their exclusion from network time, evangelicals formed the National Association of Evangelicals (NAE) in 1942. Two years later the same coalition created another organization, the National Religious Broadcasters. It, along with the Southern Baptist Convention's Radio and Television Commission, promoted a rapid expansion of religious radio stations that already in the 1950s gave conservative evangelicals a clear lead in overall airtime.

After 1950 the battleground shifted to television. Again the affiliates of the National Council started with a commanding advantage. The Federal Council started working with NBC in the late 1930s, before television had any commercial reality, to develop future formats for religious programs. A televised church service, it was argued, would not make the best use of the new medium. Programming concepts shifted toward discussions, documentary, and drama. None of the Protestant programs developed for network TV in the 1950s (*Directions*, *Lamp Unto My Feet*, and *Frontiers of Faith*) relied on preaching. Innovative programming was expensive to produce, but its National Council sponsors retained the luxury of free time. The NAE churches found themselves struggling against a triple disadvantage. In most cases, they could not buy television time. When they could, it was much more expensive than radio time. And they had to pay expensive production costs as well.

Understandably, the first efforts on TV by conservative evangelicals were bare-bones operations that depended on revival-style preaching to stimulate viewer interest. Rex Humbard, who started televising his services from Akron, Ohio, in 1952, proved that it could be done. In 1955 Oral Roberts also entered the television ministry and broadcast healing services to audiences who watched as much out of curiosity as conviction. Without a grotto or apparitions of the Virgin, Roberts had come up with an American version of Lourdes. The critics came down hard. The historically minded among them saw the hysteria of the famous Cane Ridge revival happening all over again, although they convinced themselves that the modern version was fraudulent. Somehow an ecstatic convert barking at trees in 1800 was a more "genuine" phenomenon than a person who felt better when touched on the head by Oral Roberts. Actually what Roberts claimed to do stretched credulity no farther than the "miraculous" healings of Peale's positive thinking. Roberts found plenty of takers for his Pentecostal business and entered "Blessing Pacts" with many in his television audience. They mailed him a hundred dollars, which he promised to refund if they did not within a year receive the gift back from an unexpected source.

In the 1960s, even after the FCC ruling that promised to break the network monopoly of the National Council, evangelicals made their way on television by buying up bankrupt UHF stations. That was the origin of Robertson's CBN, which became the first television station to devote more than 50 percent of its time to religious programming. The story of how Robertson built CBN into one of the largest cable networks, of how he devised *The 700 Club* program with Jim and Tammy Bakker, and of how the latter pair left CBN to found the PTL cable network and Heritage USA has been told many times with varying degrees of animus.[14] Bakker's spectacular downfall in 1987 that started in the arms of Jessica Hahn eventually brought down his fellow Pentecostal Jimmy Swaggart and damaged Jerry Falwell's enterprises that included the Liberty Broadcasting Network. Many read the story with satisfaction, convinced that media religion would go back to something respectable.

Without the benefit of French sociology, our common sense tells us that "respectable" is in the eye of the beholder. It is easy to forget that Jim Bakker represented a turn in evangelical broadcasting toward a classier act with appeal to well-dressed and economically secure audiences. Those who despise Pat Robertson ought to despise him not for encouraging spontaneous uncontrolled emotion (which is what Pentecostalism is all about) but for his cleverness in making it an efficiently orchestrated business. Robertson is a preacher. He is also a professional in the business of entertainment. The sort of "serious" religious program produced by the National Council was dead even without reduced amounts of free airtime. The audience for it had not grown, which in media terms means it did not exist. Robertson proved that religion could build an audience, not shrink it. Religious liberals could gnash their teeth and hope that his commercial success was temporary. The fact remained that he had outclassed them by doing better what they had wanted to do.

Individual televangelists retained their individual styles in the 1970s and 1980s, but the trend was toward structured programs. Most dramatically, Oral Roberts folded up his tent, built a university and medical school, and became a Methodist. A totally new television program followed in 1969. According to an admiring Ben Armstrong, the enthusiastic head of the National Religious Broadcasters, "it was a sparkling new TV presentation that had everything that would guarantee success for any series—bright contemporary music, attractive young people, a fast pace, superb technical quality, and a well-known personality at the center."[15] Armstrong became an ardent proponent of the views of Marshall McLuhan. Understanding media was the key to proselytizing the world in its end times. Armstrong spotted a scriptural allusion to the appearance of satellite discs. They were prefigured in the angel mentioned in

Revelation 14:6,7. An angel "weighing forty-seven hundred pounds, measuring eighteen feet in width, flying in geosynchronous orbit twenty-two thousand miles above the earth" appealed to the statistical bent in premillennial prophecy.[16]

The success of televangelism prompted liberal Protestants to raise one especially irrelevant charge. With embarrassing forgetfulness of fears they had ridiculed in the heady days of *The National Radio Pulpit*, they claimed that television ministers robbed local churches of their congregations and diverted donations. The charge appears to have been no truer in the 1980s than it had been in the late 1920s. No one knows the exact size of the audience for television religion. Some think that as many as twenty million people watched religious television regularly at the end of the 1980s. One sensible review of the evidence placed the figure at no higher than thirteen million.[17] That would be about 6 percent of the national television audience and perhaps a quarter of the people who claim to be born-again Christians. Most surveys suggest that the majority of viewers are over fifty and female, that they belong to a church, and that they make no contributions to the televised ministry. In any case, the audiences for Jerry Falwell and Pat Robertson are not the people who have been leaving Protestant denominations that report membership declines. Southern Baptist churches would have suffered from the competition of televangelism before any others. Instead of losing support, they have stayed a growth industry with a strong appreciation for the possibilities of the media.

The amount of money that ran through the television ministries during the 1980s was substantial, but religious liberals were in a compromised position when they raised the cry of hucksterism. Doubtlessly it was vulgar for Jim Bakker to boast for his PTL appeals: "We have a better product than soap or automobiles. We have eternal life. . . . That's why I use the most effective means of communication known today. . . . I believe that Christian television will be the tool that ushers in the triumphant return of Jesus Christ."[18] With the exception of the last line, Bakker's words could have come from any of the church advertisement manuals sponsored by Social Gospel enthusiasts earlier in the century. Armstrong defended the "show biz" qualities of television preaching in terms that were as old as Protestant revivalism. Entertainment caught people's attention and put them at ease. It prepared the way for their receiving the gospel message.

What annoyed the descendants of liberal Social Gospelers was their belief that the political meaning of church boosterism had changed. The Republican politics of Billy Sunday appeared to have triumphed on Sunday-morning television. Although much too much can be made of Pat Robertson's and Jerry Falwell's claims to have elected Ronald Reagan, they certainly did everything in their power to re-situate the Social Gospel on the political Right. Even the televangelists who stayed clear of politics, actually most of them, helped steer many southern evangelicals into the Republican party wherein northern moralistic evangelicals had earlier been comfortable.[19] Evangelicalism in African-American churches was much more resistant to political conservatism, but there have been exceptions. The Reverend Joseph Jackson, not to be confused with Jesse Jackson, headed the predominantly black National Baptist Convention from 1953 until 1983 and stood on the side of Richard Nixon. The flamboyant Reverend Ike has preached a gospel of materialism in Harlem ("I want my pie with ice cream on top") that dismayed black activists who wish to use African-American churches to mobilize social protest.

The political activism of fundamentalists and Pentecostals has struck some observers as an anomaly. They asked: are not most of them premillennialists who see the near approach of the Rapture followed in seven years by Armageddon? Why should they care who governs the mass of mortals who are doomed to extinction? Anyone who has studied the logic of strict predestination as it affected the work ethic of seventeenth-century Puritans knows that trying to find logical connections between theology and behavior is risky business. The closeness of Armageddon, the coming divinely orchestrated showdown between good and evil, fascinated Ronald Reagan and got him up from his naps to attend to foreign policy. Strong belief energizes people. With respect to the politics of the 1980s, signs that the world had entered the "end times" brought various enemies into sharp focus for Protestant fundamentalists. Politics was a way of holy revenge that separated those who knew why Christ was coming again from those who did not.

Ben Armstrong had a simple reason to commend conservative politics. *Laissez-faire* capitalism had enabled evangelical Protestant broadcasters to achieve their media victories. Religion, he said, was dying in Europe because of the restrictions placed upon it by state-owned broadcasting. The "great genius of the American system," he wrote, was that it provided a "choice of TV and radio stations, each working to capture its share of the audience. Broadcasting in this country is unique because it operates as part of the competitive system of private enterprise."[20] God blessed America for keeping its markets free. That did not mean that Armstrong and his allies were prepared to countenance unregulated traffic in all areas of the cultural marketplace.

Christian Diversification

The collapse of Jim Bakker's PTL ministry brought many things to public attention, including the distinction between Pentecostals and Baptist fundamentalists. Jerry Falwell, the fundamentalist, took over Bakker's Pentecostal empire and discovered that he was out of place. Unseemly quarrels ensued and tarnished the reputation of televangelists among the faithful. With respect to the viability of religious broadcasting, Bakker's uncovered scandals did not deliver a knock-out blow. The enterprise involved too many people and had taken too many diversified forms. The activities launched by the money raised from the television ministries had spread in a number of directions and widened the contacts of conservative evangelicals with commercial culture. Bakker had wanted to be Walt Disney as well as Johnny Carson. His vision of a Christian theme park expanded into the multifaceted complex of Heritage USA, located close to the border separating North and South Carolina. Although mismanaged, it was a potentially profitable cluster of amusement attractions, a conference center, a health spa, a campground, and luxury hotels. Unlike Falwell and Oral Roberts, Bakker and his wife Tammy were unapologetic and conspicuous consumers. Heritage USA included a shopping mall with stores that sold religious books, records, and framed prayers along with ones specializing in jewelry and clothing.[21]

Bakker's effort to create a total Christian environment was an exuberant and incautious update of a long-standing aim of American Protestants to control the uses of leisure time. Bakker advertised Heritage USA to Christian families as the ultimate in a pleasurable vacation. They did not have to forgo any of the things that their non-Christian neighbors enjoyed. Bakker gave the Pentecostal emphasis on joy frank commercial expression. The goal was to recycle the old Methodist camp meetings into Six Flags Over Texas. To Jim Bakker's many critics, a circle of people that included some fundamentalists, Heritage USA was orgiastic Christianity. It was of a piece with his sexual misconduct, his taste for luxury, and his financial mismanagement. The many charges against Bakker recalled a long series of populist-inspired religious movements of the past. Bakker was the white Father Divine. Heritage USA and the PTL were efforts to make money by selling religion, but they were not, for all that, merely exploitative. Try telling Bakker's supporters that they were people on the economic edge who sacrificed their faith to the oppressive god of consumerism. Such condescension was precisely what Bakker knew how to exorcise. That much, at least, he shared with Jerry Falwell. Bakker told people that they did not have to prove their Christianity by making the contemporary world an enemy. The world belonged to them if they would just take it. Like his wife, they could paint their faces, collect shoes, and love the sounds of country-western music. Only by enjoying in Christian form the full range of pleasures offered by commercial culture could they signal their control over modern technology. Bakker's world was a sort of reckless Pentecostal antinomianism.

Pat Robertson has some of the same instincts, but his moral standards are legal and orderly. His control over his enterprises has made him a preacher/politician with a claim to influence in high government circles and a successful businessman. It is easy to see why Robertson and the Bakkers worked well together in the early days of CBN. Their common aim was to release an old-fashioned, conversion-oriented Christianity from its cultural inferiority complex. Robertson was by far the better manager of the aim. CBN, a non-profit organization, is now the chief stockholder in Robertson's International Family Entertainment Corporation. The latter owns the Family Channel, a cable operation that has roughly the same number of viewers as MTV, the rock-video cable network. Robertson has profitably pursued diversification. The Family Cable Channel carries *The 700 Club*. It also carries news programs, movies, sit-com reruns, and adventure series.[22] All are purportedly wholesome, but most are the products of Hollywood and network television. Viewers browsing the Family Channel offerings are unlikely to spot immediately the Christian sponsorship.

Robertson continues to act on his belief that the spread of Christianity depends upon an aggressive use of the media. In 1992 he made a six-million-dollar cash bid, acting for his U.S. Media Corporation, to buy the bankrupt United Press International.[23] Were Robertson looking for other ways to invest his money, he could do worse than turn to Christian publishing. Despite the attention given to the newer media of television and film, the Protestant world of print had never stopped growing. True, some of the most famous institutions of religious publishing in the nineteenth century went out of business before the twentieth century began. The American Tract Society and the American Bible Society still exist, although we do not hear much about them. The largest denominational publishing empire may well belong to the Jehovah's Witnesses, a group with an astounding record of producing and distributing print material.

Other facts have taken the spotlight off religious publishing. Most religious journals are targeted for specific denominations rather than for general readers. There are exceptions; for example, the *Christian Science Monitor* (a newspaper especially strong in international coverage despite its link to a church unusually secretive in reporting on itself) and the *Washington Times* (owned by Reverend Sun Myung Moon's Unification

Church, which calls even less attention to its religious sponsor). The journals most closely associated in broad terms with America's major religious faiths, *Commonweal* (Roman Catholic), *Commentary* (Jewish), *Christian Century* (liberal Protestant), and *Christianity Today* (evangelical Christian) do not circulate widely and are hard to find even at well-stocked newsstands.[24]

Another major reason why the extent of religious publishing goes unnoticed is the policy of the secular press not to count sales made in religious bookstores when compiling the best-seller lists. If we truly want to know what Americans read, the policy has done a considerable disservice. Religious books are very popular. Fleming H. Revell (1849–1931) was among the first entrepreneurs to become wealthy by specializing in religious literature, most of it produced by opponents of liberal Protestantism. Revell was Dwight Moody's brother-in-law, and he made his initial profits by printing Moody's tracts and sermons. By the turn of the century, the Fleming H. Revell Publishing Company was a large operation. Revell moved it to New York City in 1906 and diversified the output to include maps, banners, and picture post cards.

What Revell accomplished is apparent in Christian bookstores across the United States. There are over six thousand of them, mostly affiliated with the Christian Booksellers Association that was formed in 1949. Gross sales approach two hundred million dollars. An astonishing number of the book titles deal with prophecy and the final days before Christ's Second Coming.[25] If it is at all plausible to imagine that people take what they read seriously, we probably have as a proportion of the population as many Americans anxiously awaiting the end of the world in the 1990s as in the heyday of the Millerites. Hal Lindsey's *The Late Great Planet Earth* (1970) was the publishing phenomenon of the last twenty years.

The Bible, of course, has a special place in the history of printing. All by itself it is big business. That was true in the nineteenth century when, for example, the Revised New Testament, a scholarly edition requiring eleven years of work, was published in 1881 and hawked by newsboys on the streets of New York City.[26] It remained true in the twentieth. The Revised Standard Version ran up mammoth sales in the 1950s until people discovered that they did not like it. Bruce Barton's firm appropriately handled the advertising campaign for the Revised Standard Version. His preferred slogan, "The Bible Jesus Would Have Loved," gave way to the more modest "Biggest Bible News in 341 Years." Printing a new edition is an increasingly useful strategy to keep an old book selling. Many editions of the Bible were available in the 1970s, including the popular *Good News Bible* ("This Can't Be the Bible—I Can Understand It").[27] Formats are as varied as the text. Christian publishing companies have brought out the Bible in every size, shape, and color, with an endless choice of bindings and inscriptions for any occasion. The young heroine of Susan Warner's *Wide, Wide World* faced a relatively easy task of consumer selection in 1850 when she wrestled with choosing the Bible right for her. In the 1980s, she would have had a choice of colors including taupe, mauve, Snow White, Lollypop, and eight shades of black; she could select a binding in flush cut kivar, easily washable vinal, or bluejean denim or such unusual editions as the world's smallest Bible on a microfiche that fit into a gold pendant, a large-print volume, one with cartoon-like illustrations, a cassette Bible, or a gold-and-leather edition marketed for thirty five hundred dollars. *Books in Print* in 1983 needed fifty-five pages to list Bibles and Bible-related entries. Food took only fifteen pages; sex, fourteen.[28]

Not that evangelical Christian book merchants neglected sex and food. How could they when the 1983 annual Christian Booksellers Association convention had three hundred fifty exhibitors spread out over 275,000 square feet of space? The decade of the 1980s produced a flourishing market in Bible-based diet books (*More of Jesus. Less of Me*), lovemaking manuals, jogging and exercise books, and the Christian equivalents of Harlequin romances. All Christian bookstores have greatly expanded their stock of "Christian goods." They carry T-shirts (a picture of a basketball team in action with half its members disappearing from the court in the Rapture—the label is "Fast Break"), bumper stickers ("Jesus is my Rock and My Name is on the Roll"), greeting cards, coffee mugs, table mats, and frisbees with inspirational messages. The video selection is extensive and includes games and Christian drama. Donald Thompson is a particularly well-known evangelical filmmaker who has won a number of "Christian Oscars."[29]

It is, in fact, difficult to wander through these bookstores and imagine any aspect of popular culture that has been left uncloned. Perhaps most surprising to the uninitiated is the burgeoning market in Christian rock music. We have, of course, long recognized the importance of African-American religious music to the development of rhythm and blues. Stories about Jerry Lee Lewis standing outside of black churches to hear the music and of a young Elvis Presley learning his body movements from Pentecostal preachers are part of rock legend. On the other hand, we have been accustomed to think that the churches regarded rock 'n' roll as the devil's perversion of sacred sound. Some still do, but a tide has turned. Evangelical pop record sales run about three hundred million dollars annually, perhaps 8 percent of the total record market. Names of some of the "heavy metal" groups are Barren Cross, Resurrection Band, Bloodgood, and Stryper. The last is the best known, a "heavenly music rock group" that performs in skin-tight black-and-yellow spandex and throws Bibles into the audience. For "punk rock," Christian bookstores carry the sounds of Youth Choir and the Altar Boys; and for "rap," the records of the Rap-Sures. Few radio stations other than the Christian ones play this music, but the network of distribution and marketing is nonetheless well-established. Christian groups tour and hold music festivals.[30]

A sizable portion of the Protestant evangelical community has made its peace with commercial culture by deciding to become "a bigger road side attraction."[31] If that requires arranging church services to accommodate televised sports on Sunday, building Christian massage parlors and nightclubs atop space needles, or equipping churches with skating rinks and bowling alleys, then so be it. The promoters of Christian commercial culture in Orange County, California, wisely decided to publish its own Yellow Pages.[32] That was the only easy way to distinguish the Christian product from the competition.

Selling the New Age

Conservative evangelicals have earned some considerable blame for the commodification of religion over the past twenty years; this despite the protests and the quarrels they have maintained with various aspects of popular culture. They threaten to boycott the sponsor of a particular television-network program, incurring the wrath of a Norman Lear, and then rush to find a Christian equivalent of the offending program. Their populism has trapped them into compromising the urgency of Armageddon. Christ is coming, but it is no longer necessary to await him on your knees garbed in a white robe. He will just as easily recognize the purity of your heart if you are plummeting down a Christian water slide. (The one at Heritage USA fell 163 feet.) This may seem awkward theology, but contemporary conservative evangelicals, we need to remember, did not invent the processes of religious commodification. Maybe I ought to add, lest liberal Protestants be left unfairly twisting in the wind, that no one did. Religion in Western societies has always had commercial aspects. Luther was not the first to notice them, nor did he eliminate them. Somehow the situation was different when churches had an articulated official realm to themselves. That arrangement at least made plain what was a spiritual commodity and what was not. The American system shattered the distinction, eventually making a member of the Jehovah's Witnesses who peddled religion door-to-door on a Sunday morning much the same as a vacuum cleaner salesman. The only difference is that judicial interpretations of the First Amendment render it difficult to regulate what the members of the Jehovah's Witnesses do. Selling a religious commodity, once construed as a religious practice, has its privileges.

Those who argue with alarm that the "public square" is naked of religion.[33] Religion is everywhere. What they ought to worry about, even if nothing can be done about it short of amending the Constitution, is that religion in the marketplace of culture has become an ordinary commodity. It might seem a high-class product or a low-class product, just like automobiles and cheeses. Jim Bakker is Velveeta; Norman Vincent Peale is sliced Swiss in plastic wrap; Reinhold Niebuhr is Brie. Without an official role to play, religion's power lies in what can be claimed through advertising. Conservative evangelicals and liberal Protestants are essentially doing the same thing. Imitation breeds imitation, and so it will go into the future. In the actions that commodify religion, Christians of all stripes have recently seen their efforts surpassed by new competitors. As the cultural landscape now lies, the reigning champions of religious salesmanship are the proponents of the New Age.

The contemporary religious scene in the United States is no longer completely accessible by perusal of the annual *Yearbook of American and Canadian Churches*. Once regarded as a quick reference to identify even the smallest religious organizations and denominations, it reads in the world of the 1990s like a directory of the "mainstream." No reference work, in fact, can hope to run down all the independent churches in the United States and say something reasonably accurate about them. Ride down the back roads of Pennsylvania or Ohio or Oregon for two hours and you can bring back a list of signboard announcements that will baffle any panel of experts. Just who are the "Jews for Jesus" singers? Who runs the "Faith for Today" chapel at the entrance of a trailer park? What tradition are we to make out in signs welcoming "questers" after religious and psychic counseling?

Thumbing through J. Gordon Melton's *Encyclopedia of American Religions* is a humbling exercise.[34] In addition to the more or less standard categories, we find thick chapters labeled "Christian Science and Metaphysical Family," "Spiritualist, Psychic, and New Age Families," "Ancient Wisdom Families," and "Magick Families." Melton's book is not a historical catalogue. It is a guide to the present. His categories break down further before we get to a listing of individual churches. Under "Magick Families," we are directed to different groups under the subcategories "Ritual Magick," "Witchcraft and Neo-Paganism," "Voodoo," and "Satanism." Within the "Spiritualist, Psychic, and New Age Families" category, we find "Channeling" churches (which include such names as the Church of the White Eagle Lodge, the Divine Word Foundation, the Fellowship of the Inner Light, and New Age Teachings), "Flying Saucer Groups," and "Drug Related Groups." A miscellaneous subcategory "Other Psychic New Age Groups" turns out to include some of the most familiar names: the Church of Scientology, the Lorian Association, and the Holy Spirit Association for the Unification of World Christianity (a.k.a. the Unification Church or the "Moonies"). These categories do not yet touch the multiple Asian creeds and practices that non-Asians have taken up and adapted in the United States. These run to many more pages in Melton's reference work. In addition to the new, readers will find groups that they assumed were long extinct (Theosophy and the "I-Am" Movement) manifested in half a dozen or more ongoing churches.[35]

Even the best known of these groups, the International Society for Krishna Consciousness, for example, are small. Most are, in fact, tiny, reporting neither a leader nor a permanent address. Each time Melton's updated encyclopedia gets to a library shelf, dozens of the references have already become defunct and other candidates for inclusion have been born. According to a survey commissioned by the Graduate School of the City University of New York and published in 1991, no more than twenty eight thousand Americans were attached in any serious way to groups identified as New Age.[36] Statistically they do not matter; so why care? For one thing, proliferation is the American way of religion. It is not a particular group that is of interest; it is the process. What has gone on since the mid-1960s bears a resemblance to what happened during the decades preceding the American Civil War. Americans from 1820 to 1850 also paid inordinate attention to a large number of very small religious groups. Many disappeared. Some did not and reshaped the geography of the American religious landscape. What may be especially interesting about that period as well as our own is that much of the division had relatively little to do with ethnic or national pluralism, not when compared to the period from 1850 to 1920. Mostly native-born whites, Christians and Jews, went about reconstituting themselves in religious denominations far removed from the faiths of their parents.

The seekers in our own times who have captured most of the attention are not only white and native-born but also young—of college age but not yet college graduates—and the scions of economically comfortable middle-class families. Perhaps the most striking thing about recruits to some New Age groups—the Moonies and the Hare Krishnas—is that they are male. One explanation for media attention might be that society always pauses when the sons of prominent families begin to disappear into "obscure" cults. Ten times as many daughters might abandon the straight and narrow path to success without causing the same alarm.

Interest in these groups derives from another fact. Many of them have blurred the distinction between religion and various forms of professionally organized psychotherapies. Blurring was already apparent when churches before World War II urged ministers to read psychology and perhaps take some courses in professional counseling. What has happened more recently has changed the rules in ways that threaten massive headaches for the legal system. New Age religions and New Age therapies have grown up together, both constituting a large element in what the historian and social critic Christopher Lasch has called our "therapeutic culture." Fifty years ago we were fairly sure that we could distinguish a clinic organized by disciples of Carl Jung from a Christian Science church. The line is less certain now when we try to decide which of the following has qualified for religious tax exemption: the Esalen Institute, the Rolf Institute, the Erhard Seminars, the Institute of Esoteric Transcendentalism, the American School of Mentalvivology, the Life Study Fellowship Foundation, Inc., and the Institute for the Development of the Harmonious Human Being. Melton lists only the last four in his *Encyclopedia of American Religions*, but slight re-packaging could shift any of them in and out of the categories "religious" and "secular."

The protean term "New Age" is unlikely to have much utility in the long run. It appears to have become faddish in 1972 when the ex-Harvard psychologist Richard Alpert re-created himself as Baba Ram Dass. Much that is supposed to typify the "New Age" predates the early seventies, by centuries if not millennia. We need not be taken in by the advertising. What best holds the concept "New Age" together is the claim to alternative and "better" paths to mental and physical health. That brings us to the main point. The New Age, despite its many proponents who oppose competitive capitalism and its rapacious uses of the planet, has a product to sell. Religious groups may call the product "transcendent awareness"; secular institutes, "holistic healing." In fact, many use these and related terms more or less interchangeably. What is being sold is a technique or a method, "transformative tools." Institutes and religions alike provide training courses for a fee. These purport to give people "practical guides" for self-improvement, for control over all aspects of daily life, for success. People often get certificates or degrees, and there is always a higher level to attain. It is a market of intense product differentiation. Each group's technique is unique. Each group's technique is best.

The Church of Scientology is almost a prototype. It is ancient by some contemporary standards, forty years old. When L. Ron Hubbard published *Dianetics. The Modern Science of Mental Health* in 1950, he did not imagine himself a religious prophet. He wished to establish a new school of psychotherapy, one with its own language of "auditing," "reactive mind," "engrams," and "clears." Initially he enjoyed considerable popular success. *Dianetics* sold well and prompted a sort of parlor game of Hubbardean therapy across America. Hubbard also organized the Dianetic Research Foundations in various cities, marketing his ideas rather like a franchise operation.

In 1953 and 1954, Hubbard moved to reorganize his enterprises into a church. Its center was Washington, D.C. Several things prompted the alteration. For starters, Hubbard ran into a stone wall of opposition from the American Psychological Association. Rollo May wrote a dismissive review of *Dianetics* in the *New York Times*. ("It so clearly illustrates the most common fallacy of our time in regard to psychological ills.")[37] What had been healthy profits in 1951 and 1952 turned into debt and financial disaster by 1953. According to some accounts, Hubbard would have moved toward religion even without these reverses.[38] His mind naturally gravitated toward the fantastic and hints of unexplored mental realms where the perfectly rational mind, Hubbard's ideal, and the cosmic mind became one. Perhaps only one thing about Hubbard's life is not disputable. Prior to his writing *Dianetics*, he was a gifted science-fiction writer, of the same generation as Robert Heinlein and A. E. Van Vogt. His close friend and an early proponent of *Dianetics* was John Campbell, Jr., the editor of *Astounding Science Fiction*, one of the most significant journals of postwar American popular culture. Science fiction need not become religion any more than Jungian therapy. Hubbard set out to demonstrate that there was no necessary separation either.

To Hubbard's critics, the sudden move to organize a church was simply a ploy to gain tax exemption and to throw government regulators off the trail of his embezzlements. Religious healing is, in general, not subject to regulations of public health and medical practice that the Food and Drug Administration establishes. A lot depends on what is claimed and how. Hubbard, as part of his auditing therapy, sold a form of skin galvanometer that he called an E-Meter. Some of the claims made for E-Meters came perilously close to the claims that the psychologist Wilhelm

Reich made in behalf of his "orgone box." Reich advertised his product as a cure for cancer, and The Food and Drug Administration took him to court in 1954. Not having church status to protect him, he went to prison in 1956. Selling E-Meters under the guise of religious practice was arguably a move of prudence, not of faith. Although Hubbard's Church of Scientology seemed to have little to do with what many people understood as organized religion, the odd name provided a layer of protection.

As it turned out, the layer was not thick enough. Hubbard had to struggle to establish the religious status of his church. Religious groups founded since Scientology have both benefited and suffered from the controversy that followed his career. His troubles as a church leader began in 1958 when the FDA seized twenty-one thousand tablets of "Dianazene" from an agency associated with Hubbard's Washington church. More seriously, government agents raided the church offices in 1962, carting off E-Meters and literature used to promote them. The charge was that Hubbard was selling E-Meters under the false claim that they cured arthritis, eye problems, bursitis, and the common cold. The legal suit stalled in the courts until 1967, when a lower court ruling upheld the FDA action. It authorized the destruction of the seized E-Meters and the revocation of the Church of Scientology's tax-exempt status.

The battle was not over. A landmark appeals-court decision in 1969 reversed a major portion of what the lower court had done. It ruled that the Church of Scientology had established a *prima facie* case as a religion and that it used E-Meters as part of its religious practice. The E-Meters, therefore, had to be restored. The court did stipulate that they could be used only for religious counseling and could not be advertised as effective in treating physical illness. That part of the ruling still left boundaries confused. The distinction between healing and religious counseling was exactly what groups like Scientology tried to erase. Although Hubbard was barred from advertising the therapeutic value of E-Meters in newspapers, he did not have to. Courts could not stop faithful Scientologists from believing in the healing efficacy of E-Meters any more than they could stop Christian Scientists and Pentecostals cured by faith from believing that their religion made doctors and hospitals unnecessary. Since for many believers the whole point of religious practice in the Church of Scientology was to effect a psychosomatic cure, people who had been "duped" by Scientology before the ruling were likely to go on being "duped."

Hubbard's legal troubles were not confined to the United States. Authorities in England and Australia launched more aggressive assaults against his operations. The actions prompted Hubbard to take some steps to give Scientology more of the "aura" of religion. He now called counselors of the church "ministers" and gave them a sort of clerical garb to wear. The organizational units formerly called "Orgs" and "Centers" became "churches" and "missions." Scientology still held no worship services. Its literature made scant reference to God, focusing instead on the various programs of "auditing" and the cost. The religion of Scientology was not a lifetime faith for many. Like psychological counseling, people stayed with it until they had gotten what they wanted for their money.

The early seventies provided a breathing spell for Scientology, and Hubbard was left to sell his expensive services "with all the more aggressive techniques of modern salesmanship."[39] Then, in 1977, the FBI moved again, breaking into church offices to find evidence that Scientologists had been stealing government documents relevant to investigations of the church. Indictments handed down in 1978 and subsequent plea bargaining resulted in the fining and jailing of several high church officials, including Hubbard's wife. Hubbard died in 1986, an event that may enable the church to get beyond its bad reputation. But not yet. Despite its ability to attract the support of celebrities, including the film actor Tom Cruise, its legal problems continue to suggest the confusions of the New Age. California in 1984 revoked the tax-exempt status of Scientology.

Several sociologists have called Scientology a "manipulationist" movement.[40] It is a useful concept. "Manipulationist" cults supposedly promise adherents something other than salvation from the world or even a way to gain knowledge of what lies beyond human experience. They offer instead a superior, esoteric means to succeed within this life, a way to manipulate rather than simply to protest the status quo. The techniques taught by such cults are supposed to improve people's station in life, to enhance their performance in high-pressure secular roles. Those who join the cult make better grades. They close more deals. They have better sex. The only problem with the sociological label, one that can become a legal conundrum, is that any religious group using prayer is inevitably "manipulationist." What does Hubbard manipulate that Norman Vincent Peale does not? On that question, disputants can go on splitting hairs forever.

After Scientology came transcendental meditation. Introduced into the United States by the Maharishi Mahesh Yogi in the 1960s and accorded legitimating testimonials by Mia Farrow, Jane Fonda, and the Beatles, TM promised a bargain-basement nirvana. Not that it was cheap. The bargain lay in the amount of effort required. For most of the people attracted to TM, attendance at a weekend seminar costing a week's salary was the only investment they made to gain their personal mantra. Additional steps existed for the serious-minded, but for most TM was a technique of home repair. The Maharishi presented himself as a religious leader even if the World Plan Executive Council that he founded in 1972 did not sound much like a church. At least one court case has held that TM is a religion and cannot be taught in public schools. The World Plan Executive Council, which runs the Maharishi International University in Fairfield, Iowa, still has a listing in Melton's *Encyclopedia of American Religions.* Its status will surely undergo legal wrangling if it gains again in popularity.

Borderline cases are a staple of contemporary religious news. In September 1992, the *New York Times,* reported on the legal tangle resulting from divorce proceedings between J. Z. Knight, an extremely successful "spirit channeler" in Yelm, Washington, and her fifth husband. The perplexed judge was trying to get Knight's alleged "spirit channel," a warrior named Ramtha from the Cro-Magnon era, to take the stand to see whether he was a "god, a spirit, or a fake." What was not in question were the profits that Knight had gotten from running the Ramtha School of Enlightenment on a fifty-acre ranch. Her celebrity coterie had at one time included Shirley MacLaine and Linda Evans. The problem is not, in the end, whether Knight is a fake, for the law cannot look closely at that issue. The question is how to regulate and tax churches that are also businesses selling videos, books, and personal counseling on matters of health. The question of Knight's sincerity as a religious leader is quite apart from the two-million-dollar house she built for herself or the Arabian horse-breeding operation that she ran.[41]

The paradox in many New Age manifestations that hover between religion and creative therapy is that, on the one hand, they promise to make us less tense, less ambitious, less obsessed with ourselves as evil, more inwardly harmonious. They release us from our "Type-A" personalities and the illusion that happiness lies in the satisfying of consumer desires. On the other hand, the big spenders for New Age services are hard-driving college students, lawyers, and Wall Street analysts who have no intention of renouncing their careers. Michael Rossman, a jaundiced observer of the market demand for professional upgrade through meditation, noted: "Throughout the 1970s there was not a running show more comic, nor more passionate and deeply meaningful to many people, than this motley, brilliant cavalcade of entrepreneurial gurus provided as they traversed the land, performing in main tents and side shows, vying to entice the populace to retreats and inductions, spinning off so many local franchise operators that the psychic crossroads of each significant cultural center came to appear in a maze of holy Kentucky Fried Chickens, McDonald's, and Jack-in-the-Boxes."[42]

In a more sympathetic review of the New Age scene, a book by Michael D'Antonio provides selected glimpses of a sub-culture of "hundreds of church-like congregations" tied in to radio stations, magazines, publishing houses, businesses, resorts, hotels, healing centers offering holistic health care, restaurants, and a music industry.[43] A few towns, like Sedona, Arizona, have become meccas of New Age products and services, offering crystals, videos of channelers, audio-cassettes, 900 phone numbers, and seminars. In almost all cases, even at the altogether admirable ice cream operation run by Ben Cohen and Jerry Greenfield in Newport, Vermont, something relatively expensive is for sale: undreamt of varieties of yoga mats, meditation cushions, microbiotic cookware, health foods, natural vitamins, and incense. It is an upscale market that invites only the well-heeled.

Even in the case of new religions that are not selling techniques for personal aggrandizement, money is a central issue. For example, the Unification Church of Reverend Sun Myung Moon is in principle a prophetic, world-renouncing movement. Unlike Scientology or TM, it does not promote the personal development of individuals. Under a strict discipline appoaching authoritarianism, it seeks the welfare of the collective defined in spiritual terms. Young men who want to make money do not become Moonies. The same can be said about ISKCON or the International Society for Krishna Consciousness that gathers adherents in a monastic, world-renouncing environment. For all that, the Unification Church in its visible operations is about money—a luxurious headquarters, ownership of a hotel and other valuable property in New York City, a financial pipeline to South Korea, an outlet for ginseng tea, a fleet of fishing boats, and a Washington, D.C., newspaper. Despite vigorous support of Reverend Sun Myung Moon from many religious leaders worried about increased IRS scrutiny of religious activity, a jury convicted him of tax evasion and sent him to prison. Both the Unification Church and the Hare Krishnas have invited controversy by their strategies for raising money through donations. What is troublesome is not merely their desire to proselytize in public places but also their practice of concealing their identity when making an approach, their practice of "heavenly deception."

When does raising money, defined by a sect as a religious duty, become an activity distinguishable from the practice of proselytizing and spreading the faith? The Moonies and Hare Krishnas who labor eighteen hours a day in airports and on street corners are not always trying to convert others. They concentrate on people who are totally outside the demographic range of people who are likely to listen with interest to their message.[44] They expect that the token literature sometimes given in exchange for a donation will be immediately discarded. It does not matter to the fund-raisers; nor does it matter that people give them money to get rid of them. The only thing that counts is the donation. To critics, who have had some recent successes in restricting the public activities of these groups, religion should not be a matter of such cold-blooded calculation.

Yet raising church finances has been a cold-blooded calculation for a long time. The Moonies and Hare Krishnas respond to criticism with a version of an affirmative-action argument. We are late starters in the market, they say, discriminated against by people who do not like new-comers. We need special protections and privileges to overcome resentment. Our methods are deceptive only in the sense that "new measures" always change the rules and upset people who like the old ways. What we preach is in no way harmful to anyone. We promote codes of righteous living, seek a personal connection to God, hold an apocalyptic view of the future, and believe in metaphysical healing. On those grounds we are not so different from many evangelical Protestant churches.

They have a point, and it is an uncomfortable truth. The closer they get to the point, the greater is the scandal it poses to proselytizing. Methodists do not want to be reminded of the controversy that George Whitefield started. Poking around in history has its dangers. Once churches began to do something other than tending the faithful, once they started beating the bushes in search of new members, once they took on the holy mission of converting the world, they were in the business of selling. Selling breeds entrepreneurs who will do whatever the law allows and will press the limits. The religious proselytizing generated by free markets and competition will always in someone's opinion be hucksterism. Those who cry "hucksterism" with respect to someone else's religion are usually no less engaged in selling. They only imagine that their selling is more professional, more tasteful.

Arguably, as a matter of policy, the law ought to leave the New Age churches alone. Their market is limited. Their product is expensive. Their appeal is to people who ought to be able to fend for themselves. Caveat emptor works better in this situation than legal aggression. Before we foolishly bear down with the law, we ought at least to recognize that the mass market for more settled religions may become an equally appropriate target. If the intention is to reduce religious hustling in order to protect the innocent and gullible, we are not likely to accomplish that aim by scapegoating a few "cults." When young people disappear into them, it is too easy to believe that they have been "brainwashed" rather than that they have found something wrong with the world they live in. What they have found wrong is often the same shoddy practices that the cults use to establish their financial viability. The cults, though, did not pick up their practices from Asia or from any New Age.

Epilogue

One may say that to be reared a member
of a national Church is in itself a lesson of
religious moderation, and a help towards
culture and harmonious perfection. Instead
of battling for his own private forms for
expressing the inexpressible and defining
the undefinable, a man . . . has leisure
and composure to satisfy other sides of his
nature as well.

Matthew Arnold, *Culture and Anarchy*

Charleston, South Carolina, is a beautiful city that pays elegant respect to its past. The spires of St. Michael's Episcopal Church, completed in 1761, and of St. Philip's Episcopal Church tower over its commercial and residential buildings. Once upon a time such a vista signaled that human beings counted on religion to lift them toward heaven. And so it still seems to say something calmingly reassuring about the arrangement of priorities, even to the non-religious mind.

From Charleston's harbor the skyline offers a glimpse of the tops of many churches, not all of them Episcopal, not all of them Protestant. On Hasell Street, between the two main thoroughfares of Meeting and King, stands St. Mary's Church. The present structure, dating from 1839, rises from the same site as the original church of 1789 that became a haven for French settlers fleeing the Santo Domingo slave revolt in 1793. Directly across the street is Kahal Kadosh Beth Elohim, the fourth oldest Jewish congregation in the United States, originally Sephardic and especially famous as the birthplace of American Reform Judaism in 1824. The congregation traces its origin to 1749 and built the present handsome Greek Revival synagogue in 1840. Not far away, on Calhoun Street, is the home of the Emanuel African Methodist Episcopal Church, an 1891 edifice built by the descendants of slaves and free African Americans. Early in the nineteenth century, blacks in Charleston had organized the independent African Methodist Association that counted Denmark Vesey, the slave rebel leader, among its adherents.

It is hard to come away from Hasell Street and Charleston without taking a certain pride in American religion and its diversity. Majorities and social elites built the big churches. But outside the main focus of public attention, small groups—groups that often had no allies outside their own societies—found ways to preserve their traditions. In pre-Revolutionary South Carolina, church pluralism happened in haphazard fashion, encouraged as much by the absence and lax enforcement of laws as by the positive encouragement of toleration. The First Amendment and many state constitutions made religious pluralism the law of the land, but it was loose social arrangements that made virtually endless pluralism a force in American history. That was contrary to anyone's expectations.

We offer the view from Charleston's harbor in part to elevate the reputation of American religious life above the image of tacky hucksterism. In haphazard pluralism we recognize a civilized accomplishment that remains impressive however we tally up the losses and gains of what accompanied it. American religious leaders, self-saddled with responsibility for protecting the nation's morals, bereft of a unified voice and of legal authority to do much, faced with competition from an increasing number of activities that occupied people's time, began early in the nineteenth century to make control of the marketplace of culture a major priority. Whether culture was defined as an attitude of refined taste; as mastery of the highest moral and artistic sensibilities; as ways of passing time pleasantly in self-improvement; or as customs, beliefs, and symbols that unified the nation, its component parts were increasingly for sale and increasingly market-sensitive to democratic desires.

Many entrepreneurs of commercial culture, through print material and oral performance, promised a product that raised the quality of life in the United States. Clerics were sceptical, especially since amusements, broadly construed, quickly became the biggest business in popular commercial culture. To halt what they viewed as a decline in moral and religious seriousness, they descended into the marketplace to erect some competition. As authors and lecturers, they contributed to commercial culture. In their own churches and in forums outside the regular market, they invented, and used as enticements, Christian forms of fun. They enjoyed considerable success, although ultimately their efforts, even though many of them sharply criticized the culture industry and sought to regulate it, served to place religion on the cultural shelves as another commodity. They sought ways to make religion attractive to a consuming public that they had helped create. Advertising became vital to their task of guiding the choices of consumers toward moral ends.

Summarizing the argument in the above manner casts the verb forms that propel the story in the active voice. Ministers and their allies chose their strategies. We can, with blame-reducing effect, relate the narrative in the passive voice. Religion, this version asserts, was done in by the market juggernaut. Spiritual goals that looked to a transcendent God were coerced into secular programs by inexorable forces unleashed by an expanding, industrializing society. Subsistent communities that had had the time to imagine a sacred power working independently of the limited aspirations of their residents were doomed by ambitions stirred in rising networks of trade. When markets had been merely places where people came together in face-to-face contact to exchange something for something else, they had a significance limited by a specific occasion. When they became a system that facilitated exchanges between people who never saw one another, their power pushed through geographic and temporal barriers to make its amorality universal.

Religious leaders perceived the decline of spiritual power and decried the loss in their sermons. Piteous breast-beating, however, was not an effective reaction. Along with everyone else, clerics were left with no choice except to slip by steady degrees into an affectionate embrace of the world. They were forced into postures of selling annually updated religious doctrines that could keep up with the competition. Religious leaders could either give in to the sway of the market or watch as their churches died. Even in some extraordinary cases in which religious groups managed to survive through exaggerated acts of world rejection, their quaintness served the fortunes of others. American Shakers shrank in numbers, but antique dealers slapped a value on their simple spirituality that boosted the price of Shaker artifacts in a costly market. Promoters of tourism in Lancaster County, Pennsylvania, used the horse-drawn buggies of the Amish to draw people to the motels, restaurants, and well-known outlet stores of the area. The Amish religion, in effect, sells "seconds" for Levi-Strauss, Hamilton watches, Pfaltzgraff china, and a hundred other manufacturers.

Readers will recognize caricature in the above. Even so, the passive account is not perversely untrue and keeps us mindful of how difficult it is for people to make a creative stamp on broad forces of economic change. The story is sufficiently complicated, with enough seemingly unrelated activities to keep track of, that it needs both the active and passive voice to tell. People *chose* and *forced* values into market operations. At the same time, their actions were seriously constrained. The mystery of agency haunts us because we want to judge the quality of the product the past has served up and to wonder whether anything we might do from this point will matter. Many who do not like the business and commercial side of religion nourish the thought that it is never too late to do something. Others see the fatal mistake as lying too far back in time, indeed in the First Amendment itself, to permit remedial action. Those who originally defended religious establishments against America's First Amendment predicted that somewhere down the line the need for churches to think constantly about ready cash and endowments would dissipate their spiritual powers. But their foresight might not have saved the day. Besides, there were other things to predict and fear that weighed in favor of the American Constitution. How could even the most careful planners have engineered the right balance?

What are the negatives of religious disestablishment? Some of the original nay-sayers expected disestablishment to eclipse organized religion altogether. For evaluative purposes, we can forget them, since events quickly proved them wrong. Matthew Arnold, England's sage Victorian poet and social critic, harbored misgivings of a different sort. He did not question that legalization and full encouragement of religious "dissent," steps that in fact stripped "dissent" of any meaning, led to earnest religious striving. He was well apprised of facts about the growth of churches in the United States. However, in Arnold's mind parochial battles to advance "our own fancies and feelings," were not the same thing as balanced spiritual development. People consumed energy inventing and fighting for their own faiths and left themselves without the "leisure and calm to steady our view of religion itself."[1]

Arnold missed the degree to which American churches under the thunder of their doctrinal quarrels emphasized the moral consequences of religion. That by itself might have pleased him, but too much else, in his mind, was wrong. For Arnold, culture either embodied the best products of the human mind, which took time and quiet reflection to deliver, or it was nothing. Busy religion, which American churches surely exemplified, was merely "philistine." Even the sometimes crushing dullness of church establishment was preferable. Arnold's idea of culture did not allow for the concept of "popular culture." His term was "barbarism." When religion had to shout shrilly in the marketplace, the potentially ennobling aspects of spirituality had·no chance to develop.

Arnold's biases were conservative; but since he directed them at unrestrained liberalism, they easily carried over into any number of Marxist-informed, general critiques of bourgeois society. I have already related Max Horkheimer's and Theodor Adorno's low estimates of the culture industry and all that it influenced. They were no longer foreseeing disastrous consequences; they were recording them. More recently the English literary critic Raymond Williams has posed the dilemma of whether educated men and women can simultaneously encourage democracy and work to clear the landscape of "bad culture" so dear to the democratic masses. For Williams, preserving a cultural hierarchy that distinguishes art from kitsch is a vital task. What makes it an all but impossible one is the capitalist market. Markets drop the question of what is good for people, taken collectively, into a deep, dark hole and provide, in the realm of culture, a steady stream of meretricious horror films, rape novels, and moronic Tin-Pan Alley "drool."[2] Williams did not, like Arnold, turn his critique of the forces that degrade "culture" into poorly produced items of mass consumption against America's non-establishment religion, though much in this account would give him grounds to do that.

However, what about the other side of what might have been foreseen or analyzed later as an inevitable consequence of religious disestablishment? Without even needing to attack Arnold and his heirs with probing questions about the social construction of good and bad taste, liberals can use the market model of disestablishment to answer critics on their right and left. Their case goes beyond Arnold's concession that competitive religious groups, like competitive producers of any sort, produce a lot of energy. Where the market side of American religious life proved itself a godsend, figuratively speaking, was in supplying a frame of orderly interaction for what might have been a frightfully vicious situation. Socialist critics of capitalism who extol the virtues of a pre-market moral economy focus on economic injustice. Whether moral economies, with their inward-looking, parochial concepts of traditional rights, can prevent the sort of religious strife that tears apart Ireland, Iraq, Bosnia, India, Afghanistan, and other large sections of the world is another question. In traditional societies, it is sufficient argument against a claim to say that it is foreign, alien, outside the web of ancient and honored personal relationships. Market logic recognizes no aliens. In that sense, Americans were fortunate that it stepped in to regulate their religious disputes.

Without committing ourselves to the editorial line of *The National Review*, we can surely understand why "conservatives" who insist on a confluence between capitalism, democracy, and religious freedom, have a forceful point. In following the historian Thomas Haskell, we can also recognize a link between the expansion of capitalism in the nineteenth century and the origins of humanitarian reform. Haskell disconnected the link from class interests. For example, capitalists did not support abolitionism to mask their own preference for an oppressive system of wage labor; they did so because market discipline had inculcated in them "altered perceptions of causation in human affairs." By vastly increasing the general credibility of promise-keeping, far-flung markets created a reliable network of strangers who recognized a mutual need for conscientious behavior. At the same time, markets made people aware of the long-range consequences of their actions and of the possibility of coordinating activities in places at great distance from one another. As the world of markets expanded, so did the realm in which human ambition and invention could operate. Markets multiplied the "recipes" for effective human actions, economic ones to be sure but also moral and benevolent ones.[3]

Keeping the verbs of the story in the active voice and the tone upbeat, we may say that religious leaders delightedly seized upon market logic implicit in disestablishment because it brought their mightiest dreams for doing God's work into the realm of possibility. Some of them wanted to create disciplined workers for factories, but that was a relatively minor part of a scheme to reshape the world according to Christian values. The transformations that market logic could effect over vast distances broke Christianity loose from a parochial setting. Church leaders saw the means to give reality to their humanitarian charities. Their sphere of influence went beyond local churches. Revivals became businesses because markets showed the way to evangelize the far corners of the globe. Market logic promised universal redemption.

As a way of overcoming parochialism, the urge to widen religion's influence through a market model of advertising and distribution networks incorporated huge amounts of ethnocentrism. Christianity was a sure-sell product because it was the best. Christian liberals have more recently muted that boast and for an interesting reason. Market choices made at home and abroad proved them wrong. To get back to the point about the confluence of capitalism, democracy, and religious freedom, the market model assisted the spread of toleration by legitimating competition. At the macro-level of social operations, it helped to neutralize antagonisms. When people think of religion as something to be sold rather than as something imposed—something advanced in the prospect of a mutually beneficial contract, which parties are free at all times to accept or reject—religious toleration advances.

The involvement of religion in commercialization is important. The preceding observations, in fact, go well beyond the main issues of this book, suggesting that market logic infiltrated into American religion in broader ways than have been described. The marketplace of culture was only one convergence point. However, the very importance of the phenomenon of commodification, its capacity to fixate our attention, requires us to stop for a moment and remind ourselves that religion is much else besides a commodity. Religion is not for sale at the local handy mart. You cannot find the daily price of religion in the *Wall Street Journal*, even if some religious leaders organize private enterprises that issue stock. The average American religious service does not try to provide on Sunday morning what people had wanted on Saturday night. Churches must raise money if they are to exist at all. But expansion is a relative drive, and most American religious leaders are not attempting to build an empire comparable in size to a state university system. They leave that to a few Texas Baptists. Jews do not proselytize; neither do American Catholics, at least not in the ways that have been described herein. Even many Protestant churches run their membership drives in a low-key fashion. Aggressive proselytizing in some forms, like that done by the Jehovah's Witnesses, has very little to do with building membership or raising money. When all is said and done, the ordinary activity of most American religious groups is to minister to the people already there, to shore up their faith, and to supply them with the strength to live their lives.

To be sure, Rembrandts, diamond necklaces, and even running shoes are also something more than commodities; and our reminder is not advanced to do what we insisted we should not do (that is, to privilege religion as a unique category of human experience) but to keep us in possession of our common sense so that we may evaluate soberly whether the commercialization of religion was such a dismal departure from previous "secular" incarnations of religion. Despite the examples discussed in this book, many American religious groups were small and poor. Many still are. Think of the plight of orthodox Jewish immigrants who struggled on the Lower East Side of New York City, not always successfully, to find a minyan. Think of individual Catholic churches, integrated, some might think, into one of the largest corporate structures in the world, that cannot raise the money to sustain basic and desperately needed parish churches. Think, perhaps above all, of African-American churches that *faute de mieux* became economic resources for the communities they served but often had to make emotional fulfillment substitute for hard cash. The pageant of American religious history reveals people who have found in their faith a social identity, a source of ethnic and racial pride, an assurance of salvation, and a basis for protest against injustice. Surely, as users of religion, they ought to be remembered as something other than ordinary consumers, their faith as something more than the only commodity on the shelves they could afford.

As for wealthy churches, the ones with the well-dressed communicants and large budgets, they are doing something more than running market concessions. "Non-profit" is a slippery concept since all organizations, however the IRS treats them, must cover the bills for their activities. Whether profit or non-profit, most of them seek ways to raise extra funds to set aside for a rainy day and to plow back into growth. Yet constitutional interpretations of the First Amendment permit tax exemption as a major exception to the rule of no state aid to churches. Why? Because the United Presbyterian Church really does have a different set of concerns than General Motors. Financial growth for wealthy religious organizations means, once building campaigns and staff salaries are taken care of, having more money for charitable activity. Their agencies work with the poor, the homeless, the battered, and the abused. They provide food, money, and education. The "nonprofits" of churches build hospitals and nursing homes.

Having issued these tardy reminders about the charitable activities and spiritual life of American churches, we must still wonder whether they have been rendered less effective by the processes of commercialization that support them. Is religion somehow not religion in the way it once was? Is it, in fact, nothing but a shallow appendage of secular life? Many readers will surely think so. And it would be disingenuous of me to deny the critical points suggested by a good part of the narrative. This book brings to the fore aspects of religious life that taint the credibility of religion's moral influence, the very thing that organized churches in their projects of public outreach wanted to enhance. Middle-class Protestants have inevitably been tarnished the most. They have many good reasons to protest and many ironies to think about in the attacks made upon them. Catholics invented many of the business tricks of the Christian world. American Judaism, from Orthodox to Reform, was a veritable training ground for success in commerce and the entertainment world. Churches of the poor carried religious competition to extremes undreamt of by middle-class congregations. Inner-city pastors looking for customers lined up their storefront faiths side by side down city blocks. Theirs was a high-risk domain with a low-cost entry level and a daunting rate of failure. Yet churches that did not belong to the Protestant, white, middle class somehow managed to retain more of an aura of spirituality, perhaps because of stronger emotional ties among the communicants and more joyous services of celebration. Orderly, well-mannered Protestants, who raised enormous amounts of money for the cause of social justice, were somehow more easily left with the reputation that they had no faith stronger than what lay in the collection plate.

In many ways the major churches of American Protestantism were saddled with associations that predated settlements in Massachusetts Bay and Virginia. The reformist cleansing of Protestantism was from the beginning an exercise in efficiency and bureaucratic streamlining that appealed to Europe's commercial bourgeoisie. A Protestant church was a material structure, nothing more. For Protestants to condemn materialism often looked like comic self-parody, a guilt-ridden striking out at what they had made the very soul of their faith. Protestant churches had no choice but to go into the world and meet it on terms that they and their privileged business sponsors both regarded as natural. To do otherwise (for example, to try to pretend that religion had no "business" in the marketplace of culture alongside so-called "secularists") would have seemed to Protestant leaders a return to monasticism.

American Protestants have some consolations. Social and legal conditions in the United States worked to equalize the various faiths with respect to market forces, normalizing what Protestants did in the world as one kind of effective church-building. If non-Protestants were to keep Protestants from determining what cultural options were available to everybody else, they had to pay attention to the marketplace of culture as well. The desire and the opportunity to count in the world brought American Catholics and Jews out of their ghettos, proudly displaying their faith in architecture, in sophisticated journalism, in well-financed fraternal organizations, and in spiritual advice books written for the mass market. The measure of their faith also became its power to push people up the economic scale. In our times, it is hard to imagine a religious organization whose operations are totally outside a market model. Granted, to say that loads the dice since it assigns the market the primary position of influence. For balance, we need to remember that it is almost equally difficult to imagine market operations, at least in the realm of commercial culture, that totally escape the moral reach of religion.

So what are we to think? Final judgments must rest with the reader, but I will allow myself brief space to say something cautious and then something dire. The cautious part is simply a reminder to go slowly before assuming that one kind of secularity, the one pronounced in our own times, somehow has a special ability to corrupt or undermine what we call religion. To say that churches are partly secular institutions is as neutral a statement as statements can get. It should astonish or upset no one. No organized church, in fact, ever imagined itself as a totally non-secular institution. Although the nature of organized religion's "secularity" has changed in the past two hundred years, that, too, is not by itself a reason for scandalized outcry. The particular form of worldliness that churches in the United States have exhibited by entering the marketplace of culture has only displaced earlier forms of church worldliness: direct political involvement in the domestic and foreign policy of states, conspicuous displays of non-bourgeois pomp and wealth, and heavy investment in the higher forms of philosophical and scientific knowledge.

I would even spin some strongly positive statements about the ventures of American religious leaders into the marketplace of culture, at least as correctives to things that are often said about religion. The most important is that American religious leaders, taken collectively, were not brakesmen on change in the American past. They deserve more credit than they usually get as major architects of American experience. Like everyone else who built successful institutions, they skillfully adopted from their historical environments the elements that suited their needs and that gave them a creative edge in making change serve their purposes. To have learned to operate effectively in the marketplace of American culture, to have made that marketplace respond to their concerns, was no mean feat. They did not triumph over circumstances, but they were not defeated either. Like American politics, religion stayed lively and relevant to national life by reflecting popular taste and commanding media coverage. Despite the many complaints that are still made about rabble-rousers and media circuses, it is possible to think about the democratic and commercial purveyors of American religion, usually the same people, as generous facilitators of American pluralism. The serene view from the Charleston harbor is only part of an impressive story. And Matthew Arnold was a fuddy-duddy.

If only. To adapt Thomas Kuhn's language, "normal" religion is alive and well in American life. The downside of that statement is that wellness does not carry with it transformative power. The paradigm-busters are nowhere in view. Those people who wait in these times for the numerically impressive organizations of American religion to coalesce into a powerful redemptive force are bound to find the present circumstances profoundly unsatisfying. Where are the real religious prophets? Can there be any in a country whose self-image rests on fast, friendly, and guiltless consumption? It is not the taste of a Big Mac that sells it; it is the way it feeds the low-down common desire to be democratically unpretentious. Would-be religious prophets have to learn the ways of Disneyland in order to find their audience, but even that popular touch cannot give them the capacity to reach the many Americans who would feel perfectly comfortable at a prayer breakfast held under McDonald's generous golden arches. How can the prophets among us terrify those people with an apocalyptic vision of a planet left desolate by careless stewards who have used up its fields, wasted its energy, and blackened its air and waters? How can they make them understand that when Adam and Eve broke a commandment against a forbidden consumption in the Garden of Eden, forbidden because it was needless, they were pointing humankind toward its final agony? Probably they cannot. So we are left with nothing new under an unforgiving sun whose burning rays carry cancer and God knows what else through an ozone-depleted atmosphere.

Notes

Introduction

1. John Corry, "Preachers: Mastery of Medium," *New York Times*, Apr. 2, 1987.
2. Report on a survey conducted by the Graduate School of the City University of New York, *New York Times*, Apr. 10, 1991.
3. Harry S. Stout, *The Divine Dramatist. George Whitefield and the Rise of Modern Evangelicalism* (Grand Rapids, 1991), xvii.
4. Peter Berger, *The Sacred Canopy* (New York, 1967), 138; Berger, "A Market Model for the Analysis of Ecumenicity," *Social Research*, 30 (Spring 1963): 77–93.

Chapter One

1. For historical arguments that challenge the "liberating" effects of reading, see, for example, Robert Muchembled, *Popular Culture and Elite Culture in France, 1400–1750* (Baton Rouge, 1985), and Harvey J. Graff, *The Legacies of Literacy. Continuities and Contradictions in Western Culture and Society* (Bloomington, 1987).
2. For a superb discussion of antebellum debates about reading, see Isabelle Lehuu, "Changes in the Word. Reading Practices in Antebellum America," Ph.D. dissertation, Cornell Univ. 1992.
3. Carlo Ginzburg, *The Cheese and the Worms. The Cosmos of a Sixteenth-Century Miller* (Baltimore, 1980); Michel de Certeau, *The Practice of Everyday Life* (Berkeley, 1984).
4. An enormous literature has grown up on this point, but for some sum-

mary positions consult various works by Roger Chartier: ed., *A History of Private Life. Passions of the Renaissance* (Cambridge, Mass., 1989), 69–159, 327–95; *The Cultural Uses of Print in Early Modern France* (Princeton, 1987); *The Culture of Print. Power and the Uses of Print in Early Modern Europe* (Princeton, 1989).

5. Scholars continue to debate the literacy rate in colonial America. See, for example, Kenneth Lockridge, *Literacy in Colonial New England. An Enquiry into the Social Context of Literacy in the Early Modern West* (New York, 1974); Lee Soltow and Edward Stevens, *The Rise of Literacy and the Common School in the United States. A Socioeconomic Analysis to 1870* (Chicago, 1981); William Gilmore, *Reading Becomes a Necessity of Life. Material and Cultural Life in Rural New England, 1780–1835* (Knoxville, 1989); David Hall, *Worlds of Wonder, Days of Judgment. Popular Religious Belief in Early New England* (New York, 1989).

6. For the reading tastes of colonial Americans, north and south, see James D. Hart, *The Popular Book. A History of America's Literary Taste* (New York, 1950).

7. The best discussion of colonial New England's reading habits, including the way in which people consumed both pious and worldly literature, is David Hall, *Worlds of Wonder*. See especially the chapter entitled "Uses of Literacy." See also Marion Stowell, *Early American Almanacs. The Colonial Weekday Bible* (New York, 1977).

8. If Jon Butler is right, this was true almost everywhere in the seventeenth century and only slightly less true in the eighteenth century. See his *Awash in a Sea of Faith. Christianizing the American People* (Cambridge, Mass., 1990).

9. Richard Beale Davis, *A Colonial Southern Bookshelf. Reading in the Eighteenth Century* (Athens, Ga., 1979), 24.

10. A rigid division between secular and religious books mars what is in many ways a pioneer social history of reading in America, Gilmore's *Reading Becomes a Necessity of Life*.

11. Nathan Hatch, *The Democratization of American Christianity* (New Haven, 1989), 125.

12. Despite the established church in Great Britain, English clergy were waging analogous struggles to control the tenor of popular print material. American ministers adopted many of their strategies. See Richard D. Altick, *The English Common Reader. A Social History of the Mass Reading Public, 1800–1900* (Chicago, 1957); Jon P. Klancher, *The Making of English Reading Audiences, 1790–1832* (Madison, 1987).

13. David Paul Nord, "The Evangelical Origins of Mass Media in America, 1815–1835," *Journalism Monographs* (1984); Lawrance Thompson, "Printing and Publishing Activities of the American Tract Society from 1825 to 1850," *Papers of the Bibliographical Society of America*, 35 (2nd quarter, 1941): 81–114.

14. See editorial, Aug. 1, 1828.

15. Hatch, *Democratization of American Christianity*, 141.

16. Quoted in Lawrance Thompson, "Printing and Publishing Activities of the American Tract Society," 96.

17. Nord, "Evangelical Origins of Mass Media," 21.

18. Quoted in Lewis Leary, *The Book-Peddling Parson. An Account of the Life and Works of Mason Locke Weems, Patriot, Pitchman, Author and Purveyor of Morality* (Chapel Hill, 1984), 156. Many of Weems's letters have been collected by Emily Ellsworth Ford Skeel, *Mason Locke Weems. His Works and Ways*, 3 volumes (New York, 1929). Also see Marcus Cunliffe, "Parson Weems and George Washington's Cherry Tree," *Bulletin of the John Rylands Library Manchester*, 45 (Sept. 1962): 58–96.

19. Weems to Carey, Mar. 10, 1798, in Skeel, *Mason Locke Weems* Vol. 2, 97.

20. Quoted in Leary, *Book-Peddling Parson*, 25.

21. Mason Locke Weems, *The Drunkard's Looking Glass* (Philadelphia, 1813).

22. Mason Locke Weems, *God's Revenge Against Murder, or the Drown'd Wife* (Philadelphia, 1808)

23. Mason Locke Weems, *God's Revenge Against Adultery* (Philadelphia, 1815)

24. Weems to Carey, Mar. 15, 1823, in Skeel, *Mason Locke Weems*, Vol. 3, 256.

25. Weems to Carey, May 31, 1810, in Skeel, *Mason Locke Weems*, Vol. 3, 22–23.

26. Mason Locke Weems, *God's Revenge Against Murder*.

27. Mason Locke Weems, *The Bad Wife's Looking Glass, Or, God's Revenge Against Cruelty to Husbands* (Charleston, 1823).

28. Victor E. Neuberg, *The Penny Histories. A Study of Chapbooks for Young Readers Over Two Centuries* (New York, 1969).

29. Hall, *Worlds of Wonder*, 132ff.

30. Ian Watt, *The Rise of the Novel. Studies in Defoe, Richardson, and Fielding* (Berkeley, 1957), 115, 152.

31. Ibid., 281. Samuel Pickering, *The Moral Tradition in English Fiction, 1785–1850* (Hanover, N.H., 1976).

32. Cathy N. Davidson, *Revolution and the Word. The Rise of the Novel in America* (New York, 1986), 17.

33. Joan Brumberg, *Mission for Life. The Story of the Family of Adoniram Judson, the Dramatic Events of the First American Foreign Mission, and the Course of Evangelical Religion in the Nineteenth Century* (New York, 1980). See especially Brumberg's discussion of Emily Chubbuck Judson, *Memoir of Sarah B. Judson* (New York, 1848). Chubbuck, Judson's third wife, was "Fanny Forester," one of the most successful women writers of sentimental fiction.

34. Pickering, *Moral Tradition*, 59.

35. Anne Scott MacLeod, *A Moral Tale. Children's Fiction and American Culture, 1820–1860* (Hamden, Conn., 1975).

36. See especially Jane P. Tompkins, *Sensational Designs. The Cultural Work of American Fiction, 1790–1860* (New York, 1985).

37. Ann Douglas, *The Feminization of American Culture* (New York, 1977).

38. Hart, *Popular Book*, 98–99; David S. Reynolds, *Faith in Fiction. The Emergence of Religious Literature in America* (Cambridge, Mass., 1981); Robert W. Weathersby, *Joseph Scott Ingraham* (Boston, 1980).

39. Rev. Wesley Cochran, "General Reading," *Ladies' Repository* (Dec. 1851).

40. "Religious Fiction," *American Quarterly Church Review*, (Oct. 1855).

41. Lippard did claim that they incited a mob to block a theatrical presentation of his book. As we shall see in subsequent chapters, theater raised somewhat different issues. David Reynolds, *George Lippard* (Boston, 1982); Reynolds, ed., *George Lippard, Prophet of Protest. Writings of an American Radical, 1822–1854* (New York, 1986).

42. One of Lippard's odious clerics was modeled on the Reverend Benjamin T. Onderdonk. We shall come to the story of this unfortunate man in Chapter 5.

43. I use the phrase "democratization of Christianity" with acknowledgments to Nathan Hatch.

44. *The Quaker City* was first published over the fall and winter of 1844–45 in ten paper-covered installments.

45. See the preface to James Everett Seaver, *A Narrative of the Life of Mary Jemison* (Canandaigua, 1824).

46. Samuel G. Drake, *Indian Captivities, or Life in the Wigwam* (Auburn, 1851).

47. John Todd, *The Moral Influences, Dangers and Duties Connected with Great Cities* (New York, 1841), 203.

48. Richard K. Fox took over the failing *Gazette* in 1876 and turned it increasingly toward sensational illustrations and sports news. Critics viewed it as even more salacious than the original. Yet even at that date, Fox insisted that "no illustration and not a line of printing of immoral tendency is suffered to appear in its columns. So far from pandering to vicious tastes, its object is to delineate vice in its proper odious character." Edward Van Every, *Sins of New York. As "Exposed" by the Police Gazette* (New York, 1930).

49. One should not underestimate Sue's reputation. His famous book on Paris drew, as it promised, on the seamier side of life. Nonetheless, Margaret Fuller viewed Sue as an ally in her intellectual/spiritual effort to uplift the human race: "Sue has the heart of a reformer, and especially towards women; he sees what they need, and what causes are injuring them. From the histories of Fleur de Marie and La Louve, from the lovely and independent character of Rigolette, from the distortion given to Matilda's mind, by the present views of marriage, and from the truly noble and immortal character of the 'humpback Sempstress' in the 'Wandering Jew,' may be gathered much that shall elucidate doubt and direct inquiry on this subject" (from *Woman in the Nineteenth Century* (New York, 1971), 149).

50. The Harper and Brothers edition, which was translated by Charles H. Town, appeared in 1843.

51. James Dabney McCabe (Edward Winslow Martin), *The Secrets of the Great City* (Philadelphia, 1868). See also George G. Foster, *New York by Gas-Light* (New York, 1850); and *New York Naked* (New York, 1854).

52. We will probably never have a satisfactory interpretive biography of Judson, but for the best available summary of facts see Jay Monaghan, *The Great Rascal. The Life and Legend of Ned Buntline* (Boston, 1952). Also Peter Buckley, "To the Opera House. Culture and Society in New York City, 1820–1860," Ph.D. dissertation, SUNY Stony Brook, 1984.

53. David Reynolds, *Beneath the American Renaissance. The Subversive Imagination in the Age of Emerson and Melville* (New York, 1988), 90–91.

54. Isaac Clark Pray, *Memoirs of James Gordon Bennett and His Times* (New York, 1855), 264ff. Douglas Fermer, *James Gordon Bennett and the New York Herald. A Study of Editorial Opinion in the Civil War Era, 1854–1867* (New York, 1986), 58.

55. Pray, *Memoirs of Bennett*, 249, 277–78, 282.

56. Charles Nordhoff, *Reminiscences of Some Editors I Have Known* (Coronado, Calif., 1900). For useful background see David Paul Nord, "Teleology and News: The Religious Roots of American Journalism, 1630–1730," *Journal of American History*, 77 (June 1990): 9–38.

57. Eugene Exman, *The Brothers Harper. A Unique Publishing Partnership and Its Impact Upon the Cultural Life of America from 1817 to 1853* (New York, 1965); *The House of Harper. One Hundred and Fifty Years of Publishing* (New York, 1967).

58. See Chapter 7 for a further discussion.

59. This particular assortment appeared in the 1843 Harper and Brothers' edition of Sue's, *The Mysteries of Paris*.

60. Colin Campbell, *The Romantic Ethic and the Spirit of Modern Consumerism* (Oxford, 1987), esp. 69–76, 123–37.

Chapter Two

1. Arnold Dallimore, ed., *George Whitefield Journals* (London, 1960), p. 42.

2. Dallimore, *Journals*, 39. The best short biography of Whitefield is Harry S. Stout, *The Divine Dramatist. George Whitefield and the Rise of Modern Evangelicalism* (Grand Rapids, 1991). Also see Frank Lambert, "'Pedlar in Divinity': George Whitefield and the Great Awakening, 1737–1745," *Journal of American History*, 77 (Dec. 1990): 812–37.

3. Dallimore, *Journals*, 63.

4. Quoted in David Reynolds, *Beneath the American Renaissance. The Sub-*

versive Imagination in the Age of Emerson and Melville (New York, 1988),
25. Lewis O. Saum, *The Popular Mood of Pre-Civil War America* (Westport,
1980), 36–38.

5. Albert M. Lyles, *Methodism Mocked. The Satiric Reaction to Methodism in the Eighteenth Century* (London, 1960), 134. See also C. Harold King, "God's Dramatist," in *Studies in Speech and Drama, in Honor of Alexander M. Drummond* (Ithaca, 1944); Dallimore, *Journals*, 340.

6. Stout, *Divine Dramatist*, xxi–xxii, 35, 68, 242, passim..

7. Lawrence Levine, *Highbrow/Lowbrow. The Emergence of Cultural Hierarchy in America* (Cambridge, Mass., 1988); Kenneth Cmiel, *Democratic Eloquence: The Fight Over Popular Speech in Nineteenth Century America* (Berkeley, 1990); Garry Wills, *Lincoln at Gettysburg. The Words that Remade America* (New York, 1992).

8. Harry S. Stout, *The New England Soul. Preaching and Religious Culture in Colonial New England* (New York, 1986), 4.

9. Donald Scott, "Print and the Public Lecture System, 1840–60," in William L. Joyce, ed., *Printing and Society in Early America* (Worcester, 1983); David D. Hall, "The World of Print and Collective Mentality in Seventeenth-Century New England," in John Higham and Paul Conkin, eds., *New Directions in American Intellectual History* (Baltimore, 1979).

10. Walter J. Ong, *The Presence of the Word. Some Prolegomena for Cultural and Religious History* (New Haven, 1967), 30, 128.

11. Charles A. Johnson, *The Frontier Camp Meeting. Religion's Harvest Time* (Dallas, 1955), esp. chapter 11.

12. William W. Woodward, *Surprising Accounts of the Revival of Religion in the United States of America* (Philadelphia, 1802); Joshua Bradley, *Accounts of Religious Revivals in Many Parts of the United States, from 1815–1818* (Albany, 1819); Bennet Tyler, *New England Revivals as They Existed at the Close of the Eighteenth and Beginning of the Nineteenth Centuries* (Boston, 1846); Rev. R. S. Smith, *Recollections of Nettleton and the Great Revival of 1820* (Albany, 1848); Adam Rankin, *A Review of the Noted Revival in Kentucky . . . in the Year 1801* (Lexington, 1802); Ebenezer Porter, *Letters on the Religious Revivals which Prevailed about the Beginning of the Present Century* (Boston, 1858); Menzies Rayner, *A Dissertation Upon Extraordinary Awakenings, or Religious Stirs* (Hudson, N.Y., 1816); Otis A. Skinner, *Letters to Rev. B. Stowe, R. H. Neale and R. W. Cushman, on Modern Revivals* (Boston, 1842); William Claiborne Walton, *Narrative of a Revival of Religion, in the Third Presbyterian Church in Baltimore* (Northampton, 1826).

13. Daniel W. Patterson, "Word, Song and Motion: Instruments of Celebration Among Protestant Radicals of Early Nineteenth-Century America," in Victor Turner, ed., *Celebration. Studies in Festivity and Ritual* (Washington D. C., 1982); Clarke Garrett, *Spirit Possession and Popular Religion. From the Camisards to the Shakers* (Baltimore, 1987), 221–22.

14. Rev. B. Weed Gorham, *Camp Meeting Manual. A Practical Book for the Camp Ground* (Boston, 1854), 32.

15. Catherine Cleveland, *The Great Revival in the West, 1795–1805* (Chicago, 1916), 77.

16. Dickson D. Bruce, Jr., *And They All Sang Hallelujah. Plain-Folk Camp-Meeting Religion, 1800–1845* (Knoxville, 1974), 86–87.

17. Leigh Eric Schmidt, *Holy Fairs. Scottish Communions and American Revivals in the Early Modern Period* (Princeton, 1989); Bruce, *And They All Sang Hallelujah*, 54.

18. Schmidt, *Holy Fairs*; Paul Conkin, *Cane Ridge. America's Pentecost* (Madison, 1990).

19. Richard Carwardine, *Transatlantic Revivalism. Popular Evangelicalism in Britain and America, 1790–1865* (Westport, 1978), 103.

20. Lyman Beecher, *Letters of Rev. Dr. Beecher and Rev. Mr. Nettleton, on the "New Measures" in Conducting Revivals of Religion* (New York, 1828); Sandra S. Sizer, *Gospel Hymns and Social Religion. The Rhetoric of Nineteenth-Century Revivalism* (Philadelphia, 1978), 63.

21. See, for example, W. P. Strickland, ed., *Autobiography of Peter Cartwright, The Backwoods Preacher* (New York, 1857), 90, 132, 141, 146.

22. Victor Turner, *The Ritual Process. Structure and Anti-Structure* (Chicago, 1969); Turner, *The Anthropology of Performance* (New York, 1986).

23. John W. Nevin, *The Anxious Bench* (Chambersburg, Penn., 1844), 40, 64, 108.

24. Skinner, *Letters to Rev. B. Stowe. . . ,* 11.

25. Catharine Read Williams, *Fall River, an Authentic Narrative* (Boston, 1833), 166–67; 188–90.

26. Bruce, *And They All Sang Hallelujah*; Sizer, *Gospel Hymns*. A number of hymnbooks were compiled. See, for example, Hugh Bourne, *A Collection of Hymns, for Camp Meetings, Revivals* (Bemersley, 1829); Jacob Knapp, *The Evangelical Harp; A New Collection of Hymns and Tunes, Designed for Revivals of Religion* (Utica, 1845); Orange Scott, *The New and Improved Camp Meeting Hymn Book* (Brookfield, Mass., 1831); *The Spiritual Songster; Containing a Variety of Camp Meeting and Other Hymns* (Fredricktown, Md., 1819); John C. Totten, *Hymns and Spiritual Songs, with Choruses Affixed, as Usually Sung at Camp Meetings* (New York, 1818). John Winebrenner, *A Prayer Meeting and Revival Hymn Book* (Harrisburg, 1825).

27. Gorham, *Camp Meeting Manual*, 166.

28. Charles Grandison Finney, *Lectures on Revivals of Religion* (Cambridge, Mass., 1960; first published in 1835), 218.

29. Ibid., 220.

30. John Witherspoon, *A Serious Inquiry into the Nature and Effects of the Stage, and a Letter Respecting Play Actors* (New York, 1812), 107–10.

31. Charles Booth Parsons, *The Pulpit and the Stage; or, the Two Itineraries, by One Who Knows,* (Nashville, 1860), 373.

32. Henry J. Ripley, *Sacred Rhetoric; or, Composition and Delivery of Sermons to Which Are Added Hints on Extemporaneous Preaching by Henry Ware, Jr.* (Boston, 1849), 193–94.

33. Abel Stevens, *Essays on the Preaching Required by the Times, and the Best Methods of Obtaining It; with Reminiscences and Illustrations of Methodist Preaching. Including Rules for Extemporaneous Preaching* (New York, 1855), 76.

34. Albert Barnes, *Miscellaneous Essays and Reviews*, Vol. 2 (New York, Phinney, 1855), 242; Henry C. Fish, *Handbook of Revivals for the Use of Winners of Souls* (Boston, 1874).

35. Rev. Calvin Colton, *History and Character of American Revivals of Religion* (London, 1832), 273.

36. John Dowling, *The Power of Illustration. An Element of Success in Preaching and Teaching* (New York, 1850); David S. Reynolds, "From Doctrine to Narrative: The Rise of Pulpit Storytelling in America," *American Quarterly*, 32 (Winter 1980): 479–98.

37. Kenneth Silverman, *A Cultural History of the American Revolution* (New York, 1976); Phoebe Stanton, *The Gothic Revival and American Church Architecture. An Episode in Taste, 1840–1856* (Baltimore, 1968).

38. Henry Ward Beecher, *Yale Lectures on Preaching* (New York, 1872), 118ff., 143.

39. Beecher's career spans the Civil War, and we will return to his "playhouse church." William McLoughlin, *The Meaning of Henry Ward Beecher. An Essay on the Shifting Values of Mid-Victorian America, 1840–1870* (New York, 1970).

40. Henry W. Bellows, *An Address Upon the Claims of the Drama Delivered Before the President and Members of the American Dramatic Fund Society* (London, 1857), 22–23.

41. Ibid., 20.

42. Ibid., 18

43. Ibid., 26. Karen Halttunen, *Confidence Men and Painted Women. A Study of Middle-Class Culture in America, 1830–1870* (New Haven, 1982).

44. Rev. Herrick Johnson, *A Plain Talk about the Theatre* (New York, 1882); Witherspoon, *Serious Inquiry into the Nature and Effects of the Stage;* D. Hayes Agnew, *Theatrical Amusements, With Some Remarks on the Rev. Henry W. Bellows' Address* (Philadelphia, 1857).

45. James H. Dormon, *Theater in the Antebellum South, 1815–1861* (Chapel Hill, 1967), 270ff.; Clement E. Foust, *The Life and Dramatic Works of Robert Montgomery Bird* (New York, 1919)

46. Donald M. Scott, "Itinerant Lecturers and Lecturing in New England, 1800–1850," in Peter Benes, ed., *Itinerancy in New England and New York* (Boston, 1986); Scott, "The Public Lecture and the Creation of a Public in Mid-Nineteenth Century America," *Journal of American History*, 66 (Mar. 1980): 791–809. Carl Bode, *The American Lyceum. Town Meeting of the Mind* (Carbondale, 1968).

47. Peter Dobkin Hall, *The Organization of American Culture. Private Institutions, Elites, and the Origins of American Nationality, 1700–1900* (New York, 1982).

48. Donald M. Scott, "Knowledge and the Marketplace," in James Gilbert et al., eds., *The Mythmaking Frame of Mind. Social Imagination and American Culture* (Belmont, Calif., 1993).

49. John B. Gough, *Autobiography and Personal Recollections of John B. Gough, with Twenty-Six Years Experience as a Public Speaker* (Chicago, 1869), 143.

50. Sydney. E. Ahlstrom, *A Religious History of the American People* (New Haven, 1972), 603.

51. Mary Kupiec Cayton, "The Making of an American Prophet: Emerson, His Audiences, and the Rise of the Culture Industry in Nineteenth-Century America," *American Historical Review*, 92 (June 1987): 597–620. My remarks on Emerson are based on Cayton's insights.

52. Scott, "Public Lecture and the Creation of a Public,"808–9.

53. Robert C. Fuller, *Alternative Medicine and American Religious Life* (New York, 1989); Whitney Cross, *The Burned-Over District. The Social and Intellectual History of Enthusiastic Religion in Western New York, 1800–1850* (Ithaca, 1950).

54. Anne M. Boylan, *Sunday School. The Formation of an American Institution, 1790–1880* (New Haven, 1988).

55. Raymond B. Culver, *Horace Mann and Religion in the Massachusetts Public Schools* (New Haven, 1929), 170.

56. "Common Schools" in Horace Bushnell, ed., *Building Eras in Religion* (New York, 1881).

57. John H. Westerhoff, *McGuffey and His Readers. Piety, Morality, and Education in Nineteenth-Century America* (Nashville, 1978), 62.

58. Westerhoff, *McGuffey and His Readers*.

59. Ruth Miller Elson, *Guardians of Tradition. American Schoolbooks of the Nineteenth Century* (Lincoln, 1964); John Alfred Nietz, *Old Textbooks . . . As Taught in the Common Schools from Colonial Days to 1900* (Pittsburgh, 1961).

Chapter Three

1. A version of this chapter was written in the spring of 1988 and appeared in Thomas Kselman, ed., *Belief in History. Innovative Approaches to European and American Religion* (Notre Dame, 1991). In revising it, I have benefited from several important works not available to me for the earlier version: Mark A. Noll, ed., *Religion and American Politics. From The Colonial Period to the 1980s.* (New York, 1990); Nathan O. Hatch, *The Democratization of American Christianity* (New Haven, 1989); and Daniel Walker Howe, "The Evangelical Movement and Political Culture in the North during the Second Party System," *Journal of American History*, 77 (Mar. 1991): 1216–39.

2. The literature on church and state in the United States is enormous. For bibliographical help, see John F. Wilson, ed., *Church and State in America. A*

Bibliographical Guide, 2 volumes (New York, 1986–87), and Clarence Chisholm et al., *Religion and Politics in the 1980s. A Selective Bibliography* (Monticello, Ill., 1987).

3. For diametrically opposed historical interpretations of the First Amendment, see Gerard V. Bradley, *Church-State Relationships in America* (New York, 1987), and Leonard W. Levy, *The Establishment Clause. Religion and the First Amendment* (New York, 1986).

4. For a comparative perspective between England and the United States, see Richard Carwardine, "Religion and Politics in Nineteenth-Century Britain: The Case Against American Exceptionalism," in Mark A. Noll, ed., *Religion and American Politics.*

5. Tocqueville's most important remarks occur in chapter 17 of the first volume of *Democracy in America,* edited by Phillps Bradley (New York, 1945). For one extended discussion of Tocqueville's views, see Cushing Strout, *The New Heavens and New Earth. Political Religion in America* (New York, 1974).

6. From *The Domestic Manners of the Americans* (London, 1984; First published in 1832). Trollope's views and those of other Europeans are collected in a useful compendium: Milton Powell, ed., *The Voluntary Church. American Religious Life (1740–1865) Seen Through the Eyes of European Visitors* (New York, 1967), 69. 71.

7. George Bush at the 1992 Republican convention in Houston. Pundits argue that the convention's featured addresses by members of the Christian right backfired. The deliberateness of the strategy is nonetheless noteworthy.

8. Marshall Frady, *Billy Graham. A Parable of American Righteousness* (Boston, 1979).

9. Mary T. Hanna, *Catholics and American Politics* (Cambridge, Mass., 1979).

10. Allen D. Hertzke, *Representing God in Washington. The Role of Religious Lobbies in the American Polity* (Knoxville, 1988); Mark Silk, *Spiritual Politics. Religion and America Since World War II* (New York, 1988); James L. Adams, *The Growing Church Lobby in Washington* (Grand Rapids, 1970); Luke Eugene Ebersole, *Church Lobbying in the Nation's Capitol* (New York, 1951); Aaron I. Abell, *American Catholicism and Social Action. A Search for Social Justice, 1865–1950* (Garden City, 1960); John R. Bodo, *The Protestant Clergy and Public Issues, 1812–1848* (Princeton, 1954); Paul Goodman, *Towards a Christian Republic. Antimasonry and the Great Transition in New England, 1826–1838* (New York, 1988); John L. Hammond, *The Politics of Benevolence. Revival Religion and American Voting Behavior* (Norwood, N.J., 1979); Harold E. Quinley, *The Prophetic Clergy. Social Activism Among Protestant Ministers* (New York, 1974).

11. Richard R. John, "Taking Sabbatarianism Seriously: The Postal System, the Sabbath, and the Transformation of American Political Culture," *Journal of the Early Republic,* 10 (Winter 1990): 517–67.

12. Steve Bruce, *The Rise and Fall of the New Christian Right. Conservative Protestant Politics in America, 1978–1988* (New York, 1988); Robert Booth

Fowler, *A New Engagement. Evangelical Political Thought, 1966–1976* (Grand Rapids, 1982); Samuel S. Hill and Dennis E. Owen, *The New Religious-Political Right in America* (Nashville, 1982); Robert C. Liebman and Robert Wuthnow, eds., *The New Christian Right. Mobilization and Legitimation* (Hawthorne N.Y., 1983).

13. An intriguing issue relates to the question of whether an unavoidable clash exists between the "free exercise" clause and the "establishment" clause of the First Amendment. See, for example, Jesse H. Choper, "Defining 'Religion' in the First Amendment," *University of Illinois Law Review*, Vol. 1982: 579–613, and "The Religion Clauses of the First Amendment: Reconciling the Conflict," *University of Pittsburgh Law Review*, 41 (Summer, 1980): 673–701.

14. Conrad E. Cherry, ed., *God's New Israel. Religious Interpretations of American Destiny* (Englewood Cliffs, 1971); James West Davidson, *The Logic of Millennial Thought. Eighteenth-Century New England* (New Haven, 1977); Winthrop Hudson, *Nationalism and Religion in America. Concepts of American Identity and Mission* (New York, 1970); James H. Moorhead, *American Apocalypse. Yankee Protestants and the Civil War, 1860–1869* (New Haven, 1978); Ernest Tuveson, *Redeemer Nation. The Idea of America's Millennial Role* (Chicago, 1968); Nathan O. Hatch, *The Sacred Cause of Liberty. Republican Thought and the Millennium in Revolutionary New England* (New Haven, 1977).

15. Robert Bellah, "Civil Religion in America," in William G. McLoughlin and Robert N. Bellah, eds., *Religion in America* (Boston, 1968), 3–23; first published in *Daedalus* (Winter 1967). For some of the debate, see John F. Wilson, *Public Religion in American Culture* (Philadelphia, 1979), and Gail Gehrig, *American Civil Religion. An Assessment* (Storrs, 1981).

16. Robert Kelley, *The Cultural Pattern in American Politics. The First Century* (New York, 1979).

17. Richard John Neuhaus, *The Naked Public Square. Religion and Democracy in America* (Grand Rapids, 1984); A. James Reichley, *Religion in American Public Life* (Washington, D.C., 1985).

18. Charles G. Sellers, *The Market Revolution. Jacksonian America, 1815–1846* (New York, 1991).

19. Ronald P. Formisano, *The Transformation of Political Culture. Massachusetts Parties, 1790s–1840s* (New York, 1983); Formisano, *The Birth of Mass Political Parties, Michigan, 1827–1861* (Princeton, 1971); Paul Kleppner, *The Cross of Culture. A Social Analysis of Midwestern Politics, 1850–1900* (New York, 1970); Kleppner, *The Third Electoral System, 1853–1892: Parties, Voters, and Political Cultures* (Chapel Hill, 1979); Kleppner et al., *The Evolution of American Electoral Systems* (Westport, 1981); Joel Silbey, *The American Political Nation, 1838–1893* (Stanford, 1991); Silbey, *The Partisan Imperative. The Dynamics of American Politics Before the Civil War* (New York, 1985); Lee Benson, *The Concept of Jacksonian Democracy. New York as a Test Case* (Princeton, 1961); and Michael Holt, *Forging a Majority. The Formation of the Republican Party in Pittsburgh, 1848–1860* (New Haven, 1969).

20. Donald G. Mathews, "The Second Great Awakening as an Organizing Process, 1780–1830," *American Quarterly*, 21 (1969): 22–43. For a sociologist's discussion of issues pertaining to American religion and capitalist order, see George M. Thomas, *Revivalism and Cultural Change. Christianity, Nation Building, and the Market in the Nineteenth-Century United States* (Chicago, 1989).

21. Nathan O. Hatch, *The Democratization of American Christianity* (New Haven, 1989).

22. Frederick Marryat, *A Diary in America, with Remarks on its Institutions*, edited by Sydney Jackman (New York, 1962; first published in 1839), 302.

23. Dickson D. Bruce, Jr., *And They All Sang Hallelujah. Plain-Folk Camp-Meeting Religion, 1800–1845* (Knoxville, 1974); Bernard Weisberger, *They Gathered at the River. The Story of the Great Revivalists and Their Impact upon Religion in America* (New York, 1958); Richard Carwardine, *Transatlantic Revivalism. Popular Evangelicalism in Britain and America, 1790–1865* (Westport, 1978); T. Scott Miyakawa, *Protestants and Pioneers. Individualism and Conformity on the American Frontier* (Chicago, 1964); John B. Boles, *The Great Revival, 1787–1805* (Lexington, 1972).

24. Richard Hofstadter and Michael Wallace, eds., *American Violence. A Documentary History* (New York, 1970).

25. Paul E. Johnson, *A Shopkeeper's Millennium. Society and Revivals in Rochester, New York, 1815–1837* (New York, 1978).

26. See Chapter 5.

27. Daniel Walker Howe, "Religion and Politics in the Antebellum North," in Noll, ed., *Religion and American Politics*.

28. David Paul Nord, "The Evangelical Origins of Mass Media in America, 1815–1835," *Journalism Monographs* (1984); Lawrance Thompson, "The Printing and Publishing Activities of the American Tract Society from 1825 to 1850," *Papers of the Bibliographical Society of America*, 35 (2nd quarter, 1941): 81–114.

29. R. Laurence Moore, "Religion, Secularization, and the Shaping of the Culture Industry in Antebellum America," *American Quarterly*, 41 (June 1989): 216–42.

30. Garth M. Rosell, "Charles G. Finney: His Place in the Stream," in Leonard I. Sweet, ed., *The Evangelical Tradition in America* (Macon, 1984).

31. On the persistence of certain revival techniques, see William G. McLoughlin, *Modern Revivalism. Charles Grandison Finney to Billy Graham* (New York, 1959); McLoughlin, *Billy Sunday Was His Real Name* (Chicago, 1955); McLoughlin, *Billy Graham, Revivalist in a Secular Age* (New York, 1960); David E. Harrell, *Oral Roberts. An American Life* (Bloomington, 1985); Jeffrey K. Hadden and Anson Shupe, *Televangelism, Power, and Politics on God's Frontier* (New York, 1988); J. D. Cardwell, *Mass Media Christianity. Televangelism and the Great Commission* (Lanham, Md., 1984).

32. Reverend A. P. Mead, *Manna in the Wilderness; or, The Grove and Its*

Altar, Offerings, and Thrilling Incidents, Containing a History of the Origin and Rise of Camp Meetings, and a Defence of This Remarkable Means of Grace (Philadelphia, 1860).

33. Rev. B. Weed Gorham, *Camp Meeting Manual. A Practical Book for the Camp Ground* (Boston, 1854); Rev. E. H. Stokes, compiler, *Ocean Grove. Its Origins and Progress, as Shown in the Annual Reports Presented by the President* (Philadelphia, 1874–87); Ellen Weiss, *City in the Woods. The Life and Design of an American Camp Meeting on Martha's Vineyard* (New York, 1987).

34. Joe L. Kincheloe, Jr., "Similarities in Crowd Control Techniques of the Camp Meeting and Political Rally: The Pioneer Role of Tennessee," *Tennessee Historical Quarterly*, 37 (Summer 1978): 155–69.

35. Nathan Hatch, "The Democratization of Christianity and the Character of American Politics," in Noll, ed. *Religion and American Politics*, 105.

36. Richard P. McCormick, *The Second American Party System. Party Formation in the Jacksonian Era* (Chapel Hill, 1966), 349 and passim.

37. Fred Somkin, *Unquiet Eagle. Memory and Desire in the Idea of American Freedom, 1815–1860* (Ithaca, 1967), 194.

38. Jean H. Baker, *Affairs of Party. The Political Culture of Northern Democrats in the Mid-Nineteenth Century* (Ithaca, 1983). 270–74.

39. Ibid., 269.

40. Ruth Bloch, "Religion and Ideological Change in the American Revolution," in Noll, ed., *Religion and American Politics*, 45–47.

41. Richard Hofstadter, *The Idea of a Party System. The Rise of Legitimate Opposition in the United States, 1780–1840* (Berkeley, 1969).

42. Joseph Charles, *The Origins of the American Party System* (Williamsburg, 1956); Leonard Levy, *Jefferson and Civil Liberties. The Darker Side* (Cambridge, Mass., 1963); James Morton Smith, *Freedom's Fetters. The Alien and Sedition Laws and American Civil Liberties* (Ithaca, 1956); William Lee Miller, *The First Liberty. Religion and the American Republic* (New York, 1985).

43. Harry S. Stout, "Rhetoric and Reality in the Early Republic: The Case of the Federalist Clergy," in Noll, ed., *Religion and American Politics*, 65–67.

44. David L. Jacobson, ed., *The English Libertarian Heritage, from the Writings of John Trenchard and Thomas Gordon* (Indianapolis, 1965), 272–73. For background on eighteenth-century English politics and American attitudes toward party, consult Isaac Kramnick, *Bolingbroke and His Circle; the Politics of Nostalgia in the Age of Walpole* (Cambridge, Mass., 1968); Bernard Bailyn, *The Origins of American Politics* (New York, 1968); Caroline Robbins, *The Eighteenth-Century Commonwealthman* (Cambridge, Mass., 1959).

45. Jefferson to Dr. Benjamin Waterhouse, June 26, 1822, in Merrill D. Peterson, ed., *Thomas Jefferson. Writings* (New York, 1984), 1458–59.

46. On the general question of political fictions, see Edmund S. Morgan, *Inventing the People. The Rise of Popular Sovereignty in England and America* (New York, 1988).

47. Formisano, *Transformation of Political Culture*, 150–70; *Birth of Mass Political Parties*, 104ff. See also Goodman, *Towards a Christian Republic*.

48. Alexis de Tocqueville, *Democracy in America*, 1:311.

49. Hofstadter, *Idea of a Party System*, 125.

50. Charles A. Johnson, *The Frontier Camp Meeting. Religion's Harvest Time* (Dallas, 1955), 214.

51. David W. Wills, "Beyond Commonality and Plurality: Persistent Racial Polarity in American Religion and Politics," in Noll, ed., *Religion and American Politics*; Eric Foner, *Reconstruction. America's Unfinished Revolution, 1863–1877* (New York, 1988), 90–95, 281–91; Clarence G. Walker, *A Rock in a Weary Land. The African Methodist Episcopal Church during the Civil War and Reconstruction* (Baton Rouge, 1982); James M. Washington, *Frustrated Fellowship. The Black Baptist Quest for Social Power* (Macon, 1986).

52. The stereotype of the strong-willed and strong-armed man of God is richly present in the *Autobiography of Peter Cartwright* which was first published in 1856. Cartwright, one of the most famous of the Methodist circuit riders, was converted during an early wave of revivals in 1801. His career as a preacher fed naturally into a minor political career in Illinois. Twice elected to the lower house of the Illinois General Assembly, he lost a bid for Congress in 1846 to the Whig nominee Abraham Lincoln. For a profile of Methodist circuit riders, see Johnson, *Frontier Camp Meeting*, 145–69, 226–29.

53. Curtis D. Johnson, *Islands of Holiness. Rural Religion in Upstate New York, 1790–1860* (Ithaca, 1989).

54. Don H. Doyle, "The Social Functions of Voluntary Associations in a Nineteenth-Century American Town," *Social Science History*, 1 (Spring 1977): 333–55.

55. Carroll Smith-Rosenberg, "The Cross and the Pedestal," in *Disorderly Conduct. Visions of Gender in Victorian America* (New York, 1985).

56. Howe, "Evangelical Movement and Political Culture," 1223. See also Johnson, *Shopkeeper's Millennium*; Anthony Wallace, *Rockdale. The Growth of an American Village in the Early Industrial Revolution* (New York, 1979).

57. Johnson, *Islands of Holiness*.

58. Doyle, "Social Functions of Voluntary Associations," 344ff.

59. C. C. Goen, *Broken Churches, Broken Nation. Denominational Schisms and the Coming of the American Civil War* (Macon, 1986).

60. Morgan, *Inventing the People*, 174–208.

61. Thomas, *Revivalism and Cultural Change*.

62. Michael Walzer, *The Revolution of the Saints. A Study in the Origins of Radical Politics* (Cambridge, Mass., 1965).

Chapter Four

1. Richard Butsch, ed., *For Fun and Profit. The Transformation of Leisure into Consumption* (Philadelphia, 1990); Neil McKendrick et al., *The Birth of Consumer Society. The Commercialization of Eighteenth-Century England*

(Bloomington, 1982); J. H. Plumb, *The Commercialization of Leisure in Eighteenth-Century England* (Reading, 1973).

2. George M. Thomas, *Revivalism and Cultural Change. Christianity, Nation Building, and the Market in the Nineteenth-Century United States* (Chicago, 1989).

3. Michael T. Gilmore, *American Romanticism and the Marketplace* (Chicago, 1985).

4. Rev. Henry Morgan, *Music Hall Discourses, Miscellaneous Sketches, Ministerial Notes* (Boston, 1859).

5. Foster Rhea Dulles, *A History of Recreation. America Learns to Play* (New York, 1965); Harry B. Weiss and Grace M. Weiss, *Early Sports and Pastimes in New Jersey* (Trenton, 1960).

6. Edmund S. Morgan, *American Slavery. American Freedom. The Ordeal of Colonial Virginia* (New York, 1975), esp. chapters 3 and 4; W. J. Rorabaugh, *The Alcoholic Republic. An American Tradition* (New York, 1979).

7. The literature of "Republicanism" is enormous. For intelligent summaries as well as critiques of various positions, consult Daniel T. Rodgers, "Republicanism. The Career of a Concept," *Journal of American History*, 79 (June 1992): 11–38; and James T. Kloppenberg, "The Virtues of Liberalism: Christianity, Republicanism, and Ethics in Early American Political Discourse," *Journal of American History*, 74 (June 1987).

8. Edmund Morgan, "The Puritan Ethic and the American Revolution," *William and Mary Quarterly*, 24 (Jan. 1967): 3–43.

9. Bertram Wyatt-Brown, *Yankee Saints and Southern Sinners* (Baton Rouge, 1985).

10. Ted Ownby, *Subduing Satan. Religion, Recreation, and Manhood in the Rural South, 1865–1920* (Chapel Hill, 1990); T. H. Breen, *Tobacco Culture. The Mentality of the Great Tidewater Planters on the Eve of Revolution* (Princeton, 1985); Dale A. Somers, *The Rise of Sports in New Orleans, 1850–1900* (Baton Rouge, 1972).

11. Frances Trollope, *Domestic Manners of the Americans* (London, 1984; first published in 1832), 175.

12. Roy Rosenzweig, *Eight Hours for What We Will. Workers and Leisure in an Industrial City, 1870–1920* (Cambridge, Mass., 1983), 70.

13. Rex A. Skidmore, "Mormon Recreation in Theory and Practice: A Study of Social Change," Ph.D. dissertation, Univ. of Pennsylvania, 1941, p. 33. See R. Laurence Moore, "Learning to Play. The Mormon Way and the Way of Other Americans," *Journal of Mormon History*, 16 (1990), 89–106.

14. Henry Ward Beecher, *Lectures to Young Men, on Various Important Subjects* (Salem, 1846), 122 and passim.

15. David Brion Davis, "The New England Origins of Mormonism," *New England Quarterly*, 26 (June 1953): 147–68.

16. In addition to Skidmore, see Leonard J. Arrington, *Brigham Young. American Moses* (New York, 1985); George D. Pyper, *The Romance of an Old Playhouse* (Salt Lake City, 1928); Myrtle E. Henderson, *A History of the The-*

atre in Salt Lake City from 1850 to 1870 (Evanston, 1934); John S. Lindsay, *The Mormons and the Theatre* (Salt Lake City, 1905).

17. Leona Holbrook, "Dancing as an Aspect of Early Mormon and Utah Culture," *Brigham Young University Studies*, 16 (Autumn 1975): 117–38; Davis Bitton, "'These Licentious Days': Dancing Among the Mormons," *Sunstone*, 2 (Spring 1977): 16–27; *Times and Seasons*, 5 (Mar. 1, 1844): 459.

18. "Remarks by President Brigham Young, February 9, 1862," *Journal of Discourses*, 9 (1862): 194; Michael Hicks, "Notes on Brigham Young's Aesthetics," *Dialogue*, 16 (Winter 1983): 124–30.

19. "Discourse by President Brigham Young, July 18, 1869," *Journal of Discourses*, 9 (1862): 60.

20. "Remarks by President Young at the Dedication of the New Theatre, March 6, 1862," *Journal of Discourses*, 9, (1862): 243.

21. Frederick W. Sawyer, *A Plea for Amusements* (New York, 1847).

22. James Leonard Corning, *The Christian Law of Amusement* (Buffalo, 1959), 18, 94.

23. Horace Bushnell, *Work and Play or Literary Varieties*, (New York, 1864).

24. Ibid., 15, 36.

25. Lawrence Levine, *Highbrow/Lowbrow. The Emergence of Cultural Hierarchy in America* (Cambridge, Mass., 1988).

26. Samuel Miller, "A Sermon Delivered January 19, 1812, at the Request of a Number of Young Gentlemen of the City of New York," (New York, 1812).

27. Bruce A. McConachie, "Pacifying American Theatrical Audiences, 1820–1900," in Butsch, ed., *For Fun and Profit*.

28. Peter Buckley "To the Opera House. Culture and Society in New York City, 1820–1860," Ph.D. dissertation, SUNY Stony Brook, 1984. The riot was extensively covered in the press and was the subject of a number of contemporary pamphlets.

29. Clement E. Foust, *The Life and Dramatic Works of Robert Montgomery Bird* (New York, 1919).

30. Buckley, "To the Opera House"; Olive Logan, *Before the Footlights and Behind the Scenes* (Philadelphia, 1870).

31. "Ministers' 'Introductory Address'" in John Witherspoon, *A Serious Inquiry into the Nature and Effects of the Stage* (New York, 1812), 19.

32. Logan, *Before the Footlights*, 535, 543.

33. Roy Rosenzweig and Elizabeth Blackmar, *The Park and the People. A History of Central Park* (Ithaca, 1992).

34. Ibid., 104–15, 234ff.

35. Ian R. Stewart, *Central Park, 1851–71. Urbanization and Environmental Planning in New York City* (Ithaca, 1973), 343.

36. Ibid., 83. Compare with Reid Badger, *The Great American Fair. The World's Columbian Exposition and American Culture* (Chicago, 1979), 97.

37. Ellen Weiss, *City in the Woods. The Life and Design of an American Camp Meeting on Martha's Vineyard* (New York, 1987).

38. Rev. B. Weed Gorham, *Camp Meeting Manual, A Practical Book For the Camp Ground* (Boston, 1854), 17.

39. Ibid., 32.

40. Weiss, *City in the Woods*, 117–118.

41. Rev. E. H. Stokes, comp., *Ocean Grove. Its Origins and Progress, as Shown in the Annual Reports Presented by the President* (Philadelphia, 1874–87).

42. Daniel T. Rodgers, *The Work Ethic in Industrial America, 1850–1920* (Chicago, 1978), 96.

43. Charles Coleman Sellers, *Mr. Peale's Museum. Charles Willson Peale and the First Popular Museum of Natural Science and Art* (New York, 1980).

44. Neil Harris, *Humbug. The Art of P. T. Barnum* (Boston, 1973); Buckley, "To the Opera House."

45. P. T. Barnum, *Struggles and Triumphs or, Forty Years' Recollections*, edited and abridged by Carl Bode (New York, 1981), 394.

46. John Dillenberger, *The Visual Arts and Christianity in America. The Colonial Period through the Nineteenth Century* (Chico, Calif., 1984), 73; Diane Apostolos-Cappadona, "The Spirit and the Vision: The Influence of Romantic Evangelicalism on Nineteenth-Century American Art," Ph.D. dissertation, George Washington University, 1988.

47. John F. Sears, *Sacred Places. American Tourist Attractions in the Nineteenth Century* (New York, 1989).

48. "The Creed of Art," *The Crayon* (Nov. 1855).

49. Barbara Novak, *Nature and Culture. American Landscape and Painting, 1825–1875* (New York, 1980), 42.

50. Jane Tompkins, *Sensational Designs. The Cultural Work of American Fiction, 1790–1860* (New York, 1985), especially chapter 1.

51. For this information, I am indebted to the excellent unpublished paper of Janice M. Coco, "Hiram Power's *Greek Slave:* White Silence Finding a Voice."

52. Richard Stott, *Workers in the Metropolis. Class, Ethnicity, and Youth in Antebellum New York City* (Ithaca, 1990), especially chapter 6.

53. George Sherwood Eddy, *A Century with Youth. A History of the Y.M.C.A. from 1844 to 1944* (New York, 1944); C. Howard Hopkins, *History of the YMCA in North America* (New York, 1951); Paul Boyer, *Urban Masses and Moral Order in America, 1820–1920* (Cambridge, Mass., 1978); Samuel Wirt Wiley, *History of the YMCA-Church Relations in the United States* (New York, 1944); Mayer N. Zald, *Organizational Change. The Political Economy of the YMCA* (Chicago, 1970).

54. William H. Ball, "The Administration of Athletics in the Young Men's Christian Association," *American Physical Education Review*, 16 (Jan. 1911): 21; Richard C. Cabot, "The Soul of Play," *The Playground*, 4 (Dec. 1910): 285–92; A. Holmes, "The Soul and Body in Physical Training," *American Physical Education Review*, 14 (Oct. 1909): 479–89; Millicent Hosmer, "The Development of Morality Through Physical Education," *American Physical Education*

Review, 19 (Oct. 1914): 20–27; Henry S. Curtis, "Public Recreation and the Church," *Religious Education*, 8 (Apr. 1913): 47–52; "Play and the Church," *The Christian Advocate*, 85 (July 7, 1910): 958.

55. Fred Eugene Leonard, *A Guide to the History of Physical Education* (Philadelphia, 1923); C. W. Hackensmith, *History of Physical Education* (New York, 1966); Aileene S. Lockhart and Betty Spears, eds., *Chronicle of American Physical Education. Selected Readings, 1855–1930* (Dubuque, 1972).

56. Laurence Locke Doggett, *Man and a School. Pioneering in Higher Education at Springfield College* (New York, 1943), 122.

Chapter Five

1. Frances Trollope, *The Domestic Manners of the Americans* (London, 1984; first published in 1832), 175, 121–26.

2. Ibid., 60.

3. Ibid., 66–7, 143.

4. D. Michael Quinn, *Early Mormonism and the Magic World View* (Salt Lake City, 1987); David S. Reynolds, *Beneath the American Renaissance. The Subversive Imagination in the Age of Emerson and Melville* (New York, 1988).

5. I am indebted to Neil Harris for his discussion of the "operational aesthetic" in *Humbug The Art of P. T. Barnum* (Boston, 1973).

6. Charles Poyen Saint Saveur, *Progress of Animal Magnetism in New England* (Boston, 1837). The best account of mesmerism in the United States is Robert C. Fuller, *Mesmerism and the American Cure of Souls* (Philadelphia, 1982). But also see Robert Darnton, *Mesmerism and the End of the Enlightenment in France* (Cambridge, Mass., 1968).

7. George Bush, *Mesmer and Swedenborg* (New York, 1847). Many translated editions and versions of Swedenborg's books were available in the United States. See Emanuel Swedenborg, *A Treatise Concerning Heaven and Hell* (Baltimore, 1812); *The Nature of Intercourse Between Soul and the Body* (London, 1832); *The True Christian Religion* (Boston, 1843).

8. Andrew Jackson Davis, *The Magic Staff. An Autobiography of Andrew Jackson Davis* (Boston, 1857). On Davis, see Robert W. Delp, "Andrew Jackson Davis: Prophet of American Spiritualism," *Journal of American History*, 54 (June 1967): 43–56; "Andrew Jackson Davis's *Revelations*, Harbinger of American Spiritualism," *New York Historical Society Quarterly*, 55 (1971): 211–34; Catherine L. Albanese, "On the Matter of Spirit: Andrew Jackson Davis and the Marriage of God and Nature," *Journal of the American Academy of Religion*, 60 (Spring 1992): 1–17.

9. George Bush, *'Davis' Revelations' Revealed* (New York, 1847).

10. R. Laurence Moore, *In Search of White Crows. Spiritualism, Parapsychology and American Culture* (New York, 1977).

11. Ann Braude, *Radical Spirits. Spiritualism and Women's Rights in Nineteenth-Century America* (Boston, 1989).

12. For the changing views of educated elites, see Keith Thomas, *Religion and the Decline of Magic* (New York, 1971), and David D. Hall, *Worlds of Wonder Days of Judgment. Popular Religious Belief in Early New England* (New York, 1989); Jon Butler, *Awash in a Sea of Faith. Christianizing the American People* (Cambridge, Mass., 1990).

13. For an outline of what was new about Mormonism, see Jan Shipps, *Mormonism. The Story of a New Religious Tradition* (Urbana, 1985).

14. For a discussion (and useful references) of the extent of the controversy, see Charles A. Cannon, "The Awesome Power of Sex: The Polemical Campaign Against Mormon Polygamy," *Pacific Historical Review*, 43 (Feb. 1974): 61–82.

15. Ray Allen Billington, *The Protestant Crusade, 1800–1860.* (New York, 1938); Billington, "Maria Monk and Her Influence," *Catholic Historical Review*, 22 (Oct. 1936): 283–96. Maria Monk, *Awful Disclosures of Maria Monk* (New York, 1836).

16. Peter Gardella, *Innocent Ecstasy. How Christianity Gave America an Ethic of Sexual Pleasure* (New York, 1985), 25–32. William Hogan, *Auricular Confession and Popish Nunneries* (Hartford, 1845); Samuel B. Smith, *The Downfall of Babylon, or, The Triumph of Truth over Popery* (Philadelphia, 1834); Charles Chiniquy, *The Priest, the Woman, and the Confessional* (Chicago, 1880); George Bourne, *Lorette, the History of Louise, Daughter of a Canadian Nun, Exhibiting the Interior of Female Convents* (New York, 1833).

17. David Richard Kasserman, *Fall River Outrage. Life, Murder, and Justice in Early Industrial New England* (Philadelphia, 1986).

18. Reynolds, *Beneath the American Renaissance*, 260–62.

19. For information on the "other" Onderdonk, see Horace Binney, *The Case of the Right Rev. Henry U. Onderdonk* (Philadelphia, 1853).

20. Alonzo Potter, *No Church Without a Bishop. Or, A Peep into the Sanctuary, Being a Succinct Examination of the Right Rev. B. T. Onderdonk* (Boston, 1845). See also James C. Richmond, *The Conspiracy Against the Late Bishop of New York* (New York, 1845); "Laicus," *The Trial Tried, or the Bishop and the Court at the Bar of Public Opinion* (New York, 1845); John Jay, *Facts Connected with the Presentment of Bishop Onderdonk* (New York, 1845).

21. *Herald*, Jan. 11, 25, 31, and Feb. 3, 1845.

22. Ibid., Jan. 10, 1845.

23. Ibid., Jan. 21, 1845.

24. Christopher Hill, *The World Turned Upside Down. Radical Ideas During the English Revolution* (New York, 1968); Stephen Marini, *Radical Sects of Revolutionary New England* (Cambridge, Mass., 1982).

25. Potter, *No Church Without a Bishop.*

26. Ann Douglas, *The Feminization of American Culture* (New York, 1977), 88ff.

27. *Autobiography of Peter Cartwright, The Backwoods Preacher*, edited by W. P. Strickland (New York, 1857), 144–46.

28. *The Autobiography of Charles G. Finney*, condensed and edited by Helen Wessel (Minneapolis, 1977), 144–46.

29. Robert David Thomas, *The Man Who Would Be Perfect. John Humphrey Noyes and the Utopian Impulse* (Philadelphia, 1977), 88.

30. John F. Sears, *Sacred Places. American Tourist Attractions in the Nineteenth Century* (New York, 1989).

31. Maren Carden, *Oneida. Utopian Community to Modern Corporation* (Baltimore, 1969), 80–83.

32. *The Complete Works of Charles F. Browne, Better Known as 'Artemus Ward'* (London, 1871), 73–77, 138, 144–45, 171–246, 331–403, 514–18.

33. William Mulder and A. Russell Mortensen, eds., *Among the Mormons. Historic Accounts by Contemporary Observers* (New York, 1958).

34. Leon Festinger et al., *When Prophecy Fails* (Minneapolis, 1956).

35. Nathan O. Hatch, *The Democratization of American Christianity* (New Haven, 1989), 145.

36. For a useful sketch of his life, see David T. Arthur, "Joshua V. Himes and the Cause of Adventism," in Ronald L. Numbers and Jonathan M. Butler, *The Disappointed. Millerism and Millenarianism in the Nineteenth Century* (Bloomington, 1987).

37. See the discussion in Malcolm Bull and Keith Lockhart, *Seeking a Sanctuary. Seventh-day Adventism and the American Dream* (New York, 1989), 3–7.

38. For a comparison of the living conditions of European and American urban workers in the antebellum period, see Richard B. Stott, *Workers in the Metropolis. Class, Ethnicity, and Youth in Antebellum New York City* (Ithaca, 1989).

39. Charles Rosenberg, *The Cholera Years. The United States in 1832, 1849, and 1866* (Chicago, 1962); Rosenberg, *The Care of Strangers. The Rise of America's Hospital System* (New York, 1987); Joseph F. Kett, *The Formation of the American Medical Profession. The Role of Institutions, 1780–1860* (New Haven, 1968).

40. The best general survey is Robert C. Fuller, *Alternative Medicine and American Religious Life* (New York, 1989). See also Catherine Albanese, *Nature Religion in America. From the Algonkian Indians to the New Age* (Chicago, 1990).

41. Hatch, *The Democratization of American Christianity.*

42. Madeleine B. Stern, *Heads and Headlines. The Phrenological Fowlers* (Normon, 1971); Fuller, *Alternative Medicine*, 26–30.

43. Stephen Nissenbaum, *Sex, Diet, and Debility in Jacksonian America. Sylvester Graham and Health Reform* (Westport, 1980).

44. Albanese, *Nature Religion*, 125.

45. Graham, *A Lecture to Young Men on Chastity* (Providence, 1834), 28.

46. Fuller, *Alternative Medicine*, 68–90.

47. Sarah Stage, *Female Complaints. Lydia Pinkham and the Business of Women's Medicine* (New York, 1979).

48. By far the best account is Ronald Numbers, *Prophetess of Health. A Study of Ellen G. White* (New York, 1976), 189.

49. I am indebted to Professor Ronald Numbers for this information.

50. Charles G. Sellers, in *The Market Revolution. Jacksonian America, 1815–1846* (New York, 1991), has reduced this argument almost to a caricature. Even so, the general outline of his position about religion and other resistance to market pressures in America must be reckoned with.

51. Reinhold Niebuhr, *The Irony of American History* (New York, 1952).

Chapter Six

1. Jonathan Baxter Harrison, *Certain Dangerous Tendencies in American Life and Other Papers* (Boston, 1880), 7–8, 11.

2. David S. Reynolds, *Faith in Fiction. The Emergence of Religious Literature in America* (Cambridge, Mass., 1981), 1.

3. Richard Stott, *Workers in the Metropolis. Class, Ethnicity, and Youth in Antebellum New York City* (Ithaca, 1990), 242.

4. *Tribune*, Oct. 22, 1867.

5. Robert Wiebe, *The Search for Order, 1877–1920* (New York, 1967).

6. Curtis Johnson, *Islands of Holiness. Rural Religion in Upstate New York, 1790–1860* (Ithaca, 1989).

7. Rev. George Hughes, *Days of Power in the Forest Temple. A Review of the Wonderful Work of God at Fourteen National Camp Meetings from 1867 to 1872* (Boston, 1873), 26. On the Holiness movement and the development of Pentecostalism, see Robert Mapes Anderson, *Vision of the Disinherited. The Making of American Pentecostalism* (New York, 1979).

8. John H. Vincent, *The Chautauqua Movement* (Boston, 1886), 4.

9. Ibid., 13, 16, 54, 89.

10. Theodore Morrison, *Chautauqua. A Center for Education, Religion, and the Arts in America* (Chicago, 1974), 57ff.

11. For a list of speakers, see Jesse Lyman Hurlburt, *The Story of Chautauqua* (New York, 1921), 395–402.

12. Vincent, *Chautauqua Movement*, 127–57.

13. R. Laurence Moore, "Learning to Play. The Mormon Way and the Way of Other Americans," *Journal of Mormon History*, 16 (1990); Richard Wightman Fox, "The Discipline of Amusement," in William R. Taylor, ed., *Inventing Times Square. Commerce and Culture at the Crossroads of the World* (New York, 1991), 83–98.

14. Washington Gladden, "Christianity and Popular Amusements," *The Century*, 29 (Jan. 1885): 388–92.

15. Washington Gladden, *Applied Christianity. Moral Aspects of Social Questions* (Boston, 1891).

16. Ibid., 258–70.

17. Ibid., 271–83.

18. Morrison, *Chautauqua*, 50.

19. *The Chautauquan*, Mar. 1886, 358.

20. The membership of the WCTU was 150,000 in 1890 and somewhere close to 250,000 in 1910. See Jack S. Blocker, Jr., *"Give to the Winds Thy Fears." The Women's Temperance Crusade, 1873–1874* (Westport, 1985); Ruth Bordin, *Woman and Temperance. The Quest for Power and Liberty, 1873–1900* (Philadelphia, 1981); Ruth Bordin, *Frances Willard. A Biography* (Chapel Hill, 1986).

21. Willard, *How to Win. A Book for Girls* (New York, 1886), 102.

22. Ibid., 104.

23. Frances E. Willard, *Do Everything. A Handbook for the World's White Ribboners* (Chicago, 1895), 80–81. Bordin, *Women and Temperance*, 70–71.

24. Willard, *How to Win*, 108–9.

25. Bordin, *Women and Temperance*, 90–91.

26. Willard, *Do Everything*, 76.

27. Ibid., 115.

28. Dagobert D. Runes, ed., *The Diary and Sundry Observations of Thomas Alva Edison* (New York, 1948), 63–65.

29. Wyn Wachhorst, *Thomas Alva Edison. An American Myth* (Cambridge, Mass., 1981), 122–28.

30. Charles Musser, *Before the Nickelodeon. Edwin S. Porter and the Edison Manufacturing Company* (Berkeley, 1991), 429. Andre Millard, *Edison and the Business of Innovation* (Baltimore, 1990).

31. Charles Musser, *High-Class Moving Pictures. Lyman H. Howe and the Forgotten Era of the Traveling Exhibition, 1880–1920* (Princeton, 1991); Musser, *The Emergence of Cinema. The American Screen to 1907* (New York, 1990).

32. The filmed version of the Oberammergau Passion Play is worth a note. The Eden Musee had inherited props and script from a theatrical producer who had unsuccessfully tried to stage Salmi Morse's *Passion Play* in 1883 in New York City. Morse's play had successfully been staged in San Francisco but ran into a storm of clerical protest in New York. Anti-Semitism apparently played some role in blocking Morse's play (Morse's parents were Russian Jews), but there was a more general objection to having an actor play Christ. In 1884 a despairing Morse threw himself into the Hudson River. He should have waited for the movies. Somehow a filmed version of an "enacted" Christ got by. Huge crowds of church members and ministers in New York City turned a nice profit for the Eden Musee.

33. For the strongest statement of the view, see Paul E. Johnson, *A Shopkeeper's Millennium. Society and Revivals in Rochester, New York, 1815–1837* (New York, 1978). Also see the interesting essays on northern conscience in Bertram Wyatt-Brown, *Yankee Saints and Southern Sinners* (Baton Rouge, 1985).

34. Bertram Wyatt-Brown, *Southern Honor. Ethics and Behavior in the Old*

South (New York, 1982). Ted Ownby, *Subduing Satan. Religion, Recreation, and Manhood in the Rural South, 1865–1920* (Chapel Hill, 1990).

35. Ownby, *Subduing Satan*, especially Part One.

36. James H. Dormon, *Theater in the Ante Bellum South, 1815–1861* (Chapel Hill, 1967).

37. Wyatt-Brown, *Southern Honor*, 342.

38. Quotes are taken from C. Vann Woodward, *Origins of the New South, 1877–1913* (Baton Rouge, 1951), 169.

39. Ibid., 170.

40. Ownby, *Subduing Satan*, chapter 9.

41. Jack Temple Kirby, *Rural Worlds Lost. The American South, 1920–1960* (Baton Rouge, 1987). Wyatt-Brown, *Southern Honor*, 367ff.

42. On slave religion, see Albert Raboteau, *Slave Religion. The "Invisible Institution" in the Antebellum South* (New York, 1978), Mechal Sobel, *Trabelin' On. The Slave Journey to an Afro-Baptist Faith* (Westport, 1979); Margaret Washington Creel, *"A Peculiar People." Slave Religion and Community-Culture Among the Gullahs* (New York, 1988); Jon Butler, *Awash in a Sea of Faith. Christianizing the American People* (Cambridge, Mass., 1990).

43. C. Eric Lincoln and Lawrence H. Mamiya, *The Black Church in the African American Experience* (Durham, 1990), 8.

44. Du Bois, *The Souls of Black Folk* (New York, 1989; first published in 1903), 157.

45. Lawrence Levine, *Black Culture and Black Consciousness. Afro-American Folk Thought from Slavery to Freedom* (New York, 1977).

46. G. D. Pike, *The Jubilee Singers, and Their Campaign for Twenty Thousand Dollars* (Boston, 1873), 47.

47. J. B. T. Marsh, ed., *The Story of the Fisk Jubilee Singers with Their Songs* (London, 1877), 32.

48. Pike, *Jubilee Singers*, 28–29.

49. Ibid., 141.

50. J. B. T. Marsh, *The Story of the Jubilee Singers* (Boston, 1880).

51. Compare Pike, *Jubilee Singers*, 153, with Marsh, *Story of the Jubilee Singers*, 39.

52. Higginson, "Negro Spirituals," *Atlantic Monthly*, 19 (June 1867): 685. The first book-length collection is William Francis Allen, *Slave Songs of the United States* (New York, 1867). Howard W. Odum, *The Negro and His Songs. A Study of the Typical Negro Songs in the South* (New York, 1925).

53. William W. Austin, *"Susanna," Jeanie," and "The Old Folks at Home." The Songs of Stephen C. Foster from His Time to Ours* (Urbana, 1987).

54. Eileen Southern, *The Music of Black Americans. A History* (New York, 1971); James H. Cone, *The Spirituals and the Blues. An Interpretation* (Maryknoll, 1991); Charles Keil, *Urban Blues* (Chicago, 1966); Dena Epstein, *Sinful Tunes and Spirituals. Black Folk Music to the Civil War* (Urbana, 1977); Imama Amiri Baraka, *Blues People. Negro Music in White America* (New York, 1963).

Chapter Seven

1. Leon Fink, *Workingmen's Democracy. The Knights of Labor and American Politics* (Urbana, 1983). On "artisan republicanism," see Sean Wilentz, *Chants Democratic. New York City and the Rise of the American Working Class, 1788–1850* (New York, 1984), 61–103.

2. Herbert Gutman, "Protestantism and the American Labor Movement: The Christian Spirit in the Gilded Age," *American Historical Review*, 72 (Oct. 1966): 74–101.

3. Henry J. Browne, *The Catholic Church and the Knights of Labor* (Washington, D.C., 1949), 149, 151.

4. Eric Foner, "Class, Ethnicity, and Radicalism in the Gilded Age. The Land League and Irish America," *Marxist Perspectives*, 1 (Summer 1978): 26.

5. Browne, *Catholic Church*, 278.

6. Quoted in Gary Kornblith, "From Artisans to Businessmen: Master Mechanics in New England, 1789–1850," Ph.D. dissertation, Princeton University, 1983, p. 411.

7. George M. Thomas, *Revivalism and Cultural Change. Christianity, Nation Building, and the Market in the Nineteenth-Century United States* (Chicago, 1989).

8. Paul E. Johnson, *A Shopkeeper's Millennium. Society and Revivals in Rochester, New York, 1815–1837* (New York, 1978), 106, 121, 138–39.

9. For the popular side of evangelicalism, see Nathan Hatch, *The Democratization of American Christianity* (New Haven, 1989).

10. H. Richard Niebuhr, *The Social Sources of Denominationalism* (New York, 1929); Stuart Blumin, *The Emergence of the Middle Class. Social Experience in the American City, 1760–1900* (New York, 1989); Mary Ryan, *Cradle of the Middle Class. The Family in Oneida County New York, 1790–1865* (New York, 1981).

11. Cynthia J. Shelton, *The Mills of Manayunk. Industrialization and Social Conflict in the Philadelphia Region, 1787–1837* (Baltimore, 1986).

12. Gary B. Kulik, "The Beginnings of the Industrial Revolution in America: Pawtucket, Rhode Island, 1672–1829," Ph.D. dissertation, Brown University, 1980.

13. Jama Lazarow, "A Good Time Coming: Religion and the Emergence of Labor Activism in Antebellum New England," Ph.D. dissertation, Brandeis, 1982.

14. Paul G. Faler, *Mechanics and Manufacturers in the Early Industrial Revolution, Lynn, Massachusetts, 1780–1860* (Albany, 1981), 100–38.

15. Phoebe B. Stanton, *The Gothic Revival and American Church Architecture. An Episode in Taste, 1840–1856* (Baltimore, 1968).

16. Sean Wilentz, *Chants Democratic*, 77–87, 226–27, 277–281, 300. Bruce Laurie, *Working People of Philadelphia, 1800–1850* (Philadelphia, 1980).

17. Steven J. Ross, *Workers on the Edge. Work, Leisure and Politics in In-*

dustrializing Cincinnati, 1788–1890 (New York, 1985); Peter Knights, *The Plain People of Boston, 1830–1860* (New York, 1971).

18. Jay Dolan, *The Immigrant Church. New York's Irish and German Catholics, 1815–1865* (Notre Dame, 1983); Kerby A. Miller, *Emigrants and Exiles. Ireland and the Irish Exodus to North America* (New York, 1985); Randall M. Miller and Thomas D. Marzik, eds., *Immigrants and Religion in Urban America* (Philadelphia, 1977); Robert Orsi, *The Madonna of 115th Street. Faith and Community in Italian Harlem, 1880–1950* (New Haven, 1985).

19. Miller and Marzik, *Immigrants and Religion*, xv.

20. Kevin J. Christiano, *Religious Diversity and Social Change. American Cities, 1890–1906* (Cambridge, Mass., 1987), 19–21.

21. For other statistics suggesting an increase of working-class church membership between 1840 and 1875, see Ken Fones-Wolf, *Trade Union Gospel. Christianity and Labor in Industrial Philadelphia, 1865–1915* (Philadelphia, 1989), and Laurie, *Working People of Philadelphia*.

22. Richard Henry Edwards, *Christianity and Amusements* (New York, 1922), 39.

23. Ibid., 143.

24. Among the fifty names were Charles Eliot, Richard Ely, Daniel Gilman, Washington Gladden, Seth Low, Francis Peabody, and Carroll Wright. The list was heavily Protestant, but it included one Catholic, Father Thomas Conaty of Catholic University, and one non-Christian, Felix Adler.

25. Raymond Calkins, *Substitutes for the Saloon* (Boston, 1901), 138ff.

26. Ibid., 3, 25, 70, 110, 131, 146.

27. Ibid., 126.

28. Darrel M. Robertson, *The Chicago Revival, 1876. Society and Revivalism in a Nineteenth-Century City* (Metuchen, N.J., 1989), 44.

29. Ibid., and Marion L. Bell, *Crusade in the City. Revivalism in Nineteenth-Century Philadelphia* (Lewisburg, 1977). Both books discount Moody's impact on industrial workers.

30. Bell, *Crusade in the City*, 240.

31. Lyle Dorsett, *Billy Sunday and the Redemption of Urban America* (Grand Rapids, 1991).

32. Fones-Wolf, *Trade Union Gospel*.

33. Ibid., 138–39, 184–90.

34. On the work of urban missions, see Paul Boyer, *Urban Masses and Moral Order in America, 1820–1920* (Cambridge, Mass., 1978).

35. Robertson, *Chicago Revival*, 86–109.

36. James Gilbert, *Perfect Cities. Chicago's Utopias of 1893* (Chicago, 1991).

37. For comparative perspective, see E. P. Thompson, "Patrician Society, Plebian Culture," *Journal of Social History*, 7 (Summer 1974): 381–405; Gareth Stedman Jones, "Working-Class Culture and Working-Class Politics in London, 1870–1900. Notes on the Remaking of a Working Class," *Journal of Social History*, 7 (Summer 1974): 460–508; J. M. Golby and A. W. Purdue, *The Civil-*

ization of the Crowd. Popular Culture in England, 1750–1900 (New York, 1985).

38. Lawrence Levine, *Highbrow/Lowbrow. The Emergence of Cultural Hierarchy in America* (Cambridge, Mass., 1988).

39. Splendid historical accounts cover all these activities. See Elliott J. Gorn, *The Manly Art, Bare-Knuckle Prize Fighting in America* (Ithaca, 1986); Michael T. Isenberg, *John L. Sullivan and His America* (Urbana, 1988); Roy Rosenzweig, *Eight Hours for What We Will. Workers and Leisure in an Industrial City, 1870–1920* (New York, 1983); Michael Denning, *Mechanic Accents. Dime Novels and Working-Class Culture in America* (New York, 1987); Robert W. Snyder, *The Voice of the City. Vaudeville and Popular Culture in New York* (New York, 1989); Bruce A. McConachie and Daniel Friedman, eds., *Theatre for Working-Class Audiences in the United States, 1830–1980* (Westport, 1985). Other important accounts covering working-class uses of leisure include Melvin L. Adelman, *A Sporting Time. New York City and the Rise of Modern Athletics, 1820–1870* (Urbana, 1986); Susan G. Davis, *Parades and Power. Street Theatre in Nineteenth-Century Philadelphia* (Philadelphia, 1986); Ann Fabian, *Card Sharps, Dream Books and Bucket Shops. Gambling in Nineteenth-Century America* (Ithaca, 1990); Stephen Hardy, *How Boston Played. Sport, Recreation and Community, 1865–1915* (Boston, 1982); John Kasson, *Amusing the Million. Coney Island at the Turn of the Century* (New York, 1978); Kathy Peiss, *Cheap Amusements. Working Women and Leisure in Turn-of-the-Century New York* (Philadelphia, 1986); Steven Riess, *City Games. The Evolution of American Urban Society and the Rise of Sports* (Urbana, 1989); Steven Riess, *Touching Base. Professional Baseball and American Culture in the Progressive Era* (Westport, 1980); Jeffrey Sammons, *Beyond the Ring. The Role of Boxing in American Society* (Urbana, 1988).

40. Gorn, *Manly Art*, 132.

41. Quoted in Ibid., 243.

42. Perry Duis, *The Saloon. Public Drinking in Chicago and Boston, 1880–1920* (Urbana, 1983); Lewis Erenberg, *Steppin' Out. New York Nightlife and the Transformation of American Culture, 1890–1930* (Westport, 1981).

43. Rosenzweig, *Eight Hours for What We Will.*

44. Levine, *Highbrow/Lowbrow.*

45. Bruce A. McConachie, "'The Theatre of the Mob': Apocalyptic Melodrama and Preindustrial Riots in Antebellum New York," in McConachie and Daniel Friedman, eds., *Theatre for Working-Class Audiences.*

46. Deane L. Root, *American Popular Stage Music, 1860–1880* (Ann Arbor, 1981).

47. Parker Zellers, *Tony Pastor. Dean of the Vaudeville Stage* (Ypsilanti, 1971); Myron Matlaw, "Tony the Trouper: Pastor's Early Years," *Theatre Annual*, 24 (1968): 72–90.

48. From the *Clipper*, as quoted in Zellers, *Tony Pastor*, 72.

49. Snyder, *Voice of the City*, 29–30, 132.

50. Quoted in Zellers, *Tony Pastor*, 99.

51. Bruce McConachie, "Pacifying American Theatrical Audiences, 1820–1900," in Richard Butsch, ed., *For Fun and Profit. The Transformation of Leisure into Consumption* (Philadelphia, 1990).

52. Robert Snyder, "Big Time, Small Time, All Around the Town: New York Vaudeville in the Early Twentieth Century," in Butsch, ed., *For Fun and Profit*.

53. Madeleine B. Stern, ed., *Publishers for Mass Entertainment in Nineteenth-Century America* (Boston, 1980).

54. Michael Denning, *Mechanic Accents*. Also see Albert Johannsen, *The House of Beadle and Adams and Its Dime and Nickel Novels. The Story of a Vanished Literature*, 3 vols. (Norman, 1950–62).

55. Theodor W. Adorno, *The Culture Industry. Selected Essays on Mass Culture* (London, 1991), 85.

56. See the discussion in "Christianity and Amusements. A Symposium," *Everybody's Magazine*, X (May 1904): 697. The language is taken from a proposed change in Methodist rules to drop the 1872 list of banned amusements. The itemized list was still in effect in 1912 although many Methodists clearly ignored it. See "The Methodist Amusement Ban," *Literary Digest*, 44 (June 15, 1912): 1260.

57. Steven A. Riess, *Touching Base*, 27, 137.

58. See the shrewd discussion by Richard Fox, "The Discipline of Amusement," in William R. Taylor, ed., *Inventing Times Square* (New York, 1991).

59. Davis, *Parades and Power*.

60. Peiss, *Cheap Amusements*. In addition to dance halls, Peiss analyzes Coney Island, the movies, and vaudeville.

61. Frances G. Couvares, "The Plebian Movement: Theatre and Working-Class Life in Late Nineteenth-Century Pittsburgh," in McConachie and Friedman, *Theatre for the Working Class*.

62. Cited in Albert F. McLean, *American Vaudeville as Ritual* (Lexington, 1965), 89.

63. On one case of commercialization see Sam Kinser, *Carnival, American Style. Mardi Gras at Mobile and New Orleans*, (Chicago, 1990). Orsi, *Madonna of 115th Street*; Irving Howe, *World of Our Fathers* (New York, 1976); Elizabeth Ewen, *Immigrant Women in the Land of Dollars. Life and Culture on the Lower East Side, 1890–1925* (New York, 1985).

Chapter Eight

1. For general background, see J. M. Golby and A. W. Purdue, *The Making of the Modern Christmas* (Athens, Ga., 1986); James H. Barnett, *The American Christmas* (New York, 1954); Clement A. Miles, *Christmas in Ritual and Tradition, Christian and Pagan* (London, 1912).

2. For an ingenious analysis of class dimensions in this invention, see Ste-

phen Nissenbaum, "Revisiting 'A Visit from St. Nicholas': The Battle for Christmas in Early Nineteenth-Century America," in James Gilbert et al., eds., *The Mythmaking Frame of Mind. Social Imagination and American Culture* (Belmont, Calif., 1993). Also, Susan G. Davis, "'Making Night Hideous': Christmas Revelry and Public Disorder in Nineteenth-Century Philadelphia," *American Quarterly*, 34 (Summer 1982): 185–99.

3. See the charming piece by Simon Schama, "Whose Tree Is It Anyway?" *New York Times*, Dec. 24, 1991, p. A19.

4. On the importance of children to Christmas marketing, see William Leach, "Child-World in the Promised Land," in Gilbert et al. *Mythmaking Frame of Mind*. The first Macy's Thanksgiving Day parade was in 1924, although John Wanamaker had introduced the idea of a fantasy parade in the fabulous toy department of his Philadelphia store.

5. Colin Campbell, *The Romantic Ethic and the Spirit of Modern Consumerism* (Oxford, 1987), 101. For an earlier discussion of Campbell, see Chapter 1.

6. Clifford E. Clark, Jr., *Henry Ward Beecher. Spokesman for a Middle-Class America* (Urbana, 1978).

7. Donald Scott, "Knowledge and the Marketplace," in Gilbert et al., *Mythmaking Frame of Mind*.

8. William G. McLoughlin, *The Meaning of Henry Ward Beecher. An Essay on the Shifting Values of Mid-Victorian America, 1840–1870* (New York, 1970), 140–48.

9. Ann Douglas, *The Feminization of American Culture* (New York, 1977).

10. Paula Baker, *The Moral Frameworks of Public Life. Gender, Politics, and the State in Rural New York, 1870–1930* (New York, 1991); Donna A. Behnke, *Religious Issues in Nineteenth Century Feminism* (Troy, N.Y., 1982); Karen J. Blair, *The Clubwoman as Feminist. True Womanhood Redefined, 1868–1914* (New York, 1980).

11. Robert A. Schneider, "Voice of Many Waters: Church Federation in the Twentieth Century," in William R. Hutchison, ed., *Between the Times. The Travail of the Protestant Establishment in America, 1900–1960* (New York, 1989), 97.

12. John A. Hutchison, *We Are Not Divided. A Critical and Historical Study of the Federal Council of the Churches of Christ in America* (New York, 1941), 99.

13. Susan Curtis, *A Consuming Faith. The Social Gospel and Modern American Culture* (Baltimore, 1991).

14. For Barton's background in liberal Protestantism and the Social Gospel, see Leo P. Ribuffo, "Jesus Christ as Business Statesman: Bruce Barton and the Selling of Corporate Capitalism," *Right Center Left. Essays in America History* (New Brunswick, 1992).

15. Guy Lewis, "The Muscular Christianity Movement," *Journal of Health, Physical Education, Recreation*, 37 (May 1966): 27–28.

16. Harry Emerson Fosdick, *The Manhood of the Master* (New York, 1913), 4, 53–54, 57, 135, 140, 162.

17. For two excellent studies of American churches and business methods, see Ben Primer, *Protestants and American Business Methods* (Ann Arbor, 1979), and Rolf Lundén, *Business and Religion in the American 1920s* (Westport, 1988).

18. Mathews, *Scientific Management in the Churches* (Chicago, 1912), 42.

19. Ibid., 34, 44–45.

20. Ibid., 58.

21. Francis H. Case, *Handbook of Church Advertising* (New York, 1921), 177, 184.

22. Albert F. McGarrah, *A Modern Church Program. A Study in Efficiency* (Chicago, 1915), 100.

23. Charles Stelzle, *A Son of the Bowery. The Life Story of an East Side American* (New York, 1926).

24. For an excellent discussion of Stelzle's career, see Curtis, *Consuming Faith*, 257–65.

25. Stelzle, *Son of the Bowery*, 121–26.

26. Case, *Church Advertising*, 20.

27. Ibid., 53.

28. C. Howard Hopkins, *John R. Mott. A Biography* (Grand Rapids, 1979).

29. Lundén, *Business and Religion*, especially chapters 1 and 2.

30. Ibid., 65.

31. Ibid., 79.

32. For material on Reisner, see Curtis, *Consuming Faith*, 234–36, and Lundén, *Business and Religion*, 80–82. Many churches other than St. Bart's in New York City would like to do something similar now if they could negotiate their way around historic preservation panels.

33. Jack Anderson, "Crusading Clergy Shape the Course of Dance," *New York Times*, Sept. 27, 1992, p. H6.

34. Thorstein Veblen, *Absentee Ownership and Business Enterprise in Recent Times. The Case of America* (New York, 1923), 319–25.

35. Walter Lippmann, *Drift and Mastery. An Attempt to Diagnose the Current Unrest* (New York, 1914).

36. *Christian Century*, May 12, 1937, 617.

37. Daniel Czitrom, "The Politics of Performance: From Theater Licensing to Movie Censorship in Turn-of-the-Century New York," *American Quarterly*, 44 (Dec. 1992): 534.

38. Neal Gabler, *An Empire of Their Own. How the Jews Invented Hollywood* (New York, 1988).

39. Czitrom, "Politics of Performance," 535–36.

40. Ibid., 543.

41. For an excellent analysis of Griffith, see Lary May, *Screening Out the Past. The Birth of Mass Culture and the Motion Picture Industry* (New York, 1980), 60–95.

42. The National Board of Review still operated in the early 1930s. According to a report prepared by the Federal Council that was published in 1931 (*The*

Public Relations of the Motion Picture Industry) (New York, 1931), it had 350 voluntary members with a paid secretarial staff of five and a stenographic force of three. Griffith directed films through the 1920s.

43. May, *Screening Out the Past*, 209–36.

44. On the importance of the boards in pressuring Hollywood to change its policies in the 1920s and 1930s, see Lea Jacobs, *The Wages of Sin. Censorship and the Fallen Woman Film, 1928–1942* (Madison, 1991), 20–22, 31–35, and passim.

45. Stephen Vaughan, "Morality and Entertainment: The Origins of the Motion Picture Production Code," *Journal of American History*, 77 (June 1990): 39–65; Francis G. Couvares, "Hollywood, Main Street, and the Church: Trying to Censor the Movies Before the Production Code," *American Quarterly*, 44 (Dec. 1992): 584–97.

46. "A Year at the Movies," *Christian Century*, Dec. 31, 1930, p. 1618; "The Federal Council Weighs the Movies," *Christian Century*, July 15, 1931, pp. 918–20.

47. May, *Screening Out the Past*, 205.

48. Catheryne Gilman, "Government Regulation of the Movies," *Christian Century*, Aug. 26, 1931, pp. 1066–68. Leonard J. Leff and Jerold Simmons, *The Dame in the Kimono. Hollywood, Censorship, and the Production Code from the 1920s to the 1960s* (New York, 1990), and Jacobs, *Wages of Sin*. Also see two reports issued by the Federal Council: Reverend Charles Newton Lathrop, *The Motion Picture Problem* (New York, 1922), and *The Public Relations of the Motion Picture Industry* (New York, 1931).

49. Maxwell Stewart, "Deflating the Movies," *Christian Century*, Aug. 13, 1930, p. 987.

50. For the text of the code and a practical discussion of what it meant to filmmaking in the 1930s, see Olga J. Martin, *Hollywood's Movie Commandments. A Handbook for Motion Picture Writers and Reviewers* (New York, 1937). Martin was secretary to Joseph Breen, and her account, though informative, is a defense of the code.

51. *Christian Century*, June 20, 1934, p. 823.

52. Ibid., Mar. 20, 1940, p. 373. For a defense of the Legion's position, see Martin Quigley, *Decency in Motion Pictures* (New York, 1937).

53. Leff and Simmons, *Dame in the Kimono*, chapter 7.

54. Dennis N. Voskuil, "Reaching Out: Mainline Protestantism and the Media," in Hutchison, *Between the Times*, 81–82.

55. "What Hath God Wrought," *The Wireless Age*, 10 (Feb. 1923): 22.

56. "Radio and the Pulpit," *Review of Reviews*, 71 (Feb. 1925): 203–4.

57. "The Radio Cathedral," *The Wireless Age* (Sept. 1923), 42.

58. Spencer Miller, Jr., "Radio and Religion," *American Academy of Political and Social Science. Annals*, 177 (Jan. 1935): 135–40.

59. The Federal Council's gratitude to NBC and RCA was evident in a gala dinner held at the Waldorf in May 1938 to celebrate the fifteenth anniversary of National Religious Radio. NBC, it was calculated, had given "millions and mil-

lions of dollars' worth of free facilities." Federal Council, *The Church in the Sky* (New York, 1938).

60. See, for example, "The Air is Reserved for Conventional Religion," *Christian Century*, Jan. 20, 1932, p. 78; "Freedom for Radio Pulpit," *Christian Century*, Jan. 27, 1932, pp. 112–13.

61. Roger Ward Babson, "Church Use of the Radio," *Literary Digest*, Oct. 13, 1928, p. 31; Babson, *Religion and Business* (New York, 1921).

62. Federal Council, *The Church in the Sky*.

63. Everett C. Parker et al., *Religious Radio. What to Do and How* (New York, 1948).

64. J. Fred MacDonald, *Don't Touch that Dial! Radio Programming in American Life, 1920–1960* (Chicago, 1979), 106.

Chapter Nine

1. *Newsweek*, Sept. 26, 1949; *Newsweek*, Oct. 1, 1956.

2. Henry Herx, "Religion and Film," in Charles H. Lippy and Peter W. Williams, eds., *Encyclopedia of the American Religious Experience* (New York, 1988), 1341–58.

3. *Time*, June 29, 1953; *Newsweek*, July 5, 1954; *Newsweek*, Aug. 7, 1961.

4. The first Luce puff of Billy Graham was *Life* magazine's report of his revival in Los Angeles, Nov. 21, 1949. Also see *Life*, Mar. 27, 1950. William Randolph Hearst was really the first media magnate to publicize Graham. On Oral Roberts, see *Life*, May 7, 1951. Reliable biographies exist for both Graham and Roberts. See William McLoughlin, *Billy Graham. Revivalist in a Secular Age* (New York, 1960); Marshall Frady, *Billy Graham. A Parable of American Righteousness* (Boston, 1979); David Harrell, *Oral Roberts. An American Life* (Bloomington, 1985).

5. Carol V. R. George, *God's Salesman. Norman Vincent Peale and the Power of Positive Thinking* (New York, 1993).

6. Norman Vincent Peale, *The Power of Positive Thinking* (New York, 1952), viii.

7. A. Roy Eckardt, "The New Look in American Piety," *Christian Century*, Nov. 17, 1954.

8. Reinhold Niebuhr, "Varieties of Religious Revival," *New Republic*, June 6, 1955. Also see Niebuhr's article in the *New York Times Magazine*, Nov. 19, 1950.

9. Will Herberg, *Protestant, Catholic, Jew* (Garden City, 1955), 260.

10. Dean M. Kelley, *Why Conservative Churches Are Growing* (New York, 1972).

11. George Marsden, *Reforming Fundamentulism. Fuller Seminary and the New Evangelicalism* (Grand Rapids, 1987).

12. George Marsden, ed., *Evangelicalism and Modern America* (Grand Rap-

ids, 1984); George Marsden, *Understanding Fundamentalism and Evangelicalism* (Grand Rapids, 1991); George Marsden, *Fundamentalism and American Culture* (New York, 1980); Martin Marty, *Modern American Religion*, Vol. 2, *The Noise of Conflict, 1919–1941* (Chicago, 1991); James Davison Hunter, *Evangelicalism. The Coming Generation* (Chicago, 1987); Richard Quebedeaux, *The Young Evangelicals. Revolution in Orthodoxy* (New York, 1974).

13. For an excellent summary, see William Martin, "Mass Communications," in Lippy and Williams, *Encyclopedia of the American Religious Experience*, 1711–26. Ben Armstrong, *The Electric Church* (Nashville, 1979) is a partisan but useful account.

14. By far the most sympathetic reliable account of Robertson is David Harrell, *Pat Robertson. A Personal, Religious, and Political Portrait* (New York, 1987). For a less friendly view, see Larry Martz and Ginny Carroll, *Ministry of Greed. The Inside Story of the Televangelists and their Holy Wars* (New York, 1988). Also see Steve Bruce, *Pray TV. Televangelism in America* (London, 1990); Jeffrey Hadden and Anson Shupe, *Televangelism, Power, and Politics on God's Frontier* (New York, 1988); Peter Horsfield, *Religious Television. The American Experience* (New York, 1984).

15. Ben Armstrong, *The Electric Church*.

16. Ibid., 173.

17. Martin, "Mass Communication," 1719.

18. Quoted in Armstrong, *The Electric Church*, 108.

19. Samuel Hill and Dennis Owen, *The New Religious-Political Right in America* (Nashville, 1982); Steve Bruce, *The Rise and Fall of the New Christian Right. Conservative Protestant Politics in America, 1978–1988* (New York, 1989), Mark Noll, ed., *Religion and American Politics. From the Colonial Period to the 1980s* (New York, 1990); Garry Wills, *Under God. Religion and American Politics* (New York, 1990); Mark Silk, *Spiritual Politics. Religion and America Since World War II* (New York, 1988).

20. Armstrong, *The Electric Church*, 134.

21. The best description of Heritage USA is Frances FitzGerald, "Reflections. Jim and Tammy," *The New Yorker*, Apr. 23, 1990, pp. 45–87; also see FitzGerald, *Cities on a Hill. A Journey Through Contemporary America* (New York 1986).

22. *New York Times*, Apr. 18, 1992, p. D33, 35.

23. Ibid., May 13, 1992, p. D1, 22.

24. Martin Marty, "The Religious Press," in Lippy and Williams, *Encyclopedia*, 1697–709.

25. Paul Boyer, *When Time Shall Be No More. Prophecy Belief in Modern American Culture* (Cambridge, Mass., 1992).

26. Kenneth Cmiel, *Democratic Eloquence. The Fight Over Popular Speech in Nineteenth-Century America* (Berkeley, 1990), 216–17.

27. Wayne Elzey, "Popular Culture," in Lippy and Williams, *Encyclopedia*, 1729.

28. Ibid., 1730–31. Elzey lists many other examples.

29. Randall Balmer, *Mine Eyes Have Seen the Glory. A Journey into the Evangelical Subculture in America* (New York, 1989), 48–70.

30. *New York Times*, Dec. 1, 1987, p. C17. Carol Flake, *Redemptorama, Culture, Politics, and the New Evangelicalism* (New York, 1984), chapter 8.

31. Carol Flake, *Redemptorama*, 18.

32. Ibid., 61.

33. Richard Neuhaus, *The Naked Public Square. Religion and Democracy in America* (Grand Rapids, 1984).

34. J. Gordon Melton, *The Encyclopedia of American Religions*, third edition (Detroit, 1989).

35. Catherine Albanese, *Nature Religion in America. From the Algonkian Indians to the New Age* (Chicago, 1990); Mary Farrell Bednarowski, *New Religions and the Theological Imagination in America* (Bloomington, 1989); Marilyn Ferguson, *The Aquarian Conspiracy. Personal and Social Transformation in the 1980s* (Los Angeles, 1987).

36. *New York Times*, Apr. 10, 1991, p. A1.

37. Ibid., July 2, 1950.

38. Harriet Whitehead, *Renunciation and Reformulation. A Study of Conversion in an American Sect* (Ithaca, 1987).

39. Roy Wallis, *The Road to Total Freedom. A Sociological Analysis of Scientology* (New York, 1977), 4.

40. Ibid., 4.

41. *New York Times*, Sept. 25, 1992. Knight's present operations are apparently not tax exempt, although earlier she had organized a tax exempt "Church I am."

42. Michael Rossman, *New Age Blues. On the Politics of Consciousness* (New York, 1979), 151.

43. Michael D'Antonio, *Heaven on Earth* (New York, 1992).

44. E. Burke Rochford, Jr., *Hare Krishna in America* (New Brunswick, 1985), 171.

Epilogue

1. Matthew Arnold, *Culture and Anarchy. An Essay in Political and Social Criticism* (New York, 1883), xix–xxvii.

2. Raymond Williams, *The Long Revolution* (London, 1961), 336ff.

3. Thomas Haskell, "Capitalism and the Origins of the Humanitarian Sensibility," *American Historical Review*, 90 (Apr. and June, 1985): 342ff.

Index

Abbott, Lyman, 210
Addams, Jane, 210
Adorno, Theodor, 200, 202, 270
Advertising, 213-18, 233
African Americans, 35-36, 163, 166-71, 250, 267, 273
Ahlstrom, Sydney, 58
Albaugh, Gaylord P., 19
Albee, Edward F., 196-97
Alden, Mrs. G. R. ("Pansy"), 154
Alderman, Edwin A., 165
Aldrich, Maude M., 226
Alger, Horatio, 199
Allen, Richard, 167
Allston, Washington, 109
Alpert, Richard (Baba Ram Dass), 258
American Bible Society, 18, 75-6, 252
American Broadcasting Company (ABC), 233
American Federation of Labor, 187, 219
American Museum of Natural History, 104
American Tract Society, 17-20, 26, 75-76, 252
Amish: as objects of commercialization, 11, 269
Anti-Masons, 78
Antinomianism, 15, 73, 78, 131-32
Arbuckle, Roscoe (Fatty), 225
Armour, J. Ogden, 187
Armstrong, Ben, 248-50
Armstrong, Herbert W., 246
Arnold, Matthew, 266, 275: defines culture, 5, 269-70
Arthur, Timothy Shay, 29
Arts, visual: commercialization of, 110-11, Protestant worries about, 109-12
Astor Place Riot, 101
Avery Ephraim K., 129-30

Babson, Roger W., 234
Bakker, Jim, 3, 150, 248-49, 251-52
Bakker, Tammy, 3, 248, 251-52
Bangs, Nathan, 78-79
Baptists, 26, 37, 49, 52, 75, 83, 88, 161, 164-65, 179, 188, 209, 226, 247, 250
Bara, Theda, 224
Barnes, Alfred S., 216
Barnhouse, Donald Grey, 246
Barnum, Phineas Taylor, 106-9, 117-18, 121, 185, 196, 201, 222; and family entertainment, 108; religious critics of, 108, 159
Barton, Bruce, 211-12, 218, 253
Beadle, Erastus, 18
Beadle, Irwin, 18
Beadle and Adams, 198
Beecher, Henry Ward, 26, 66, 95-6, 106, 169, 210; and consumerism, 206-8; and the theater, 53-55
Beecher, Lyman, 47, 53, 207
Bell, Daniel, 243
Bellamy, Edward, 204, 209
Bellows, Henry W., 54-55, 103
Benjamin, Park, 198
Bennett, James Gordon, 18, 33, 130-31
Berger, Peter, 7
Bible: as commodity, 34-35, 253-54
Bicycle Thief, The, 230-31
Black Crook, The, 147
Blithedale Romance, The, 122-23
Boxing, 191-94
Brace, Charles Loring, 104
Breen, Joseph I., 228-29
Brown, R. R. , 245
Buntline, Ned. See Judson, Edward Zane Carroll

Arghame is argued by showing how engagement in cultural market had effects -- not always intended (or even anticipated), not always welcomed, ~~but identifiable and~~ & not always as strong as ~~retrogor~~ the actors wished their influence to be, but still strong.

Interesting that only sociologist cited is George Thomas -- a clue that the connection between this book & soc. is via a new institutionalism that is concerned with the cultural roots of ~~organizate~~ social life (or something).